The Clean Pet Food Revolution

THE CLEAN PET FOOD REVOLUTION

How Better Pet Food Will Change the World

Ernie Ward, Alice Oven, and Ryan Bethencourt

Lantern Books ● Brooklyn, NY

2020

Lantern Books
128 Second Place
Brooklyn, NY 11231
www.lanternbooks.com

Printed in the United States of America

Library of Congress Cataloging-in-Publication Data

Names: Ward, Ernie, author. | Oven, Alice, author. | Bethencourt, Ryan, author.
Title: The clean pet food revolution : how better pet food will change the world / Ernie Ward, Alice Oven, and Ryan Bethencourt.
Description: Brooklyn : Lantern Books, 2019. | Includes bibliographical references and index.
Identifiers: LCCN 2019035027 (print) | LCCN 2019035028 (ebook) | ISBN 9781590566022 (hardcover) | ISBN 9781590566039 (ebook)
Subjects: LCSH: Pet food industry—United States.
Classification: LCC HD9340.U52 W37 2019 (print) | LCC HD9340.U52 (ebook) | DDC 664/.66—dc23
LC record available at https://lccn.loc.gov/2019035027
LC ebook record available at https://lccn.loc.gov/2019035028

Contents

Introduction

Our Evolving Responsibilities as Pet Owners

NAME AN ANIMAL, any animal. Did you first think *dog* or *cat*? Over the last fifty years, the number of cats and dogs kept as domestic pets in the Western world has increased exponentially. Today, over half of all U.S. households have at least one companion animal,[1] compared to just 22 percent in 1967.[2] As we humans have become increasingly urbanized and affluent, able to feed ourselves with little effort, we've also evolved to support four-legged friends. Over time, that relationship has blossomed, with the result being that today there are nearly 180 million pet dogs and cats in the United States and 20 million in the United Kingdom.

Most people consider their pets family and treat them as such. Bernard Rollin, professor of philosophy and animal sciences at Colorado State University, explains that "the bond initially based in pragmatic symbiosis has turned into a bond based in love."[3] Our relationship with animals has shifted from our considering them an asset or income source to their being something (or even some*one*) to spend money on. And do we splurge on our pets! In 2018, pet expenditure in the United States was estimated to exceed $72 billion (£55.3 billion),[4] more than the combined GDP of the thirty-nine poorest countries in the world. The market is growing elsewhere, too. Chinese pet owners are forecast to lavish about $2.6 billion (£2 billion) on their pets by 2019, double the amount spent three years earlier. So, where is all this money going?

Most of the money spent on pets is being poured into their food bowls. In the United States alone, almost $30 billion (£23 billion) goes to *feeding* dogs and cats.[5] U.K. dog owners each drop nearly $520 (£400) a year on food, totaling nearly $3 billion,[6] and Brazilian pet lovers spent almost $5 billion (£3.8 billion) on feeding their pets in 2018.[7] By 2022, the global pet food market is estimated to be worth almost $100 billion (£77 billion).[8] That's a lot of bowls to fill. And what's the main ingredient filling them? Meat. Animal meat is where our story begins.

Why Our Pets' Meat Consumption Is a Serious Problem

In October 2018, the world was sent reeling by a report from the U.N. Intergovernmental Panel on Climate Change (IPCC), which revealed that global warming is going to have a devastating impact on our planet even sooner than scientists originally projected.[9] The report concluded that humans have approximately twelve years to reverse our environmental impact if we want to avoid severe, long-term consequences to Earth's ecosystems. It urged "rapid, far-reaching, and unprecedented changes in all aspects of society" to avoid extinction-level disaster. Saving ourselves and our planet will require enormous changes in the way we power our cities and industries, what we build, the energy we use, how we get around, and, most significant, what we *eat*. The report concluded that if temperatures rise to 1.5 degrees Celsius above pre-industrial levels over the next eighty years, we'll be facing tens of millions of premature deaths, massive loss of biodiversity, and many millions of climate refugees. The scientific panel warned that if we are to survive, emissions of CO_2 and other greenhouse gases (GHGs) must be slashed and our food supply systems radically changed.

Additional research published immediately after the U.N. report concluded that the United States and Europe would need to reduce their current animal-meat intake by 90 percent in order to sustain the nearly ten billion people who will be alive by 2050.[10] The consensus of the global scientific community is that the farming of animals is contributing to the destruction of the world's ecosystems: the GHGs produced by beef, pork, poultry, and fish farming are helping to push the planet closer to the 1.5-degree threshold. The farming of livestock destroys huge areas of forest and consumes vast amounts of potable water, threatening both our natural resources and ecosystems. It's clear we must drastically reduce human meat consumption if we want to save the planet and preserve our species. But what people *haven't* been discussing is how feeding our pets is contributing to this threat to our very existence.

The impact pet food is having on climate change has received little attention. Yet pets eat an estimated *one-quarter* of all the meat consumed in the United States, equivalent to the meat devoured by twenty-six million Americans. That makes U.S. dogs and cats equal to the fifth largest country in the world in terms of animal protein consumption.[11] It's no longer enough to evaluate only the human population and its food consumption when calculating environmental impacts: we *must* include pets in our dietary footprint. We won't be able to save the planet if we ignore the climatological change our companion animals create. Because dogs and cats have become an integral part of human society, the way we care for them, specifically how we feed them, must also become part of the changes we make.

According to the latest Yale Climate Opinion report, about 70 percent of U.S. adults believe global warming is happening, and 68 percent think corporations should do more to help.[12] Unfortunately, most pet owners aren't aware of the impact the pet food industry has on the environment. The rapid growth of "high-protein," "meat as first ingredient," and "ancestral meat-based" pet diets reflects a disconnect between concern about global warming and the market for meat-intensive pet food. Dog and cat owners demand ever greater meat content, resulting in increased beef, chicken, pork, and fish production for pet foods.

In addition to filling pet food bowls with meat-centric diets, pet owners are increasingly offering meat-based treats. Seventy-one percent of U.S. pet owners say they enjoy buying "indulgent" pet treats and products, especially pig-ear and bacon snacks. "What's more indulgent than pork or bacon?" asked David Sprinkle, research director for Packaged

Facts, at the 2019 VMX State of the Veterinary Profession conference. Apparently not much. Bacon enjoys an 80 percent market penetration on human dining menus[13] and is now a frequent ingredient in premium pet foods. Further worsening the direct environmental impacts of pet food is the trend of using "human-grade meat" in pet foods. Making all that meat for pets creates about sixty-four million metric tons of GHGs each year, matching the equivalent of the annual exhaust puffed out by over fourteen million cars.[14] We need to radically rethink what we're putting into our pets' food bowls. We need a clean pet food revolution.

Meat-Based Pet Food Consumption Is on the Rise

Over the next thirty years, we'll need to feed an estimated ten billion humans and between two and three billion pets. There are currently close to one billion pet dogs and cats worldwide.[15] The United States leads the way, caring for about ninety-four million cats and ninety million dogs. The United Kingdom boasts an impressive eleven million cats and nine million pet dogs, even though the land mass is only the size of Michigan.[16] China shares its homes with as many as 100 million dogs and cats, and that number is projected to grow 15 percent each year for the next five to ten years.[17] There are at least fifty-five million pet dogs and cats in Russia and Brazil. And to put this in context, we don't have exact estimates on global pet populations because the world is only just beginning to fall in love with pets.

Since 2008 there has been a significant jump in U.S. dog ownership, especially among millennials (eighteen- to thirty-four-year-olds), rising from 35 percent to 41 percent in 2016.[18] More people are becoming dog owners earlier in life, instead of waiting for the proverbial "white picket fence and two children." In the majority of modern homes, indoor dogs are no longer taboo but the norm. Alice just invested in a king-sized bed, not because she has kids but because her Cavalier King Charles spaniel needs more sleeping space. Ernie and his wife go one better: a California King bed to accommodate their two border terriers and cats. They're not outliers. Fifty to 71 percent of Americans proudly proclaim that their pets sleep with them.[19] In a report by the American Animal Hospital Association (AAHA), 40 percent of the women interviewed said they received more affection from their dogs than from their husbands or children.[20] This emphasis on dog ownership is important because, as we'll explain in detail later, dogs do not biologically require animal meat to thrive. Man's best friend may be our best hope to help save the planet.

Animal meat. How many of us think much about the animal that became our pets' meaty chunks? As we've elevated dogs and cats to the status of "family members," we've largely forgotten the billions of farmed animals we kill for their food. The closer we've grown to dogs and cats, the more physically and emotionally distant we've become from the animals we eat and feed our pets. We've ordained ourselves guardians of a few privileged species of animal, and, in order to feed those lucky cats and dogs, we've banished other animals to a relentless and cruel factory production line. Although bacon might be touted as an "indulgent" ingredient in pet food, most of the pigs that become bacon live in factory farms and die in industrialized slaughterhouses.

The suffering of animals in our modern farm system is discussed later in this book, but it's likely you're already at least vaguely aware of it through social media or the increasingly vocal animal welfare movement. We tend to think about animal agriculture as an ideological matter for human diets, but, as Jessica Pierce points out in her book *Run, Spot, Run*, we shouldn't just consider "what" our pets eat, but *who* they eat.[21] Living, breathing, feeling beings have been reduced to an ingredient listed in small print on a pet food label. We lovingly give one type of animal a name, an identity, a personality, and feelings, while hiding other animals under inanimate nomenclature. We, the authors, don't believe one animal needs to be harmed and sacrificed to feed another. Indeed, for many, feeding our pets another animal creates an ethical dilemma we call ethical feeding friction. The third and fourth chapters of this book delve into the ethical questions of modern pet foods.

This confused attitude to different categories of animal, to whom we attribute different traits and rights, extends to another group of domestic creatures: the dogs and cats we use to test pet foods. For a pet food to pass an AAFCO (Association of American Feed Control Officials) feeding trial, purpose-bred dogs and cats penned in "kennel farms" have traditionally been used. These outdated and inaccurate methods can be modernized and made more humane, as we'll share in the final chapter of this book.

When it comes to the welfare of farmed animals, there are other immediate concerns for the conscientious pet owner. Although these staple "ingredients" of the pet food industry are rarely thought about in life, their bodies are conspicuously present in our pets' food. When dogs and cats eat other animals, they also consume any toxins those animals ate, along with supplements, hormones, and antibiotics routinely used to keep the overcrowded and stressed cows, chickens, pigs, and fish alive and growing. Pet food meats also contain potential contaminants, such as the euthanasia drug pentobarbital, which triggered a massive nationwide recall in 2018. We explore all of these food-safety issues in the first chapter.

Two things have been holding back change when it comes to excluding meat from our pets' diets, even for vegan or vegetarian owners. First, there is a lack of quality or viable alternatives to traditional animal meat–based pet food. Food biotech is changing this. We've dedicated the largest part of this book to the exciting new innovations in the pet food industry that are going to revolutionize pet diets. In Chapters 7 and 8, we explore the benefits and challenges for plant-based pets. Chapters 9 to 12 are devoted to the stories of companies developing everything from new plant-based proteins, to clean cellular meats and finless fish and mouse meats for cats, to fungal and yeast proteins, and beyond.

The second barrier to eliminating animal meats from pet food is ideological. What right do humans have to impose our values on our pets? How can we interfere with what is "natural" for a wolf-descendent or predator? Chapters 6, 7, and 8 debunk the mythology that our pets *need* animal meat to survive and show that both dogs and cats can thrive on animal-free diets. After all, as we're about to see, eating animal meat is not necessarily the healthiest dietary option for humans or pets.

The question for the next decade is whether we feed pets less animal meat, or feed fewer pets. We're past the point where individual ideology and personal beliefs can be the main motivator. Changing our pets' eating habits is a practical necessity for survival. The evidence is clear: if we continue consuming and feeding animal meat as we do currently, we're not going to be able to sustain ourselves, much less our pets. It's not science fiction to suggest that the dogs and cats snuggling in our beds will no longer be a viable expense in the looming climatological dystopia where our heated oceans are dead and our scorched fields bare. A world without pets? That's not a scenario any dog or cat owner wants, so we need to radically rethink the way we produce our pet food. Scientists are calling for a "global shift" toward reducing meat in our diets, and this shift *must* include what we feed our dogs and cats.

What Does a Responsible Pet Owner Look Like?

Let's consider our responsibilities as pet owners. Valuing animals as our friends or family rather than as servants or helpers means rethinking how we view them and their abilities. Philosopher Bernard Rollin points out that the concept of "friendship" requires some morality-based, self-less exchange on the part of *both* friends. As part of their "deal" with us, our pets must agree to not "misbehave" and to abide by our rules. In return, humans offer pets love and, more practically, food, shelter, protection, and medical care. It's not a dissimilar relationship to that of a parent and child, and Cary Cooper, professor of organizational psychology and health at Manchester Business School, believes would-be parents are actually using pets to test how they cope with the responsibility of caring for an infant.[22] In the United States, the number of cats and dogs now exceeds the number of children under the age of eighteen by almost two to one, and 90 percent of dog owners consider their animals to be part of their "family."[23] This means we now want *human* or *human-like* products for our pets. That includes human-grade, meat-rich, freshly cooked pet food, often tailored to each pet and delivered via online subscription. As we'll explore in detail, this purchasing pressure is having alarming consequences for our planet and all the other animals, in addition to not always being the healthiest choice for our pets.

Translating the overwhelming affection we feel for our pets into responsible care is a core part of the evolution of the human–animal bond. The good news is that research shows we're becoming more responsible pet owners. Not only has there been a decline in unwanted animals entering American shelters and being euthanized, but we're also adopting more homeless animals.[24] Over the past decade, people have become more likely to get a pet "purposefully" (62 percent) rather than "serendipitously" (26 percent). Ten years ago, those numbers were 46 percent and 37 percent, respectively.[25] Researchers believe this is attributable to a "cultural shift" in how society and pet owners relate to their animals. The increased level of commitment and care that pet owners provide for their pets, as well as the growing perception of dogs and cats as family members, are indicators of an improving human–pet relationship. Clearly, we're more responsible and caring pet owners than ever before.

This book doesn't suggest that all pets are treated like princes or princesses. The reality is that too many people continue to mistreat pets. Purchasing or adopting animals without fully understanding pet care responsibilities often leads to cats and dogs being abandoned in shelters or out on the streets. Pets may be abused and tormented, trained to be unnaturally aggressive, or used as a fashion statement. Some people who claim to love dogs and cats crop their ears, dock their tails, or amputate their claws so they will fit more conveniently into their human lives. These owners are treating their dogs and cats as "accessories" rather than as autonomous beings with rights and needs of their own. Hal Herzog rather cynically states in his book *Some We Love, Some We Hate, Some We Eat*: "The terms companion animal and pet guardian are linguistic illusions that enable us to pretend we do not own the animals we live with."[26]

Whatever we choose to call the human–animal relationship, even if we do consider an animal our friend, we must remember that we still *own* him or her. That's why, throughout this book, we refer to our dogs and cats not just as "companion animals" but also as "pets." Whereas many of us may prefer to see ourselves as "guardians" or "companions" rather than as "owners," the reality is that our animals live in our care, under our rules and restrictions. Ownership bestows a certain freedom to treat our "property" how we choose, within cultural bounds. Unfortunately, this means we can choose to euthanize an animal because we can't afford his medical treatment, punish a cat for urinating on a bed, or train a dog using fear-motivated or dominance methods. We're also free to choose compassionate options, provide our pets with responsible end-of-life care, train a dog with positive reinforcement and rewards, and welcome them into our families as valued individuals. We can't say it any better than the words often attributed to Mahatma Gandhi: "The greatness of a nation can be judged by the way its animals are treated."

We can also choose what and how we feed our pets. Food is one of the most obvious ways we show our love for our pets, but how do we know that a diet is truly healthy and ethically sourced? Although many pet owners believe feeding a premium, raw meat, or home-prepared diet is best for our pets, it's certainly not best for the animals killed to feed them. No matter what you feed your pets, chances are you're pretty adamant about it.

In her chapter "Feeding Frenzy" in *Run, Spot, Run,* Jessica Pierce describes how our pets' diets have become "a veritable circus of conflicting opinions, to which adherents cling with surprising violence."[27] In Chapter 5 of this book we look at the rise of premium pet foods and investigate how healthy such options really are. Responsible pet owners are bombarded with advice from friends, recommendations from veterinarians, instructions from raw-meat zealots, advertising from pet food companies, home-baked cat treat recipes from websites, campaigns from vegan dog owners, and horror stories from news agencies on pet food recalls. How can we sift through the clutter and determine what our dogs and cats actually need? It's safe to say our pets aren't losing sleep worrying about global warming and the suffering of broiler chickens, but we should. In Chapters 2, 3, and 4, we'll look at our wider responsibilities as pet owners, both as inhabitants of a struggling planet and as ethical consumers in a food system built on animal suffering. We believe there are healthier ways to care for pets without harming the planet or other animals.

Fido Isn't Free to Choose

By treating our cats and dogs more like "family members" than "animal companions," we've developed a deeper emotional bond than when our animals worked for us. Unfortunately, this compelling human–animal bond doesn't always lead us to make the best decisions for our pets. Deborah Linder, a veterinarian at the Tufts Obesity Clinic for Animals, highlights how the veterinary field is starting to understand that "pet obesity is much more about the human–animal bond than the food bowl."[28] We'll explore this in detail later, delving into our responsibilities as loving, but disciplined, pet feeders. As much as our pets benefit from our care, we must remember they are captive animals. We're in control of nearly every aspect of their lives, including what goes into their bodies. Ethologist Marc Bekoff has repeatedly pointed out that domestic dogs are highly restrained and confined creatures. He critiques the phrase "It's a dog's life," turning it into "Would you *really* want to live a dog's life?"

Perhaps living as a domestic dog in a human environment is actually more stressful to animals than we realize, even when that home is an extremely loving one. Roughly 80 percent of the world's dogs are free-ranging, and recent research has suggested that these animals might be happier than their domestic cousins. It was found that, on Bali Island, dogs who have lived free-roaming for thousands of years were less aggressive and calmer than pet dogs kept inside houses and backyards.[29] The researchers concluded that living in a confined environment might have negative consequences for some canine personality traits. Jennifer Arnold agrees. In her book *Love Is All You Need*, she writes that pet dogs live in an environment that "makes it impossible for them to alleviate their own stress and anxiety."[30] As for cats, the Humane Society of the

United States (HSUS) insists that all pet cats should be kept inside to protect them from danger. However, animal experts Dennis Turner and Patrick Bateson argue that this policy is not good for feline welfare, as do several European veterinary organizations. These experts claim an animal's belief that it is in control of its surroundings is essential for avoiding stress.[31]

Our pets are always attempting to adapt to a human world in which their desires and needs are secondary to ours. Indoor dogs must be granted permission and access to urinate or defecate and are often restrained on a leash when outdoors. They are only allowed to play with the toys we give them and the playmates we introduce them to. They must eat what we feed them, *when* we feed them. It's clear we have created companions wholly dependent on us. To fully understand our responsibilities to them, we must first accept that pets are captive, domesticated animals. As we'll see later, we haven't "rescued" wild creatures from lives of hardship; we've deliberately bred dogs and cats to be entirely dependent on our care over thousands of years. As Bekoff says, this is "the crucial starting point for understanding our relationships with, and responsibilities to, our furry friends, relationships that very often favor us."[32]

Whether or not you believe that we can, or should, "own" a dog or cat, it's clear that we can, and must, offer them stewardship. While we restrict their freedom, we also offer our pets veterinary care, comfortable beds, shelter, and of course regular water and food. We also need to allow our pets to be individuals and learn about their unique personalities and needs. That extends to the food we give them. We must evaluate what is right for our own particular pet, and this means being as informed as possible about the benefits and pitfalls of all the various diets and products out there, and those about to come.

Ultimately, we've taken the stress of hunting and scavenging their own food away from cats and dogs, but we have also removed their choice. That means we have to take our responsibility to feed them the healthiest, tastiest, most *sustainable*, and most *ethical* foods very, very seriously. Hopefully, this book will help pet owners navigate the marketing minefield of the modern pet food industry and introduce the innovations that are shaking up traditional pet food production in the best possible way. In this sense, we hope that this book will take some of the stress away from you, too.

1

A Dollop of Deadly

How Animal Ingredients Are Harming Our Pets

IN SEPTEMBER 2018, following the devastation of Hurricane Florence, at least 3.4 million chickens and turkeys and over 5,500 pigs were drowned in North Carolina. Fearing financial ruin for farmers and enormous payouts from agricultural insurers, the North Carolina Department of Agriculture devised a special "disposal plan" to deal with such a catastrophe.[1] With the stroke of a pen, millions of dead and decomposing animal corpses were deemed acceptable for rendering and eventual sale as animal feed ingredients. At the same time state officials were approving drowned pigs and poultry for use in food for animals, they issued a declaration that flooded crops were unsuitable for human consumption.[2] No one knows for sure how many, if any, of those rotten animal carcasses ended up in our pets' food bowls, but it certainly reinforced how rancid the world of animal ingredients in pet food has become.

Scarily, many commercial pet foods contain ingredients that would shock most pet owners. Toxic chemicals, animal hormones and antibiotics, and a multitude of harmful bacteria may accompany animal meats in both wet and dry food.[3] In addition to these unhealthy contaminants, the evidence continues to prove that a diet high in animal meats is unhealthy. In humans, eating a diet rich in animal meat is strongly correlated with the onset of preventable diseases,[4] estimated to cost $314 billion a year for interventional medicine.[5] The situation has become so dire for humans that the World Health Organization (WHO) issued a warning in 2015 linking processed red meat consumption to cancer, urging that we decrease animal proteins in our own diets.[6] In animals, we have less research, but obesity,[7] kidney and liver disease,[8,9] and certain cancers[10-15] have been correlated with commercial diets high in animal meat.

Of course, there's more to this dilemma than health alone. Vegan and vegetarian readers may already be struggling with the ethical and moral aspects of including animal meat in their pet's diet. The next three chapters of this book explore the ethical challenges pet food poses in terms of environmental concerns and farmed-animal welfare. However, ideology aside, there are a host of immediate, practical reasons for taking animal proteins out of the pet bowl. Whether or not you're worried about the planetary impact of pet food, or care much about pigs and chickens, we're willing to bet that you *do* care deeply about your dog or cat's health and safety. There begins the struggle to solve the pet food problem.

The UFOs (Unidentified Furry Objects) in Pet Food

Most pet owners are aware (unless they are in blissful denial) that most commercial pet foods aren't made of the juiciest cuts of meat but rather of "byproduct," a euphemism for the leftover animal body parts that slaughterhouses can't or won't sell to humans. The Association of American Feed Control Officials (AAFCO) defines a "meat byproduct" as follows:

> The non-rendered, clean parts, other than meat, derived from slaughtered mammals. It includes, but is not limited to, lungs, spleen, kidneys, brain, livers, blood, bone, partially de-fatted low temperature fatty tissue, and stomachs and intestines freed of their contents. It does not include hair, horns, teeth and hoofs. It shall be suitable for use in animal feed.[16]

It's some relief to know that our dogs aren't munching on hair, teeth, and hooves, but it's unlikely that many people relish the idea of their pet chowing down on horse brain or pig colon. In their book *Feed Your Pet Right*, Marion Nestle and Malden Nesheim explain how the animal meat used for pet food primarily comes from parts rejected from human food production, usually flesh removed from mechanical deboning or other cuts not fit for human consumption.[17]

There are currently nine AAFCO ingredient terms used to classify "meat" in pet food, and three do not require the animal species to be identified. The AAFCO-approved term *meat* can include the flesh of cattle, pigs, sheep, and goats. This meat is most often a "meal" made up of a combination of different animals, with rendered animal protein making up to 40 percent of the protein and fats in commercial pet foods. Rendering is a process in which animal parts are chopped into small pieces and boiled until the mass of flesh is an unrecognizable lumpy stew. The stew is then dehydrated, and the fat and proteins removed. The protein fraction is ground into a "meal" and used in pet foods. About 31 percent of rendered proteins and 15 percent of rendered fats are used as pet food ingredients in the United States and Canada.[18]

The most problematic meat ingredients in pet food are not the whole food byproducts but rather the rendered animal material. Rendering allows pet food companies to potentially use what many call "4-D meats": flesh from animals that were dead, dying, diseased, or disabled, as well as expired human retail meats. Despite the fact that using decomposing animal tissue in pet food is a direct violation of the Federal Food, Drug, and Cosmetic Act, which categorizes 4-D meats as "adulterated," this law is rarely enforced. The FDA's Center for Veterinary Medicine (CVM) publicly admits:

> CVM is aware of the sale of dead, dying, disabled, or diseased (4-D) animals to salvagers for use as animal food. Meat from these carcasses is boned and the meat is packaged or frozen without heat processing. The raw, frozen meat is shipped for use by several industries, including pet food manufacturers, zoos, greyhound kennels, and mink ranches. This meat may present a potential health hazard to the animals that consume it and to the people who handle it.[19]

The reality is that a large percentage of animals in the factory-farming industry don't make it to slaughter, instead dying from disease, during transportation, or because of stress. The flesh of these dead animals is no longer able to be sold for human consumption because it's often contaminated with pathogens. As we saw after Hurricane Florence, the animal farming industry would suffer huge economic losses if these masses of prematurely deceased animals weren't put to profitable use. This is why rendering is salvation for animal farms facing these losses. Aside from the illegal packaged or frozen meat sales cited by the FDA, approximately two billion pounds (938 million kilograms) of food animals that die before slaughter are rendered and approved as fit for animal food.[20]

Gene Baur, co-founder and president of Farm Sanctuary, has seen first-hand the type of meat that goes into pet food. Speaking at the Plant-Powered Dog Food Summit in 2019, he revealed the following:

> I've been to rendering plants and seen carcasses that are decayed, that are being eaten by maggots. Those products will go into the rendering industry and will ultimately, in many cases, end up as pet food.

Baur and others want pet owners to know that dogs and cats are likely being fed diseased animal corpses. The National Renderers Association assures the public that they are taking potentially unsafe food ingredients and making them safe again.[21] They make this claim based on the fact that rendering heat-sterilizes bacteria-laden 4-D meat. So why, as we're about to see, are bacterial pathogens including *Listeria* and *Salmonella* still found in pet food? It seems that even though the rendering process *should* make the meat safe for consumption, some contamination is still happening, especially during pet food production, where processing standards are lower than those for human foods. Are you really happy with the idea of feeding your beloved dog or cat meat that was once potentially cancerous, decaying, or infected? Chillingly, veterinarian Richard Pitcairn presented to veterinary conference delegates that meat inspectors at the slaughter line will remove parts of diseased animals not fit for human consumption, such as abscesses and tumors, and allow them for pet food.[22]

A huge problem with today's meat byproducts is that we don't know exactly what's going into our animals' food. Perhaps the chicken was raised as humanely as possible under ideal conditions, or perhaps it drowned and rotted after a flood. There's simply no way currently to verify where, or sometimes what, animal protein source you're feeding your pet. A research team at Chapman University in 2015 analyzed fifty-two commercial pet food products to identify meat species present as well as any instances of mislabeling.[23] Out of the tested products, thirty-one were labeled correctly, twenty were potentially mislabeled, and one contained a non-specific meat ingredient that could not be verified. This isn't good enough. If we buy "beef dog food," we trust it contains cow meat. We no longer toss our dog dinner scraps; we pay a hefty fee for his pet food to be high-quality, safe, and nutritious. When we purchase a "dog food," we expect it to be formulated for a dog's specific nutritional needs, not just a mixture of the cheapest byproducts of the human food industry. Regardless of the type of pet food we prefer, we deserve to know exactly what is in the bag or can, not an ingredient list of questions.

Some people believe that animal byproducts and rendered meats are not only acceptable, but also environmentally responsible. Frank Mitloehner, professor and air quality extension specialist at the University of California Davis Department of Animal Science, says: "The whole rendering business is one of the biggest recycling businesses out there."[24] The authors of a 2015 article for the National Renderers Association, entitled "Rendered Ingredients Significantly Influence Sustainability, Quality, and Safety of Pet Food,"[25] stress that without rendering, there would be huge biosafety problems and we'd waste a huge amount of food nutrients that could be eaten. We agree that rendering waste animal meat is far better than letting it decompose and release additional greenhouse gases. If we're going to kill animals for meat, we have a moral responsibility to use as much of their bodies as possible.

If we're going to kill animals for meat. The National Renderers Association study inadvertently makes the point that in the absence of the pet food industry, animal agriculture as we know it (i.e., factory farming) *could not exist*. About 20 percent of all U.S. meat is used in pet food, most of this as byproducts for rendering. The researchers admit that the amount of meat considered inedible by humans, such as bones, fat, blood, feathers, and some internal organs, "is a large volume of byproduct that would quickly overtake landfills if not rendered. . . . The sustainability of animal agriculture depends on a reasonable and practical use of the byproducts generated."[26] Author Ted Kerasote comes to a similar conclusion in his book *Pukka's Promise: The Quest for Longer-Lived Dogs*: "There would be no modern meat industry without rendering, because the leftovers of slaughterhouses would soon overwhelm landfills and create an enormous health hazard as billions of tons of organic waste rotted."[27] As we'll explore in the next three chapters, by feeding our pets animal meat we are often unwittingly supporting the cruel, environmentally damaging practice of factory farming animals.

Others would argue that we've been feeding dogs leftovers since the beginning of domestication, so meat byproducts are no big deal. The theory that dogs evolved from the most docile and submissive wolves by scavenging our food scraps is commonly accepted. Yet recent research has challenged the idea that early-domesticated dogs were simply scavengers, as we'll explore in Chapter 6. Either way, it's clear that humans have made distinctions between human and animal foods for hundreds, if not thousands, of years. Some of the earliest recorded food regulations in modern civilizations included these partitions, with some codifying which "impure" foods were considered unsafe for humans and safe for dogs. This list includes food tainted as "carrion,"[28] or the rotting corpses of any "beast" (that is, any animal other than human). Although ancient regulators discouraged humans from eating decomposing animals, it was perfectly fine for dogs, according to these early food inspectors. Sound familiar? Despite the passage of hundreds of years, we seem to be living in a state of perpetual pet food confusion.

How do we overcome the concern that if we stop using leftovers in pet food, we would create more food waste? If we eliminated meat byproducts from pet foods, would we decrease the number of animals raised for slaughter? No one knows for sure, but the authors of this book believe dogs and cats deserve better quality and safer proteins—and we're sure you do, too. Dog and cat feed-grade ingredients should be more similar to human-grade food. And that doesn't have to mean more human-grade animal meats. If we switched all pets to a human-grade animal-meat diet, we would increase the number of farmed animals, and the associated environmental and animal welfare costs. That was the old way of solving the protein problem. Later in this book we'll see that human-grade protein doesn't need to come from animals; but first let's explore the problems that arise when it does.

The ambiguous animal protein ingredients we discussed earlier not only confuse consumers, but they also make it harder for improved animal welfare to be part of our purchasing decisions, even when we buy "human-grade meat." Pet owners who proudly purchase "organic grass-fed beef kibble" for their dogs may unknowingly be paying for byproducts of cage-bound chickens within the same bag. Distressingly, even expensive foods labeled "organic" and "free-range" are particularly vulnerable to fraud and obfuscation. Operation Opson, a 2011 investigation targeting ten European ports, airports, and retail outlets, found that about half of the goods seized were counterfeit brands and the other half counterfeit foods. The sting uncovered products such as "wild salmon" that was actually farmed salmon; fake coffees made from ingredients such as corn, barley, and sugar; and "caviar" created from seaweed and lumpsucker fish. "Organic soybeans" were coated in pesticides. Today, rising food prices, long supply chains, confusing label terminology, and high mark-ups have made food fraud more profitable and easier to get away with. So much for transparency. The watchwords when buying pet food these days should certainly be *caveat emptor*.

Most people tend to believe that the animal-meat supply chain has four parts: 1) family farm, 2) slaughterhouse, 3) meat-packing plant, and

4) grocer. The reality is dramatically different. The vast majority of animals raised for meat are born and die on massive factory farms. Many animals are bought and sold at huge livestock markets before they are carted off to the slaughterhouse, introducing additional stress, disease exposure, injury, and suffering. After the slaughterhouse, the animal remains may be shipped to another facility to be cut and processed, introducing more risk of contamination. If the meat is imported, it might have been slaughtered in one country, sent to another plant, and then processed at a third plant before arriving at the manufacturer. Each country may have different food safety regulations and inspections, making quality assurance and biosecurity nearly impossible. Finally, the meat ends up at the food manufacturer, with little hope of fully tracing its circuitous journey. This convoluted food supply chain leaves ample room for contamination and corruption. When we evaluate that supply chain for pet food, the process is even more recent, less regulated, and more poorly enforced, resulting in greater risk.

The concept of specialized pet food basically started in the 1860s when an entrepreneurial electrician, James Spratt, created meat and vegetable biscuits "specially designed for dogs." Spratt recognized that people were beginning to feed their pets not only leftover dinner scraps, but entire helpings of their own meals. He guessed that if these dog owners had a special food to feed their pet, he might have a market. Spratt developed a concept based on taking human food and animal feed leftovers and producing dog food during downtime at livestock feed production facilities. The first "pet foods" were born and now top nearly $80 million (£60 million) globally in annual sales.[29] The more cynical of us might say that the very notion of "pet food" is an elaborate marketing tactic enacted by a savvy industry intent on exploiting our bond with our companion animals. Although that's not an entirely accurate summation, the pet food industry certainly takes advantage of our unique interspecies relationship. Later, we'll look at the advantages and disadvantages of feeding your pet homemade "human food" as an alternative to food specifically formulated for dogs or cats. But, for now, let's explore whether most commercial pet foods are truly "special."

The Unsettling Matter of Mass Recalls

If the only rogue ingredients in pet foods were simply unwanted animal byproduct proteins, that wouldn't be the end of the world. As a veterinarian focused on nutrition, Ernie has found the majority of contemporary pet foods in grocery and pet stores to be nutritionally complete and balanced, at least according to accepted nutritional guidelines. Whereas we might feel confident that our dogs are getting the amount of nutrients they need, is it being served with a helping of bad stuff they *don't* need? The fact that modern pet foods are full of healthy nutrients is wonderful, but we also need it to be free of contaminants such as antibiotic residues, hormones, toxins, pesticides, physical particulates, or disease-causing pathogens. The FDA doesn't require that pet food products have pre-market approval, but their guidelines are meant to ensure the ingredients used are "safe and have an appropriate function in the pet food."[30] But what does that really mean?

On average, there are thirty-eight ingredients in dog food and thirty-four ingredients in cat food, according to data from Petnet. It's pretty standard for processed foods, whether for pets or people, to contain thirty-eight ingredients. Generally, "whole" ingredients start off the list, and then you get into the more indecipherable extras. Those "extras" aren't necessarily good or bad, but you still need to pay attention to them. The problem is that even if you understand what all the ingredient terms mean, it's still a mystery where each one comes from. After receiving more than 8,500 reports of pet deaths following the melamine pet food recall by Menu Foods in March 2007, Congress promised a new law in the FDA Amendments Act, called "Ensuring the Safety of Pet Food." Lawmakers assured consumers that no later than October 2009 regulated pet food ingredient standards and definitions would be established, including processing and labeling standards that have more comprehensive nutritional and ingredient information.

A decade later, there is no sign of this promised law, and in 2018, Section 306 of HR 5554 completely eliminated these federal pet food safety promises. This means it continues to be the private pet food industry organization AAFCO, and not the FDA, that helps create state-specific regulations and model pet food safety legislation. Although the AAFCO guidelines emphasize nutritional minimum and maximum allowances, the organization has no interest in how pet food ingredients are *sourced*. The AAFCO guidelines openly state that fact:

> AAFCO does not regulate, test, approve or certify pet foods in any way. AAFCO establishes the nutritional standards for complete and balanced pet foods, and it is the pet food company's responsibility to formulate their products according to the appropriate AAFCO standard.[31]

The fact is there is minimal governmental or regulatory oversight to prevent U.S. pet food companies from sourcing their animal material from pigs, cows, and chickens in poor health or killed in unsanitary slaughterhouses.

Back in 1958, U.S. federal law required all "food," whether for humans or pets, to be sourced *only* from USDA-inspected and -certified/-passed meat facilities. That's not the case today. As we saw earlier, the FDA's compliance policies have explicitly informed the pet food industry that federal food law will *not* be enforced, allowing nonviable, diseased, or decaying animals to be rendered into pet food without disclosure to the consumer. When regulatory authorities choose to ignore the law, we see cases such as the 2010 incident of Bravo Packing, Inc., a pet food manufacturer that turned out to be an animal carcass removal agency. After their "Performance Dog Food" was recalled for *Salmonella* contamination, an undercover investigation revealed that the pet food company was actually based at a horse slaughterhouse. Although it's not illegal in the United States to slaughter horses for animal consumption, in this case the manufacturer was not only misinforming consumers but was also found to be mistreating and abusing their horses and confining them in "unspeakable conditions."[32] Pet food manufacturers and dog and cat owners were naïvely feeding their pets euthanized horsemeat that potentially contained a euthanasia drug. It's not necessarily the ingredients on the pet food label you need to worry about; it's those unlisted or hidden that may pose the most danger.

The most prominent and successful pet foods, the ones lining supermarket and grocery store shelves, tend to be the brands with the biggest marketing budgets: J. M. Smucker (Nutrish, Ol' Roy, 9-Lives, Meow Mix, Kibbles 'n' Bits, Milk Bone, Natural Balance, Skippy, Pup-Peroni, Gravy Train, Milo's Kitchen); Mars Petcare (Pedigree, Whiskas, Nutro, Iams); Nestlé Purina (Purina, Fancy Feast, Alpo, Friskies, Beneful, One); or Colgate Palmolive (Hill's Science Diet, Prescription Diet). These companies source their ingredients from the same global suppliers, meaning the essential composition of most commercial pet foods is very similar, especially animal meats. This means that when there's a problem with one of these major suppliers, it can escalate *fast*.

In 2007, 180 different brands used pet food ingredients supplied by Menu Foods. Menu Foods was sourcing its protein from a Chinese company that decided to cheat. Instead of adding real animal proteins, this Chinese company discovered that adding toxic melamine would trick chemical analyzers into reporting higher animal protein levels than were actually present. As most pet owners know, the company added melamine in order to skimp on animal proteins and boost their bottom line. Hundreds, perhaps thousands, of pets were poisoned after melamine-induced crystals formed in their kidneys. A subsequent lawsuit estimated that over 13,000 pets died in the United States as a result of eating the tainted food. The following year, China's Sanlu Group had to recall human baby formula because it was also contaminated with melamine, making around 294,000 babies sick (54,000 were hospitalized) and killing at least six infants.[33]

Since 2007, there have been over two hundred pet food recalls in the United States alone. In 2018, J. M. Smucker was forced to recall over 107 million cans of poisoned pet food, this time for potential pentobarbital contamination, an animal euthanasia drug. Also in 2018, Advance Dermocare was pulled from Australian store shelves after more than a hundred dogs were diagnosed with and died from megaesophagus, a disease that causes a dog's esophagus to lose its elasticity and ability to contract, making it difficult, if not impossible, to swallow. It's certainly good we're seeing more pet food recalls; they help keep our pets safer. However, the bad news is that these recalls are still occurring and are only initiated after a problem is reported by consumers, industry watchdogs, or retailers. Most of these pet foods were recalled not because the FDA identified a problem before it occurred, but because an official complaint was lodged. The same was true in the extensive 2007 melamine and 2018 Smucker euthanasia drug recalls; the problem was only identified after dogs died. We must do better.

Responsible pet owners should be alarmed that there's so much pet food contamination. The majority of pet food recalls are due to disease-causing bacteria that thrive on animal meat. *Salmonella* is one of the leading causes of food poisoning in the United States, according to Foodsafety.gov, followed by *E. coli*, *Listeria*, and vitamin or mineral imbalances. Although many animals eating contaminated pet food may not become sick themselves, they can become carriers and expose their human family members to pathogenic bacteria. In March 2018, two children became ill with a high pathogenic strain of *Salmonella* that matched the strain found in samples of the family dog's pet food. Three years earlier, J. J. Fuds had to recall their Chicken Tender Chunks Pet Food because it was potentially contaminated with *Listeria monocytogenes*, an organism that can cause serious and sometimes fatal infections in young children and frail or elderly people, as well as lead to miscarriages and stillbirths among pregnant women.

It's not just the animal meat in traditional pet food that's putting pets at risk. Bioethicist and animal advocate Jessica Pierce points out that even stranger "ingredients" derive from modern agribusiness: yellow plastic ID ear tags, the poop that drains from slaughtered cow intestines, rat poison, animal microchips, and sawdust are included in some pet foods.[34] Used restaurant grease is often recycled and rendered along with animal flesh, complete with high concentrations of hazardous free radicals and harmful trans-fatty acids, to make pet food ingredients. Farm Sanctuary's

Gene Baur told the following to delegates at the 2019 Plant-Powered Dog Food Summit:

> [After rendering] there are perhaps heavy metals, or other toxins, that could be entering the food supply and getting into pet food that are not tested for. This is an industry that has taken a "don't look, don't find" approach. . . . There's a very strong economic interest in not finding problems, so they don't really look very closely.[35]

Plastic meat and poultry wrapping have been documented in pet foods. These plastics have been shown to contain triclosan (TCS), a manufacturing chemical used as an antimicrobial ingredient in more than two thousand consumer products. Scientists recently reported that even brief exposure to TCS, at relatively low doses, can cause low-grade colonic inflammation and colitis and exacerbates colitis-associated colon cancer in mice.[36] Veterinarian and former Humane Society of the United States (HSUS) vice president Michael W. Fox believes TCS exposure may be a contributor to dysbiosis and inflammatory bowel disease in dogs and cats, and has called pet food manufacturers to demand their suppliers remove all plastic wrappings on discarded meat and poultry parts before processing.[37] Chronic exposure to and ingestion of TCS may also contribute to skin and thyroid problems and food allergies in dogs and cats. Unsurprisingly, TCS isn't the only chemical in our pet food. Quaternary ammonium compound mixture, an antimicrobial chemical used for cleaning food processing equipment, was recently discovered in dog chews, leading to two nationwide recalls. Another recall was attributed to fragments of metal, and one was for rubber pieces that could present a choking hazard to dogs and cats.

What else is in factory-farmed animals that we shouldn't feed our pets? Antibiotic residues in animal meats are an obvious concern. Currently, about 80 percent of all antibiotics in the United States are fed to livestock to keep them alive and growing in unnaturally crowded and contaminated conditions (a situation we'll look at in more detail in Chapter 3). Scientists are predicting that by 2050 more humans will die due to antibiotic resistance than from cancer and diabetes combined, and they caution that drug resistance begins with farmed animals. Antibiotic-resistant bacteria develop in the gut of the farmed animals and are transferred onto meat during slaughtering and processing. We risk exposure to the antibiotic-resistant bacteria by handling contaminated meats and products, including pet food.

Hormones are another pet food pollutant resulting from factory farming. Growth and reproductive hormones are often administered to cattle, poultry, swine, and fish that we consume or feed to our pets. There is increasing evidence and concern that even trace residues of these hormones, antimicrobials, and anthelmintics (drugs used to treat internal parasites) may be causing disruptions in a pet's normal hormonal secretions and cycles, altering normal gut microflora and leading to increased drug resistance.[38]

Let's return to that massive 2018 pet food recall involving the animal euthanasia drug, pentobarbital. Countless pet owners were shocked to learn from their local news media that pentobarbital had been discovered in dozens of pet foods. Later, it would be revealed that this had been a persistent problem for over twenty years. In both 1998 and 2000, the FDA conducted studies to determine the "safe" level of pentobarbital for pet food. The FDA concluded: "The low levels of exposure to sodium pentobarbital (pentobarbital) that dogs might receive through food is unlikely to cause them any adverse health effects."[39] In other words, if it didn't immediately kill or sicken the pets that ate it, it must be okay.

Hold on a minute! There's no way a euthanasia drug should be present in pet food in *any* amount. Farmed meat animals are not euthanized: they're killed without the use of drugs, either through blunt force or electrocution in most cases. If there are euthanasia drugs in your pet food, it means that food includes animals that shouldn't be in pet food. The FDA report states that the origin of 2018 contamination was most likely due to improperly slaughtered cattle or horses: "[I]t is assumed that the pentobarbital residues are entering pet foods from euthanized, rendered cattle or even horses."[40] Are you worried about the safety of animal meats yet?

Some pet food critics suggest an even more sinister origin for pentobarbital in pet foods: "protein meal" could be euthanized pets. This somewhat sensationalist conspiracy theory has been repeatedly denied by the FDA, but not everybody is convinced. In an undated video, the 1998 president of AAFCO Hersch Pendell informs a news reporter that there was no specific regulation that prevented rendered dog or cat meats from being included in pet food under the listing "meat meal." He said: "There's no way to really tell that, because if the ingredient says meat and bone meal, you don't know if that's cattle or sheep or horse—or Fluffy."[41]

In 2013, *Slate* carried out an investigation, entitled "Does Your Pet's Food Contain Dead Pets?" It found the answer to be a murky "Maybe." In March 2018, after the pentobarbital-triggered pet food recall, the Ohio legislature debated a bill requiring pet food to be free of any euthanized animal, including dogs and cats. Shockingly, this was the first time state lawmakers in the United States had considered the issue.

The Food Safety Modernization Act (FSMA) won't do much to prohibit or prevent pentobarbital in pet food as long as the FDA allows pet food manufacturers to use ingredients that include "animals which have died otherwise than by slaughter." These animals include pentobarbital-euthanized animals. Susan Thixton, former AAFCO Pet Food Committee member, investigative blogger, and author of the popular website truthaboutpetfood.com, asked the FDA why they do not enforce every violation of the law. Their response was telling:

> Due to competing priorities and resource limitations, government agencies cannot act against every violation of the law. . . . The use of enforcement discretion allows the FDA to concentrate on the most egregious violations and the ones that present the highest risk to animal and human health.

In September 2018, Dr. Steven Solomon, the director of the FDA's Center for Veterinary Medicine (CVM), told a packed audience at an industry trade event that "new evidence" showed that pentobarbital may be "a much more pervasive problem in the animal food supply than originally thought."[42] If we can't rely on the FDA to ensure manufacturers don't use euthanized animal meat in their products, and if the FDA doesn't have the budget to inspect and prevent diseased animals and non-slaughtered animals from becoming pet food, it seems risky to continue feeding animal meat–based foods to our pets. In the last half of this book, we'll share with you the exciting future foods that will usher in an era of safer and more nutritious non-animal proteins.

Why Are We Feeding Our Pets Animal-Grade Feed?

Responsibility for the standards for what can and cannot be included as pet food ingredients lies, as we have seen, with AAFCO, a group of animal feed and agricultural industry representatives. Note the term *animal feed*. Perhaps the most ironic element in the whole story about what we feed our pets is that most of the ingredients in dog and cat foods are literally (and legally) the same as those used to feed pigs, chickens, and other livestock. From the perspective of AAFCO and other animal feed regulatory bodies, anything not fit for humans is animal feed. That is beginning to change, but for now, all animal feed is a totally separate category from human food.

Food nomenclature is powerful, at least when it comes to regulations and public perceptions. In upcoming chapters, we'll examine the ethical problem with assigning greater value to one group of animals than another. When it comes to how we feed our pets, we're actually being less discriminatory than we think, relying on the same regulations and protections for our pets as those used for livestock. We protect our pets from abuse and suffering in ways we don't extend to farmed animals, but we don't apply this protection to what our companions are *eating*.

Advisors to AAFCO's Pet Food Committee include representatives from meat-industry interest groups such as the National Renderers Association and the American Feed Industry Association. According to the National Renderers Association, each year rendering converts inedible animal byproducts and "other materials" into eleven billion pounds of reclaimed animal fat, a concentrated source of energy for both livestock and domestic pet feed.[43] This fact presents a real conflict of interest. Although the meat industry doesn't need food animals to live long, healthy lives, the pet food industry is supposed to care deeply about companion animals doing exactly that. The sad fact is that it doesn't matter to meat producers if the antibiotics and growth hormones in a pig lead to that animal developing disease or cancer. Long before those side effects occur, that pig has become bacon, his sad fate buried forever within a frying pan or between the halves of a bun. But if that same feed, or breed of animal, is fed to your dog, year after year, your pet has to live, or die, with the consequences of your choices. What you feed your pet today matters for the rest of their life.

Almost *half* of all U.S. dogs alive today will develop cancer after the age of ten, according to the American Veterinary Medical Association (AVMA). A growing number of veterinarians are linking these high cancer rates to poor quality meat-based pet foods. Events such as the 2007 melamine crisis are relatively rare, but many more dogs and cats suffer from the subtle, long-term damage of bioaccumulation that results from eating contaminated or nutritionally deficient foods. In humans, research by the Broad Institute suggests that less than 10 percent of all cancer cases are caused by faulty genetics; the vast majority result from environmental factors such as exposure to toxins, obesity, and diet. Although genetics are likely to play a bigger role in pet cancer cases due to decades of irresponsible breeding, we shouldn't rule out the contribution of diet. Chemical toxins in the environment increase (bioaccumulate) in animals the higher we move up the food chain. When our pets eat other animals, they also consume the accumulation of toxins those animals ingested. We've already seen that most of the animals used in pet food are considered unfit for human consumption, including some animals that may be sick or diseased.

There is growing concern that hidden contaminants and chemicals in animal meats fed to pets may be triggering a wide variety of diseases and disorders, including cancer. At the end of 2018, it was discovered that plastic residues found in animal feed could pose a risk to people eating the animals. British farmer Andrew Rock noticed plastic shreds in his animal feed but was told by the suppliers that this was a legal part of the recycling process that turns waste food, still wrapped and packaged, into animal feed.[44] They were right. In the United Kingdom, a limit of 0.15 percent of plastic is allowed by the Food Standards Agency; according to AAFCO guidelines on allowed ingredients in animal feed, polyethylene plastic in pellet form may be used as a roughage substitute in cattle feed.[45] When this food is eaten and metabolized by cows, harmful microplastic compounds can be released, along with a variety of biologically disruptive chemicals. Those molecules end up distributed throughout a cow, pig, or chicken's body, and then we eat it or feed it to pets.

Andrew Knight, a small-animal veterinarian and professor of animal welfare at the University of Winchester, describes commercial pet foods as constituting "a vast industrial dumping ground for slaughterhouse waste products," including old or spoiled supermarket meat, large numbers of rendered dogs and cats from animal shelters, and damaged or spoiled fish (complete with potentially dangerous levels of mercury, PCBs, and other toxins and antibiotics), all of which are made irresistible to pets by the addition of "digest," a soup of partially dissolved intestines, livers, lungs, and miscellaneous viscera of chickens and other animals.

Human-grade animal meat is also far from risk-free. In 2015, the World Health Organization (WHO) classified all processed ("meat that has been transformed through salting, curing, fermentation, smoking, or other processes to enhance flavour or improve preservation" such as "hot dogs [frankfurters], ham, sausages, corned beef, and biltong or beef jerky as well as canned meat and meat-based preparations and sauces") and red meats ("all mammalian muscle meat, including, beef, veal, pork, lamb, mutton, horse, and goat") as Group 1 and 2A carcinogens, based on the International Agency for Research on Cancer's assessment of a "sufficient" and "strong" link between these meats and the mechanistic evidence for carcinogenicity.[46] The WHO noted that it wasn't simply the protein that posed a health risk, but the processing. Although the WHO doesn't comment on pet food, many of these statements translate directly to the health of dogs and cats, and vice versa. Even if your meat is labeled "organic," more often than not the factory-farm environment is saturated with persistent chemicals that bioaccumulate, giving meat-eating humans and pets a potential dose of toxins. These chemicals have been shown to contribute to degenerative diseases, including many forms of cancer, kidney disease, and neurological conditions. Scientists have also found that vegans are considerably less likely to die at a young age than people who ate meat, eggs, and dairy-based foods.[47]

* * *

When we feed our pets the flesh of other animals, we're gambling with their health. We, the authors, don't believe pet owners should take the risk when there are healthier dietary options. This book is about to explore the moral issue of how society uses—and abuses—sentient animals in modern animal farming systems, as well as the impact farming animals has on the environment, which, of course, affects our future survivability and quality of life. Ultimately, the impetus is on each of us to demand the most ethical, nutritious, and safest foods for both people and pets. Based on what we've learned so far, the best diet must surely be one without animal meats.

2

How Pet Food Is Destroying the World

OUR PRIMARY CONCERN so far has been the safety of a conventional animal meat–based diet for dogs and cats. We've explored how farmed-animal beef, pork, poultry, and fish often carry risk of contamination, potentially leading to illness and disease. High consumption of processed and red animal meats has also been shown to pose health threats for both people and perhaps pets. But that's not our only worry. Animal-meat pet foods may also be the most destructive diet for the health of our planet.

A few years back, an episode of the popular British quiz show *QI* showed contestants a photograph of a typical happy family with two children, a car, and a dog. The host asked, "What could this family do to reduce their carbon footprint?" Their answer was "Get rid of the car." Nope. The correct answer was "Get rid of the *dog*!" The contestants didn't realize that the family pet, fed two predominantly animal meat–based meals a day, was contributing to more carbon emissions than either the automobile or the human family's meals. Getting rid of the dog doesn't have to be the answer; a simpler solution is a meat-free diet.

Modern pet diets high in animal protein are now a major contributor to anthropogenic (human-induced) climate change, yet the overwhelming majority of pet owners aren't aware of that fact. Most have largely ignored the increasing environmental impact of their high-protein, "ancestral," "biologically appropriate," or "human-grade" and raw meat diets. According to a recent report from the World Resources Institute, beef, a key ingredient in meat-based dog food, is the most greenhouse gas (GHG)–intensive animal-based food product consumed today.[1] To complicate matters further, emissions from intensively raised beef (factory-farmed cows) are actually lower than premium cuts from outdoor-grazed, free-range cattle. This is because grain-fed cows produce less methane than do grass-fed ones. We're faced with a challenging trade-off: what is best for farmed-animal welfare, and arguably healthier for our pet, may actually be worse for mitigating climate change.

Climate change is now accelerating at an alarming rate, and the fate of our planet has never been more in the balance. On November 23, 2018, the U.S. government released an official report[2] confirming that climate change is significantly affecting the natural environment, agriculture, energy production and use, land and water resources, transportation, and human health and welfare across the United States and its territories. Everything essential to human life as we know it is in imminent danger. Everything. This dire warning doesn't issue from the hyperbolic shouts of tree-hugging activists; this is the U.S. National Climate Assessment cautioning that the world is about to become significantly more ecologically unstable. Climate change, in the most basic sense, is the long-term alteration of temperatures and weather patterns that makes rainfall patterns more irregular, makes intense heat and cold more extreme and frequent, and threatens highly biodiverse and complex ecosystems, such as the Amazon River Basin and the Great Barrier Reef.[3] Climate change will shortly undermine not just individual lives and millions of species but also the very foundation of life on our planet. It is our greatest existential threat. And it's happening *now*.

Technological advancements of the last two centuries have allowed humans to exploit natural resources to the extent that scientists are predicting not just the destruction of coral reefs and rainforests, but also the imminent shrinking of the economy and the deaths of hundreds of thousands to millions of people. Climate change is expected to reduce global food availability, resulting in around *half a million additional deaths* by 2050.[4] That's downright horrifying. Perhaps that's why the 2018 U.S. climate report was released on "Black Friday." The irony of announcing the impending destruction of our planet on a day celebrating mass consumption and unbridled consumerism wasn't lost on everybody. Many environmentalists suggested the U.S. government had deliberately "snuck out" the report while Americans were too busy shopping to notice.[5] They may be right. News stories reported the bleak future forecast just before they announced spectacular retail-spending results. Who had time to think about climatic disaster when there were steep discounts on BBQ grills and video games?

Humanity doesn't have time to ignore these warnings any longer. The government report's comprehensive, evidence-based survey announced the threat of "cascading impacts of climate change" to the natural, built, and social systems Americans rely on, both within and beyond our borders. The government experts stated that rising temperatures, extreme temperature shifts, droughts, wildfires on rangelands, and heavy downpours are expected to increasingly challenge the quality and quantity of U.S. crop yields, livestock health, price stability, and rural livelihoods. They warned that many communities should expect higher costs and lower property values to result from sea-level rise.

The researchers outlined that climate change threatens the health and well-being of all Americans by causing the spread of new diseases by insects, wildlife, and pests, and leads to the reduced availability of food and fresh water. Lack of available water will increase risks and costs to agriculture, energy production, industry, and recreation. Finally, the report concluded that humans are not doing anything close enough to challenge, much less slow, this terrifying future. Current efforts to respond to climate change were criticized as utterly inadequate to avoid substantial damage to the economy, environment, and human health over the coming decades. Apparently, most Americans ignored these "hysterical extremists" and "liberal scientists" and continued going their own gas-guzzling, steak-and-bacon-eating ways.

To prove this environmental indifference, in 2018 the United States ranked twenty-seventh in the 2018 Environmental Performance Index (EPI), trending downward since 2016. This reputable metric ranks 180 countries across ten categories, covering environmental health and ecosystem vitality. America is moving in the wrong environmental direction. In fact, humanity is about to reach a crisis point. Over the next fifty years, if we continue to do little to nothing to reverse climate change, we will struggle to find potable water and to prevent emerging diseases; war and revolutions will break out, and food will become scarce. As climate change progresses over the next two to three decades and pressure for natural resources escalates, what will be one of the first "luxuries" to go? We believe it will be our pets.

The Diagnosis Is In: Twelve Years to Turn Things Around

In around thirty years the global human population will reach ten billion, according to the latest projections. A 2018 report by the U.N. Intergovernmental Panel on Climate Change (IPCC), the undisputed global scientific authority on this issue, has concluded that global warming is going to have a devastating impact sooner than we think.[6] The worldwide consensus is that we currently have less than twelve years to keep global temperatures at 1.5° Celsius (2.7° Fahrenheit) below pre-industrial levels. After this point, the IPCC report states, we will be on a path to 2° Celsius, and perhaps higher—much higher. Each increase of half a degree means orders of magnitude greater environmental destruction, widespread social disruption, and wholesale species extinction. Should our planet exceed these climatological tipping points, humanity will begin a desperate attempt not to preserve our current way of life, but to survive shocks that could potentially end civilization.

The U.N. report urges governments around the world to take "rapid, far-reaching and unprecedented changes in all aspects of society" to avoid extreme drought, wildfires, floods, and food shortages for hundreds of millions to billions of people. Coral reefs and the oxygen-producing phytoplankton we rely on to breathe are already compromised, with between 70 and 90 percent expected to collapse and die. The impact on aquatic and terrestrial wildlife will be nothing short of extinction-level. The data prove we're already two-thirds of the way to this apocalyptic future. Global temperatures have already warmed about 1°C since the industrial age.[7]

Scientists agree that in order to slow or stop the planet from further overheating, we need to lower global net emissions of carbon dioxide by 45 percent from 2010 levels, and reach "net zero" by no later than 2050. The Paris Agreement, signed by the United States in 2016, aims to bring all nations into a common cause to combat climate change; namely by keeping a global temperature rise this century well below 2°C and to pursue efforts to limit the increase even further to 1.5°C. On June 1, 2017, U.S. President Donald Trump announced that America would cease all participation in the Paris Agreement, a withdrawal scheduled to take full effect in 2020. Things don't look good. But with or without governmental support, there are things that we, as individuals, can do.

It's true that society needs to make enormous changes to the way we power our industries, what we build, the energy we use, how we get around, and what we *eat*. When it comes to the last few points, we all have opportunities to make these changes. Scientists have known for years that animal meat–heavy diets are a major contributor to global GHG emissions and to global deforestation and land clearing.[8] A controversial 2009 article from the Worldwatch Institute estimated that over *half* our global GHG emissions could be attributed to animal agriculture products.[9] In a 2018 strategic paper,[10] Harvard farmed-animal law and policy fellow Dr. Helen Harwatt concluded that the rapid GHG reduction required to meet the goals of the Paris Agreement "allows no sector to maintain business as usual practices."

How can we change animal farming to eliminate or reduce emissions? Controversial supplements such as chloroform can be added to the feed of cattle, sheep, and goats to reduce their methane output, but this adversely affects their welfare, and creates additional risks to food safety. Environmental scientist Tobias Thornes concludes: "[T]here is no ethical, environmentally friendly way to reduce methane emissions from ruminants at the same time as maintaining or increasing the availability of meat and dairy produce."[11] Creating a genetically modified cow or other ruminant that somehow produces fewer toxic gases or adding feed chemicals to produce fewer emissions may be nearly impossible in the next decade.

Of course, there's a far simpler solution, but nobody seems to want to hear it, much less implement it. Harwatt unequivocally states that "animal to plant-sourced protein shifts offer substantial potential for GHG emission reductions." Switching to an animal meat–free vegetarian diet could reduce food-related emissions by 63 percent; becoming vegan (including no animal byproducts) could increase that to 70 percent.[12] At the start of 2019, the medical journal the *Lancet* published the findings of the EAT–*Lancet* Commission on healthy and sustainable diets. Their verdict was that civilization is in imminent crisis, Earth is at risk, and it's time to put the planet on a better, more sustainable meal plan:

> The dominant diets that the world has been producing and eating for the past 50 years are no longer nutritionally optimal, are a major contributor to climate change, and are accelerating erosion of natural biodiversity.[13]

Reducing animal-meat production and consumption is a necessity and not simply a lifestyle choice. According to the Organization for Economic Cooperation and Development (OECD), the global average meat consumption per person, per year is seventy-five pounds: the equivalent of approximately three hundred quarter-pounders.[14] Americans consume *a lot* more than seventy-five pounds a year. In 2017, Americans ate an average of 214 pounds of meat each, overtaking Australians for the first time. This figure is expected to rise to over 222 pounds for 2018. It's not just America and Australia that are bumping up the stats. The average European resident devours 153 pounds of meat per annum. It's unsurprising that research suggests Westerners must slash meat intake by 90 percent in order to feed an anticipated ten billion people by 2050.[15] Unfortunately for the future of humanity, the OECD report predicts that global meat consumption per capita is expected to *increase* to seventy-eight pounds per person by 2027. World, we have a problem. We're eating too much animal meat.

If we don't change our diet, Harwatt calculates that the livestock industry could account for 37 to 49 percent of total GHG emissions allowable under the 2°C and 1.5°C targets by 2030. If we continue eating the same amount of animal meat, we'll need to make substantial GHG reductions in other areas such as manufacturing, housing, and transportation, far beyond what are planned, or what the authors think realistic. Simply put, reducing animal-meat production is the easiest way to save our planet.

What Does Pet Food Have to Do with All This?

Even though more than 60 percent of U.S. households have pets,[16] the diets of our companion animals are rarely included in calculations of the environmental impact of meat consumption. Why not? In 2017, UCLA professor Gregory Okin published research showing that about 25 percent of calories from all animal meats consumed in the United States are now eaten by pets.[17] Put it this way: if dogs and cats had their own country, it would rank *fifth* in terms of total animal protein consumption. It's clear that unless we take the meat out of pet food, we're not going to achieve the 60 to 70 percent reduction in food-based GHG emissions needed to slow climate change. Okin's answer to the unsustainable business of pet food production is that humans would do better not to own dogs and cats at all, or to switch to vegetarian pets such as birds, hamsters, or even small horses. The authors don't view this as a realistic or acceptable resolution. We owe it to our animal companions to find another solution to our shortsightedness, other than their eradication. As we'll see later, humans and animals have been living together for tens of thousands of years and, if we can stop eating and feeding animal meats, we may continue doing so for thousands more. There's a choice here: we can own fewer pets, or we can feed our pets fewer animal meats.

Hopefully, you're convinced by now that current pet food production is bad for the planet. Although pet food uses lots of the "waste" material from animals killed for human consumption, Okin challenges the argument that dog and cat environmental impacts are obviated by the fact that they eat animal byproducts. He points out that this assessment relies on the assumption that these same byproducts couldn't be made suitable for human consumption after appropriate processing. Okin explains that most animal byproducts could, and he believes *should*, be eaten by people as well as pets. He claims that if just one-quarter of the estimated 25 percent of animal-derived calories in pet food was approved and used for human consumption, this alone would feed 26 million Americans. Okin's conclusion is that if humans are going to continue eating meat, Americans must do a better job optimizing animals for human consumption. Waste not, want not: save the planet.

Pet food meats, leather goods, cosmetics, and other animal byproducts are also essential for the animal farming industry to remain profitable. Due to the intense price pressure and global competition for human-edible meat, poultry, pork, and fish, the U.S. meat industry would not be nearly as lucrative without these "value-added" byproducts. According to the USDA Economic Research Service, beef, veal, and pork byproducts account for up to 19 percent of the industry's total value. These byproducts help keep "human foods" cheap and allow the animal farming industry to thrive. Remove animal meats from pet foods, and their entire economic system is threatened.

The reality is that more pet owners are demanding and buying human-grade animal meats for their dogs and cats. It seems almost certain that this trend will continue, with market surveys indicating young pet owners are more likely to purchase premium "human-grade" pet foods than standard fare.[18] What the pet-owning public wants, the pet food industry provides, regardless of nutrition or sustainability. A 2013 pet industry publication found that many commercial "premium" pet foods are formulated primarily to meet consumer demand rather than a pet's nutritional requirements. Pet food fashion sells, and the hottest food trend is a diet high in animal protein. The 2013 study demonstrated that many of the most popular pet foods provide nutrients in excess of established requirements, especially animal proteins. These premium and super-premium pet foods tend to use ingredients that compete directly with the human food system or are overfed to pets, resulting in food waste and obesity.[19] If there are more animal proteins in pet foods, how come so many brands are relatively cheap?

The primary reason why high-protein animal-meat pet foods are inexpensive is because they're heavily subsidized by U.S. taxpayers. The U.S. Farm Bill does an excellent job of incentivizing certain crops and keeping staple foods low-cost for American consumers. Most Americans don't realize that the reason fast food restaurants can sell you a cheap hamburger, chicken nuggets, taco, shake, or bacon platter is because tens of billions of their tax dollars suppress prices. Kept out of the headlines is the fact that the Farm Bill artificially lowers the price of beef, poultry, pork, dairy, and farmed fish either through direct subsidies or indirectly through subsidies on animal feed, such as corn, soy, and wheat. These, along with most major U.S. plant crops, also benefit from government payouts.[20–22] As long as U.S. taxpayers keep funding factory-farmed animal meats, animal proteins will continue to be the cheapest food solution for both producers and consumers. The authors question the U.S. food and animal feed industry's dependence on taxpayer donations to falsely lower prices, creating unsustainable market expectations.

Pet food companies greatly benefit from U.S. Farm Bill taxpayer handouts. The plants used in pet food are subsidized by the U.S. taxpayer. Animal feed for livestock and poultry is subsidized. The raising of animals for meat is subsidized. All of these subsidies artificially lower pet food prices. If the U.S. government began reducing taxpayers' contributions to the food industry, Americans would see dramatic increases in their grocery bills, and the cost of feeding their pets would rise. Furthermore, the U.S. Farm Bill is unintentionally supporting environmental damage by propping up these damaging industries. Shouldn't our tax dollars be used to preserve our future and quality of life rather than to threaten it in the pursuit of a cheap burger, fries, and milkshake? We don't believe we should continue subsidizing animal-meat pet foods, knowing it's bad for the planet. Big animal-meat pet food means big environmental damage.

America's approximately 180 million dogs and cats have a considerable dietary and "environmental pawprint." Meat-based pet food causes environmental impacts from animal farming in terms of the use of land, water, fossil fuels, phosphates, and biocides. Okin's UCLA report shows that dog and cat animal-product consumption is now responsible for the release of up to 64 million metric tons of CO_2—the equivalent of two powerful greenhouse gases, methane and nitrous oxide. As was noted in the introduction, feeding dogs and cats in America equals the exhaust of nearly fourteen million cars, or approximately 162 billion miles driven in a year.[23] That's a lot of trips to buy pet food.

What if pet owners switched to pet foods that only use non–factory farmed meats, poultry, or fish? Would that help the environment? We're afraid not. Even if we ignore the animal welfare concerns presented in the next chapter, these food animals *need to be fed*. Food animals consume enormous numbers of plants, crops that could be fed directly to humans or pets. Those crops also require land. Enormous swaths of forests are bulldozed to grow plants to feed livestock. Over 260 million acres of forest have been cleared to make room for crop fields in the United States alone, most of which are used to exclusively grow livestock feed.[24] Cutting down forests to grow animal-feed crops is a losing situation. When we eliminate trees that absorb carbon dioxide by chopping them down (loss #1), we turn them into carbon-emitting sources (loss #2). When a forest is cleared to make way for wheat fields, corn, or soy, the carbon stored within the forest biomass is released back into the atmosphere, either through decomposition, burning, or processing into lumber or paper (loss #3). If that deforested land is used to raise cattle, pigs, or other farmed animals, hydrating these animals uses unsustainable amounts of water (loss #4). That's a lot of losses for so few wins.

Making animal meat–based pet food requires a *lot* of drinking water. One pound of beef requires about 2,500 gallons, compared to 250 gallons for a pound of soy or 25 gallons for wheat. One researcher found that a diet containing more animal products (one or more servings of animal protein per week compared with less than one serving per week) necessitated an additional 2,700 gallons (10,252 liters) of water; 9,910 kJ of energy; 7 ounces (186 grams) of fertilizer; and 0.2 ounces (6 g) of pesticides per week.[25] In a year, animal meats need an additional 140,400 gallons of water, 23 pounds of fertilizer, and almost a pound of pesticides. At this rate, experts are warning that potable fresh water may become our most valuable resource after clean air within the next century. Future wars will most likely be waged for drinking water, not oil or land.

Producing animal proteins for pets is not only draining our fresh water reservoirs, it's also polluting existing water supplies and killing entire ecosystems. All that corn, soy, and wheat grown for animal feed requires a tremendous amount of artificial fertilizer. The U.S. Environmental Protection Agency (EPA) found that approximately 20 percent of 50,000 lakes surveyed had been impacted by nitrogen and phosphorus pollution, common byproducts of industrialized agriculture, doubling the likelihood of poor ecosystem health. When waters are stagnant, nutrients and sediment build up, increasing the chances of harmful pollution and algal growth. According to the EPA, in 2010 30 percent of streams across the country had elevated levels of nitrogen or phosphorus. Lakes and rivers are our primary sources for drinking water, and nationwide violations of the nitrate limit in drinking water have doubled over a ten-year period.[26]

Animal agriculture is also partly responsible for the creation of massive oceanic and river "dead zones," which are spreading around the globe. Concentrated Animal Feeding Operations (CAFOs), an industry term for factory farms, require colossal cesspools to store animal wastes, and they frequently leak into nearby waterways. These animal wastes are rich in nitrates, pathogenic microbes, and drug-resistant bacteria. When these animal wastes are legally, accidentally, or even illegally dumped into estuaries, they can cause both immediate toxicities as well as algal blooms, eventually resulting in aquatic dead zones. CAFOs have been proven to contribute 72 percent of phosphorus and 63 percent of nitrogen pollution (eutrophication), all resulting from farmed-animal manure and chemical fertilizers applied to farmed animal–feed crops.[27]

There are now over 550 documented aquatic dead zones around the world—vast areas of rivers and oceans in which life has been largely destroyed by these agricultural wastes. Water contamination is already having a direct impact on human health. High levels of nitrates in drinking water have been linked to spontaneous abortions and "blue baby syndrome" (methemoglobinemia), and pathogenic bacteria from polluted water have been responsible for several disease outbreaks across the United States. The once fertile crescent of the Mississippi Delta has become a dead zone, risking the lives and livelihoods of tens of millions of Americans dependent on fishing and ocean harvests. How can we stop dead zones from spreading? Shift from animal- to plant-based agriculture, reducing eutrophication by 49 percent in the process.[28]

In their book *Time to Eat the Dog? The Real Guide to Sustainable Living*, Robert and Brenda Vale estimate the specific "eco-footprints" of our pets in terms of the land required to feed and water them. Analyzing the ingredients in popular pet food brands, the authors calculate that each year a medium-sized dog is fed 360 pounds of meat and 200 pounds of cereals, and he has an eco-footprint of 0.84 hectares. For a large dog, this would increase to about 1.1 hectares.[29] Even smaller cats have large ecological footprints. It takes roughly 0.15 hectares of land to feed a housecat, or the size of about three American home yards.[30] That's a lot of land to feed our tiny pets. Of course, it's tricky to calculate these ecological footprints accurately, because much of the meat used in pet food is a byproduct of animals farmed for humans.[31]

The simple fact is that feeding our pets animal meats is endorsing and supporting animal factory farming and its associated environmental damage. In *Companion Animal Ethics*, Peter Sandøe and his co-authors also remind us of the additional energy costs incurred in pet food manufacturing, packaging, and transportation; the negative impacts of other pet care supplies such as cat litter;[32] as well as the booming pet services, clothing, and toy markets. No matter how complicated or contested the "impact math" is, the clear conclusion is that animal meat–based pet food is now a major cause of climate change.

Getting to the Meat of the Issue:
The Environmental Impact of Farming Livestock for Pet Food

Despite the fact that human-caused climate change and habitat destruction have caused populations of vertebrates to decline by an average of 60 percent in the last fifty years,[33] the global *livestock* population is at an all-time high of over 28 billion animals.[34] Double this number are actually slaughtered each year, based on the fact that a farmed animal's lifespan is typically less than twelve months. Over the past twenty years, the global farmed chicken population has risen from 14 billion to 23 billion, while cattle have increased from 1.3 to 1.5 billion.[35] This slaughter line shows no sign of slowing down, as the number of animals farmed and killed for food is expected to rise substantially as the global population grows and demand for meat increases in the developing world.

The 2019 report by the EAT–*Lancet* Commission on healthy diets from sustainable food systems presented the consensus of more than thirty of the world's leading scientists on what it means to have a diet that is both healthy and sustainable.[36] Significantly, the scientists specified a red meat intake of less than 0.5 ounces (14 grams) daily or one 3.5-ounce (100 grams) serving per week. How much is the average American eating each day? Nearly eight ounces a day (200 grams), roughly *fourteen* times the EAT–*Lancet* recommendation.[37] That level of animal-meat consumption is simply unsustainable and unhealthy.

Given the huge amounts of animal meats consumed in the United States, it's no surprise that livestock were estimated to be responsible for at least 23 percent of total global warming in 2010. This is a very conservative figure that openly admits to omitting the majority of emissions related to feed production, fertilizer use, energy, and transport.[38] The greenhouse gases produced by livestock production are pushing us closer to that 1.5°C threshold. All farmed animals need pasture to graze on or food crops to eat. To meet this need, a small group of "commodity crops" now take up the majority of the world's agricultural land. Hundreds of millions of acres of corn, wheat, and soybeans are planted each year. These crops produce high yields but are extremely vulnerable to changes in environmental conditions. As the environment warms, insects and crop infections will migrate and threaten areas previously considered safe. To protect these crops, farmers must use more synthetic pesticides, leading to potentially more environmental damage.

Modern farming of these few high-yield and profitable crops has also reduced plant biodiversity. Planting the same crops year after year requires tremendous amounts of synthetic fertilizers to replace the natural nutrients depleted from the soil by monoculture farming. The shift in modern farming from seasonal crop rotation to high-intensity monocultures indirectly causes *two-thirds* of agricultural GHG emissions, including nitrogen-emitting fertilizer production and fuel to transport crops.[39] Ironically, hyperefficient intensive farming is also a contributor to world hunger, given the inefficient use of land and crops grown exclusively for animal feed.

The sad reality is that we grow more food to feed the animals Americans eat than nutritious foods that could feed the world's human population. In 2003, scientists estimated that the nine billion animals raised for meat in the United States consumed *seven times* as much grain as the Americans who ate them.[40] Even "growing" a chicken is half as energy efficient as directly consuming the plants we feed the chicken. Unfortunately, as long as we cling to the idea that humans and dogs, both omnivores, need to get most of our protein from eating animals, we will continue wasting the world's precious calories.

A further drawback of farming animals for food is the chemicals and compounds we give meat animals to boost growth rates and combat pathogens associated with close confinement. These antibiotics, hormones, and pesticides filter into wider ecosystems and waterways. In the previous chapter, we looked at the food safety and public health issues around routinely feeding livestock antibiotics, but there are also considerable environmental concerns. Seventy to eighty percent of all antibiotics consumed by humans, pets, and, most important, farmed animals find their way into natural environments. As the saying goes, we are what we eat.

It has been reasonably argued that keeping a small number of grazed cattle on land where crops for human consumption can't be grown, and using their manure to fertilize the soil, would be more environmentally beneficial than eliminating all livestock. Rotating pasture-grazed cows with plant crops is certainly a better way forward than the current situation, and one we successfully used in the past. The problem is, this technique is no longer realistic. Despite what some popular television series claim, scaling up the few genuinely high-welfare, environmentally friendly food-animal farms that exist, while maintaining the level of care for the individual animals, would be an enormous, perhaps impossible undertaking. Besides, changing the entire animal agricultural system would require decades, perhaps a century, to achieve a scale similar to that of the current factory-farm system. According to the 2018 U.S. National Climate Assessment as well as global scientific consensus, we're almost out of time to make real, substantial change. Whether we're aiming to reduce the number of animals farmed from fifty-six billion to one billion or even zero, the first step *has* to be dietary change. Nothing less will save our planet in time.

In addition to reducing GHG emissions, Dr. Helen Harwatt believes that making the shift from consuming animal to consuming plant protein could provide "a suite of co-benefits."[41] She presents evidence that replacing beef with beans in America alone could deliver up to 75 percent of the 2020 GHG reduction target and spare an area of land 1.5 times the size of California, with no loss of protein or calories on American dinner plates. A recent analysis estimates that a global transition from animal to arable agriculture could reduce the land-use footprint of food by 76 percent.[42]

Instead of growing cows, we should grow beans. In fact, beans have a very similar amino acid profile to beef and contain more iron and calcium, as well as provide dietary fiber, B vitamins, and no cholesterol. Besides, that bean burrito could save a life: 500,000 people are at risk of starvation over the next two to three decades if climate change continues.[43] If this occurs, we'll witness mass migrations, political upheavals, and economic collapse. Global food security and sustainability will become a major concern for developed nations. Imagine millions of homeless, starving people fleeing Central and South America, equatorial Asia and Africa, and southern Europe. There are no border walls that can contain the effects of climate change. Currently, 77 percent of the world's agricultural land is used for raising livestock, which provides only 17 percent of calories and 33 percent of protein for global consumption.[44] Crops grown for human consumption, notably corn, soy, and wheat, use the remaining 23 percent of this agricultural land in exchange for 83 percent of calories and 67 percent of protein for global consumption. You do the math. It doesn't add up for our planet or humanity.

Plant-sourced alternatives to meat, including our beloved beans, require far fewer natural resources—including land, nitrogen, phosphorus, water, and energy—and result in lower GHG emissions. A third of all calories produced globally are fed to animals we eat or drink milk from, with only 12 percent of those calories being used by humans through meat, eggs, and dairy consumption.[45] That's a waste of 29 percent of all calories produced globally. Moving American agricultural systems away from animal-feed crops to crops that produce healthy alternatives for human and pet food, including legumes, fruits, and vegetables, would feed an additional 350 million people in comparison to our current food system.[46] Switching from animal to plant proteins can actually *increase* global food protein supply, in addition to reducing GHG emissions and land use and improving animal welfare.

The world would experience direct health and economic benefits if we reduced animal protein intake. The health-related costs of the consumption of red and processed meat is estimated to be $285 billion in 2020, with 4.4 percent of all human deaths linked to eating red or processed meat.[47] Neither of these statistics include the health-related *veterinary* bills and pet deaths or illnesses linked to contaminated or nutritionally inadequate pet food. It's clear that substituting animal meat on our plates *and* pet bowls with plant-sourced protein would deliver numerous benefits to the environment, improve biodiversity, increase sustainability, and potentially benefit our pets' health and longevity.

Feline Fish Failure:
There's Something Fishy About Sustainable Salmon

Cats eat a lot of meat. And they especially eat a lot of fish.

The average U.S. pet cat eats about thirty pounds of fish each year, more than the average human eats in most industrialized nations.[48] A 2008 study found that more than 2.9 million tons of fish are fed to house cats globally and predicted that by 2010 this would rise to 4.9 million.[49] But it's not only felines that feast on fish. Dogs are also catching a bite as people choose to feed them seafood diets. The rationale tends to be that fish is healthier and less allergenic than beef or chicken. Whether that's true is debatable, but, sadly, little consideration is given to where all that fish comes from. There's also little discussion about contaminated water found in fish farms, the added antibiotics and hormones used to grow the fish, or even the welfare and the living conditions of these fish. That's a shame, because this book will soon share the evidence that fish feel a lot more than most people know.

Unfortunately, it takes many more killed fish than killed cows to feed the average dog or cat. This leads to more individual animal pain, suffering, environmental damage, and slaughter. Fish-based cat food is typically made from small fish like anchovies, mackerel, herring, and sardines caught specifically for that product, not as a byproduct of fishing for human consumption. Demand for these small fish from pet food companies is putting pressure on this natural resource and competing with natural predators. Carnivorous fish, mammals, and seabirds currently depend on a diet consisting of about 12 to 13 percent small fish.[50] Every can or bag of wild fish–based cat food potentially starves an ocean animal.

In addition to being food for other animals, these small fish play a vital, protective role in ecosystems by preying on other smaller organisms, maintaining a healthy food chain, and regulating sedimentary processes and the flow of carbon and nutrients. Even though we've known of this fragile balance for decades, we continue to harvest our planet's small-fish species at increasing rates. In an article assessing the impact of the pet food industry on world fish and seafood supplies, Sena S. De Silva and Giovanni M. Turchini state that the cat food industry used 2,478,520 metric tons of raw forage fish in 2002.[51] In a world where about 90 percent of marine fish are either fully or over-exploited,[52] this statistic needs to be taken seriously. A 2006 analysis[53] predicted a global collapse of all species fished in 2048, perhaps earlier, given the acceleration in aquaculture and fisheries in the last fifteen years. In our lifetime, we could see large expanses of fishless oceans. The more we insist on feeding dogs and cats diets full of fish, the sooner we will kill our blue planet.

What if we switched to farmed fish? The aquaculture industry, in which fish are farmed for food in ponds, tanks, and open-water pens rather than caught in the wild, has grown substantially over recent decades. This is mainly because we've overfished our rivers and oceans, yet the increasing consumer demand for fish meat continues.[54] What many people don't realize or appreciate is that our pets, especially cats, represent a big group of "consumers," exacerbating the collapse of our water ecosystems. The Food and Agriculture Organization (FAO) is worried about fish farms. According to FAO data adjusted for growth since 2010, there are 50 to 170 billion fish farmed annually worldwide. As you can see, these numbers are widely variable and arguably imprecise because no one is keeping track. Although the FAO carefully monitors the number of land animals farmed, fish are only reported in tons produced. Carp is the most numerous farmed vertebrate animal in the world, with an estimated 25 to 95 billion raised and killed every year. In second place, 62 billion chickens are farmed every year. However, most chickens are farmed for just five to eight weeks, compared to carp, which are raised for twelve to fourteen months. This means that far more carp are alive in factory-farm ponds at any given time.[55]

In 2013, Swedish researchers Jenny Bergqvist and Stefan Gunnarsson reviewed the growing aquaculture industry. They concluded the following:

> The general agreement is that current aquaculture practices are neither meeting the needs of fish nor environment. Thus, the obvious environmental and animal welfare aspects of finfish aquaculture make it hard to ethically defend a fish diet.[56]

Today, aquaculture accounts for the majority of fish consumed by humans and their pets. Sadly, very little effort or progress has been made in addressing the welfare and environmental issues of aquaculture. The chemicals used in aquaculture often seep into surrounding human aquifers, polluting potable water with pesticides, fertilizers, disinfectants, antibiotics, and oxidants and harming or killing wild aquatic animals by exposing them to antibiotics, hormones, or toxins. Toxic nitrogen leaks into nearby waterways, while wastewater contaminated with feces and excess feed and antibiotics pollutes surrounding shallow waters. These spills and leaks can lead to human and animal infections, but also increase the risk of bacterial antibiotic resistance. Many common fish-farm medicines and antibiotics have also been shown to seriously damage the oceanic environment. One recent example is teflubenzuron, a commonly used anti-parasitic drug fed to farmed Atlantic salmon, which has been discovered to be lethal to oceanic lobsters and shrimp. By the time scientists figured out what was killing the crustaceans, huge losses had occurred.

Aquaculture also often involves clearing *land* to create saltwater ponds, irreversibly altering the natural environment. In Chile, aquaculture production of Atlantic salmon has led to a loss of biodiversity by 50 percent on fish-farm sites. Fish farms are often built adjacent to oceans and rivers, allowing for easier water replenishment. This close proximity to wild fish also means new and exotic diseases can be introduced and spread from farmed fish. Parasitic infections such as sea lice have become a hazard to wild fish in many regions. A single salmon farm has been shown to cause a fivefold increase in wild fish infections. Sometimes farmed fish escape, becoming a part of the ecosystem and competing with wild fish for food, mating with them and weakening their genetics, *eating* them, or infecting them with disease.

Farmed Atlantic salmon are constantly escaping into the wild, and now constitute almost half the "wild salmon" caught in the North Atlantic. Because these farmed Atlantic salmon are selected for fast growth, they are more aggressive and risk-taking than their wild counterparts, which makes them tough competition for food. It's highly possible that soon *all* wild salmon will have descended from farmed fish, meaning a huge loss of natural genetic diversity. The use of natural ocean habitats as sites for aquaculture pens poses further risk to wild fish. Mangrove forests cultivated for "wild-caught" fish farming have led to the loss of nursing grounds and shelter for other free fish species, and also have disrupted sediment transport and killed downstream coral reefs. These open-water fish farms cause the collateral killing of numerous aquatic animal and plant species. Fish farms are not the solution to our planet's food crisis.

In perhaps the weirdest twist imaginable, wild-caught fish are being used to feed farmed fish, amplifying environmental destruction. Wild fish are fed in the form of fishmeal and fish oil in both aquaculture and livestock production. Why?

Economics. We've been focusing on what we feed our pets, but let's not forget what we feed farmed animals—*other animals*. The amount of fish used to feed house cats still falls well below the amount used to feed farmed animals. Whereas omnivorous fish such as carp can be fed cereals and grains, more diners favor carnivorous fish species such as salmon, tuna, and mackerel. The problem is these "fishy" fish need to eat other fish. About a third of wild-caught fish are fed to farmed animals, including farmed fish, chickens, pigs, and cows. We've essentially introduced a "middle man"—or rather, "middle fish"—into animal factory farming. By feeding farmed carnivorous fish other fish, we recreate the huge caloric inefficiencies encountered in terrestrial meat production. We feed cows loads of food and barrels of water to produce relatively few calories for human and pet consumption. Then we do the same thing in our oceans, wasting billions of lives and tons of natural resources to produce small amounts of edible calories. Once again, the math doesn't add up: not for the planet, not for humans or pets, and certainly not for the sentient creatures we sacrifice to "feed the world." Once again, we find this is done in the pursuit of cheap animal proteins.

In the early days of aquaculture, fish in "intensive production systems," or fish-factory farms, were being fed two to five times the amount of fish protein that was actually being produced by the farm.[57] This made no economic or production sense at all. The only reason it worked was because small fish are astonishingly cheap. This "fed protein to produced protein" ratio is slowly improving in aquaculture as a whole, but it remains alarmingly high for the most popular and desired farmed fish, the Atlantic salmon. Economics aside, the fish-based feed we supply to the farmed fish carries additional risks. Contaminated fish feed, which usually consists of wild fish products imported from different parts of the world, is more common than we'd like. Many of the countries producing fishmeal have little, if any, regulatory oversight, and enforcement is largely nonexistent. Because these imported small fish are often harvested under questionable circumstances, there are significant problems created by the fish-based feed system. In their 2013 review of the industry, Bergqvist and Gunnarsson wondered:

With wild fish populations declining, the world's climate changing, and sites of fish farms becoming damaged, the question is whether an industry that is dependent on captured wild fish as feed and a healthy environment for production, should be counted on, and invested in, for future economic gain.[58]

Today, this question has become even more critical. Why raise fish and feed them animal or plant proteins that could feed humans directly, without the energy losses and increased risk potential? It's the same question we ask about animal meat. Put simply, environmentally sound eating means eating as low as possible on the food chain to optimize health, longevity, and quality of life while minimizing detrimental impacts on the environment and other animals. Regardless of whether humans and pets begin eating lower on the food chain, time is running out for feeding fish to other animals.

The Cruelty of Wild-Caught Fish

Many well-meaning consumers and pet owners select food claiming "wild-caught" fish to bypass the harms of fish farms. But is feeding your cat wild-caught fish any better? Unfortunately, no. The main reason for the growth of aquaculture is because there aren't enough fish in the sea. Overfishing has led to the dramatic decline of not only wild fish, but also, because of "bycatch" or "trash catch," a decimation of various species, including sharks, rays, dolphins, sea turtles, crustaceans, and even seabirds. Some research estimates that 40 percent of the global fish catch is wasted bycatch, and in some fisheries it can be as large as 90 percent.

It's distressing to think a dolphin or sea turtle probably died for a cat's "gourmet fish dinner." When we imagine what it might be like to be caught in a net, dragged until we drown, or impaled on a hook, "wild-caught" becomes an inhumane and barbaric idea. Long-line fishing uses thousands of hooks on a single line, thirty to sixty miles long (fifty to a hundred kilometers). When fish take the bait, they remain hooked for hours or days, slowly bleeding to death as they're dragged through the ocean, before the line is hauled aboard.[59] And those are the lucky fish. The hearty ones that survive the hook and line are forced to "drown" on the deck or hold of the boat, suffering even more.

Another common commercial fishing technique uses walls of nearly invisible, razor-sharp netting to ensnare schools of fish. Colloquially referred to as "gill nets," the opening in the netting is designed to be just large enough to allow the fish's head to pass through. Once the fish realizes it's trapped, it desperately tries to swim backward or sideways, only to become stuck on its gills, macerating this highly sensitive organ with each thrust of its tail. With their gill "lungs" swollen and bleeding, fish struggle to breathe for hours before the nets are pulled in and they're put out of their misery. These wild-caught fish don't enjoy a speedy or painless death; it's slow and excruciating. Studies have shown that cod and haddock stored in holds on boats remain conscious and in pain for at least two hours, slowly suffocating.[60]

Research in 2009 predicted that as a result of the decline of wild fish populations, aquaculture will soon need to depend on plant proteins to feed farmed fish.[61] As we'll see in later chapters, the future development of alternative sources for fish proteins, such as cellular agriculture and proteins from microorganisms, may lead to more sustainable fish farming. We, the authors, propose eliminating farmed fish and animal meats and using plant-based and alternative protein sources for pet food.

* * *

The state of our planet as we approach the third decade of the twenty-first century isn't pretty. But what does this impending environmental catastrophe actually mean for our pets and for those of us who work hard to feed them? The estimated lifetime cost of pet ownership is about $8,000 (£6,200) for a medium-sized dog and $10,000 (£7,700) for a cat. That's a lot of money for most folks. Author Hal Herzog asks: "But what happens when the bottom falls out? Do people still spend money on pets when times get hard?"[62] In the past, the answer has seemed to be, "Yes!" Even as the U.S. economy was collapsing in 2008, total sales at PetSmart, the country's largest retail pet specialty chain, increased 8.4 percent, to over $5 billion. But what happens when the environment collapses?

Environmental collapse is a completely different proposition. Science tells us that if we continue living as we do today, we're going to struggle to feed and protect ourselves over the next twelve to twenty years. That means it will be a resource challenge to have and care for dogs and cats as companions. Although the very wealthy will still be able to afford to keep their Yorkies in rhinestone collars, regular mutts and house cats may become less common for the rest of us. If we're to avoid this nightmare scenario, we need to radically rethink the way we produce pet food. As more people become pet owners in developing countries, including China, Brazil, and India, pets will further intensify climate change and competition for food ingredients. The environmental damage of pet food will be magnified if the trend toward higher animal-protein foods continues.

It doesn't have to be this way. Rather than reducing the rate of future dog and cat ownership, why not simply reduce or remove the amount of animal meats in pet food? According to the calculations of animal nutritionists Richard and Susan Pitcairn, transitioning a seventy-pound dog from a raw meat–based diet to a plant-based diet could save, *every day*, 2,200 gallons of water, about sixty square feet of rainforest, about ninety pounds of grain, and two farmed animals' lives.[63]

Right now, many of us are worried about climate change, but we're still feeding our pets other animals. We want to survive, we want our pets to thrive, and we don't know what other choices we have. This chapter has shown how pet food is currently part of the problem. But pet food *can* become part of the solution. Alice spoke to Klaus Wagner, CEO of the German pet food company Green Petfood, about his company's mission to produce truly sustainable pet food. He said the following:

Everyone's talking about the footprint that we leave on this world, but pets are rarely considered in this equation. Consequently, we at Green Petfood aim to provide an innovative and ecological food alternative for people who want to keep their pet's pawprint as small as possible. Our sustainable philosophy is also constant throughout our entire production process—from choosing the ingredients over efficient production measures to the final product. In doing so, we use alternative proteins such as peas, red lentils, or even insects.

One of the most impressive things about Green Petfood is that they offset their carbon dioxide emissions via forest preservation in Tanzania. This is part of their ambition to become climate neutral by 2020. But their contributions also help preserve the habitat of the country's largest chimpanzee population and support social outreach. Wagner is also committed to finding alternative packaging options and accessories and equipment to make everyday life with our pets more environmentally friendly. Green Petfood's mission is to make the world *more* sustainable every day, directly through pet food, but also indirectly in the pet owner's daily life.

In 2016, Dr. Joseph Wakshlag, then associate professor at Cornell University's College of Veterinary Medicine, told Petfood Forum attendees in Kansas City that if pet food companies are to stay in business, they're going to need to change their unsustainable ingredients. What sustainable foods did he suggest? He urged the industry to explore novel proteins, "like kangaroo meat."[64] Although kangaroo meat may be novel, it is hardly sustainable. From 2014 to 2019, the pet food industry wiped out nearly half of the state of Victoria's kangaroo population as a result of bribery and fraud. During court proceedings held in March 2019, prosecutors revealed that illegal permits and harvesting practices caused a 250 percent increase in the number of kangaroos killed in the region. Approximately one million kangaroos died during the five-year program, often in cruel, brutal ways.[65] Wakshlag and Ernie are friends, and Ernie respects Wakshlag's dedication to improving pet nutrition. But on this issue, Ernie concludes that kangaroo meat is neither ethical nor sustainable as a pet food.

Wakshlag was correct in declaring that traditional animal meats are unsustainable, but why should we look for proteins from kangaroos, cod, and other nontraditional animal sources? That's not the sustainable solution we need. Wakshlag also suggests feeding dogs the highly abundant and underutilized aquatic duckweed, *Landoltia punctata*, because it is rich in healthy proteins and is already used in pig and poultry diets. Plant-based feeding is certainly an excellent option, as we'll explore in Chapter 7. However, there are other alternative proteins only a few daring food biotech companies are beginning to openly discuss. Companies like Green Petfood, as well as some of the other exciting startups explored later, are showing that there *are* other ways to feed pets.

Wagner declares:

We want to be a partner in supporting pet owners in finding innovative and ecological pet food that gives animals everything they need. Simultaneously, we see ourselves in the role of pushing this issue further. Because the question regarding environmental issues doesn't stop at the pet's bowl.

He's right, but our pet bowls are a great place to start.

3

Who Are We Feeding to Our Pets?

DURING HER KEYNOTE presentation at the 2018 Conference on Human Behavior Change for Animal Welfare, Anne McBride, senior lecturer in human–animal interactions at the University of Southampton, related an exchange she'd had with a lady buying dried pig's ears in the pet shop.

The shopper observed, "It's wonderful how they're making these smaller these days, much more convenient for my little dog."

"Yes," McBride replied. "That's because they kill the pigs much younger."

The shopper looked aghast at McBride, shaking her head: "No, no, no, they just make them smaller!"

Although this level of cognitive dissonance might seem extreme, how many pet owners really want to know where the meat in pet food comes from? It's much easier (and more pleasant) to imagine that Fido's beef kibble or Felix's gourmet chicken chunks are magically "produced" than to explicitly connect these to the life and death of a living, breathing, feeling animal. The question then veers from "*What* are we feeding our pets?" to "*Who* are we feeding our pets?" Unfortunately, ignoring a problem doesn't make it go away. It also doesn't make it less harmful or damaging. When we feed our dog or cat an animal meat–based food, hundreds or thousands of sentient animals suffer the consequences.

As Jacy Reese summarizes in his book *The End of Animal Farming*, there are up to one hundred *billion* farmed animals alive at this moment. Over 90 percent of the world's farmed animals, and over 99 percent in North America, live in factory farms. When we open a bag or can of conventional pet food, we're affirming that these thousands of intensively farmed animals, bred into miserable conditions and sacrificed to feed our dogs and cats, are somehow less valuable or meaningful than the lives of our pets. As author Julian Baggini points out: "[T]he only animal welfare that seems to count when buying pet food is that of the beast being fed."[1]

In the United States, about three hundred manufacturers produce more than seven million tons of pet food each year, a large percentage of which is animal meat: beef, poultry, pork, or fish mixed with cereals, grain, and added vitamins and minerals. Alarmingly, 30 percent of intensively farmed animals are bred and slaughtered for our companion animals, who consume more than a quarter of all animal-derived calories in the United States.[2] As we've seen, much of this is byproduct from animals killed for human food—but not all. A rapidly growing market for human-grade meat and diets high in animal protein for dogs and cats means that the pet food industry now plays a significant role in supporting factory farming.

Many consumers wrongly assume that "human-grade" means high animal welfare. They want to believe that an expensive pet food made from the highest-quality animal meats must guarantee better welfare standards than a cheap brand of pet food. Not at all. In fact, a label claiming "human-grade pet food" has absolutely nothing to do with animal welfare. The high cost doesn't alleviate any pain and suffering, nor does it improve the horrific lives of the animals killed to fill the bag, can, or container. In a nation such as the United States, where almost all animals are raised in factory farms,[3] the fact that *humans* eat them doesn't mean the food animals are treated humanely. America has earned an embarrassing "D" rating in animal welfare standards from World Animal Protection,[4] abysmal for any civilized nation.

Pet food companies rarely make any animal welfare claims. Pet food packages are festooned with edited images of glistening chicken breasts, pork loins, and steaks, but scarce attention is given to how these ingredients are sourced. Those enticing food photos hide the cruel conditions in which "pet food animals" are born, suffer, and die. Sadly, these voiceless victims of the pet food industry are rarely mentioned, even among academics and veterinary professionals. In their 268-page textbook on *Companion Animal Ethics*, Peter Sandøe and his co-authors dedicate roughly six pages to the environmental impact of pet food[5] and make no mention of the contribution of the pet food industry to the welfare issues associated with intensive livestock farming.

Surely "companion animal ethics" should include the ethics of how we feed our pets! Each time we browse the supermarket aisles and purchase animal meat–based pet food, we run the risk of promoting and paying for the suffering of these other animals. Those of us who are pet owners and lovers are in the special position of having inherent sympathy toward animals, yet our buying behaviors don't reflect these wider concerns. Reese describes how, in 2016, just 1.5 percent of conventional fresh meat sales in America were for organic cuts and only 0.9 percent for grass-fed labels.[6] Ironically, our focus on the well-being of dogs and cats is preventing pet owners from thinking too much about the animals we kill to feed them.

When we *do* think about these "other animals," making the connection can help us broaden our circle of compassion. Popular pet-nutrition author Diana Laverdure-Dunetz's rescue dog Chase helped open her eyes to the plight of abused and suffering animals of *all species*, inspiring her to become vegetarian and then vegan. She writes: "From that development arose the contradiction in my mind of wanting to help heal dogs but not wanting to contribute to the torture and slaughter of other intelligent, feeling animals."[7] Laverdure-Dunetz went on to launch the first ever plant-based dog food summit in 2019, inspired by the health improvements she saw in Chase after removing meat from his diet. Introducing the summit, Laverdure-Dunetz told delegates how, as a rescue dog, Chase taught her a lot more than just canine nutrition; he also taught her about the plight of *all* abused and suffering animals. She's not alone. In a study of 233 pet owners in Austria, Germany, and Switzerland, 90 percent of those participants feeding their pets meat-free diets said moral, ethical, and animal welfare concerns had motivated their decision.[8] In Chapter 4 we'll examine the link between love of companion animals and broader concern for farmed animals.

Why Don't We Know About the Suffering in Our Pet Bowls?

It's an obvious question, but given our progress in understanding animal sentience and the revulsion most people feel when it comes to animal cruelty, how is this still happening? Why don't we see more images and videos from inside cattle and hog farms or chicken houses? The reason you don't see farmed animals suffering is because it's illegal for people to show you.

In June 2011, animal welfare advocacy organization Mercy For Animals shocked U.S. citizens when it released undercover footage taken inside chicken and hog farms. Over hours of secretly recorded videos, the organization exposed the horrific living conditions of chickens raised for McDonald's Chicken McNuggets. The group also recorded the deplorable conditions endured by pigs raised for bacon and pork, including painful castrations and tail amputations performed without any anesthesia or pain relief. It detailed just how small the gestation crates were for pigs, showing videos of animals unable to turn around for their entire adult lives. In response to these undercover investigations, McDonald's, Sam's Club, and Target discontinued using the suppliers. Sounds like a victory for animal welfare, right? Unfortunately, this set off an industry-coordinated governmental and regulatory response that would potentially prevent the public from ever seeing these images again. The age of Ag-Gag had begun.

Mercy For Animals had embedded an investigator in a pig farm in rural Iowa. The large-scale, corporatized pork industry nets over $6 billion (£4.6 billion) per year in Iowa and makes up about one-quarter of total U.S. pork production. The following spring, the pork industry lobby went to work to make sure these whistleblowers would never succeed again in their state. By spring, the Iowa state legislature had passed the first of a flurry of new nationwide ag-gag laws. Within a year, nearly every cattle-, hog-, and poultry-producing state had passed similar laws prohibiting anyone from working "under false pretenses" in order to expose criminal acts or objectionable practices.

These laws clearly violate our First Amendment right to freedom of speech. Lawmakers knew this when they passed the legislation, but they also knew it could take years for the law to reach the Supreme Court to be deemed unconstitutional. Over the past eight years, every "agricultural gag" law that has been challenged has been ruled unconstitutional, a blatant violation of an individual's right to free speech. Each time an ag-gag law is repealed, another variation is introduced, and the cycle begins again. An investigative journalist could remain in prison for years awaiting the Supreme Court to overturn the unconstitutional law they allegedly broke. The result is few are willing to risk committing a felony in order to document animal abuse in factory farms.

Surely the public deserves to see what goes on inside the steel sheds of dairy, beef, pig, and chicken farms. Journalists have historically been the public's eyes and ears, revealing legitimately bad practices, dangerous conditions, and threats to society. Without journalists' exposés, many workplace protections and food safety acts would not have been passed or enforced. The ability to conceal the conditions inside animal factory farms inevitably leads the public to believe whatever the industry tells them. They simply don't have access to any other information. It also allows the industry to portray undercover investigators as "extremists," "criminals," and "animal rights weirdos." By controlling access, the animal-farm industry controls the narrative. By controlling the narrative, they control the public's perception, which may contribute in part to where most people donate to animal causes.

Each year, millions of pet lovers donate enormous amounts of money to pet charities, sacrificing hard-earned cash to ensure our "furry family members" are free from abuse and well cared for. About 66 percent of donations to U.S. animal charities go directly to companion animal shelters. But how much do we spend on farmed-animal charities? How much do we donate to raise awareness of domesticated animal welfare issues beyond our favored dogs and cats? Almost nothing. A mere 0.8 percent of donations go specifically to farmed-animal organizations, despite the fact that for every dog or cat euthanized in a shelter, about 3,400 farmed animals are confined and slaughtered.[9] Our wallets clearly imply that humans have abandoned farmed-animal welfare.

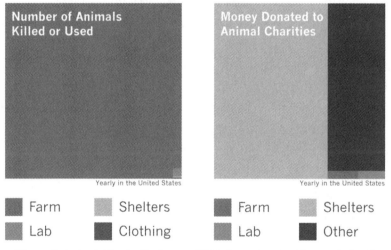

Figure 1: Animal Charity Evaluators, 2016. Reproduced with permission.[10]

Few of us *want* to support animal factory farms. More than seven in ten American adults consistently support improvements in farmed-animal welfare, such as freeing animals from cages and establishing more humane methods of slaughter,[11] even if this doesn't necessarily translate to our purchasing habits. So why haven't more pet owners demanded improvements in animal welfare for the animals they fed their pets? Maybe it's because very few of us actually know how bad things really are.

The Unpalatable Truth About the Animals in Pet Food

Sadly, the words "torture and slaughter" are no exaggeration when it comes to describing the conditions in factory farms. In the majority of cases, the animal that fills our pet's bowl did not live a life we'd feel comfortable knowing about, even if that information were freely available. But should uncomfortable truths really be a barrier to change? A good way to ease into this issue is to ask whether you'd allow your dog or cat to live and die in similar conditions. As Lucille Claire Thibodeau writes in an essay entitled "All Creation Groans," more animals suffer today at the hands of humans than at any other time in history.[12]

Particularly in America, factory farming is a highly sophisticated, mechanized industry of staggering scale. The massive routine suffering of animals in intensive farming systems has been well documented, most famously in Peter Singer's *Animal Liberation* and Ruth Harrison's seminal *Animal Machines*, and more recently in a series of documentaries that includes *Earthlings* and *Dominion*. It's impossible to read or watch these revelatory stories and not agree that "[i]n their numbers and in the duration and depth of the cruelty inflicted upon them, factory-farmed animals are the most widely abused and most suffering of all creatures on our planet."[13] What's not well documented is the fact that approximately one in four animals killed in factory farms today dies to feed a pet. Is that a cost another animal should pay for with their life each time we say, "Food is love"?

It seems that when it comes to the multitude of domesticated animals under our care, we're stuck in biblical times. "Everything that lives and moves about will be food for you," God tells Noah and his sons in Genesis, at least through the court-appointed and closely supervised interpreters of King James. But apparently God didn't mean it was okay to eat cats and dogs, at least in the Western world. Our laws reinforce the "you can't eat pets" ethos while sanctioning the suffering of nearly every other animal.

In 1977 Joyce Tischler, co-founder of the Animal Legal Defense Fund (ALDF), described domesticated dogs and cats as "a higher form of life, having the ability to feel and express their pain and pleasure, and the ability to reason and to desire."[14] She asserted that the law should recognize these abilities and afford these "special animals" legal rights, introducing a guardianship model based on "care and compassion." Thanks to the ALDF, we now have laws that protect our companion animals from neglect and abuse, legal rights that extend beyond the perception of cats and dogs as "property." You also can't eat them. This legal protection provided for our companions is striking when we consider that farmed animals do not share these privileges, despite being scientifically proven to share "the ability to feel and express their pain and pleasure, and the ability to reason and desire."[15] There are only two federal laws protecting farmed animals in America: the 28-Hour Law governing live animal transport, and the Humane Methods of Slaughter Act, which was written expressly to exempt chickens, the most farmed animal in America. In the United States, you can do almost anything to a farmed-animal species and get away with it. And, of course, the very reason for their existence is to feed us and our pets: their "fate" is to be eaten; how they end up on the menu is largely ignored.

The sad reality is that these two laws are rarely, if ever, enforced. The Slaughter Act's purported purpose is to ensure that animals are killed humanely and quickly. That's simply not the case in today's high-tech, highly automated slaughterhouses. The "killing line" moves so quickly that the captive bolts or electrocution baths fail to stun or kill every animal. Videos and court testimonies prove that many animals are alive and conscious for as long as seven minutes after their throats have been cut. Too graphic? We're afraid that the next sections of this chapter are going to describe some of the routine, and to us barbaric, realities of intensive farming. We, the authors, believe you'll agree that if we're paying for these animals to be bred and killed for our pets' food, we deserve to know how they're treated. Still, if you're not ready to learn about these atrocities, or you're already familiar with them, feel free to skip ahead to Chapter 4.

Suffering Is Standard

We domesticated livestock just as we did dogs and cats, yet we treat them very differently. Similar to our pets, modern food animals have little in common with their wild ancestors; they have different genetics, behaviors, growth rates, sizes, and lifespans. Yet whereas our "creation" of domestic dogs and cats has resulted in a greater sense of moral responsibility, we seem to have erased all ethics and morals regarding our farmed-animal creations. The consequences of this cognitive compartmentalization are devastating for the cows, chickens, pigs, fish, and other "animal inventory" that suffer and die to feed our pets.

Although the law can place limits on farmed animals as "property" to ensure responsible use, it does little to protect their care. A factory farm in America cannot be prosecuted for an abuse deemed "standard farming practice." Of course, "standard farming practice" covers nearly anything imaginable, from humane to horrific.

Pet owners like to fantasize that the meat we feed our dog or cat comes from a family farm: bucolic pastures, ample sunshine, and fresh air. The images used by pet food companies reinforce this myth: friendly farmers donned in overalls and straw hats petting the cows and pigs under their care. Marketing terms such as *free-range*, *cage-free*, and *organic* instill a false confidence that the animals used to feed pets were cared for humanely. Nothing could be further from the truth. The Humane Society of the United States (HSUS) estimates that over 99.5 percent of farmed animals in the United States are born and suffer on factory farms before dying in highly mechanized, cruel, and torturous slaughterhouses. Mercy For Animals estimates that 60 percent of *all mammals* are raised to be food for pets or people.

The terms *free-range* and *cage-free* are primarily fabricated marketing terms designed to reduce consumer guilt and carry little, if any, regulatory oversight or enforcement. Much of the responsibility lies with food corporations that create incentives to value productivity over all else, including animal cruelty. If we're going to eliminate the cruelty and suffering associated with animal-meat production, we need to hold these companies accountable. To accomplish this, we need to change what we eat and feed. As individuals, we have the direct means to show that we don't think the current food systems are acceptable, not just when we buy our own meals, but when we buy food for our pets.

It would be impossible to write this chapter without highlighting some of the "standard" and legally protected abuses that occur every second of every day inside locked metal sheds housing thousands of caged animals. Take, for instance, the 50 million male piglets born every year in the United States, castrated without anesthetic or pain relief. The males are neutered to avoid the "gamey" taste produced by the male sex hormone, testosterone. The pig industry's objective is to grow a hog to be turned into bacon or pork as quickly, and cheaply, as possible. This means feeding the minimum amount of nutrients, dosing the animal with plenty of antibiotics and hormones, and performing endless genetic manipulation.

Piglets who don't grow fast enough are swung, alive and kicking, by their hind legs against the concrete floor, their brains bashed in until they cease to move. This may sound exaggerated and extreme, yet it's actually an accepted technique known as "thumping." When an HBO documentary[16] showed Ohio farmers "thumping" piglets and using forklifts to strangle them, the pork industry claimed that all of this was "common agricultural practice" and thus exempt from the animal cruelty law. Their defense was corroborated by veterinarians and accepted in court. Suffering really is the standard in animal farming.

The Cruelty of Beef and Dairy

Burgers and shakes, beef dog diets, and cheesy cat treats: the cow has become symbolic of the American human and pet diet. Hidden within every fictional "happy cow" is a truth buried in suffering. To make the milk that produces whey proteins and creates the cheeses pets and people crave, calves are separated from their mothers almost immediately after birth (industry standards recommend no more than an hour). The reason for the act and the speed is because the mother's first milk, rich in antibodies and nourishing colostrum, is also the most valuable milk a dairy cow makes. A long-time dairy farmer describes the immediate separation of mother from calf as "one of the biggest affronts against animal welfare in the dairy industry, as evidenced by the bawling of both cow and calf."[17]

Since milk can only be produced by female calves, what happens to the baby boys? Male calves are often slaughtered immediately after being taken from their mother, or worse, raised for veal. The life of a veal calf is short, but far from sweet. Confined to a tiny crate with barely enough room to turn his head to the side, the male calf will be nutritionally deprived to ensure his meat remains soft and tender. Any movement would risk turning his muscles lean and strong as nature intended, but that's not what discerning diners desire. As his nutritional deprivation continues, his iron restriction causes cravings so strong that he will desperately lick his cage slats soaked with his own urine. After eighteen to twenty weeks of living immobilized in this torture chamber, he is sent to slaughter to be plated as veal marsala.

Do the girl cows fare better? The fate of a female calf is to be raised on cheap "milk replacer"[18] while her mother's milk is sold for human and pet consumption, and then to be artificially impregnated as soon as she is old enough to bear offspring of her own. We find it ironic that "milk cows" are not fed their own mother's milk. Once again, it's simple economics. It's less expensive to grow cows on a dilution of whey protein and water than on their own mother's milk. The goal is to grow calves as efficiently and profitably (cheaply) as possible so they can "continue the production cycle" at twenty-four months of age. And in order to calve, they must be bred.

Breeding a heifer (female cow) is not a pleasant experience for them. The device used to restrain the female during impregnation is called a "breeding box." It was once referred to as a "rape rack" until the cattle industry's term (and practice) came under fire from animal welfare groups. Whatever you want to call it, it's a horrible contraption and practice. If the heifer isn't mated "naturally" by a bull while she's strapped to a breeding rack, she is increasingly artificially inseminated (AI). Semen is collected from a bull (male cow) using electrostimulation to force him to ejaculate. A veterinarian or AI technician inseminates a cow primed to ovulate, using their arm to reach into the cow's uterus and squirt a dosage of thawed semen through a long straw. Everything about the process is artificial, unnatural, and involves pain, no matter what the dairy industry claims.

After successfully delivering her own calf, mother and baby are once again separated. It is at this time that a dairy cow begins producing her own milk and becomes a financial asset. Her life will now consist of an unrelenting pattern of pregnancies, milking, a brief dry period, and then repeat. The next four to five years will be spent entirely in close confinement, locked away from the outside world's prying eyes. As we've learned, it's a crime in most states for the public to actually see what's happening inside these cruel "parlors," making it easy to deny their abuse. The heifer will be milked up to three times a day for ten months and impregnated again after the third month. With only about six weeks of rest, this cycle of artificial hyperlactation persists for years. After about five years of making milk, her body is depleted and no longer profitable. A cow's natural lifespan is eighteen to twenty-two years, yet modern dairy farming kills her after four to six. What is the purpose of this short life, full of suffering? To provide our pet the momentary pleasure of a treat, or a bowl of food wolfed down in seconds. We don't believe that's the purpose of any life.

Other "standard" cattle industry practices include hot-iron branding of cows without anesthesia,[19] electroimmobilization (using an electric current to paralyze a cow while they remain fully conscious—it's cheaper than using anesthetics),[20] and dehorning or "disbudding," a technique using a 600°F hot iron to burn and prevent horns from developing.[21] The latter procedure is normally conducted without anesthesia or pain relief, as is the castration of young male calves, a procedure causing minutes of excruciating pain and weeks of discomfort.[22,23,24] It's becoming clear that the fantasy of the "happy family-farm cow" is a lie. The ugly truth is 99.5 percent of the beef in U.S. pet food comes from these shuttered animal factory farms and gargantuan feedlots.

In his book *Dead Zone*, Compassion In World Farming's CEO Philip Lymbery describes a typical feedlot he visited in Nebraska:

A thousand cattle stood motionless in muddy paddocks. An eerie hush hung over the place, as if in a hospital ward, broken only by the odd cough, sneeze or wail. Some were big, some were small. Clear shiny

fluid ran from the nose of a coughing black calf. I noticed some of the
animals discharging strangely runny cowpats. All stood in the hot sun,
without an inch of shade. Desperate for relief, they tried lying in each
other's shadow. The stench was overpowering.[25]

Lymbery's experience is similar to what Ernie has observed as a
veterinarian. This eerie quiet, occasionally punctuated by a desperate
bleat, hangs over feedlots. When animals are exposed to chronic stress,
a psychological state is produced comparable to human depression. If
the condition worsens, psychologists call it "learned helplessness" or
"resignation syndrome" in people. Animals in these conditions often
experience similar behavioral states. The psychological trauma created by
modern animal farming systems has led to billions of severely depressed
and anxious animals, reduced to nothing more than meat-producing
machines. In simplest terms, these cows have given up.

It's no wonder these animals are depressed. Cows, pigs, chickens,
and farm-raised salmon live wholly unnatural lives in captivity. Although
some veterinarians and animal industry experts insist that farmed
animals' basic nutritional and medical needs are met in industrial agriculture, restrictions of natural species-typical behavior are considered
standard practices. Nest-building and dust-bathing for chickens, mud-
bathing for pigs, play, social interaction, and natural hierarchies of cattle
herds are almost entirely eliminated in factory farms.

The Happy Chicken Mythology

Ninety-eight percent of commercially sold American eggs come from
nine billion laying hens kept in battery farms. These sweltering tin sheds
contain rows and rows of chickens crammed into tiny metal cages. The
United Egg Producers, an industry organization that creates legislative
and regulatory recommendations for lawmakers, recommends that each
hen gets sixty-seven square inches of cage space. That's about the size of
a regular-sized iPad.

In her tiny cage, the hen clings to wire mesh floors covered with her own excrement, causing her feet to weaken and her toe pads to thicken. She is in constant pain. The only time she will see sunlight is the day she is thrown into an even smaller crate and driven to the slaughterhouse. Until then, she must lay egg after egg, usually over three hundred each year, until her body fails. Nature didn't design chickens to lay this number of eggs. Wild hens are only able to produce ten to fifteen eggs a year due to the intense physiological demands of reproduction. A hen normally takes twenty-three to twenty-seven hours to form and lay a single egg, an arduous process, followed by days of rest and recuperation.[26,27]

Yet modern laying hens are artificially manipulated into infinite reproductive cycles by techniques such as "forced molting." This involves stressing the hens by depriving them of sleep or restricting food, which forces a "molt," or loss of feathers, that triggers sexual hormonal changes, causing her to produce more eggs sooner. Producing almost thirty times as many eggs as she would naturally comes at a severe physiological cost for the hen. Laying hens often suffer from ovarian cancer, prolapsed vents (leading to death by hemorrhage or shock), calcium deficiency, or a build-up of impacted egg material when the hen is unable to fully expel an egg from her body. And we haven't considered the emotional cruelty these hens must endure.

Hens are naturally compassionate mothers and, somewhat ironically, are often used in analogies to teach human parenting. We use the terms *nesting* and *nest* to define a warm and loving home environment, refer to attentive human mothers as "hens," and use "nest egg" to signify protecting something valuable and dear. Unfortunately, the nurturing instincts of real-life hens are denied. Laying hens will never parent a chick, walk or run in the sunshine followed by their clutch, teach their children to hunt for insects, or find a mate. The majority of laying hens will never be able to nest, a natural instinct proven to be more important to a hen than eating food after seventy-two hours of starvation.[28] A hen's instinctive need to nest is so great that some hens have been known to lay eggs in the bodies of their dead cage mates (it's not uncommon for cages and "cage-free" barns to be littered with the corpses of birds who have starved or collapsed).

There's little, if any, veterinary care for these hens, because the economics of treating an individual animal in these massive operations would make no financial sense. Their sores, infections, and prolapsed vents (their egg-laying organ similar to the uterus) remain untreated, and many hens die well before their two years of laying are over. Because the U.S. Humane Slaughter Act doesn't apply to chickens or turkeys, these animals often go into scald tanks still alive, inhaling boiling water as they drown, their slaughterhouses immune from prosecution. What is the purpose of their suffering? Cheap chicken meat. Chicken nuggets for a buck. High-protein pet food. Two years of suffering for food our pets gobble up in less than a minute.

Perhaps the most distressing case of all is the life of the modern-day broiler chicken, a product of intensive genetic selection, growth-promoting antibiotics, hormones, and food additives. As we've learned, chickens are naturally affectionate animals; they love to play, peck, dust-bathe, and cuddle up to each other and even humans. They also appear to be intelligent. Chickens have been proven to have "object permanence" as early as two days old. Object permanence is the fairly sophisticated understanding that an object still exists when it is taken away or hidden, something that only begins to develop in human children at six to seven months.

No matter, we still abuse and exploit these caring and clever birds. We pump broiler chickens full of drugs and supplements and manipulate their genetics, creating super-sized birds that gain weight rapidly on a minimum of nutrients. Constant artificial light in these indoor, stagnant sheds tricks the birds' biology into thinking it is always time to eat.[29] Genetically designed to grow extremely quickly, many chickens collapse under the excessive weight of their ballooning bodies.[30,31] If a broiler goes down, they often starve to death on the floor as they try desperately to reach food or water. The stench of ammonia in these chicken houses is suffocating, and antibiotics are routinely overused to help birds survive contagious infections until slaughter.

Sitting in the toxic, damp ammonia stench of his own excrement, the time a broiler chicken has on this earth is spent in absolute misery. Mercifully, that time is shorter than ever. A traditional "broiler" chicken would take eighty-four days to reach ideal size in the 1950s. Today, this time period has been drastically reduced:[32] modern broiler chickens are slaughtered when they reach about four pounds, which can be as soon as forty-nine days old. Breeding broilers are similarly genetically engineered to grow quickly and crave enormous amounts of food, but these birds need to be kept slimmer so they can live long enough to breed. This means they're kept perpetually hungry. Farmed chickens can't catch a break.

Another popular pet food protein is turkey. Every year, the president of the United States officially pardons two turkeys at Thanksgiving, sparing them from slaughter. In 2017, two lucky turkeys were named "Drumstick" and "Wishbone" (humans easily reduce these intelligent birds to edible "pieces"). In 2018, the turkeys were called "Peas" and "Carrots," and "Wishbone" and "Drumstick" were already dead, unable to outlive their altered genetics. A spokesman said the passing of the 2017 turkeys was "not surprising given the short life expectancy of domestic turkeys."[33] Wild turkeys are known to live up to ten years, far longer than the factory-farm turkey's one to two. Similar to any other animal, turkeys are far more than their constituent body parts. They are extremely maternal, carrying their young chicks on their backs to keep them safe. Turkeys have been bred to grow artificially fast, compromising their health and well-being. Veterinarian professor John Webster explains the consequences:

> On the balance of this evidence, we must conclude that approximately one quarter of the heavy strains of broiler chickens and turkeys are in chronic pain for approximately one third of their lives. . . . This must constitute, in both magnitude and severity, the single most severe, systematic example of man's inhumanity to another sentient creature.[34]

Can you imagine being in constant agony for over a third of your life? Karen Davis, founding director of United Poultry Concerns (UPC), shares her opinion on the plight of farmed chickens and turkeys:

> I think chickens are in hell and they are not going to get out. They already are in hell and there are just going to be more of them. As long as people want billions of eggs and millions of pounds of flesh, how can all these animal products be delivered to the millions? There will be crowding and cruelty—it is just built into the situation. You can't get away from it. And we are ingesting their misery.[35]

The food we provide for our pets is supposedly an expression of love. So why are we feeding them misery and death? Do we really want to feed our pets the suffering of other animals?

Sad as a Pig on Concrete

These examples aren't anomalies or exaggerations; they are standard animal production practices. Occasionally, a "nonstandard" abuse will make the news, shining a brief light on the abuses of animals farmed for human and pet food. One example is the exposure of animal abuse at Tosh Farms, a supplier to JBS USA, the world's largest meat company, which also supplies meat for pet food. JBS USA's rendering facility, MOPAC, holds the distinction of being one of the largest renderers on the East Coast.

In 2017, undercover video—shot once again by a Mercy For Animals investigator—exposed what the animal welfare group calls the "malicious and systemic abuse of mother pigs and piglets." It's painful to watch, but we think you should. Following publicity and public outcry from the video, JBS suspended shipments from Tosh Farms, but Mercy For Animals is now calling on the company to end factory-farm cruelty across its global pork supply chains, including the housing of sows in tiny gestation crates. It's not hyperbole to describe gestation crates as one of the cruelest inventions in agricultural history.

Gestation crates are standard practice for U.S. pork production. They're given their name because they're where pregnant sows are sentenced to live. These cold metal cages measure 6.6 by 2 feet and are so small that pigs forced inside can't lie down or turn around. They can't even turn their heads to see if a piglet is crying. The leg muscles of pigs confined in gestation crates atrophy from lack of use, and their skin develops abscessed sores from constantly scraping against rough steel bars. A pregnant sow will spend 124 days trapped inside this steel coffin, after which she will give birth in a farrowing crate and have her piglets removed from her after a few days. She will then be immediately artificially inseminated again, a cycle that is repeated at least eight times before she dies or is sent to slaughter.

This pig, along with another 5.5 million breeding sows in the United States alone, will never be able to move freely. She will suffer immense and prolonged mental and emotional pain, gnawing at her crate and banging her body back and forth in frustration. Would we ever allow a dog or cat to be so cruelly confined?

Of course not. That would be considered a clear case of animal cruelty. As professor of philosophy Jeff Johnson puts it: "We need only ask what we might think of subjecting our dogs and cats to such confinement to see the issues that might arise."[36] We believe this is a marker we can use as a moral standard when it comes to what we should and should not do to farmed animals: Would you do it to your dog or cat? If not, why do we allow it to happen?

Can't We Just Buy Better Meat for Pets?

Many people think the solution is to buy more humanely raised animal meats. We can try. German company Green Petfood is trying to go where most conventional pet food companies haven't: to produce sustainable and humane pet food.

CEO Klaus Wagner is proud that "the meat we use in our animal-based products stems from chicken [sic] that grow up in a more species-appropriate husbandry. In this way, we want to call attention to the problem of intensive animal husbandry and support an improvement of the status quo." While Green Petfood also sells vegetarian and insect-based pet foods, they are aware that some customers want to feed their pets farmed-animal proteins. These consumers want to know where these animals come from and how they were raised, which is where their high-welfare brand FarmDog comes in. Wagner says:

> Besides a trustworthy regional source, one of [FarmDog's] top priorities are the conditions in which the animals are kept, in terms of space, feeding, and medication. Thanks to FarmDog, we provide pet food that meets exactly these expectations. Our chickens come from regional farmers in Southern Germany, deeply committed to the issue of animal welfare. The quality standards have been developed by the German Society for Animals. In order to ensure the high welfare, the farms undergo several hours of initial inspection as part of the certification process. This is followed by regular third-party inspections, which are both announced and unannounced by an independent testing laboratory several times a year.

The Green Petfood staff regularly visits these farms themselves for personal reassurance that their high-welfare criteria—such as more space, a more natural coop structure, and a covered porch—are implemented on the farms. They are transparent about these experiences on their social media channels and website, conscious that the origin of food plays a role in the purchasing decision. Still, concerns remain about purpose-breeding and killing any animals to feed a pet.

Philosopher Julian Baggini[37] considers that as demand for higher-welfare meat for people grows, the byproducts of that meat will be available to pets. The argument is that if we insist on only eating and feeding animals that are well cared for, all will be well, moral, and ethical in the grocery store. If we can somehow overcome price, increase the scale, and improve animal-farm environments, we can solve our pet food dilemma.

Yet this is a tall order in practical terms. A study estimates that if we were to only farm slow-growing broiler chickens, as many as 68 percent more birds than the current production levels would be needed to produce the same amount of breast meat as conventional birds.[38] Not only does this illustrate how dramatically removed modern broilers are from "real" or "legacy" chickens, but it also proves that making chicken farming more "humane" would have significant negative environmental and economic impacts. As such, it's doubtful that the idealistic vision of "humane meat for all" will offer an actual solution to the animal welfare problems associated with pet food.

Even if we could somehow make raising animals for food sustainable, current farming systems are a long way from achieving this goal, especially in the United States. In an independent assessment by Business Benchmark on Farm Animal Welfare (BBFAW) in early 2019, not a single major poultry producer attained their top Tier 1 status in animal welfare. The majority of poultry companies sat on Tier 3, which means that although welfare is an established goal, there's much more work to be done. Sanderson Farms, the third largest U.S. poultry producer, was only at Tier 5, showing limited evidence of *any* implementation of welfare measures. Clearly, "humane meat for all" isn't happening anytime soon. More concerning, if companies that keep fast-growing strains of broilers permanently packed inside enclosed barns can gain Tier 3 recognition, we must critically question what "humane" really means.

Humane animal farming is difficult to define. There are no official federal guidelines for the definition of "humanely raised," so producers are free to write their own definition of "humane," which the USDA and Food Safety and Inspection Service (FSIS) then approves by verifying that that producer follows the arbitrary standards it set itself.[39] On most "humane" animal farms in the United States, castration without pain relief, hot iron branding, and dehorning without anesthesia are accepted and stamped HUMANE. In U.S. "cage-free" and "free-range" environments, hens actually have greater risk of contracting and transmitting infectious diseases and are more likely to experience severe feather pecking than in more restrictive environments.[40] Even in many of these "cage-free" environments, chickens never get to see the light of day, much less "roam freely." The Humane Society of the United States describes it this way:

"Most cage-free hens live in very large flocks that can consist of many thousands of hens who never go outside."[41]

Even when hens have the luxury of outdoor space, things are often far from rosy. In *The End of Animal Farming*, Jacy Reese describes his visit to an award-winning organic farm outside of San Francisco.[42] The chickens were truly free-ranging, with ample space to stretch their wings, move around, and engage in natural behaviors. Surprisingly, Reese found these birds were in worse health than any he had seen in the factory farms he'd investigated for Animal Charity Evaluators (ACE). Many chickens had a common contagious viral infection called Marek's disease that causes partial blindness. Others had swollen abdomens that he described as "some with over a pound of fluid build-up in their less-than-five-pound body." He also observed fungal infections, lice, and other preventable conditions. Despite being kept outside, these chickens had the same genetics as the birds raised in factory farms. That means they also had the same physiological problems that come with hyperactive reproductivity and ultra-rapid growth adaptations. After witnessing this horror scene, Reese wondered: "What was the farmer's main concern? Not the welfare of his diseased chickens, but how many birds he had lost to predators."[43]

Another welfare concern not limited to inhumane or "bad" chicken farms is that in order to prevent feather pecking, chicks have part of their beaks cut off without anesthetic or pain relief, often resulting in a syndrome compared to "phantom limb" in amputees.[44] This practice is approved even in Certified Organic and Certified Humane farms. A chicken's beak is its primary sensory organ, no different than our nose, tongues, hands, or eyes. Brutally amputating a chick's beak has very serious consequences and creates intense pain. Furthermore, even free-range egg operations rely on chicks obtained from commercial factory-farm hatcheries. In a very real sense, by purchasing female chicks from these chicken houses, people are supporting the practice of killing billions of unwanted male chicks.[45]

The painful reality of modern animal farming is that everything is dictated by profit. It's easier and cheaper to grind up a living male chick and raise another female broiler than to find a use for smaller males.[46] This practice, known as "culling," has been a poultry-industry standard for decades. Why grind them up? Because macerating a live male chick is the most profitable solution. By literally killing the proverbial "two birds" with one macerator, producers get rid of unwanted males and grind them into meal to feed other animals, including other chickens.

Sadly, these dirty secrets of modern farming can happen even in "free-range," "cage-free," and "organic" farms; otherwise, there would be no way to make a profit. Of course, there are genuinely humane animal farms where the animals are treated well, their behavioral needs are met, and they are given adequate veterinary care, although certain treatments are banned on organic farms, which causes inadvertent suffering. But for every good animal farm, there will be a bad one, and how can consumers know the difference? Max Elder summarizes this dilemma at the end of his chapter in *Ethical Vegetarianism and Veganism*: "When it comes to the ethics of our dinner table, the question we ought to ask ourselves is not which animals can be consumed but why we need to consume animals at all."[47] High-welfare or not, the rationale for leaving animals out of pet foods is increasingly convincing.

Walking Our Pets Away from Omelas

Readers may be familiar with Ursula K. Le Guin's famous short story, "The Ones Who Walk Away from Omelas." Within a few pages, Le Guin depicts an idyllic society called Omelas. It is the happiest place a reader could possibly imagine; its residents enjoy guilt-free, carefree, jubilant lives. Except beneath this utopia lurks a deep, dark secret. The secret all its citizens must bear is that their joy requires the sacrifice of a single child. This innocent being is locked away at birth inside a room, without light, adequate food, comfort, or care. Le Guin describes the child this way:

> The child . . . is so thin there are no calves to its legs; its belly protrudes; it lives on a half-bowl of corn meal and grease a day. It is naked. Its buttocks and thighs are a mass of festered sores, as it sits in its own excrement continually.

Recall the chickens collapsed in their soiled cages, the calves forced from their mothers, or the pigs locked in tiny gestation crates. We know they exist but are happier when we ignore them. Le Guin writes of this tortured child: "They all know it is there, all the people of Omelas." We learn that when a citizen of Omelas comes of age, they must go and see the child and bear brief witness to its suffering. After the initial feelings of shock, disgust, anger, and impotence, most people rationalize that the price of their happiness is only one small child. They can live with that. They return from their penance to their carefree lives, secure in the knowledge that they never have to see it again. But not everyone.

Even in sublime Omelas, there is always a small percentage of conscientious people that walks away, their lives changed forever. No matter how they try to rationalize the suffering of this one small child, they can't justify it. When we give up eating animals, we walk away from our own version of Omelas. Industrial animal agriculture has made life for most of us extraordinarily comfortable. Farmed animals contribute to almost every facet of our modern lives. They provide the cheap and convenient food we eat, the clothes we wear, the reliable shoes we walk in, the upholstery in our houses, our car seats, cosmetics, and we even test products and medications on them, theoretically to avoid harming humans. Modern civilization is built on the suffering of animals. Many people work hard to keep the truth hidden and help others justify the abuse. Yet once you've witnessed the suffering, you have the choice to help by changing what you eat and feed your pets.

Despite the best efforts of Big Ag, this book has probably told you very little about factory farming that you haven't already heard, seen on the Internet, or watched in documentaries. We're not talking about one fictional child; we're talking tens of billions of *real* lives locked out of sight and suffering. An estimated sixty billion farmed animals are sent to slaughter every year, most of whom have lived in appalling conditions in order to be killed for cheap food and products for pets and people. This has become an ethical issue impossible to ignore. In their book *Ethical Vegetarianism and Veganism*, Andrew and Claire Linzey state the following:

In terms of our relations with animals, it is difficult to think of a more urgent moral problem than the fate of literally billions of sentient creatures killed every year for human consumption.[48]

It's becoming harder to maintain the façade of civilized society while condoning the brutal and shameful suffering of animals. Social media reports and a growing vegan activist movement are breaking down the walls of slaughterhouses, defying ag-gag laws, and risking incarceration in their mission to free others from concrete prisons. Metrics like the Voiceless Animal Cruelty Index (VACI) are revealing so-called civilized Western society as the worst abuser of sentient animals. The 2018 VACI evaluates and ranks fifty countries based on the welfare of farmed animals and places the United States forty-ninth, with the grade "extremely poor."[49]

Terrifyingly, the violence and cruelty of slaughterhouses are beginning to spread into human society. Studies have shown a direct correlation between communities where animal farms and slaughterhouses are located and increased rates of assault and domestic violence.[50] As we'll explore later, the resources needed to maintain these animals in the dark corners of human society are destroying the planet and poisoning our morality. The tremendous moral cost of upholding our current way of living, our real-life "Omelas," is becoming too huge to bear.

Even those of us who have chosen to "leave Omelas" and lead animal-free vegan lifestyles often find it hard to take our pets. That moral epiphany we saw at the start of this chapter, when Diana Laverdure-Dunetz consciously connected human and pet animal-meat consumption, is fairly unusual. After all, it's far easier to maintain a divide between pets and the animals we eat. Why is that?

4

Four Legs Good, Four Legs Bad

INDUSTRIALIZED AGRICULTURE'S SUCCESS in hiding farmed animals is a key reason for the contradiction between the animals we love and protect and the animals we abuse and eat. In the mid-twentieth century, the industrialization of agriculture evicted cows, pigs, and chickens from pastures and fields, where they had been cared for on small family farms for hundreds of years, into densely packed facilities capable of housing thousands of animals. More meat could be "grown" more quickly, with less human involvement.

This transition also signaled the death and decline of thousands of small, family-owned U.S. farms. When family farms were replaced by massive corporate factory farms, a part of the American dream was lost, along with concerns about animal welfare. We also began losing touch with nature and animals, other than the pets in our homes. The majority of our human population now lives in urban and suburban areas, and most people have never seen or touched an actual farmed animal. The closest most schoolchildren will ever be to living livestock is at a staged "petting zoo." We saw in the previous chapter that the agriculture industry has taken great care to maintain this distance, keeping farmed animals out of view. How did we get to the point where not only is it illegal to visit a hog or chicken farm, but also that our children don't believe a hamburger is made from a dead cow?

Our author Ryan Bethencourt recalls that until he moved to the United Kingdom in his teens, he'd never seen a cow in real life. In his mind, cows were cute little animals a little bigger than dogs. Driving past a meadow one day, he exclaimed, "What is that? Is that a *giant cow*?" He'd never considered the reality of a cow, never considered his burgers as anything but burgers. The collapse of family farms and the rise of industrialized animal systems have altered society's historical closeness and access to animal agriculture. Ryan and hundreds of millions of other children grow up innocent of the dissonance between how people perceive and treat different types of animals. Ryan's generation rarely witnessed farmed animals, never saw inside a factory farm, and was brainwashed by cartoon cows and talking pigs. Dogs and cats were to be loved; all the rest eaten.

Aren't Pet Lovers More Likely to Be Animal Lovers?

Those of us who already have empathetic connections with nonhuman animals such as dogs and cats are actually in a special position to stand up for farmed animals. James Serpell, professor of ethics and animal welfare at the University of Pennsylvania, describes dogs as occupying a "kind of strange no man's land" in between animal and human, concluding that the dog has "unwittingly become a kind of an ambassador for the rest of the animal kingdom."[1] Los Angeles lawyer Lisa Bloom agrees: "Dogs are the ambassadors of the animal world sent to make us think about our choices. I would consider anyone who loves a dog to extend that compassion to other animals."[2] Our intimacy with dogs and cats unavoidably raises the question of our moral responsibility to farmed animals. Serpell summarizes:

> I think that's where the ambassador idea comes in, that they are out there representing the rest of the animal kingdom. And whenever we think about our relationships with them and how close those relationships often can get, it raises very uncomfortable moral questions about the way we treat other animals which are not so privileged and aren't so much in favor.[3]

Are Bloom and Serpell right? Is our increasing intimacy with cats and dogs changing our attitudes toward cows, pigs, and chickens? Or do farmed animals escape our responsibility because they are out of sight and out of mind?

A number of studies over the last five years have supported the assumption that people's relationships with their pets have a positive impact on their broader perception of all animals, making pet owners more likely to be receptive to broader animal welfare issues. Animal protection supporters and activists in the United States are usually either current or former pet owners.[4] In 2019, research showed that vegetarianism and veganism were more prevalent among more than 3,600 pet owners than has been reported in the general population, accounting for approximately 12 percent of pet owners in the sample group.[5] That means that in the United States alone, with its population of 325 million, 56 percent of whom own pets, there may be as many as fifteen to twenty million vegetarian and vegan pet owners. At the very least, this research indicates a larger proportion of pet owners may be sympathetic to the plight of farmed animals.

In 2013, a large-scale Humane League Labs survey asked over three thousand vegans, vegetarians, semi-vegetarians, and omnivores what most influenced their decision to give up or reduce animal products.[6] The survey found that 26 percent of vegans and vegetarians cited an interaction with a pet as being the first nudge, and 27 percent said interactions with companion animals were most helpful for keeping them motivated. Another study by psychologist Hank Rothgerber found that a major predictor of meat avoidance among pet owners was strong attachment to a pet, especially when this bond developed in childhood. Those with the strongest bonds with their companion animals tended to develop empathy for animals more broadly as a result, and their attitude to eating meat was thus more likely to change.[7] Children who grow up caring responsibly for pets have been shown to be more compassionate toward other animals. We need to make sure future generations are free to observe, interact, and bond with both farmed animals and livestock if we hope to improve animal welfare.

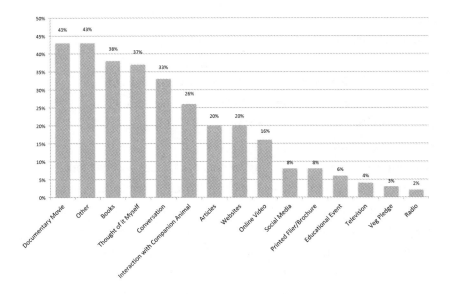

Figure 2: Reproduced from Humane League Labs Report April 2014, "Diet Change and Demographic Characteristics of Vegans, Vegetarians, Semi-Vegetarians, and Omnivores" (CC BY 4.0) https://creativecommons.org/licenses/by/4.0/.[8]

Chris Bryant, director of social science at the Cellular Agriculture Society, points out that "when we view the world through the unfiltered eyes of a child, we more easily see that we shouldn't be killing animals; but as we age and acquire cultural norms, it becomes easier to see this as being fine." Or, perhaps, we feel compelled to try to *convince* ourselves that killing animals is fine.

Other evidence shows that simple categorization of animals has a real effect on how we think about eating them. A 2011 study[9] asked participants to read about an animal in a distant nation; in some cases, the animal was categorized as food, in some it was killed, and in others a human was directly responsible for its death. The results showed that labeling an animal as "food," rather than killing or human responsibility, was sufficient to reduce the animal's perceived capacity to suffer, which lessened the participant's moral concern. The study concluded that people may be able to love animals such as dogs and cats and also love meat, simply because animals categorized as "food" are seen as insensitive to pain and unworthy of moral consideration.

Why Are Some Animals More Equal Than Others?

Serpell points out that although members of the pet-owning public tend to be morally disgusted at the thought of eating dogs and cats, "puppy mills," dog fighting, or the use of dogs and cats in biomedical research, we typically accept these treatments on non-pet species without much care.[10] This ethical disconnect creates emotional friction, requiring pet lovers to create complex moral codes to justify their actions. If you love one animal but want to eat another, you'll actually need to build up a deeper level of cognitive dissonance than people who have no relationship with animals at all. Scientists have confirmed this psychological coping scheme exists. The Rothgerber study found that many of the people who developed the strongest bonds with pets were also the people who most strongly endorsed indirect strategies to *justify* eating meat.[11] Apparently, humans are excellent at irrational rationalization.

What about feeding the animals you don't love to those you do? That's potentially an even tougher mental struggle. Chris Bryant suggests that whether or not you choose to eat meat yourself, "you might well see something perverse in chopping up one animal to give to another." With more animals intensively farmed today than ever before and pet owners feeding their companions more and more animal meat, these dissonance strategies seem to be working. It's hard not to feel that the divide between how we perceive these "categories" of food animals is widening as we grow closer to dogs and cats. The closer we grow to dogs and cats, the more we shove farmed animals away. Why? Is there any truth in the idea that farmed animals such as cows, pigs, chicken, and salmon suffer less or have fewer emotions than dogs or cats? What are the other barriers to making broader empathetic connections with all animals? Is there really any justifiable rationale to support caring for a pug instead of a pig?

In search of answers, let's go to South Korea, where the pet industry is booming. The Korean pet industry raked in $361 million in 2016 and is expected to exceed $573 million by 2022. Dog food accounts for the majority of spending (at around 60 percent), and many consumers are purchasing expensive, premium pet foods. Pets throughout South Korea are sold in shops and at traditional street markets. Along these winding streets is where the South Korean love affair with dogs gets complicated. At the very same markets where an enthusiastic new owner can buy a puppy to take home as a loving family member, he or she can also purchase a very different type of dog known as a *ttonggae*. *Ttonggae* translates literally as "shit dog." These are not dogs you *buy food for,* they are dogs you *buy for food*. As Julien Dugnoille quotes in his article "To Eat or Not to Eat Companion Dogs,"[12] "There are dogs Koreans eat and dogs Koreans don't eat." *Ttonggae* are dogs you eat.

The contradiction and hypocrisy between "dogs to love" and "dogs to eat" is everywhere in South Korea. In 2019, it was revealed that Royal Canin was building a large pet food production facility in Gimje, South Korea. Just a few miles down the road, another kind of "dog food" was being produced—human food made from *ttonggae* dogs. The dog meat trade was operating alongside a high-tech, premium pet food facility.[13] How's that for cognitive dissonance? As you'd expect, U.S. dog lovers were outraged when they found out dogs were being grown for human food next to a popular dog food company. Animal rescue red alert! As long as it's only dogs; no alerts for cows, pigs, chickens, or salmon, of course.

In 2019, Humane Society International (HSI) saved nearly two hundred dogs after a South Korean dog meat farm was forced to shut down. Shockingly, this facility doubled as a puppy mill, meaning the sixty-year-old farmer was breeding some dogs to sell as pets and others to sell for *bosintang*, a popular dog meat and vegetable stew. Inside this dog farm the dilemma between "some we love and some we eat" was never clearer. Nara Kim, HSI's Korean anti–dog meat campaigner, said: "The lines between puppy mills and dog meat farms are routinely blurred throughout South Korea, and with our latest dog farm closure we are exposing the shocking reality of that. These dogs are suffering at the hands of two abusive industries, their ultimate fate depending on whether they will sell for more money as a pet or for meat."[14]

In this high-tech, youth-oriented nation of new pet-lovers, it's estimated that as many as two million dogs are eaten every year in South Korea. The arbitrary distinction between "friend" and "food" dogs and cats is made even more startling by the blurring of boundaries between the two. Many animals bought and sold for their meat or fur are actually family pets that have been caught in the streets or even sold by their owners at the market. Indeed, "pedigree" cats and dogs (*Jindo*) are thought to have purer blood, so they fetch up to ten times the price of a "normal" pet. It's not impossible for a cash-strapped pet owner to rationalize selling their dog or cat to the highest bidder. It really happens.

Eating a dog is a shocking idea for most of us, and the Asian dog and cat meat trade has been the target of mass protests in the United States and United Kingdom. Western pet owners are particularly outraged by the thought of someone cooking and consuming the flesh of a dog or cat, despite the fact that hundreds, if not thousands, of years of Asian culture held no such prejudice. Why are some cultures incensed at the thought while others find it no different than chowing down on a chicken? Do Europeans and Americans hold the moral high ground" when it comes to *not* eating pets? The archaeological evidence indicates that humans, including North Americans and Europeans, were eating dogs for thousands of years. The Aztecs developed a hairless "edible" dog, the Xoloitzcuintli, bred to be about the size of a chicken, just as the South Koreans have bred the *ttonggae*. "Xolo" meat was a staple in the diet of many North American Indian tribes. Rumor has it that the conquistadors dined on dog without objection. Today about sixteen million dogs and four million cats are consumed each year in Asia. Dog meat is about as expensive as beef, and there are similar associations with sexual potency, virility, and overall "manliness" for those who eat it.

Now that modern civilizations have grown closer to dogs and cats, we find the idea of *farming and eating pets* revolting. But are the distinctions we make between pets and food animals any less arbitrary than those used in South Korea on their dogs? Here's professor of evolutionary biology and ethologist Marc Bekoff:

> People used to ask me why I went to China and other places where they ate dogs and cats. I simply mentioned that I had just come from the good ole U. S. of A., where they eat pigs, cows, lamb, all sorts of birds and fishes, et cetera. This got good conversations going!

Why is an American eating cows and pigs more ethical than a South Korean enjoying *ttonggae* dog meat? We can assure you it's not due to intelligence, ability to feel pain, or emotional capability.

Rosamund Young's surprise best seller *The Secret Life of Cows* gave the public a fly-on-the-barn perspective on the unique natures of each individual member of her herd. She shared tales of her trusting, thoughtful cows grieving for their dead, bonding with their calves, and playing tricks on their human farmers. We defy anyone to read Young's stories and insist cows are intellectually "slow" or "stupid." As for pigs, these incredible animals have been shown to be able to recognize themselves in a mirror, passing the benchmark self-awareness test that human children can only achieve at around three years of age. Dogs haven't been shown to recognize themselves in a mirror, instead simply barking at the mirror as if they're seeing another dog or simply ignoring it. Clearly animal intelligence isn't the main criteria for deciding who we eat.

Intelligent or not, one animal is a "food" species and one is a "pet," and we've been conditioned to accept that this is just the way it is. Only it's not so straightforward. What about the vastly different rights and privileges we assign a pet rabbit compared with a farmed rabbit? Or, as we'll explore later, the legal and regulatory rights we give a "pet beagle" compared to a "laboratory beagle." Are we in any way morally superior to South Koreans with their "food dogs" and "pet dogs"? Why do we judge an Asian man for using dog meat to affirm his masculinity when chowing down on a bleeding slab of beef is the epitome of American manliness?

The main reason we've decided it's immoral to dine on certain animals is because we've bonded with them, and thus ethically elevated them above animals we eat. We don't eat dogs and cats because we love them; we eat cows, pigs, chickens, and salmon because they're not part of the "human–animal bond." The difference between "love" and "food" boils down to an arbitrary category. Slowly, we're seeing a shift in attitudes toward all dogs in South Korea. As more South Koreans bring dogs into their homes, they are becoming less comfortable eating their beloved canine's *ttonggae* cousins. Mr. Lee, the convicted owner of the South Korean puppy mill and dog meat farm, told HSI:

> From the very beginning, my entire family has been against my dog farming. All my daughters and my wife want me to close it, and they have never wanted to visit the farm. I feel very ashamed to be a dog meat farmer and a puppy mill farmer, so I barely tell anyone what I'm doing. . . . I spend more money on this farm than I make from it. I think the dog meat trade will die soon. I feel like it's already ending.[15]

Mr. Lee signed a twenty-year contract promising to stay out of the dog meat trade and any animal-related industry. In November 2018, South Korean authorities shut down the country's largest dog slaughterhouse, the Taepyeong-dong complex, and a Gallup poll earlier that year found 70 percent of South Koreans reported they will no longer eat dog meat. The number of restaurants selling dog meat in Seoul has fallen from 1,500 to fewer than 700. As South Koreans have bonded with dogs and shared their homes, their attitudes toward eating them have changed dramatically. Does this mean that if Westerners got to know pigs and cows as we have dogs, we would feel just as bad about eating them and feeding them to our pets? We believe that's part of the solution.

Michael Mountain, co-founder and ex-president of Best Friends Animal Society, is somebody who knows these "other animals." He is vegan, and he's responsible for saving the lives of thousands of animals, not just pets. At the sanctuary, you can sponsor a rescued dog or cat, or a horse, pig, goat, or bird. Similar to the dog owner in Anne McBride's story about her trip to the supermarket, Mountain says he purchases pigs' ears for his dogs to chew on. The dogs love them, but Mountain tells author Hal Herzog that he can't stop thinking about the poor pigs. He expresses his philosophy in Herzog's book as follows: "You can't save all the animals in the world, but the ones that come into your care, you are responsible for."[16]

Yet this doesn't seem to match Mountain's veganism. Why not care for the pigs killed for the pig ear chews? Ultimately, we each choose what animals to include in our personal sphere of moral concern, and Mountain has chosen to include farmed animals that would otherwise have to die for his dinner but has yet to extend his animal-free ethos to the pets under his care. Mountain is no different from the majority of pet owners and caregivers who experience ethical feeding friction and feel powerless to do anything about it. We'll soon show you how biotech and the new generation of pet foods are collaborating to eliminate this feeding friction forever.

Our Responsibilities Toward Domesticated Animals

Responsibility is a complicated issue. Professor of philosophy Corine Pelluchon writes that responsibility changes our person from within: "It is the answer to the call of the other."[17] In this case, *another animal*. Not being personally connected to these animals isn't a valid reason to reject our duty toward them. We're not saying we should be intervening to defend prey animals from predators in the wild, but where humans have already intervened, we have a responsibility to take action. Consider Sue Donaldson and Will Kymlicka's argument in their animal rights book *Zoopolis*:

> The fact that humans have deliberately bred domesticated animals to become dependent on us generates different moral obligations to cows or dogs than we have to the ducks or squirrels who migrate to areas of human settlement. And both of these cases differ yet again from our obligations to animals in isolated wilderness who have little or no contact with humans.[18]

Despite what Mountain says, we *can* and we *are* responsible for animals who aren't directly in front of us or under our direct care. Pelluchon also points out that responsibility is a trait specific to humans. As we saw in the last chapter, our pets aren't responsible for the disappearance of 60 percent of mammalian wildlife in the last half century; *humans* are. It's our obligation because we are the ones choosing what, or who, to feed them.

Rationally and scientifically, we know that other non-companion animals are sentient and conscious. The simple fact is that animals are aware, attentive, feel pain and pleasure, experience relationships with other animals, suffer, and have intelligence. The notion that somehow "food animals" suffer less has been widely disproved countless times over the last twenty years. Science is proving that animals are smarter and more capable than we ever imagined. Almost everyone today believes animals have emotions; it's actually more logical and commonsensical than presuming they don't. Yet the scientific papers on animal emotions and intelligence that earn most headlines continue to be about dogs and cats. When the media ignore discoveries about the intelligence and emotions of farmed animals, the public continues to think of them as "dumb" and unfeeling," and easily forgets they exist by the tens of billions in captivity. Veterinarian Jeanette Thelander muses somewhat cynically: "This could be due to the fact that the public does not really want to know."[19] We, the authors, believe the public wants to know; they just aren't being shown.

For some reason, most people are reluctant to apply advances in animal behavior and emotions to the animals we eat. After all, as research psychologist Stanley Coren says in his book *The Intelligence of Dogs*: "Who wants smart food?"[20] The fact is that the pig crying out in a gestation crate ending up as bacon on our avocado toast is more intelligent than the family dog, and as smart as many young infants, but most people don't want to know that. The idea that your bacon had intelligent thoughts makes it a little less appetizing. It's easier to continue to view these "edible animals" as food, not as thinking, feeling beings, and certainly not as family members. Andrew Rowan, director of the Center for Animals and Public Policy at Tufts University, summarizes it this way: "The only consistency in the way humans think about animals is inconsistency."[21] After all, "Omelas" is pretty remarkable, as long as you can forget that suffering child.

When we feed our dog or cat the flesh of a broiler chicken who never saw the light of day, or (as we'll explore in the final chapter) canned food tested on a laboratory dog or cat, we're further reinforcing these categorical divisions. In an article for *The Conversation*, philosopher Sandra Woien considers the ethics of excessive spending on pets when other animals are suffering.[22] She cites the canine social media star Sylar, a photogenic Chinese Border Collie, who has his own mansion with a trampoline and indoor pool. Countless Instagram posts document Sylar and his dog friends frolicking about, receiving spa treatments, and enjoying massages. Woien muses: "As an ethicist, pet owner and vegetarian, I don't deny that the interests of animals matter, and while Sylar is indeed one privileged pup, his lifestyle comes with costs to others and to the planet itself." It's all too easy to lavish care and money on our pets while completely ignoring the plight of the animals we eat and feed. We believe we should start by protecting all animals from abuse. That's not to suggest that every farmed pig receive a massage like Sylar (although that would be nice); let's start simply by freeing them from gestation crates and allowing them to stand up and turn around.

Nathan Runkle, founder and former executive director of Mercy For Animals, points out what we've repeatedly shown in this book: "[C]urrently, U.S. law allows animals used for food to be routinely abused, mutilated, confined in unsanitary and inhumane conditions, and slaughtered by the billions—abuses that would land the perpetrator in jail if the victims were Fido or Fluffy." Runkle comments:

> There is no sound basis for this double standard. If not for the might of the industries that profit from their pain, farmed animals would likely enjoy, at the very least, the same protections as our dogs and cats. After

all, surveys show that the majority of Americans of all ages, genders, and political leanings believe that farmed animals do indeed deserve protection from cruelty.[23]

Our author Ernie Ward is a veterinarian, and veterinarians take an oath to uphold "the protection of animal health and welfare" and "the prevention and relief of animal suffering." For him, this is personal and means educating the public not just on the science of pet nutrition, but also on the impact our pet food choices have on other animals, especially those we eat or feed. The purchase of each bag and can of dog food represents a choice in how a cow, chicken, pig, or fish lives and dies. Currently, the secret lives of these highly intelligent, feeling, emotional animals are nothing short of nightmarish. Thousands of animals are crammed into metal sheds with barely enough space to stand and sentenced to a brutal life that ends in terror and pain. It's crucial that we begin to be more mindful of the consequences of our pet food choices. As Runkle suggests, few dog or cat owners really believe that other kinds of animals deserve to have their suffering disregarded. We therefore *have* to stop funding the cruelty of factory farming by feeding our own animals meat. There must be a more compassionate way to feed our companions.

5

Paying a Premium

M OST PET OWNERS would agree that feeding their pet is an expression of affection. After all, "Food is love" is baked into our consciousness for a reason. It's no surprise that people are spending *tens of billions* on pet food and treats each year in an effort to prove how much they love their pets. But are they getting what they're paying for? Consumers are increasingly choosing pet food brands claiming to be healthier and more "natural." Yet many of these companies are painting unrealistic pictures of our pets to encourage us to spend more. One brand might tell us that we need to feed our terrier as if he's a blood-hungry wolf, craving a fresh kill, while another brand owned by the same company will depict him as a pampered prince, whose genetics require a specialized "terrier breed diet." These mixed marketing messages are distracting us from the real issue: the irreversible damage that meat-based pet foods are wreaking on the environment, on farmed animals, and on the health of our pets.

To maintain these fantasies of pets as wild hunters or fussy toddlers, dog and cat owners are shelling out billions. The underlying hope is that by spending more on healthier pet food, they'll save money in the long term by paying less in future medical bills. But does a "wolf diet" or "terrier-specific" food save money or improve health? Are pet owners actually paying more for pretty pictures and clever stories instead of better nutrients? Over the last twenty years, we've seen pet food prices increase by up to 48 percent. The U.S. pet food market had a value of $24.6 billion in 2016 and is expected to exceed $30 billion in 2022.[1] This corresponds to a shift in spending on pets by household income. In 2003, 60 percent of spending came from lower-income households.[2] By 2017, demographic pet spending data from the U.S. Bureau of Labor Statistics (BLS) found that over 70 percent of spending on pet food was from households earning over $50,000, with the majority from the top income brackets.

So, wealthier people spend the most on pet foods: no surprises there. Well, actually there's something more interesting buried within the data. Much of the recent increase in pet food spending has come from *middle-income* households, suggesting a "spreading" of the pet food upgrade throughout society. With premium pet foods no longer reserved for the wealthy and their pampered poodles, the pet food industry has become an increasingly lucrative market, generating billions in profits. In 2017, analysts recorded a $4.6 billion increase in pet food spending, despite an extremely competitive environment. So-called upgraded or premium food is now a viable option for most pet owners, even low- and middle-income families.

The biggest gains have been in "super premium" pet foods containing high amounts of animal proteins, especially "human-grade," "fresh," and "ancestral" diets, where exorbitant prices are accepted. This is also where "grain-free" foods have made the biggest gains. These luxury brands now make up 20 percent of all pet food sales in the United States but generate over *half* of industry profits. Self-proclaimed "natural" pet food company Blue Buffalo's marketing slogan, "Love Them Like Family, Feed Them Like Family," perfectly captures the sentiment of modern pet ownership. If it's not good enough for people, it's not good enough for our pets. And these companies are charging a premium for that feeling. From 2013 to 2018, Blue Buffalo nearly doubled its annual revenue, to over $1.5 billion in annual sales.[3] A 2018 Pet Market Outlook survey by Packaged Facts also found that 75 percent of American pet owners would be willing to pay more, often much more, for healthier dog and cat foods.[4]

How do pet owners decide which food to feed? The latest Packaged Facts report shows the majority of pet owners relied on pet food advertising, family and friends' recommendations, or social media advertising. Online marketing has become a key tactic for pet food manufacturers to persuade pet owners to fork over their money. In 2012, only 28 percent of pet owners reported they bought pet products online more than they used to; in 2018, this had risen to 40 percent, and industry experts predict the market share for online pet retail will almost double by 2022. This may become problematic because online shoppers aren't exposed to as much dietary advice from veterinary professionals as are retail shoppers. Mouth-watering photos, gorgeously filmed testimonials, and catchy advertising slogans have replaced evidence-based nutritional recommendations for many pet owners. Once again, we ask if pet owners are getting their money's worth when paying for expensive ultra-premium pet foods.

The answer isn't as clear as we'd like. The FDA explicitly states that pet food "[p]roducts labeled as premium or gourmet are not required to contain any different or higher quality ingredients, nor are they held up to any higher nutritional standards than are any other complete and balanced products."[5] The FDA doesn't care if "premium" pet foods are created equally. Some very expensive and heavily advertised brands may source their base ingredients from the same third-party supplier as much cheaper pet foods use. Apparently, simply changing the packaging and marketing claims justifies higher prices for some pet owners.[6]

The truth is, it's hard to judge a food by its price or packaging. High-end pet food companies are no more transparent about their supply chains than giant corporations. In 2015, Nestlé Purina Petcare Co. sued Blue Buffalo for making a false claim that its food had "NO Chicken/ Poultry By-Product Meals." Blue Buffalo laid the blame upon its ingredient supplier, Wilbur-Ellis. The ingredient supplier pled guilty to substituting lower-cost ingredients for more expensive premium chicken and turkey meal. Clearly, Blue Buffalo wasn't able to monitor its suppliers closely enough, and we can safely assume these low-quality ingredients ended up in other "super premium" pet foods.[7] After losing the lawsuit, Blue Buffalo paid out $32 million in damages and actually saw its sales increase; it was bought in 2018 by General Mills for a whopping $8 billion.

To add to the confusion of selecting the best pet food, AAFCO (Association of American Feed Control Officials) doesn't allow pet food companies to advertise their foods as containing "high-quality ingredients," even if they genuinely do. In other words, there is no way to distinguish the best, most wholesome, and most nutritious ingredients from the worst simply by examining a pet food's packaging. High- and low-quality ingredients are listed identically on the ingredient list. These guidelines are intended to prevent inferior ingredients from being advertised as higher quality. We understand that. Unfortunately, these regulations also prevent a responsible pet food company committed to adding the best-quality ingredients from properly informing pet owners. Companies resort to quality signals such as "natural," "raw," "organic," "freeze-dried," "gluten-free," or "human-grade," but many of these terms don't have official definitions or are loosely defined in pet food, making them easy to manipulate by less reputable companies.

When "Natural" Isn't Natural

There's a simple reason why Whole Foods and Planet Organic can charge a fortune for their produce and shoppers are eager to pay it: "natural." When it comes to our own diets, we associate natural, homegrown products with health and nourishment, and artificial ingredients and additives with unhealthy junk food. For those of us willing to spend the money, this trend has transferred into premium "natural" pet food. In fact, market studies indicate about 43 percent of pet owners are willing to pay more for "natural" pet foods. According to Petfood Industry:

> While consumers once trusted science to deliver the magic mix of vital nutrients for their pets, they're putting more faith in nature these days. Just as with their own food choices, consumers increasingly prefer pet foods made in a kitchen over those made in a lab.[8]

Are consumers right to distrust science and choose nature instead? Research published in the *Journal of Animal Science* concludes: "The application of human food trends often is used to support functional health benefits of natural pet food products despite limited scientific evidence supporting the benefits in companion animals."[9] Is what's naturally good for humans also naturally good for pets? It can be, and later we'll look at the health benefits for dogs and cats of natural superfood ingredients like algae, koji, and yeast. But there are also healthy natural human foods that can potentially be toxic to our pets, including onions, garlic, grapes, and chocolate. Natural or human-grade doesn't *always* mean the food is better, or safer, for our pets. Later, we'll explore how pet food "made in a lab" might actually be the *best* food you can feed your pet in terms of safety, health, sustainability, and ethics. But for now, let's look at how "natural" these premium brands really are.

To begin with, what does "natural" mean when it comes to pet food? Not the same as it does for human food. In 2014, the Consumer Reports National Research Center conducted a nationally representative phone survey to assess consumer opinion regarding food labeling. Sixty-six percent of all respondents in the Consumer Reports survey said that a "natural" label on packaged and processed foods means that "no toxic pesticides were used." Yet "natural" is actually defined in pet food by the AAFCO as follows:

> A feed or feed ingredient derived solely from plant, animal or mined sources, either in its unprocessed state or having been subject to physical processing, heat processing, rendering, purification, extraction, hydrolysis, enzymolysis or fermentation, but not having been produced by or subject to a chemically synthetic process and not containing any additives or processing aids that are chemically synthetic except in amounts as might occur in good manufacturing practices.[10]

So, a pet food can be rendered, hydrolyzed, enzymatically treated, and processed, and contain some "chemically synthetic" elements, yet still be labeled "natural." To put it another way, as long as the pet food ingredient originates and is prepared in this universe and isn't a chemically synthesized food additive, it could be argued that it is "natural." Confused yet?

There have been several cases in which pet food companies have promoted their products as "natural" although they were fully aware that they contained harmful synthetic additives or contaminants. In August 2018, a class action lawsuit was filed against Diamond Pet Foods' "Taste of the Wild" brand for negligent misrepresentation, false advertising, and breach of warranty.[11] This premium pet food company advertises its dog food as being made of "the highest quality ingredients and products," "as nature intended," and for "nutrition-conscious pet owners." The lawsuit called Diamond Pet's marketing "deceptive, misleading, unfair, and/or false because, among other things, the Contaminated Dog Foods include undisclosed Heavy Metals, pesticides, acrylamide, and/or bisphenol A (BPA)." These toxins have been shown to accumulate over time in the dog's body and cause poisoning, injury, or disease. We're pretty sure this isn't what "nature intended."

A second lawsuit was filed against the same brand in March 2019, accusing Diamond of "misrepresenting, failing to test for, and failing to fully disclose the risk and/or presence of heavy metals, toxins, Bisphenol A ('BPA')."[12] Test results found 12,200 mcg/kg of lead in their grain-free Southwest Canyon Canine Recipe with Wild Boar dry dog food. Dangerous levels of lead have been established by the FDA to be 12.5 mcg per day for human adults. Two cups of the tested dog food would give a thirty-pound dog 2,440 mcg of lead per day. While the NRC "safe level" of lead is significantly higher for dogs at 2,000 mcg per day, this contamination is understandably concerning.

It's not just canines that are at risk. Solid Gold Pet Food faced its own class action lawsuit in 2019 that claimed "heavy metals, chemicals, and/or toxins" were present in their cat foods.[13] The company's marketing campaign promotes its pet food products as being nutritious, healthy, holistic, and high quality, possessing stringent quality controls, and containing "All that's good, nothing that's not." Arsenic is deadly to cats in doses of just one to twelve milligrams per pound of body weight, and mercury can cause long-term damage to their kidneys and neurological, cardiovascular, and nervous systems. Cadmium has highly toxic biological effects at extremely low concentrations. BPA, an industrial chemical that is a known endocrine disruptor in microdoses, has been linked to various health issues, including reproductive disorders, heart disease, diabetes, cancer, and neurological problems.

The lawsuit claimed Solid Gold didn't keep its "All that's good, nothing's that's not" promise. In the same year, Rachael Ray Nutrish Pet Food faced a $5 million class action lawsuit for deceptive advertising of "natural" products.[14] When the lawsuit was filed, Nutrish was the fastest growing U.S. pet food, with sales up 49 percent over the previous year, aggressively advertising its products as "natural" despite knowing they contained the unnatural pesticide glyphosate. Tests conducted by an independent laboratory proved that glyphosate was present in Rachael Ray Nutrish products. We're neither condemning nor condoning glyphosate as a health threat; we're just asking for transparency in advertising. These legal actions are ongoing.

In response to the high-profile lawsuits, some states are starting to improve pet food protections and safety. California holds "natural" pet foods to the long and detailed legal human-food definition of "natural," essentially assuring consumers that a pet food product labeled "natural pet food" contains no synthetic ingredients. However, pet food companies are actively lobbying the state legislature to change their definition of "natural" to match the AAFCO definition used in every other state. In April 2018, at the request of Canidae Pet Food, the State of California provided a hearing to the pet food manufacturers. The state's defense attorney pointed out that consumers don't receive a copy of the AAFCO guidelines included on the "natural" label, and they have a right to know what this term really means when they purchase the product. They propose requiring labels to state, "Made with natural ingredients with added synthetic vitamins, minerals and trace nutrients." We hope

California lawmakers will be able to withstand the intense pet food industry pressure, preserving some much-needed transparency in pet food labeling. Once again, these legal actions are ongoing.

Grain-Free Pets and the DCM Debate

An example of a premium pet food trend every bit as controversial as "natural" is "grain-free." Sales of grain-free dog food rose in the United States to nearly $2.8 billion by the end of 2017, dominating 44 percent of the market. Much of this growth has been fueled by concerns over food allergies. Although some pets may have specific food allergies, food allergies in pets are far less common than are allergies to fleabites and environmental allergens, and animal proteins have been shown to cause more food allergies in dogs than grains do. A 2016 peer-reviewed study showed that animal-meat ingredients—including beef, dairy, chicken, lamb, egg, pork, fish, and rabbit—were responsible for 236 cases of food allergies in dogs, whereas plant-based ingredients (wheat, soy, corn, rice, barley, kidney bean, and tomato) were involved in only 77 cases.[15] Whole grains such as brown rice and pseudo-grains such as quinoa, teff, amaranth, and buckwheat are packed with wholesome nutrients, which dogs have been proven to digest and utilize. Allergies and digestibility aside, the latest grain-free dispute involves a somewhat rare form of heart disease.

In July 2018, the FDA publicly announced that it was investigating a link between grain-free diets and a common type of canine heart disease, dilated cardiomyopathy (DCM), in which the heart muscle weakens and becomes enlarged. DCM is historically a rare condition most commonly limited to a handful of breeds, and symptoms include fatigue, difficulty breathing, coughing, and acute heart failure. In 2018, after surveying 150 recent cases, Chesapeake Veterinary Cardiology Associates (CVCA), a practice of nineteen veterinary cardiologists in the Baltimore–Washington, DC, area, alerted the FDA that it had begun diagnosing DCM in atypical breeds. CVCA had diagnosed golden retrievers, doodle mixes, Labrador retrievers, and Shih Tzus with this rare heart disease. The common factor, in their opinion? "Grain-free, exotic, and boutique"

dog foods, often containing kangaroo, peas, lentils, chickpeas, and potatoes (ingredients commonly used to replace grains). With little more
evidence than a handful of puzzling cases, a series of events began that
has confused pet owners and veterinarians about the safety of "grain-
free" pet foods.

The original study that initiated the grain-free/DCM debate described
the clinical and dietary features in golden retrievers diagnosed with
taurine deficiency and dilated cardiomyopathy.[16] It hoped to establish
specific dietary associations with atypical DCM. In short, the researchers
believed there was a link between grain-free diets and this rare heart
disease. They evaluated twenty-four golden retrievers with documented
taurine deficiency and dilated cardiomyopathy alongside fifty-two
healthy, client-owned golden retrievers. Twenty-three of the twenty-four
taurine-deficient dogs were fed diets that were either grain-free, legume-
rich, or a combination of these factors.

The "grain-free diet" is what triggered these cardiologists' attention.
Sixteen of the forty-three normal dogs with diet histories also had low
blood taurine levels, but not DCM. All diets included a complete and
balanced claim substantiated by formulation to meet the AAFCO Dog
Food Nutrient Profiles, but only eleven of the forty-three healthy dogs
with diet histories were fed a diet meeting the more stringent World
Small Animal Veterinary Association Global Nutrition Committee
(WSAVA GNC) recommendations. The study noted that all but one of the
DCM dogs were eating fewer calories per day ("up to 62% less"). AAFCO
regulations don't account for low- and high-activity differences in calorie
consumption, meaning these dogs would potentially be receiving fewer
nutrients from their pet food (so less methionine and cystine, the building
blocks of taurine). Once the dogs' diets were changed (seventeen were
changed to a grain-inclusive food), they showed significant improvement in their heart health, and their taurine concentrations normalized.
What's so special about taurine? In the next chapter we'll delve deeper
into the functional nutrition of pet food, but let's have a specific look at
this infamous sulfonic acid now.

Taurine is an organic compound widely distributed in animal tissues. It is also found in the large intestine, and both dogs and humans need it to conjugate bile acids. Humans can alternate between using the amino acids taurine and glycine, whereas dogs can only use taurine. This means a dog is more reliant on taurine and its precursors, cystine and methionine, for maintaining health. Increased physiological demands or decreased intestinal absorption can lead to taurine deficiency, and potentially heart disease. Even though taurine plays a critical role in heart health, pet food manufacturers are not required to conduct dietary testing or add supplemental taurine to their formulations. This is because consuming adequate methionine and cystine via its food is all a dog needs to make its own taurine and avoid these problems.

Making dry dog food can pose additional challenges to taurine adequacy. Cooking and heat can lead to a loss of naturally occurring taurine from animal meats, along with a reduction in many other amino acids. Animal muscle has typically contained the highest levels of "naturally occurring taurine," but different animals contain widely different amounts. Rabbits, for example, contain relatively little taurine, and lamb meal may be low in methionine and cystine. Plant-based diets may also require added taurine to offset the effects of certain natural proteolytic inhibitors (molecules that prevent the normal functioning of the enzymes that aid the breakdown of proteins) and phytates (which can inhibit the absorption of dietary minerals, calcium, iron, and zinc). Grains and legumes contain higher amount of phytates and fiber and can potentially reduce taurine absorption in the intestinal tract. Although some fans of animal meat–based diets criticize phytic acid for these reasons, phytates have also been associated with many of the health benefits of plant-based and fiber-rich foods. Phytic acid has been shown to serve as a potent antioxidant and protectively binds heavy metals in the gut and promotes digestive health.

The fact that "grain-free" and "boutique" pet foods were specifically targeted in the study and FDA report didn't go unnoticed. Grain-free pet foods have been steadily taking market share from traditional corn- and wheat-based pet foods for the past decade. The big pet food companies have spent tens of millions in advertising to discredit this trend. Could this be yet another attack on a competing pet food philosophy? Could this be about money? The *New York Times* points out: "The possibility that expensive food, lovingly chosen, could make one's adored pet devastatingly ill is sending shudders through dog owners."[17] Three dogs have died allegedly from being fed grain-free diets. Whether this is because of the absence of grains or some other non-diet factor, we simply don't know.

A growing number of veterinarians and pet nutrition experts are skeptical that a specific type of diet is to blame. The consensus is building that some dog foods may contain inadequate taurine levels or other nutrients, such as carnitine, methionine, or cystine, and that genetic factors play a significant role. In a special column in the March 2019 edition of the peer-reviewed *Journal of Animal Science* titled "The Association between Pulse Ingredients and Canine Dilated Cardiomyopathy: Addressing the Knowledge Gaps before Establishing Causation," a panel of veterinary experts warned veterinarians and pet owners against jumping to conclusions.[18] The golden retriever study speculated that legumes may interfere with a dog's ability to make or absorb taurine. However, there is also evidence that those commercial grain-free pet foods may not contain the required levels of methionine and cystine. In Europe, where we have yet to see grain-free diets leading to heart disease in dogs, the lowest required levels for methionine and cystine are considerably higher than in the United States. In fact, the authors of the 2019 paper urged pet food companies to continue pursuing animal protein alternatives, to continue including legumes in their formulations, and to critically review current AAFCO taurine, carnitine, methionine, and cysteine requirements and bioavailability in pet foods. In their opinion, a causal link between grain-free or "boutique" pet foods and DCM has yet to be established.

Currently, there's much we don't know about these unusual DCM cases. A third FDA update published on June 27, 2019, also failed to find causality between diet and DCM. What we do know is that the pet food industry needs to do a better job testing nutritional levels in pet foods. AAFCO should also work with European and WSAVA experts to modernize their taurine recommendations and testing procedures. The fact that these DCM cases haven't been observed in mainland Europe or the United Kingdom, despite an increase in the popularity of grain-free and vegetarian dog foods there, indicates increased nutrient oversight may be part of the solution. Simply adding more animal meat in response to a few cases risks ignoring the real problem and contributes to environmental destruction.

What's also left out of the DCM discussion is that when scientists simply added taurine to the diet of affected dogs, almost all of the animals recovered. Inadequate dietary or bio-unavailable taurine, methionine, or cystine may turn out to be the real culprit, not a specific dietary philosophy. One thing we can learn from this debate is that it's vitally important that dietary nutrients are provided at the appropriate levels. Indeed, excessive nutrients can be just as harmful as deficiencies. Vitamin D, for instance, is an essential nutrient for dogs, but high amounts can cause serious health problems, including kidney failure or even death. In December 2018, the FDA acted on complaints about dogs experiencing vitamin D toxicity after eating certain dry kibble. The government agency recalled several brands after testing confirmed that samples contained excessive, potentially toxic, amounts of vitamin D. Recalls continued into 2019.

Grain-free dog food gained popularity shortly after another pet food disaster, the 2007 melamine recall we discussed in Chapter 1. As pet owners abandoned less-expensive grain-based diets, sales of grain-free pet foods soared. By 2011, grain-free dog food accounted for 15 percent of sales in American pet specialty stores, reaching nearly $1 billion in sales. By the end of 2017, the grain-free pet food market had nearly tripled in value. And despite the recent news, it continues to grow in 2019. Even if you don't believe these health scares, Dr. Lisa Freeman, a veterinary nutritionist at Tufts University, has a warning: "Contrary to advertising and popular belief, there is no research to demonstrate that grain-free diets offer any health benefits over diets that contain grains."[19]

If grain-free pet food isn't proven to be healthier, why is it *still* growing in popularity? Two words: animal meat. "Grain-free" is a clever spin for marketers to tap into the belief that dogs lust for meat and to reaffirm "natural" marketing. In the next chapter we'll explore how some companies are promoting raw, grain-free, meat-based diets as the most "natural" pet food possible, claiming their food is "biologically appropriate" or closer to the "ancestral" diet of wolves. You probably know somebody who swears by the popular low-carb Keto diet, or the caveman Paleo regimen. As with most human diet trends, we're seeing the high-protein, grain-free trend make its way into pet foods. If only nutrition were so simple.

Human-Grade and Homemade Pet Food: Healthy or Hoax?

In the quest for the perfect pet food, dog and cat owners are turning to foods they put in their own bodies. Millennial pet owners are purchasing "people foods" for their pets. But what exactly is "human-grade," and is there a difference between "people food" and "pet food?" Once again, when it comes to pet food, it's complicated.

In simplest terms, "human-grade" pet food manufacturers do not use FDA or AAFCO pet food standards to grade the quality of their ingredients. Instead, they adhere to FDA guidelines for what is acceptable to be used in *human* foods. This means "human-grade" pet food should be more highly regulated and has stricter standards on quality, ingredients, and nutritional profiles, using USDA-approved animal-meat ingredients rather than unapproved byproducts. Human-grade pet foods should also use human-grade standards for food production as well as ingredient handling. When it comes to price, this means human-grade pet foods will often be more expensive. Much more expensive.

In addition to higher prices, using human-grade meats has significant environmental costs. But is human-grade actually healthier for our pets? The evidence is lacking. No one has done the research in animals. From a human health perspective, high-protein diets, especially animal meats, have long been associated by medical experts with cancer, obesity, kidney disease, and decreased life expectancy. Why would we think that human-grade meat is going to be any healthier for our pets when it has been shown to be unhealthy for humans? Because it's "organic"?

In addition to human-grade meats, pet owners are scrambling to find "organic" options. Even when we pick the best organic human or pet food we can buy, there's no guarantee that this means healthier. Organic pet food is regulated by the USDA as part of the National Organic Program, and like human-grade pet food, organic pet foods need to meet the same criteria as organic human foods. As with human foods, an organic label is not a guarantee of complete nutrition or safer food; it only means that there are no genetically modified organisms (GMOs) or pesticides in the product. Well, that only leaves "people foods."

Some pet owners have become so wary of commercial pet food that they feed their pet exclusively human foods. The rationale is, "If I can, and do, eat it myself, then surely it's safe for my pets." There's something reassuring about handpicking high-quality ingredients without the ominous byproducts or contaminants hidden in cans or kibbles. We can also select high-welfare human-grade meats, fresh fruits and veggies, and nutrient-rich grains and starches. What could go wrong?

A lot. Research in the veterinary journal *Topics in Companion Animal Medicine* reveals the pitfalls of homemade diets, showing that most recipes contain excessive protein because of the perception that the diet of dogs and cats should be mostly animal meat.[20] This often creates an invisible imbalance of calcium and phosphorus, leading to eventual bone and kidney disease. By the time a pet shows any symptoms, it's usually too late to reverse the condition. Cat foods made by individuals are commonly deficient in essential fats, have low energy density, or contain an unpalatable fat source like vegetable oil. Homemade pet foods are rarely balanced for most micro-minerals and essential vitamins, because over-the-counter pet vitamin and mineral supplements aren't "complete" and were never intended to balance a pet's diet. Use of uncooked meat, organs, and eggs in homemade pet food recipes can be especially dangerous for human family members, often contaminated with pathogenic microorganisms including *E. coli*, *Salmonella*, *Listeria*, *Campylobacter*, and *Clostridium*.

Even if a pet owner is following a recipe approved by a veterinarian, making a nutritionally complete meal for your cat or dog isn't as simple as it sounds. In reality, most people who make pet food at home get rushed or complacent and aren't paying due diligence, despite their best efforts. Most nutritional imbalances are imperceptible and may take months to years to cause symptoms, falsely reassuring a pet owner that a diet is working—until it's too late. In a 2013 published study, two hundred homemade dog food recipes from thirty-four sources (including websites, pet care books, and veterinary textbooks) were evaluated for nutritional adequacy.[21] *Ninety-five percent* of the diets were deficient in at least one essential nutrient, and most (84 percent) had multiple deficiencies, some of which were severe. In addition, several recipes contained dangerously *high* levels of nutrients such as vitamin D. You *can* have too much of a good thing, especially when it comes to the fat-soluble vitamins A, D, E, and K, and certain minerals, particularly phosphorus. The recipes that fared best in this study were designed by veterinary nutritionists and veterinarians.

But a good recipe doesn't guarantee a good diet. In 2014, another study[22] observed veterinary nutritionists who prescribed fifty-nine dogs nutritionally complete and balanced homemade diets made from readily available ingredients and supplements. All forty-six owners received a written recipe detailing the exact daily amount of each of the ingredients to feed, and the veterinary nutritionist stressed to the owners the importance of following the recipe exactly. Surely it shouldn't be hard to follow a pet food recipe written and explained by an expert. It was. The researchers were shocked to discover that after only six months, 30 percent of the owners admitted to modifying the recipe, 40 percent failed to control the amount of the ingredients they used, 70 percent didn't use the recommended amount of oil and salt, and 35 percent did not use the vitamin, mineral, or amino acid supplements as directed. The last is especially worrying, given that these are the essential ingredients in our pets' diets that greatly influence health and well-being. Based on the current scientific evidence and these results, it may be healthier, less expensive, and less environmentally damaging to feed our animals a commercial pet food.

Raw Meat Pet Food

Animal meat is the hot trend in pet food, and raw meat blazes the brightest. Magazines, social media, and advertisers may celebrate pets as princes and princesses, but equally strong is the marketing of dogs and cats as wolves and tigers. To manufacture this myth, advertisers use sales terms such as "ancestral," "biologically appropriate," and "raw." An extension of this trend is "fresh," encompassing the "natural," "human-grade," and "raw meat" trends. But raw animal meat has risks. According to the FDA, Centers for Disease Control (CDC), American Veterinary Medical Association, British Small Animal Veterinary Association, Canadian Veterinary Medical Association, World Small Animal Veterinary Association, and a host of other organizations, raw meat pet food is the diet most likely to introduce disease-causing bacteria into our pets and our homes. One study found that in a group of two hundred therapy dogs, the incidence of *Salmonella* in raw animal meat–fed dogs was 0.61 cases/dog per year, compared with 0.08 cases/dog per year in dogs that were not fed raw meat.[23]

Despite these risks, raw animal meat is touted by many as the "premium" of all pet diets. *Fortune* reported that the growing number of commercial raw meat–based pet foods has been accompanied by an increase in recalls,[24] and an FDA study found significantly higher levels of *Salmonella* and E. *coli* in raw pet food samples than in other types of pet foods.[25] At the end of January 2019, thirty-three days into a U.S. government shutdown (when the FDA was only in operation for "imminent threats"), the FDA issued an urgent caution to pet owners not to feed their pets a specific brand of raw food "due to *Salmonella* and *Listeria monocytogenes*." This proves that, despite being officially closed, the FDA was still worried about the public health risk of raw meat pet foods.

Does this mean the FDA is anti–raw meat pet food? No, they're pro–human health. Contaminated raw animal meats pose a serious health risk to pet owners who handle the foods, packaging, and wastes. Secondary transmission is especially dangerous to children, older persons, and immunocompromised individuals.[26] That's why so many medical organizations discourage feeding pets raw animal meats. So why are raw meat diets such a hot trend? Well, as we'll delve into in the next chapter, a lot of it has to do with astonishingly clever marketing.

Early each day, Alice watches her dog JD chase the pigeons that invade his garden. She knows he has as much chance of catching a soaring bird as he does the squirrels he joyfully pursues in his daydreams. In fact, when JD once found a dead squirrel, he had no idea what it was or what to do with it. JD's instinct wasn't to gnash and devour this "prey," but to cautiously sniff and retreat. JD's hunting drive might cause him to chase other animals, but he apparently has little desire to kill them. We'd argue that JD and most pet dogs are not killing, carnivorous canine commandos. Yet somehow the assumption that dogs are prehistoric predators lusting to kill other animals persists, and this perception is used as a key marketing message for high-animal protein, raw, and "pure-meat" pet foods. These "ancestral diets" claim that how and what a dog ate millions of years ago is best: natural is healthier. This cognitive bias is well documented by psychologists as the "appeal to nature" fallacy. It relies on the argument that because something is "natural," it must somehow be better. That's not necessarily true. Ecology and evolutionary biology professor Marc Bekoff told the authors:

> People are swayed by ridiculously misleading advertisements for dog food that go something like "Feed the wolf in your dog." Dogs aren't wolves, and if they ate like wolves there would be more of an obesity crisis because most dogs don't get near enough exercise.

As we explored earlier, modern animal meats potentially contain many contaminants, toxins, pathogenic bacteria, and added antibiotics and hormones. They're not very "natural." The "raw meat" fed to a dog or cat today has little relation to the prey a wolf or tiger killed tens of thousands of years ago (or even hundreds). For starters, in the "real wild," not the "biologically appropriate" or "ancestral" pet food fairyland created by marketers, a wolf or tiger would consume their kill immediately.

This means the fresh meat would have little chance to become contaminated by pathogenic bacteria. There would also be no added antibiotics, hormones, or growth-boosting vitamin and mineral injections. And forget about cows, pigs, chickens, or tuna and salmon. Ancient wolves and dogs had virtually no chance of eating these animals, making them a poor choice as "biologically appropriate."

The animals that dogs and cats would naturally eat if they had to kill them themselves would primarily be rabbits, squirrels, mice, and whatever dead carcass they lucked across; for cats, it would be small rodents, birds, reptiles, and insects. The species of animal meat we feed our pets today is far from "ancestral" or even "species appropriate." To compare the fresh kill or scavenging find of a wild cat or coyote with a modern grocery-store-bought "ancestral raw diet" or chicken necks from the butcher is just plain ridiculous. Our domestic dogs and cats no longer hunt for survival, nor are they wild. They are creatures of our creation: mild-mannered, cuddly versions of once proud predators and scavengers. Tens of thousands of years of careful breeding and codependence have made our dogs and cats more similar to us, and completely different from their ancestors.

Ross Lamond, founder of insect-based dog treat company Bug Bakes, sees lots of companies promoting raw meat pet food and making a lot of money—certainly more than bug-based pet food. He muses: "[T]here are some perks with raw food, in that it's probably better than some rubbish kibble." However:

> Is that the only option? Absolutely not. Is it the most ethical option? In no way, shape, or form. We humans are very fickle; we want to enjoy trends. Cats and dogs will eat what they're given, so why wouldn't we give them the most ethical and environmentally friendly option? Sure, a dog's probably going to do well on a raw meat diet, but he will also probably do well on many other diets. Raw pet food will push meat demand up massively and that's just not the way to go.

The problem is, raw animal-meat pet food isn't just hurting the environment and farmed animals; it's potentially hurting our pets and our human family, too. In modern domestic society, there are many opportunities for pathogens to contaminate meat between the time an animal is slaughtered and when it reaches the pet bowl. New research[27] shows the surprising degree to which germs and parasites can be found in commercial raw-meat products, posing potential health risks to both pets and their owners. Despite denials by raw pet food advocates, raw meat and raw eggs are known to contain harmful bacteria such as *E. coli* and *Salmonella*, and feeding excess raw egg whites can cause biotin deficiency in pets. Many proponents of raw food diets boast of their pet's more frequent poops and shinier coats, but the constant pooping is more likely due to lower fiber intake rather than the magical "enzymes" and mysterious "co-factors" purportedly in raw animal flesh. The shiny coat probably is because of high levels of dietary fat, which also has risks such as obesity.

As we saw earlier, pet food and feeding has become increasingly integrated into the human kitchen. We no longer store dog food out in the garage next to the toolbox; we keep it in the pantry next to the peanut butter. Few pet owners feed their dogs and cats in their yards anymore; we lovingly place their meals in our dining rooms and kitchens. If you're preparing raw animal meats, this humanization trend inadvertently puts your human family at risk. Wouldn't it be safer to prepare our pets' meat-free vegetable dishes alongside our own? Alice loves to bake extra butternut squash specifically for her spaniel, his favorite food, to supplement his complete, commercially formulated plant-based kibble. Ernie shares his sweet potatoes and chopped carrots with his meat-free terriers. As we'll explore in the next chapters, removing meat from canine diets may have myriad health benefits for dogs and humans.

* * *

Grain-free, super premium, human-grade, raw meat. . . . Maybe we're getting too hung up on feeding our pets the "perfect" pet food. Marc Bekoff isn't buying into any of these pet food trends. He tells us that the last dogs with whom he "shared his home and heart" did very well on a diet of bean and rice burritos, bagels with peanut butter, and other non–animal meat meals. Bekoff never worried too much about brands, labels, or trendy diets; most of the time his dogs ate whatever he ate. Was it their vegan diets that gave his dogs the energy they needed for their daily romps around the mountains in his hometown of Boulder? In the next chapter, we'll explore the idea that although dogs may benefit from the proteins and nutrients found in animal meat, those proteins no longer have to come from dead animals.

6

Where Do Your Pets
Get Their Protein?

I T's CLEAR TO us that animal-meat pet food is harming the planet, farmed animals, and possibly even our pets. At this point, you're probably asking, "Okay, but what can I do? Don't dogs and cats *have* to eat animal meat?" Recent advances in biology, veterinary nutrition, and food technology are challenging this assumption. The answer isn't as straightforward as once thought, but it's increasingly evident that pets no longer have to eat other animals to thrive. Pets crave nutrients, not ingredients. This chapter will show that, contrary to what some pet food manufacturers would like us to believe, protein doesn't have to come from the bodies of other animals. The science clearly shows that our pets, especially dogs, can thrive on plant-based food and love it as much as, if not more than, beef or chicken diets. It's true that cats are more nutritionally challenging than dogs (we'll explore the debates around "plant-based cats" in Chapter 8), and later in the book we'll look at advances in food technology that might soon allow feline fanciers to remove animal meat from their cats' diets without risk. But for now, let's focus on plant-based dogs.

From her childhood, Alice remembers her family's rescue retriever, Benson, having a very particular favorite food. It wasn't a bloody T-bone or a thick pork chop, but rather a steaming plate of spaghetti topped with tomato sauce. Benson would prance and spin in eager anticipation as soon as he spied his prized pasta splashed into a pot of boiling water. Benson wasn't an outlier. Most dog owners have observed their dog pleading for ice cream, doughnuts, potatoes, or any of myriad meat-free foods. While we don't advise pasta and doughnuts as the main ingredients for any diet (no matter how good that may sound), there is clear evidence that dogs can, and do, thrive on a balanced, nutritional meal plan without animal meat.[1] The question becomes, if humans and dogs don't need to kill animals for food anymore, why do we?

Psychologists offer the four Ns of reasoning to explain why humans insist on eating animal meat: meat is Normal, Necessary, Nice, and Natural. When it comes to feeding our *pets* meat, these four Ns take on even stronger resonance. To begin, it's completely *Normal* to give your dog or cat animal meat–based pet food, and if you don't, you risk being attacked by other dog owners for "inadequate care." The social pressure to conform and continue to feed our pets animal meat is enormous. Later, we'll look at some of the responses on social media to posts promoting meat-free diets for dogs.

Most people believe animal meat is *Necessary* for the health of our pets. It's no surprise that this is also the most common reason people give for their own consumption of meat, despite the multitude of warnings about excessive animal-meat consumption and the growing number of vegetarians and vegans in our society living healthy, active lives. You can imagine how adamantly many pet owners cling to this idea of "necessary" when discussing how their pets descended from wolves and wild cats.

Meat is also perceived as *Nice* for our pets. Owners observe pets salivating over meat as a sign they enjoy and crave eating other animals. But dogs also salivate for toxic chocolate and unhealthy ice cream, and many go bonkers for brownies. Salivation and food-enjoyment behaviors don't always indicate a healthy desire.

Finally, meat is perceived as *Natural* for dogs and cats, and so withholding animal meat must be unnatural. No matter that the "meat" in most pet foods bears little resemblance to "real" meat or even the "meat" pictured on the bag. We've already seen that the ingredients in most conventional animal meat–based pet food are far from "natural" and are generations of genetic modifications and entirely separate species from a pet's natural prey. In this chapter and the next, we'll pull apart these arguments further, exploring the importance of "natural" for the well-being of our dogs and cats.

Is Animal Meat Necessary?

Let's begin by examining the assumption that animal meat is necessary for dogs. Protein is vitally important for canine health, promoting the growth and maintenance of muscle, hair, and nails, transporting nutrients around the body, helping dogs' immune and neurological systems function correctly, and producing essential hormones. According to current nutritional guidelines, the minimum amount of protein required for growth at all canine life stages is 22.5 percent of daily food consumption, and the current AAFCO standards state that dry food for adult dogs should contain at least 18 percent protein.

Proteins are only useful to an animal if they can be digested and absorbed within the body. Whether animal or plant-based, the food must be proven to contain bioavailable nutrients. But does it matter where that protein comes from? When it comes to protein, we need to look at quality and composition, not just quantity. The total amount of protein in the food isn't the most important issue; it's whether those proteins contain all the amino acids and nutrients a dog needs for optimal health. Let's begin by examining what makes protein important for health.

Protein molecules are actually molecular "strings" comprising twenty common amino acids. The strings come in varying lengths and are folded in ways that determine how the resulting protein interacts in the body or environment. When dogs eat protein, the digestive system breaks down these proteinaceous folds and links into their amino acid building blocks.

The body then uses these amino acids to manufacture a multitude of specific proteins needed at any particular moment to build muscle, produce hormones, or fight infection. Dogs can make half of the twenty common amino acids on their own (including taurine) as long as their diet contains enough of these amino acid building blocks. However, there are ten amino acids that *can't* be created by the canine body, which means they must be eaten. The ten essential amino acids for dogs are arginine, histidine, isoleucine, leucine, lysine, methionine, phenylalanine, threonine, tryptophan, and valine, and a dog food must contain all of them in adequate levels to meet AAFCO standards. An AAFCO nutritional adequacy statement on the label of your dog food indicates that all a dog's essential acids are present.

Returning to our previous question: Is it just animal-derived products that contain these ten essential amino acids? Not at all. High-quality plant, fungal, bacterial, or algal protein sources can also contain all ten essential amino acids for dogs. One popular plant-based dog food packs 24 percent protein in its formula, with ingredients such as peas, lentils, and quinoa, and earns the same "complete & balanced AAFCO formula" label badge as animal meat–based diets. Ryan and Ernie's pet food company, Wild Earth, has created an animal-free, complete and balanced dog food with over 30 percent protein. Identical to a complete and balanced meat-free diet consumed by humans, it's possible to provide dogs with all of the nutritious proteins they need by going directly to the source: plants and organic compounds. After all, that's where the cows, pigs, and chickens we feed our dogs get *their* proteins.

The Miniature Wolf Mythology

Feed your dog's inner wolf! Satisfy your pup's need for meat! It's no surprise that modern pet dogs are mythologized as miniature, blood-thirsty wolves when many people see *themselves* as carnivorous predators. What vegetarian or vegan hasn't been lectured, "But it's the circle of life. We were born to hunt!"? While that may be true, we're much better gatherers and farmers.

If we're no longer anxious hunter-gatherers foraging for dinner, are our dogs still miniature wolves stalking prey? Of course not. Modern dogs are as similar to wolves as we are to our Neolithic ancestors. To make this point, let's explore a bit of canine evolutionary biology and DNA evidence. Today, we have a much better understanding about canine evolution based on their mitochondrial DNA. Mitochondrial DNA (mtDNA) is also referred to as "maternal DNA" and consists of genetic material passed from mother to offspring. Ancestral lines of mitochondrial DNA remain unchanged from generation to generation, until there is a genetic mutation. These mutations are the key to unlocking the emergence of a new characteristic, or even a new species.

Using canine mtDNA as evidence, we know that dogs began to diverge from gray wolves between 15,000 and 40,000 years ago. The assumption has long been that when wolves were snatching tidbits of food from a caveman's camp, the boldest and friendliest would secure the most food. This initiated selection of "tame" traits in future generations. Humans benefited from the collateral protection offered by these select wolves, further reinforcing the reciprocal relationship that exists today. During the following thousands of years, we continued domesticating dogs to work for us.

Author and dog expert Mark Derr has long advocated a slightly different theory.[2] He hypothesizes that dogs and humans were evolutionary partners, wild wolves living voluntarily within human societies and teaming up with humans to hunt game. Research published in the *Journal of Anthropological Archaeology* backs the idea that 11,500 years ago, humans and dogs probably hunted animals collaboratively.[3] Another study by Christoph Jung and Daniela Pörtl[4] similarly refutes the idea that dogs became domesticated simply by scavenging our scraps. These researchers believe the human–dog relationship was far more integrated than a primal food-centered relationship. Jung and Pörtl highlight evidence for emotional bonds and active *cooperation* between humans and dogs starting in the Upper Paleolithic period, when we were Neolithic, grunting cavemen beginning to discover tools, art, and poetry.

Supporting this theory is a 12,000-year-old skeleton of an elderly woman unearthed in northern Israel, who appears to have been buried cradling a puppy.[5] Humans don't typically bond with scavengers, and, given that early human hunters used nearly every part of the animals they killed, it's unlikely there were enough leftovers to support a group of wolves lurking outside our caves. Furthermore, if wolves were domesticated simply because they stole some scraps from humans, why wouldn't we also have domesticated jackals, hyenas, raccoons, or bears? Those species frequented our camps, too. Surely some intrepid caveman would've thought it'd be pretty cool to have a pet bear or jog alongside a jackal!

Jung and Pörtl propose that "dog domestication could be understood as an active social process of both sides." Early dogs would still have been eating human byproducts, but this was probably a deliberate act of feeding as a reward for help during hunts. According to this hypothesis, we were actively altering what dogs ate at least 15,000 years ago. As Mark Derr argues, it also shows that our enduring relationship with dogs is based not on force and enslavement, but on "a fundamental recognition of each other as sentient beings who can benefit from an alliance."[6]

Our domestication of cats followed a similar pattern, although wild cats first entered human society less than 10,000 years ago, coinciding with the introduction of farming in the Middle East.[7] The mice that took up residence in human grain stores attracted our feline friends into villages, where the tamest took advantage of human table scraps and protection. This was another reciprocal relationship, leading to the friendlier, smaller breeds of cat we now share our homes and hearts with.

Only a couple of hundred thousand gray wolves remain in the wild today, compared with about 400 million dogs. We have truly adopted and transformed a species into something more to our liking, replacing combative traits with cuddling, hunting with heeling, and independence with domesticity. A study published in the journal *Animals* compared the social and communication skills of human infants and dogs and discovered striking similarities,[8] which the scientists attributed to convergent evolutionary and domestication processes. In fact, this study found that the social intelligence of humans was more similar to dogs than to chimpanzees. Dogs and babies performed similarly on communication tests, such as the ability to follow a human finger or human gaze, whereas chimpanzees struggled. Dogs also exhibited extremely precise control over their eyelids and surrounding facial muscles, allowing them to match and project facial emotions favored by their human cohabitants. These researchers concluded that because humans and dogs are raised in the same environment, they develop similar cooperative communication skills. Tens of thousands of years have led dogs and humans to be similar in terms of social communication, energy requirements, temperature adaptation, behavior, and diet.

The creation of these extremely tame modern dog breeds began at least seven thousand years ago when humans began creating specific types of dogs to perform distinct duties. Hunters, retrievers, dogs that chase foxes out of tunnels or "point" to prey, dogs designed to herd livestock—we created them all, filtering out traits we didn't like or need in favor of more useful or desirable characteristics. Modern pet dogs exhibit these historical traits of domestication: body size, morphological features, characteristic coats, or ability to point or herd. The only truly "wolfish" characteristics that remain are color and fur texture, facial conformity, and the size of a few breeds. The majority of the dog-is-wolf myth is a fabrication of our imagination, embellished by advertising.

We haven't just changed dogs; dogs have changed us, too. The co-evolution of our two species has altered the architecture of our brains in ways that make it easier for modern humans and dogs to support each other and cohabitate.[9] This co-adaptation is evident from birth. Whereas wolves require immediate human handling and interaction after birth to prevent them from fearing us, most modern dogs can adapt to human companionship at nearly any point in their lives. Human infants welcome dogs nearly as well as they do children or adults. In fact, we're so used to our cozy co-existence with dogs and cats that nearly any other domestic animal seems "wild" to us. Even our biology bolsters this unique bond. Stroking a pet has been shown to raise levels of oxytocin in both humans and dogs. Oxytocin is known as a "feel-good" hormone, associated with pair-bonding and feelings of well-being.[10] To equate the needs and benefits of domestic dogs and cats with feral predators seems wildly off the mark. As modern-day pet owners, we need to make sure dogs and cats continue to benefit from our bond, and that means continually reassessing what we feed them and why we make these decisions. We no longer need to make food choices based on survival and scarcity. The abundance of food in Western society affords us the luxury of selecting pet foods best for the environment, animal welfare, and food safety. We don't need dogs to help us "hunt" for food anymore, unless you count riding in the grocery cart.

What Do We Feed Wolves? Dog Food

The dogs we put in strollers or grocery carts are also physiologically divergent from their ancient wolf ancestors. As domestic dogs co-evolved with humans, their biology adapted in terms of not just physical features, but also internal functionality. In 2013, a group of Swedish researchers conducted whole-genome resequencing of dogs and wolves and identified thirty-six key genomic regions associated with canine domestication.[11] Ten of the domestic dog genes were responsible for changes in starch digestion and fat metabolism. The researchers identified specific genetic mutations that allowed dogs to digest and utilize starches much more efficiently than wolves. The scientists concluded that these new genetic traits allowed the early ancestors of dogs to thrive on a diet rich in starch, much different to the diet of wild wolves.

A year later, the Swedish researchers published a second paper that confirmed that, compared with wolves, dogs have more copies of a gene called AMY2B, crucial for producing amylase, a primary enzyme that digests starch. In dogs, amylase activity is around thirty times higher than in wolves.[12] In the simplest terms, we have selected, bred, and propagated dogs that are capable of digesting and utilizing starches and many "people foods." This study also proved that modern dogs have additional genetic changes that make them efficient carbohydrate users. Dogs have a longer version of the amylase gene that makes maltase, another enzyme needed for starch digestion. This maltase gene is found in herbivores and omnivores. In dogs, the maltase gene is much longer and more active than it is in wild wolves. It's clear from the genetic science, therefore, that modern dogs are no longer strict carnivores. Dogs have important genetic mutations that have adapted them to an omnivorous diet. When did these mutations occur?

A 2018 archeological study analyzed human and animal DNA evidence to reveal that when the first farmers left the Middle East as far back as 9000 B.C.E., they took sheep and goats, and dogs to herd them. The researchers explain: "Our study shows that dogs and humans have an intertwined story—dogs followed humans during this migration across Europe. We show in this paper that dogs and humans were already really connected."[13] These migrating farmers largely replaced local hunter-gatherer populations, establishing communities and spreading crops that included wheat, barley, peas, broad beans, and lentils. These findings indicate domesticated dogs were likely eating grains and legumes along-side Neolithic humans as far back as 9000 B.C.E. In 2016, researchers discovered that ancient dog populations seven thousand years ago in southeastern Europe and southwest Asia contained duplications of the AMY2B gene,[14] further widening the digestive gap from wolves. This series of specific metabolic adaptations allowed dogs to thrive on a plant-rich diet, especially within early farming societies. Based on the preponderance of scientific evidence, it's impossible to deny that dogs have been thriving as omnivores for thousands of years. So much for those meat-heavy "ancestral diets."

Feeding a high-protein animal-meat diet to dogs is a new trend. Before the industrial revolution, meat was far too precious to waste on dogs. Pet dogs were typically fed the bottom of the stew pot (that's why dogs are called "pot lickers" in certain cultures), stale bread crusts, and the occasional scrap of sinewy meat. It was only when we came to value dogs as workers, as hunting and herding dogs, that we considered feeding them fresh beef or chicken. This serendipitously coincided with our emerging affluence as a society and the falling price of meat as industrial farming began. When people insist that dogs have "always" eaten meat, this simply isn't the case. There's evidence that even *wolves* aren't strict carnivores that need exclusive animal-meat diets:

> Captive maned wolves (*Chrysocyon brachyurus*) often consume diets high in prey and meat items even though they are omnivorous in the wild.

That quotation is the opening line from a seminal March 1994 research study published in *Zoo Biology* by nutritionists from the National Zoological Park, Smithsonian Institution, and George Washington University. In case you missed it, even wolf experts say, "They are omnivorous in the wild." If wolves are omnivorous in the wild, what do the experts recommend we feed captive wolves? Dog food. "Dietary management of maned wolves should minimize excess protein intake by limiting prey consumption and acclimating animals to extruded diets for domestic dogs."[15]

Why do we persist in believing that wolves are strict carnivores and view dogs as mini-wolves that need a similar diet? Scientists have studied these feeding habits for decades and concluded that wolves and dogs are nearly identical in terms of dietary needs. Dogs have an evolutionary advantage of tens of thousands of years of human co-habitation, but, in general, wolves are also able to eat a wide variety of non-animal foods.

Dr. Mary E. Allen is the deputy director of the FDA Center for Veterinary Medicine's Office of Research. Before moving to the FDA CVM, she served as a clinical nutritionist in the Department of Conservation Biology at the National Zoological Park in Washington, DC, for many years. Dr. Allen has spent much of her career studying what wolves eat and how to feed animals in captivity. In 1995, she wrote a chapter in *Husbandry Manual for the Maned Wolf Chrysocyon brachyurus*[16] to provide zoos and wolf sanctuaries with a reference for the best care of these wild canids. At the time, there was growing concern in the global wolf community that many U.S. sanctuaries were feeding captive wolves excessive protein, leading to low urinary pH and cystine bladder stone formation. American facilities were feeding their wolves horsemeat, roadkill, or commercial "big cat" high-protein diets, while European groups were feeding lower-protein, plant-containing commercial dog foods, including Purina Hi-Pro Dog Chow, and not encountering the same medical problems. Allen and her colleagues concluded that the evidence supported feeding captive wolves a diet

1) of low to moderate protein content, between 20% and 25% protein, DMB (dry matter basis) to reduce the amount of cystine that the kidneys must excrete;
2) that promotes oral health (dry feeds versus soft);
3) that results in well-formed stool (soybean meal may exacerbate loose stool); and
4) that results in more alkaline urine (foods with higher carbohydrate and lower animal protein contents will promote alkaline urine).

Allen advised that if a captive wolf were to be fed animal meats, a commercial dog food should also be offered to avoid any vitamin or mineral deficiencies and reduce the risk of urinary tract disease: "It is therefore recommended that nutritionally complete commercial products (e.g., dry dog foods, omnivore biscuits) represent at least 60–70% of the dry matter intake for maned wolves." She and her colleagues noted that wolf pups raised on commercial moderate- to low-protein dog food do very well, with normal stools and high acceptance. Older wolves rescued later in life may require a transition period or added oils to aid with stool firmness and acceptability. Allen's nutritional recommendations have been widely implemented by wolf rescues. In *Gray Wolf: A Comparison of Husbandry and Housing Practices*,[17] published in Canada in 2000, six out of nine evaluated wolf sanctuaries fed their wolves a commercial dog food diet.

Despite nutritional experts proclaiming that both wolves and dogs are omnivorous, convincing dog owners mesmerized by marketing slogans is a challenge, especially when the dog in question is more Samoyed than Shih Tzu.

Carnivore and Omnivore: Arbitrary and Antiquated Terminology?

If you share your home with a German Shepherd, a Leonberger, or a Siberian husky, you may be surprised, or even skeptical, to learn about their omnivorous genetic heritage. However, the majority of us have dogs that look nothing like their ancient wolf predecessors. In modern Western society we tend to breed pets with the specific goal of developing animals that look "cute," complete with flat, round faces and big, begging eyes. We even select for youthful appearance, favoring dogs that retain puppy-like features their entire lives. If such a variant, or perhaps more accurately, "mutant," had accidentally evolved in the wild, its chances of survival would have been slim. Cuteness comes at a cost.

By genetically selecting these "squashed-face" (brachycephalic) dogs, we've been unintentionally cruel, creating and perpetrating a wide range of inherited defects in the pursuit of perpetual puppyhood. This is probably a topic for another book, but, for better or worse, it's undeniable that the majority of dogs that live in our homes right now are as far removed in appearance from "natural canines," much less wolves, as we are from Cro-Magnons. Indeed, animal ethics professor James Serpell believes that "many modern companion animals are quite literally becoming anthropomorphic or paedomorphic projections of 'human wants, desires and emotions.'"[18]

Even as we create increasingly tame and babyish-looking animals, and as breeders actively erase "neophobic" traits (instinctual fear of new things and people) from the genes of dogs, we argue that dogs "desire and need" the same diets as their "wild ancestors." We treat them like babies but feed them like wolves; it's an incredibly confused logic. Katherine Grier, author of *Pets in America*,[19] believes the pet industry is playing on our desire to make our pets into "mini-me's" by framing dogs and cats as consumers themselves. We tell ourselves that our pets want—and are entitled to—all the luxuries humans enjoy, from Halloween costumes to gourmet food, forgetting they are still dogs and cats, unique species with distinct desires and needs. We purchase pet treats picturing a cute, cartwheeling cartoon puppy while simultaneously feeding diets of human-grade raw meat, insisting that our dogs are actually wolves that must eat raw flesh. Which is it? One or the other, or both? How can we be content offering starchy dog biscuits while bragging about the benefits of raw animal meat? How do we justify the hypocrisy? We need to accept that modern dogs don't require raw animal meat any more than they need doggy doughnuts or nail polish. Modern dogs need, and are capable of digesting, a wide range of nutrients, and it's our job to find the best ones for *them* and the planet, not some flesh-hungry fantasy we're projecting. Part of that fantasy stems from an outdated taxonomic term.

What Is a Carnivore?

It wasn't until the early eighteenth century that scientists, chiefly botanists and biologists, realized they needed to better standardize how they were naming and organizing the natural world. Prior attempts had been made by the Egyptians (basically labeling foods as poisonous or safe) and Aristotle (plants and animals, live birth or eggs, number of legs, whether it contained blood, and whether it was warm- or cold-blooded). During the Middle Ages, scholars tried to rank organisms based on philosophical ascension, the *scala natura* (the Natural Ladder). During each era, scientists were, and continue to be, limited by their powers of observation.

When the microscope was invented during the Renaissance, taxonomy was able to view the structural elements of life, and classification began along more discrete, and minuscule, criteria. It wasn't until the Renaissance and magnification that one of the planet's most abundant life forms, fungi, was discovered. Until a technological advancement allowed us to see microscopic organisms, we didn't acknowledge they existed, much less name them. Throughout the ages, humankind has continued naming things based on what could be observed at the time. Carl Linnaeus introduced the classification *Carnivora* based primarily on physical characteristics, not physiological requirements. And names, like history, can be hard to change.

As scientists were naming animals, they organized them into observable traits. Hooved animals, aquatic animals, animals that grazed on grass, and animals that ate each other were typically used as categories. Unfortunately, these categories were often made by scholars and scientists who had not observed the animals themselves and relied on decades-old eyewitness accounts, preserved specimens, and informed speculation. A scientist examining the physical characteristics of wolf and lion skulls would be correct in assuming they must be similar. Europeans had also been familiar with lions from Roman times, knew they hunted and killed animals, and had massive fangs. The wolf kept its distance from humans but was known to kill livestock and steal a leg of lamb from a smokehouse. Limited by visual observation and little understanding of nutritional biology, the taxonomist branded both lion and wolf "Carnivora," and we've been stuck with it for the past three hundred years.

As time progressed, clever biologists recognized that "carnivore" was inaccurate for many animals in *Carnivora*. Because they couldn't simply reclassify a wolf or panda bear (think of all the museum posters and textbooks!), they began adding unofficial adjectives. "Strict carnivore," "obligate carnivore," and "facultative carnivore" began appearing in textbooks, and later in pet food marketing. "Obligate carnivore" has become synonymous with a "true carnivore," or an animal that must derive a specific nutrient from animal sources that is not found in plants. That may be true for now, but as we'll soon see, science is about to retire, or at least redefine, that term.

"Facultative carnivore" became twisted into meaning something along the lines of "a carnivore that does best on a carnivorous diet but can survive on a non-carnivorous diet." That obviously makes little sense, so proponents began adding another phrase: "survive not thrive." Again, what does that mean? There's no scientific test for "thrive." If critics claim "dog and wolf carnivores" aren't "thriving" on omnivorous diets, why are both living far longer with fewer illnesses than their wild counterparts? We think it's abundantly clear that modern pet dogs are enjoying an incredibly high quality of life, "thriving" to the point of excess and developing obesity at alarming rates around the world.

Animal-meat advocates argue that obesity rates are soaring due to feeding too little protein, and that if we simply fed dogs and cats an all-meat diet, there would be no obesity. We wish that were even remotely factual, because then both humans and pets could be spared billions in medical bills and immeasurable suffering. High–animal meat diets are generally high-calorie diets, and calories count most when it comes to lifestyle causes of weight gain. We wish it were simply a matter of feeding an ultra–high protein diet to prevent obesity, but the scientific evidence proves it isn't. The science of obesity is complicated, but we know enough to conclude that the cure isn't a single ingredient, nutrient, or even diet. That doesn't mean all-carb, all-plant, or all-anything diets are the answer. It means it's complicated, and there are no easy answers or miracle cures found in meat. Health is multifactorial and individual, not a "one diet fits all" solution, especially not a predominantly meat-based diet for dogs.

Nutrition and food can always be better; that's the point of scientific progress. We also need to advance our nomenclature and terminology to help pet owners avoid marketing confusion and misleading dietary beliefs. It's time we stop arguing about a dog's diet using eighteenth-century language and science. The next generation of animal nutrition will be based on physiological and nutritional requirements, not ingredient composition. For now, let's return to the question of "Are dogs miniature wolves?"

As this chapter has shown, dogs are taxonomically classified as part of the eighteenth century's order *Carnivora*, which includes some carnivorans, such as felidae and pinnipeds (animals that depend on specific nutrients currently only found in animal meat), but also contains species that are omnivorous. Panda bears, perhaps the most famous of all bamboo-munchers, are part of *Carnivora*. Bears, including massive grizzlies and bellicose black bears, are also in the same outdated taxonomic classification as dogs. Bears will swat salmon from a stream and take down an occasional deer but grow to immense size on a diet mainly of fruits, vegetables, and honey. The point is that even if an animal is categorized as a carnivore, science proves it may actually be omnivorous. Which brings us back to wolves and dogs, two misunderstood carnivorans.

Because dogs are omnivores and have tens of thousands of years of physiological adaptations from living alongside humans, they can get all the nutrients they need from plant-based and animal sources. Unlike obligate carnivores, they can convert plant-based beta-carotene, also known as provitamin A, to retinol, the pure form of vitamin A. True carnivores such as cats cannot make this conversion and must obtain retinol either from animal sources or artificial supplements. Dogs can also convert linoleic acid, an omega-6 fatty acid found in plant-based sources, to the essential arachidonic acid. It's an interesting thought experiment to consider that if humans were to become extinct in the future, dogs would have an excellent chance of survival because we made them more omnivorous. Because dogs can eat plants *or* meat, they would be able to avoid dangerous competitive encounters with true terrestrial carnivores, such as lions and tigers.

Animals such as dogs and wolves eat more or less meat depending on their *habitat*. If animal prey is abundant, the species evolves to better hunt and digest those food sources. Biological adaptation occurs based on environmental influences and resource availability. The human home environment, where dogs have been raised for the past 9,000 to 35,000 years, has influenced the foods canines can best digest and utilize. Marc Bekoff points out that feeding domestic dogs a high-meat diet as if they were wolves risks making them overweight, as wolves burn about 70 percent more calories a day than typical animals of similar size, including domestic dogs. This is because wolves spend a large percentage of their time actively hunting and scavenging. Wild wolves are known to roam over fifty miles before finding or killing a meal. Few pet dogs walk one mile a day, much less roam fifty. Surveys indicate that most dogs are walked less than thirty minutes a day, with many receiving only a few five- to ten-minute "potty breaks." Despite these realities, high-calorie, high-fat, high–animal protein pet food advertised as the "ideal meal" arrives in their bowl twice a day, regardless of how hard they've "worked" for it.

Nutrients, Not Ingredients:
Living Longer, Healthier Lives Without Animal Meat

Humanizing pets doesn't have to mean misrepresenting their biological needs. Shannon Falconer, CEO of Philadelphia's animal-free pet food startup Because Animals, understands that people want to feed their pets recognizable ingredients, diets that are scientifically proven to benefit cats and dogs, but also foods that *they* would eat themselves. Starting with a Superfood Supplement for dogs and cats (which Falconer adds to her own smoothie every morning), Because Animals products are "human-grade" but are also tested to be nutritionally appropriate for pets. Their dental cookie for dogs, for instance, will be made of chickpea flour, nutritional yeast, chia seeds, and kelp. These ingredients are edible for humans *and* pets; the rich iodine content and high levels of other nutrient minerals and vitamins in kelp, including twenty-one amino acids, make it ideal for dogs.[20]

Ernie and Ryan's company, Wild Earth, are working on a similar basis. They've reevaluated dog and cat diets not from arbitrary taxonomy or legacy but based on evidence emerging from nutritional biotech. Their "microscopes" are genetic microbiome analyzers, high-tech biofermentation devices, and an army of global future-food scientists committed to solving the world's food dilemmas. They're creating animal-free pet food that is nutritionally ideal for dogs and cats. Their peanut butter–flavored dog snacks combine flax, oats, and green tea with koji, an ancient mushroom superfood, which contains all ten amino acids dogs require. They've also looked into fungal biology and discovered that yeast and fungi are excellent protein sources for dogs, and maybe cats, too.

The guiding principle of these next-generation pet companies is: *pets need nutrients, not ingredients, to thrive*. Because Animals and Wild Earth use nutrients from non-animal sources, combining them in a way that ensures the nutritional requirements for pets are met. Falconer tells us:

> These are all foods that I feed my own pets, so I can't overstate how important it is to me that this food is high, high-quality nutrition. . . . For us humans, we think about feeding ourselves antioxidants, probiotics, prebiotics, foods that have anti-inflammatory capabilities, and so on. Dogs and cats need these things just as much as humans do. Biochemically, yes, our metabolisms are different, but in terms of the aging process, in terms of the basic fundamental features of biochemistry and molecular biology, we are the same.

The "aging process" is a hugely important component of pet nutrition. The shift toward treating pets as children, or at least as part of our families, means the emphasis isn't simply on providing nutrients they need to live, but nutrients that help them *thrive*. Thriving means living long, energetic, and healthy lives. As our dogs and cats grow older, similar to humans, they become more susceptible to many forms of illness. Unfortunately, modern pets appear to be developing more cancers, kidney and liver failure, digestive diseases, and orthopedic issues than expected. It seems highly likely that, no different than human cancer, the emphasis on processed animal proteins and red meat–based diets is a contributing factor.

As discussed earlier, the AVMA estimates that over half of all dogs will develop cancer after age ten. Part of this is the result of genetics; humans have created "at-risk" dog breeds that share an underlying genetic predisposition to cancer because they shared a common ancestor during breed development. Most scientists put the contribution of inherited genetic mutations at about 5 to 10 percent of an individual's risk of developing cancer. The vast majority of cancers are caused by environmental contributors, including the potential long-term impact of the foods our pets consume throughout their lives. After examining and treating thousands of animals for around a decade, Andrew Knight, professor of animal welfare at Winchester, United Kingdom, and a small-animal veterinarian, is convinced that rates in pets of diseases such as cancer, and kidney and liver disease, are far higher than they should be. He believes our animals are being exposed, over many years, to toxins not severe enough to cause acute reactions, but sufficient to cause hidden cellular damage. Where does Knight believe many of these toxins originate? Factory-farmed animals and contemporary animal-meat processing.

The first major organ exposed to toxins after food ingestion and intestinal absorption is the liver, followed by the kidneys. In Chapter 1 we saw that animal meat in pet food is potentially unhealthy and often poses a food safety risk, with numerous documented recalls. Low-quality animal-meat pet food may turn out to be the actual cause or physiological trigger of many diseases diagnosed today, particularly in older animals. Plastics, pesticides, euthanasia drugs, added hormones, and antibiotics are just a few of the food contaminants that have been well documented in the animal meats we feed our pets.

Many veterinarians are convinced that we should be able to extend the healthy lifespan of our pets, perhaps significantly. Evidence supports that a dog's lifespan *can* be over twenty years, but most die in their early to mid-teens. In 2015, Ernie launched Project 25 (Project25.vet), an awareness campaign for veterinarians and the pet industry committed "to raise the average life expectancy of dogs and cats by 25 percent by 2025." The agenda of the organization is to help dogs and cats live, healthily and happily, to twenty-five years—and beyond. Bold and audacious? Maybe, but Ernie believes it's entirely achievable based on the current data. He also believes advances in nutrition, preventable diseases, and medical breakthroughs, especially genetic profiling and personalized immunotherapies, will make his dream a reality in the next decade.

Bramble, a blue merle Collie in the United Kingdom, is a great example of this potential. Bramble once held the Guinness World Record for being the "oldest living dog" at twenty-seven years of age. Like her owner, she lived on a strict vegan diet of rice, lentils, organic vegetables, and nutritional yeast, eating once a day and exercising regularly. The fact that the majority of our dogs are living less than half as long as Bramble suggests we can do better. Bramble also proves that eliminating animal meats doesn't mean decreasing energy or vitality. Bramble's owner said she certainly "thrived" and herded until her last day.

Another issue connecting longevity, quality of life, and pet nutrition is obesity. The issue of pet obesity was so concerning to Ernie that, in 2005, he founded the world's foremost organization dedicated to preventing obesity, the Association for Pet Obesity Prevention (APOP). Distressingly, APOP finds that more than half of all U.S. dogs and cats are overweight or obese. According to APOP's annual survey, an estimated 55.8 percent of dogs and 59.5 percent of cats were classified as overweight or diagnosed with obesity in 2018. That totals over 100 million pets at risk for weight-related disorders, including diabetes, arthritis, hypertension, kidney disease, and cancer.

Other research proves that overweight dogs live up to two and half years less than dogs at a healthy weight. A review of data provided by over eight hundred Banfield Pet Hospitals evaluated the age of death of 50,787 middle-aged dogs of twelve different breeds.[21] For all dog breeds, risk of death was greater for overweight dogs than for those in healthy body condition. Average life expectancy was shorter in overweight compared with normal-weight dogs (the difference was greatest in Yorkshire terriers). When we consider that the average dog lives a little less than fourteen years, that means being overweight reduces their life by almost 20 percent. If excess weight can reduce a pet's life expectancy, why aren't pet owners doing more to prevent obesity? As with all biology, it's complicated.

Diet, physical activity, genetics, hormonal imbalances, environmental contaminants, microbiome disorders, and many diseases play a role in the development of pet obesity. Both diet and exercise are essential for optimal health, but Ernie emphasizes that pet obesity is a multifactorial condition requiring a multimodal therapeutic approach. Ernie, along with a growing number of veterinarians, is increasingly concerned that additives hidden during animal-meat farming may play a more important role in obesity than previously recognized. As we saw in Chapter 3, farmed animals are routinely administered a variety of hormones and antibiotics to encourage rapid weight gain.

We now have evidence that these drugs and chemicals filter down the food chain, potentially ending up on our dinner plates and in our pets' bowls. Additionally, high consumption of red meats has been linked in numerous studies with obesity in humans and lab animals, and there's little rationale why this wouldn't be the same for dogs. Animal products also typically contain high amounts of fat, predominantly saturated fat, making them more calorically dense, meaning smaller portions of high-protein diets can contain more calories.

Instead of feeding our pets excess protein, high fat, and potentially harmful animal-meat diets, we should consider more closely counting calories and offering our dogs a complete and balanced plant-based diet. As a bonus, plant-based diets tend to be higher in healthy forms of fiber, which aid digestive health and help our pets feel full and reduce appetite urges. This is why most therapeutic weight-loss diets contain increased levels of soluble and insoluble fibers. Unfortunately, there's a conspicuous absence of published research on weight loss and plant-based diets in dogs. These studies have yet to be funded by traditional pet food companies that make billions off animal meat–based diets, but studies on humans suggest vegetarian and vegan diets promote ideal, healthy weight more than do diets containing animal proteins.[22,23] Emerging plant-based pet food companies such as Wild Earth are committed to conducting these studies as their products gain popularity.

The Era of "-omics"

When it comes to healthy aging in animals, we're learning a lot from human studies. Research published in the *Journal of Nutrition* as far back as 2003 stated that "this is an exciting time for biological scientists as the "-omics" era continues to evolve and shape the way science is understood and conducted."[24] Breakthroughs in genomics, nutrigenomics, nutritranscriptomics, nutriproteomics, and nutrimetabolomics are reshaping our understanding of nutrition. In 2005, a complete dog genome was sequenced for the first time by an international team of scientists led by the Broad Institute of MIT and Harvard University. As the researchers anticipated, functional genomics, including the global analysis of RNA and protein expression, protein localization, and protein-protein interactions, have emerged as important areas of academic study. The code of life was beginning to unlock the secrets of health.

The first feline genome was sequenced in 2007 by researchers from the Laboratory of Genomic Diversity at the National Cancer Institute in Maryland. Scientists have now compared the domestic cat's DNA with those of cows, tigers, dogs, and humans.[25] This analysis revealed 281 domestic cat genes that showed signs of rapid or numerous genetic changes, many playing a role in fat metabolism. These genetic adaptations are believed to be in response to domestication and dietary changes, but they haven't made cats omnivorous. Whereas dogs have evolved over tens of thousands of years to bypass the need for animal meat, the same thing can't be said for our feline companions. But evolution and domestication have changed cat genetics in ways that have potentially impacted their diet. An excellent example is that felines lost the gene linked with detecting sweet flavors.[26] This is important, as taste is an evolutionary adaptation for assessing whether something is edible or potentially toxic. Dogs might desire the sweet taste of butternut squash or peanut butter because they can metabolize the nutrients they contain; however, cats don't like those sweets because they don't contain usable nutrients. This is discussed further in Chapter 8.

Since 2005, research into canine and feline genomics has intensified, mainly with the goal of improving the health of our pets. Researchers also believe that studying canine biology could lead to a better understanding of human health and disease. Dogs and humans share many medical matters, suffer from many of the same genetic conditions, live in the same environment, and receive many of the same medical treatments. Our pets have the potential to become valuable sentinels of human health. The study of genomics and nutriproteomics has become crucial in areas such as nutrient-requirement determination, disease prevention and treatment, and functional ingredient testing. The original geneticists' prediction that "nutritional genomics and proteomics will definitely play a vital role in the future of pet foods"[27] is coming true.

The Genetics of Aging

Geroscience is a discipline that seeks to understand the relationship between the biology of aging and age-related disease. The principles of geroscience are just as important in pets as they are in human health. Because dogs "age" roughly seven to ten times more quickly than humans, we have the potential to make discoveries about the biology of aging much faster in canines. For example, giant-breed dogs experience the effects of aging about twice as fast as toy breeds. Discovering the genetic causes of why different families of the same species experience vastly different cellular changes and demise might help us extend the life expectancy of both people and pets.

It's relatively easy to identify connections between genetic variations and health by gathering enormous amounts of data over the lifespan of the animal, and the crowd-sourced pet-genomics project Darwin's Ark is aiming to do just that by collecting dog and cat DNA samples from around the United States. Another exciting initiative, The Dog Aging Project, based at the University of Washington, is creating a network of pet owners, veterinarians, and scientists to conduct both a longitudinal study of aging in dogs and an interventional trial to prevent disease and extend *healthy* longevity in middle-aged dogs. Despite the wealth of veterinary expertise in treating elderly companion animals, this is the first comprehensive, detailed study of aging in dogs or cats. Individual animals will be followed throughout their lives to understand the biological and environmental factors that determine why some dogs die early or develop diseases such as cancer, kidney failure, and dementia, while others live to a ripe old age. In less than a decade, the project hopes to identify the critical factors that can help our pets stay healthy longer.

Some of the most debilitating age-related illnesses in humans also afflict dogs. One example is Canine Cognitive Dysfunction (CCD). The clinical signs displayed by aging dogs with CCD often mirror the signs for dementia and Alzheimer's disease in humans. Symptoms in your senior dog might be forgetting commands, decreased responsiveness and interaction, disorientation, unusual sleep patterns, or accidents inside the house. In severe cases, a dog may even fail to recognize its human owners, a distressing experience for everyone. This age-related neurobehavioral syndrome affects 14 to 22 percent of senior dogs and may strike as early as nine years of age.

There is evidence that we can help our pets avoid this devastating condition by paying attention to what they eat. Studies of therapeutic diets and certain supplements suggest the right nutrition can slow down the progression of CCD.[28] Ernie and other veterinarians recommend supplements for CCD that have an antioxidant or anti-inflammatory effect, such as silybin, S-Adenosylmethionine (SAMe), omega-3 fatty acids (primarily DHA), and vitamin E.[29] Other research proves that medium chain triglycerides (MCTs) can also boost mental abilities in humans and dogs and may slow down neural degeneration.[30,31,32] The bottom line is that what we feed our dogs may enhance and extend their mental functions, and we're beginning to learn how to apply these findings to treat human diseases such as Alzheimer's.

Elinor Karlsson, director of the Vertebrate Genomics Group at the Broad Institute of MIT and Harvard, is trying to glean insights from dog allergies that could be applied to humans. After asking dog owners about their pets' eating habits, her team has begun analyzing the links between those traits and their genes. Up until now, few studies have evaluated the link between diet and aging in dogs and cats due to cost and complexity. Karlsson and her team hope to expand their studies to better understand exactly how genes, environment, and diet impact the health and longevity of humans and animals.

Caloric restriction, the practice of reducing food intake without creating nutritional deficiencies, has been proven to slow aging in many animals. There is also increasing evidence that the source and quality of those calories may also be a major contributor to improving health. For most pet owners, quality of life is just as important, if not more so, than quantity of life. "Healthspan" is the term used to describe the period of time during which an animal enjoys relatively good health, free from chronic disease and disability. Could reducing the consumption of animal meats increase a pet's "healthspan"? The vegan pet food company V-dog believes so and has scores of testimonials from owners whose dogs are fed plant-based diets.[33] V-dog reports that many of its customers boast that their dogs live energetically well into their late teens.

One particularly interesting plant-based ingredient for senior dogs is algae, a nutrient-dense organism increasingly popular in dog food. Algae are rich in vitamins, minerals, and antioxidants, and a recent study showed that algae appeared to improve cognitive function in older dogs. These findings have led many dog food manufacturers such as Health Extension to add whole-cell algae as a key ingredient to their senior dog formulas. Real innovation in pet food isn't accomplished by guessing what ancient wolves may have eaten, but rather by better understanding the unique nutritional needs of modern dogs. Food trends aren't going to help our pets remain healthy and fight disease, but essential nutrients will.

One of the most exciting things about pet food innovation is how companies are exploring more deeply the question of what *nutrition* actually is. Our understanding is evolving of how a dog's diet is linked with genetic and epigenetic adaptations and how those linkages not only affect the gut microbiome, hormones, and more, but also how all of those factors simultaneously impact health. This is part of the "big science" approach that is revolutionizing nutritional and biomedical research. Using tools developed for genetics and pharmaceutical research, researchers can learn how genes interact with food, and can gain deeper insight into our understanding of risk factors for diseases, including cancer, diabetes, and cardiovascular disease. These researchers are no longer limiting their studies to humans; they're also actively investigating dogs and cats.

The truth is that scientists don't understand human nutrition at a very deep level, and studying pets and pet food offers an opportunity to get better data faster. The scientific community is beginning to understand more about the long- and short-term health impacts of what we feed our pets, and how this translates to what we ourselves eat. Not all pets respond to dietary changes in the same way, so innovative pet food companies like Wild Earth and others are not just developing new premium pet foods, but are also trying to gain a deeper understanding of the microbiome, genome, and underlying physiology. In doing so, they will be able to understand how the food actually interacts with the canine and feline—or, one day, human—body on a cellular level.

We learned in previous chapters that although many conventional "natural" and "premium" brands will market a "whole food diet" for pets, the reality is that the leftover animal meats they use are far from whole. Understanding how higher-quality whole foods actually work and what, if any, benefits they provide would be a huge step for pet food and, beyond that, for human food. It's also important to realize that what makes a "whole food" today may not be the "whole food" of tomorrow, especially as science improves. Wild Earth co-founder Dr. Ron Shigeta explains it this way:

> The twenty-first century will create foods that have never existed before. The ability to work with microorganisms and create the molecular qualities of food, to understand how food is built molecule by molecule—biology is starting to understand how this works. We will actually be able to improve our health in a way that's much more accommodating of our individual biology. We have the equivalent of a cat's brain's worth of neurons just in our intestines! Those neurons and all the other cells, the olfactory receptors in the cavity behind the nose and in the gut, they're sensing everything about our food. The body and the brain are watching and monitoring everything that goes in and adjusting to it. It's like a handshake or saying hello to everyone in your office as you walk in.

Using pet diets as a starting point, scientists will be able to work with that "metabolic handshake" more precisely. In doing so, we'll all be able to solve many of our individual health problems simply by adjusting the nutrients in our diet.

You will recall that back in 2003 geneticists proclaimed that "genomic technologies are powerful tools that will be applied to the pet food industry in the future to optimize nutritional and health status." That future is *now*. Scientists are already able to determine the minimum nutrient requirements and mechanisms by which many nutrients function to prevent and treat many common diseases. We therefore need to stop searching for "trendy" ingredients and abandon outdated concepts of what is "natural" for our pets. Instead, pet food producers should be focusing on nutrients, not ingredients, to optimize health. The future of pet nutrition is about tailoring pet food to contain *exactly* what a pet needs to function at optimum capacity *at any given time*. It doesn't get more precise or personal than that. In the near future, we may well see diets formulated according to your dog or cat's individual genotype, and phenotype meal plans adjusted based on hormonal, metabolomic, and microbiome data and containing nutrients that can prevent, or perhaps treat, many diseases.

In 2010, Kenneth Korman, head of InterLeukin Genetic, told *Nature* that today's commercial pet foods may be a preview of the kind of food categories humans might find in future grocery stores: "Pet foods I get for my dog are age-categorized or categorized by sensitivities such as gastrointestinal problems."[34] The future holds something far more ambitious, identifying different pet populations based on their genetic adaptations and responsiveness, as opposed to physical size, age, or breed, and formulating the nutrients precisely for that individual animal—and hopefully later, for individual humans. As explored further on in this book, biotech innovations such as cell-grown meat make nutritional tailoring much easier and more realistic. Creating molecular-based foods means understanding the function of *every molecule* that humans and pets consume. This is an incredibly exciting prospect, filled with limitless potential.

By using nutritional genomics, proteomics, and metabolomics, science will be able to determine nutrient requirements for individual dogs and cats at different stages of their lives. Our pets' diets are much more controlled than ours, which means enormous insights can be gained from analyzing the impact of specific nutrient changes. This is a health journey that begins with dogs and cats and leads to humans.

* * *

Let's end this section by revisiting the definition of "natural." Andrew Knight, Ernie, and an increasing number of veterinarians and animal nutritionists advocate for animal meat–free diets for pets. There are many reasons for this recommendation, but their primary concern is a commitment to helping pets be healthy and live as long and as comfortably as possible. This conflicts with an ideology of "I want my pet to live a *natural* life." To live a long and healthy life requires many "unnatural interventions," including vaccinations, parasiticides, spaying or neutering, a safe human home environment, and food. Knight says:

> I've already accepted that the pet is a domesticated creature; it's not going to be thrown out into the surrounding bushland and asked to fend for itself in a natural way. Instead it's going to be in a home, with heating, and not be allowed outdoors at night, and have to have vaccinations and worming pills and all these other unnatural things. So the ideology of a plant-based pet diet that I think most people would agree with, if they thought about it, is it's not about "nature" and "natural"; it's about safeguarding the welfare of these animals in a responsible way, along with all the other "unnatural" things we do for them.

The fact that we have created modern-day domestic dogs and cats means we have a responsibility to care for them. It also means we have a responsibility to mitigate the impact their care has on the planet and all other life. If the food we feed our pets can be nutritionally fulfilling and tasty, and also benefit the environment and other creatures, why should we continue to kill animals for it?

7

Plant-Powered Pets

"And to all the beasts of the earth and all the birds in the sky and all the creatures that move along the ground—everything that has the breath of life in it—I give every green plant for food." And it was so. (**Genesis 1:30**)

MICHELLE CEHN, FOUNDER of World of Vegan, prolific YouTuber, and social media influencer, is one of the loudest voices of today's plant-based generation. What makes Cehn's activism particularly exciting is that her dog, Chance, a large mixed-breed, is being heard, too. Chance is thirteen years old, but he looks much younger. "I've had him for, gosh, twelve years now," Cehn tells Alice. "They said he was three years old at the shelter, but I think he was really closer to one." She fell in love with this furry giant when she was volunteering at the Berkeley Humane Society animal shelter, staying late and arriving early just to hang out with him. Cehn jokes that she "took a chance on Chance," a decision she's never once regretted.

Owning a big "wolf-like" hound inadvertently put Cehn in an ethically awkward position. She had been vegetarian since she was eight years old, when she made the connection between the sliced lamb on the dinner table and the fluffy lamb in the field. "From that point on, I made up my mind not to eat animals anymore," she says with a frown.

"I didn't want to participate in that." When Cehn started college, she began learning about the reality of factory farming and gave up animal products altogether. Her dietary ethics shifted from a personal belief to trying to impact public policy, forming the basis of a life of activism. "I just thought, this is not right; people don't know that this is going on, it's horrific," she says. "So I made it my goal to educate other people about what's going on behind closed doors."

Cehn went vegan the same summer she adopted Chance. She rejected animal products for herself based on her personal ethics but continued to buy them for her pet without considering the conflict. The breakthrough came when she began reading scientific evidence that supported the health benefits of a vegan diet, an aspect previously secondary to her ethical motivations. The affirmation of the health benefits of her vegan diet led her to wonder whether plant-based food might be healthier for Chance.

"I was like, huh! I've never thought about raising a dog vegan," she confides. "But in research mode, I thought it might be possible." Like many dog owners, Cehn was raised on the dog-is-wolf myth: "In my head I still had so many doubts, because I look at my dog and he looks like a wolf. They have big canine teeth; in the wild they'd be hunting down animals and eating them." She started transitioning Chance's diet by mixing half vegan kibble with half animal meat or rewarding him with vegan treats. Slowly, but steadily, she began to turn Chance into a complete and balanced plant-based dog.

The Evidence Is In: Vegetarian Dogs Are Healthy Dogs

Chance has had a lot of veterinarians over the years, but at every checkup, each one has praised his shiny coat, high energy, and robust health. Cehn recalls one veterinarian telling her, "Whatever you're doing, keep doing it!" When she told her veterinarians about Chance's "unorthodox" diet, they offered full support, despite neither being vegan nor vegetarian. Cehn continued eliminating animal meat from Chance's diet, making a few YouTube videos about "vegan dogs." She met people whose dogs had been vegan for years, spoke with the founder of one of the first vegan dog food companies, and studied the ingredients used in vegan dog foods. Everything she learned reassured her that she was doing something good for Chance. He was happy, loving his food, and getting great feedback from his veterinarians.

"So, I stopped worrying!" she adds with a laugh. "Everything I bought him from that point on was vegan. I've never had any issues: he's now thirteen years old, and he's thriving." Chance has been fully supportive of his plant-based diet, simply because "he loves food, whatever it is!" That includes foods Cehn eats herself, especially carrots. In fact, Chance will chew as happily on a "big honking thick carrot" as he once did on a dehydrated animal-skin rawhide. At one point, Cehn noticed that when she fed her pet rabbit cilantro, Brussels sprouts, and other vegetables, Chance would get so jealous he'd come over and beg for some, too. She grins: "You could tell by his face he was thinking, 'I'm going to eat it because I want what the bunny's getting!'"

When Cehn began buying vegan pet food for Chance, there were only one or two brands available at her pet store. Even today, the choices for plant-based pet food are limited. But as the vegan human-food market explodes throughout the Western world, there are indications that demand for animal-free pet food is growing. Philadelphia startup Because Animals is selling plant-based "superfood" supplements for cats and dogs that include seaweed, blueberries, coconut flour, and turmeric, and they're working on a vegan pet food. Meanwhile, established brands like V-dog, Benovo, Halo, Wysong, and Natural Balance are becoming more readily available.

In Europe, Green Petfood and Ami Pet Food are creating vegetarian and vegan pet foods that, as Ami Pet Food puts it, pave the way for "an ethical, eco-friendly and successful economy." Green Petfood's CEO, Klaus Wagner, observed the environmental damage caused by the pet food industry, specifically trends like raw meat diets, and concluded that there had to be another way. He reviewed the scientific evidence that dogs can be healthy on plant-based foods and realized that as long as a dog gets all the required nutrients, it's possible to feed him a vegetarian or vegan meal. After learning that many pets are allergic to animal proteins, Wagner concluded that "for many of these dogs, a vegetarian diet is a true blessing."

Although you're still unlikely to find all of these brands at your local pet or grocery stores, there's increasing support for animal-free pet food, at least for dogs. Tracy Reiman, executive vice president of People for the Ethical Treatment of Animals (PETA), states that a vegan diet is healthier and more ethical than feeding dogs "factory farmed animals who have endured miserable lives and gruesome deaths and whose dead, dying, diseased, or disabled carcasses are found in most commercial dog foods."[1] In the United Kingdom, three times as many vegetarian pet foods were launched in 2014 as in the previous three years.[2]

It's not just vegan and animal advocacy groups that are offering public support for complete and balanced animal-free pet foods. Many veterinarians strongly advocate that dogs are healthier on vegetarian or vegan diets. In March 2019, sixteen global leaders in plant-based veterinary nutrition, science, and animal activism, including Ernie, contributed presentations to the world's first Plant-Powered Dog Food Summit.[3] The event was created for people interested in learning more about feeding their dog a plant-based diet.

For his presentation, Andrew Knight reviewed his publication entitled "Vegetarian versus Meat-Based Diets for Companion Animals." Knight previously published this 2016 article in the journal *Animals*, and that paper has been downloaded about 20,000 times, the second highest in the journal's history.[4] Knight provides convincing evidence that both dogs and cats fed a nutritionally complete food can thrive on plant-based diets. Alice met with him in the quaint English town of Winchester, where they talked vegan pets over soy coffees while Alice's dog, JD, dined on apple and kale treats. In the few months before they spoke, Knight reported he had been contacted by three separate companies wanting to create new plant-based pet foods, and he's extremely excited about a plant-based future.

When it comes to human diets, the assumption that "meat is necessary" is also changing. The dietary guidelines from the U.S. Office of Disease Prevention and Health Promotion, long linked with big agricultural producers, are shifting from endorsing a traditional animal meat–based diet to encouraging more plant-based foods.[5] Canada went a step further with its dietary guidelines by refusing to specifically recommend dairy at all. It removed dairy as a separate food group and instead included it as an option within the protein category. These government-backed nutritional guidelines are moving in a new direction, recommending that proteins should come from plant sources such as tofu, legumes, and nuts.[6]

This is a big shift for U.S. agriculture and could generate huge changes for American consumers. It's also healthier. In 2019, meat giant Tyson Foods surprised meat industry analysts by announcing an earnings shortfall. They blamed the dip on Americans who moved away from traditional chicken toward proteins perceived as healthier and cited the fact that 40 percent of U.S. consumers reported eating more plant-based foods.[7] In response, CEO Noel White announced that Tyson was going to make their own alternative plant-based chicken products in 2019. This is a company with the marketing budget and shelf space to convince millions of hard-core meat lovers to try plant-based alternatives.

We're confident these changes will quickly transfer to pet foods. "People are naturally interested in seeing whether that's possible for all of their family, and they're increasingly seeing cats and dogs as family members," Knight says. "So it was inevitable that that kind of interest would translate into looking at pet food diets as well, and that's what's going on." Green Petfood's Wagner agrees:

> Although raw feeding has become a trend, many people have changed their view regarding nutrition and meat consumption over the past few years. The proportion of people who are vegetarians is continuously rising. This openness for alternative ways of feeding finally encouraged us to create our VeggieDog brand.

The evidence that dogs can thrive on animal-free diets is becoming harder to ignore. A sixteen-week study of twelve sprint-racing Siberian huskies[8] evaluated the health and performance of six of the canine athletes fed a commercial meat-based diet and six on a vegetarian diet. Sprint-racing, which involves dragging heavy sleds through freezing snow over long distances, is considered one of the most demanding sustained activities for any dog. Both diets used in the study were formulated to the exact same nutritional composition and were the dogs' sole nutrient source for the four-month study, which included a period of intensely competitive racing. The racing huskies were assessed by a licensed veterinarian at regular intervals. All the dogs showed the positive physical and physiological adaptations expected during athletic training. Most significant, throughout the study, all appeared to be extremely fit, and there were no adverse effects reported for the huskies fed the vegetarian diet. The researchers concluded that sprint-racing Siberian huskies could be maintained on a vegetarian diet with no negative effects on health or performance. This study feasibly indicates our own "backyard sprinters" would also do well on a plant-based dog food.

Despite the small number of dogs in this study, these findings are highly suggestive that plant-based canines can be healthy and fit, even when undergoing intense and prolonged physiological demands. Other anecdotal cases show pets on plant-based diets may have increased overall health and vitality; decreased incidences of cancer, infections, and hypothyroidism; improved coat condition; fewer allergic conditions; lower rates of obesity; decreased arthritis; and diabetes regression. In 2009, a veterinary publication on vegetarianism in the domestic dog concluded that as long as the animal meat–free diet is correctly formulated to meet nutrient requirements and is sufficiently palatable to ensure adequate dietary intake, "then it is a suitable diet for the dog, irrespective of the owner's motivation for feeding a vegetarian diet."[9] An earlier study compared the health of thirty-four cats maintained on vegetarian diets for over a year with that of fifty-two cats fed traditional animal meat–based diets.[10] The vegan and vegetarian cats showed no significant differences in weight gain or losses of perceived health status, with most cats described as "healthy" or "generally healthy."

Being a small-animal veterinarian and a long-time vegan, Knight has taken a special interest in whether companion animals can be maintained safely and healthily on plants alone. He spent several months researching the literature, looking specifically for evidence to support the urban myth that cats and dogs cannot thrive on plant-based diets. He wasn't able to find a single study showing that animals maintained on plant-based diets suffered any problems, other than one that was deliberately formulated to be deficient in potassium (in that study the animals showed signs of potassium deficiency, but that was all).[11]

As we wrote this book, it was indeed a struggle for us to find studies proving plant-based pet diets are less healthy than animal-meat pet food. We found only one paper, authored by animal scientists at the University of Illinois in 2000,[12] comparing the nutrient digestibility and fecal characteristics of dogs fed animal- and plant-protein sources incorporated into grain-based diets. These scientists concluded that digestibility of the plant-based dog food was marginally lower than that of the animal-protein food. Yet only *four* dogs were sampled, and the researchers stated that all diets were "well utilized" by the dogs in terms of digestibility and fecal characteristics. The study failed to find a meaningful difference between animal- and plant-based diets in terms of digestibility and utility.

On the flip side, if you research whether or not animal-meat pet diets cause harm, you'll see conclusive evidence they do. Knight points to at least eleven academic studies showing that animals fed various animal-protein diets develop a variety of health conditions over time.[13] Diseases documented to be more likely when cats and dogs eat commercial animal meat–based diets include those affecting the kidneys, liver, heart, thyroid, neurological system, neuromuscular structure, and the skin; such a diet can also lead to infectious diseases and bleeding disorders.

Knight shares his personal experience with two cats he fostered for six months. When the abandoned cats arrived, they had severe miliary dermatitis, a common feline skin condition identified by numerous scaly lesions and dull, rough coats. Within a short time of feeding them a plant-based diet, Knight observed their skin cleared up, the fur became smoother, and the lumps disappeared.

Ernie has also seen numerous medical cases improve after switching to plant-based diets. Many lifelong vegetarians and vegans who feed their own pets animal-free diets agree. In fact, these plant-based success stories are so common, with mounting scientific evidence for the positive impact of meat-free diets on allergies, that the big pet food companies have taken note. Many therapeutic dermatologic diets are made without any animal meat to reduce their allergenicity. Plant-based "prescription diets" such as Purina HA Vegetarian Canine Formula is formulated "to be less likely to cause an adverse food reaction in certain dogs." Royal Canin advertises their Canine Vegetarian Dry Dog Food as being "for dogs with food sensitivities." These therapeutic diets weren't developed for environmental or ethical reasons, but because some of the most effective protein sources for preventing and treating food allergies are plant-based.

Many pet owners are surprised to hear that many dogs and cats are allergic to animal proteins, and an animal-free diet can be a remedy for other common allergies or inflammatory conditions, such as inflammatory bowel disease (IBD). Small-animal veterinary nutritionist Cailin Heinze states that, contrary to popular opinion, "it's much more common for dogs to have allergies to meat than to grain," with chicken, beef, eggs, dairy, and wheat causing the most common allergies in dogs.[14] A recent study revealed that animal-based ingredients (beef, dairy, chicken, lamb, egg, pork, fish, and rabbit) were responsible for 236 cases of food allergies in dogs. By contrast, plant-based ingredients (wheat, soy, corn, rice, barley, kidney bean, and tomato) were responsible for only 77 cases.[15] Animal nutritionists Richard and Susan Pitcairn highlight that eight out of ten of the top allergens in pet foods are animal products.[16]

So Why Are Our Dogs Still Eating Meat?

Armed with these facts, why don't more pet owners switch to healthier, more ethical, plant-based pet diets? One issue is practicality. Complete plant-based pet foods have been hard to find. Vegan dog foods like Halo, V-dog, Natural Balance, and products from a few other smaller companies have been available but haven't been carried by most large pet retailers or grocery stores. Ryan wanted to feed his foster dogs vegan or vegetarian food, but his local pet food store rarely stocked animal-free options. When he did run across vegetarian pet foods, he didn't have many choices. Asking his vegan and vegetarian friends what brands they recommended, Ryan quickly realized that most were still feeding their pets animal meat–based foods. Their collective answer was, "There are no good plant-based options out there, so I guess I have to feed them animal meat." One of Ryan's vegan friends protested: "I've got two really big dogs, so I *have* to feed them meat. And they eat a lot of meat." This rationale was partly based on the idea that because their dogs were big, they could only thrive on animal flesh. However, price was also a factor: two large dogs require a lot of kibble.

Many vegans and vegetarians complain that animal-free pet foods are too expensive, and so they buy less expensive animal-meat pet foods. David Sprinkle, research director of Packaged Facts, told veterinarians at a conference in 2018:

> Even your most platinum pet parent is still very much looking for value. They're still comparison shopping, they're looking for discounts, they're looking for rewards. Even the most super premium pet food shopper is still very conscious of value.[17]

The adoption of plant-based pet foods has been slowed because they've been hard to find, are frequently out of stock, and are costly. Producing an affordable pet food that aligns with cruelty-free ethical values shouldn't be that difficult for pet food companies. Similar to human foods, plant-based pet foods don't need to be prohibitively expensive. As demand grows, prices should fall, and many pet food startups are already offering more affordable and accessible animal-free pet foods and treats.

Unfortunately, even affordable plant-based pet food doesn't overcome the biggest obstacle to abandoning the legacy of meat-based feeding:

public perception. It's hard to overcome the persuasive nutritional myths based in lupine ancestry, even for veterinarians. Over fifteen years ago, an article supporting alternative pet diets published in the peer-reviewed journal *Clinical Techniques in Small Animal Practice* urged veterinarians not to cling to outdated notions: "Small-animal nutrition is an ever-changing field. What veterinarians were taught 10 years ago may no longer be sound advice."[18] This statement has never been more pertinent. Our understanding of what is nutritionally sound for our pets is constantly evolving, and increasingly veterinarians like Knight and Ernie are challenging antiquated assumptions. Change takes time, especially with something as emotionally charged as food. As we saw in Chapter 2, though, our planet can't wait much longer.

If veterinarians are slow to embrace new evidence that diets high in animal protein might not be the healthiest options for our pets, the general public is even more conservative. In 2019, the first ever large-scale investigation into meat-avoidance in the pet-owner population was published, entitled "Plant-Based (Vegan) Diets for Pets: A Survey of Pet Owner Attitudes and Feeding Practices." The research team at the University of Guelph, led by Dr. Sarah Dodd, surveyed 3,673 pet owners and found that vegans were the only pet owners who omitted meat from their pets' diets (plus one vegetarian).[19] No surprises so far. Yet of the vegans surveyed, only 27 percent (58 of 212) reported feeding their pets a plant-based diet. Seventy-eight percent of vegan pet owners indicated they *would* feed a meat-free diet to their pet if one were available that met their required criteria. In fact, 35 percent of *all* survey respondents (1,083 people) who did not already feed a plant-based diet to their pet indicated interest in doing so, but 55 percent of those owners stated certain stipulations needed to be met. Forty-five percent wanted further evidence of nutritional sufficiency, 20 percent wanted veterinary approval, and another 20 percent expressed a wish for greater availability. These findings suggest that pet owners, particularly (but not exclusively) vegans, *would* be willing to try a meat-free diet for their pets if they knew there was a valid, nutritionally complete option.

Although we can always argue that there needs to be more research on plant-based (or animal-meat) pet diets, the fact is that complete and balanced, AAFCO-approved plant-based pet diets exist. There must be more to this reluctance to feed a meat-free diet than these respondents are admitting. There is: "natural." Dodd found that vegan pet owners with concerns about plant-based diets being "unnatural" for their pets were significantly less likely to remove meat from their food. Belief in the "unnaturalness" of plant-based diets for pets was the most predictive factor against feeding an animal-free diet among the survey respondents. Despite all scientific evidence, the "dog-is-wolf" myth endures. And there is another obstacle too: taste.

The Palatability Paradox

Regardless of how nutritionally complete plant-based food might be for pets, many people find it difficult to dismiss the notion that it's somehow unfair "to deprive pets of their natural food: animals." Many pet owners inexplicably worry that by eliminating animal meats, their companions will be "less happy."

Let's stick with dogs for now. Is a dog less happy eating plant-based food? Jessica Pierce admits that a big factor in her choice to return her dogs to an animal meat–based diet was their "disappointed looks" when she offered them vegetarian food.[20] Even vegetarian pet food advocate Dr. Jennifer Coates is worried: "The only issue I've seen with dogs being switched to a vegetarian food is one of acceptance. It seems to me that dogs who are used to eating diets that contain meat go through a 'where's the beef, chicken . . . etc.?' stage."[21] She reassures her clients that overcoming this is easy if you simply mix increasing amounts of the new food with decreasing amounts of the old and make the change slowly. Although concerns about "plant-based blandness" may have been true years ago, the current generation of animal-free pet foods is tastier and more satisfying than earlier versions. The bottom line is that plant-based human and pet foods are still in their infancy. If you think of this transition in terms of human culinary science, you realize plant-based pet food is in the "pre-spice" stage. In other words, most commercial plant-based dog foods manufactured today are focused on making sure their foods are nutritionally complete and balanced and aren't focused on flavor. The perceived blandness of vegetarian pet foods is changing as new protein sources and production techniques advance, and this is important to owners.

Feeding a pet should be a mutually satisfying experience, a time of intimate bonding. Most owners judge how satisfied, or happy, their dog is with a food or treat by how quickly they eat it. In fact, a dog is said to "wolf down" a delicious food, begging for more as soon as they swallow. But is the rate of eating a good indicator of satisfaction? Not really. Contrary to popular belief, *Canis lupus* was not an extraordinary hunter, certainly not nearly as capable as his purring playmate, *Felis domesticus*. Dogs and humans evolved in a world where food was scarce. Not knowing when, or what, their next meal would be, early dogs developed an enormously expandable stomach capacity in order to maximize any feeding opportunity. Even today, if needed, a dog's stomach can easily stretch to accommodate five to ten times its resting size. (By comparison, the human stomach can only swell three to four times its size.)

Because early dogs tended to roam in packs, whenever they stumbled across a dead carcass or fruiting plant, or (later) were tossed leftover food by humans, they had to eat quickly or risk missing out. Some veterinarians and physiologists believe one of the reasons dogs evolved with less salivary amylase (an enzyme that begins breaking down starches in the mouth) than other omnivores or humans is because dogs simply didn't have time to chew. Regardless, dogs have evolved to swiftly eat massive amounts of food, and are happiest when their bellies are full, whether they're full of animals, plants, insects, fungal proteins, or something else. "Wolfing down food" is normal dog behavior and has little, if any, relevancy to satisfaction or "happiness."

The perception of a dog or cat's feeding contentment is largely based on our own emotional associations with food. Professor Marc Bekoff points out: "If you've ever watched dogs eat, you may wonder whether they taste anything at all as they vacuum down snacks and meals, chomping and spraying food far and wide. Although the table or bowl manners of many dogs are appalling by human standards of etiquette, they certainly enjoy what makes it into their mouths."[22] In his book *Unleashing Your Dog: A Field Guide to Giving Your Canine Companion the Best Life Possible*, Bekoff talks about how science has tended to neglect the dog's sense of taste, disregarding it as far less sensitive than our own. Scientists initially based this on the fact that dogs only have around 1,700 taste buds compared with our 9,000. It was also believed that whereas humans can taste all five flavors—salty, sweet, sour, bitter, and umami (savory)—dogs are unable to fully detect "savory."

More recent research has challenged that hypothesis. Several studies have shown that dogs are able to detect umami, similar to humans.[23,24] Having witnessed dogs go crazy for Wild Earth's umami-flavored treats, all three of the authors believe these studies! Does the number of taste buds possessed by an animal dictate their appreciation of food? After all, cats only have around 470 taste buds but are notoriously fussy eaters. Does any of this really matter? Isn't taste preference unique to each individual, based on experience, genetics, physical characteristics, environment, and more?

Bekoff agrees that no two pets will necessarily love the same foods. Anyone who has lived with several dogs or cats will know that pets can display significant variability in taste preferences. Dogs will happily devour things we'd never touch, and certainly never put into our mouth. A dog's definition of tasty food extends well beyond grocery-store kibble, and canine concepts of edible, palatable, and nutritional are not the same as ours. But that's not what pet food companies are selling us. Pet store aisles are lined with manipulative marketing messages and pretty pictures painting a make-believe food world for shoppers. Packages plastered with images of succulent beef, toned chicken breasts, and fresh-caught salmon line store shelves. These images are designed to appeal to the tastes of humans, the ones with the actual purchasing power. Crack open a can or bag, and you quickly discover the pet food bears no resemblance to the pretty pictures. Instead, we find hard, square, brown kibbles or indiscriminate mush punctuated with chunks of, well, who knows? We're happily fooling ourselves into believing we're feeding real, whole, fresh foods, despite the evidence in front of our eyes.

That's not to say there's anything wrong with feeding kibble or canned pet foods; we just need a better understanding of what that food really is. If we insist that "dogs crave real meat" while feeding them an extruded kibble or canned food, we're contradicting ourselves. There is simply no real, whole animal meat in any kibble, and the meat in canned food is often cooked and processed far beyond recognition. In reality, it can be argued that we're already feeding our dogs a "meatless" diet.

In order to entice pets into eating this food, pet food manufacturers play some clever sensory tricks on our pets. If commercial pet foods filled their bags with only extruded meat ingredients combined with essential vitamins and minerals, cats and dogs wouldn't eat it. Dogs would need all of their 1,700 taste buds to find anything desirable in those dry, taste-less kibbles. High-quality plant-based ingredients in a vegetarian kibble can be cooked at lower temperatures for a short period of time, gently processed to better preserve the valuable nutrients, whereas animal meat requires higher heat and harsher treatment to remove contaminants and bacteria. Once animal meat has been rendered or dehydrated into safe little cubes, it tastes astonishingly bland.

This conventional-meat pet food needs a little "secret sauce." What does the FDA have to say about this "secret"?

> With respect to flavors, pet foods often contain "digests," which are materials treated with heat, enzymes and/or acids to form concentrated natural flavors. Only a small amount of a "chicken digest" is needed to produce a "Chicken Flavored Cat Food," even though no actual chicken is added to the food.[25]

The "secret sauce" turns out to be animal fat sprayed on the outside of kibbles. Essentially, meat-based pet food companies enhance the palat-ability of their dry pet foods by "enrobing" or spraying animal fat or "digest" (the entrails of chickens and other animals) onto the food. A

2015 *Journal of Animal Science* study describes common flavor additives as follows: "[R]endered fats and oils such as tallow, lard, poultry fat, and fish oil provide a supplementary source of energy, flavor, texture and nutrients in pet foods."[26]

And pets love it. "Of course, they can come to like these greatly," Knight says, "so I think there is a degree of our pets being genuinely upset when that is taken away from them. Of course, what we *ought* to do as guardians of these animals is not to give them whatever they want but try to give them whatever is *best*." He recalls his meat-quality lectures in veterinary school explaining that human consumers like the taste of fat, despite knowing it's unhealthy. If we find a piece of something full of protein, fat, or sugar, we're evolved to highly value those nutrients and to eat as many of them as possible. In their revolutionary animal rights book *Zoopolis*, Sue Donaldson and Will Kymlicka make a similar argument, but based on ethics rather than health. They write: "There is no natural diet for animal companions" and argue that what matters for our pets is to have food that is both palatable and meets all their nutritional needs. They state that while animal meat–free food might not be the first choice for a dog or cat in the wild, their owners should consider it:

There is plenty of evidence of their partiality to many vegan foods and palate enhancers (e.g., nutritional yeast, sea vegetables, and simulated meat, fish, and cheese flavors). . . . Why, in the case of diet, are we advocating that meat should not be among the choices offered to them? Because the liberty of citizens is always constrained by respect for the liberties of others. Dog and cat members of mixed human-animal society do not have a right to food that involves the killing of other animals.[27]

We've entered a time when people aren't forced to choose between healthy, ethical, or tasty food for their pets. Advances in food science are proving that the flavors associated with animal meats can be created without killing animals. The savory appeal of a steak or texture of chicken has been reduced to a series of molecular bonds and compounds.

Flavors once thought to be unique to animal flesh are being discovered in fungi, bacteria, algae, and even insects. Using bioreactors and clever food science, startups around the globe are now able to mimic, and often surpass, the flavor profiles of anything from filet mignon to hamburger. These advances are being applied to pet food to create appetizing animal meat–free dishes.

Let's re-examine the "Won't my dog miss meat?" conundrum many owners fear. The simplest answer is that dogs (or cats) don't crave specific *ingredients* or foods such as animal tissues; they crave the *nutrients* within them. As you've seen, evolution has specifically adapted animals to optimize usage of available resources, from taste buds primed for nutritious plants, to genes that trigger enzyme release. These adaptations are the result of the nutritional building blocks the body uncovers in a food through digestion and metabolism. The fact is your dog won't miss animal meat as long as it eats the nutrients its body needs.

But still, many pet owners worry about the emotional connection their dog or cat may have to a particular food. This is because humans have strong feelings associated with the food and drinks we consume. Champagne signals celebration, cake is associated with birthdays, and baked turkey is affiliated with holidays. It is these associations and the context of certain foods that binds us to them emotionally. Dogs and cats, while thrilled to be sharing Christmas dinner with us, are unlikely to be able to make the executive-function brain connections required to experience this deeper food relationship. To humans, the saying "Food is love" is true. For our pets, "Food is good" is more accurate.

Furthermore, modern plant-based foods for pets and people are delicious. Newer plant-based pet foods are nearly indistinguishable in taste and texture from, and are nutritionally superior to, their animal-meat competitors. Wild Earth's plant-based dog treats and foods use the savory flavors of yeast and fungi to satisfy canine taste buds. Philadelphia startup Because Animals is working on an animal-free palatant as an alternative to the tasty chicken fat used in most commercial pet food. Not only are these animal-free pet food ingredients delicious to our dogs and cats, but they have unique health benefits not found within animal meats, in addition to avoiding the potential harmful contaminants. By choosing animal-free options, owners are able to choose pet foods that are naturally tasty, healthier, safer, more nutritious, and better for the planet and animals. It's up to us to make better choices.

Shannon Falconer, CEO of Because Animals, acknowledges that pet owners tend to have a mindset entrenched in the idea that their "pets are carnivores and need to eat meat." Despite this "conventional wisdom," we, the authors, are optimistic that pet owners will switch to plant-based pet foods based on quality, health benefits, cost, and safety. Falconer puts it this way:

> We're not going to convince people by just *telling* them that it's possible for pets to thrive without meat. That's why it's really important for us to focus on creating foods that have a high nutritional value so people can see the benefits and build that trust.

Because Animals started its company with a "superfood" pet supplement that emphasizes nutritional elements uncommon in commercial pet foods, such as seaweed, marine minerals, sprouted legumes and seeds, and probiotics. By emphasizing the positive ingredients in its own unique foods rather than the missing animal meats, Because Animals and other alternative-protein pet food companies are hoping to create an animal meat–free pet food industry recognized for providing positive health benefits, rather than simply for being "meat-free." Falconer hopes that at least a small cohort of pet owners will see the health benefits in their pets, as well as witness how much they *enjoy* the food, and that others will follow. This is the beginning of the inevitable clean pet food revolution.

8

Challenges for Plant-Based Feeding

"Vegan food for dogs . . . quite ridiculous! What next?"

"If you are feeding your dog a vegan diet you deserve to be punished by law."

"Dogs were never designed to be vegans though. . . ."

"What's this shite dogs are supposed to eat meat don't make them eat vegan shite just cause u are."

I T'S CLEAR WHY most animal meat–free pet food companies are wary of the word *vegan*. The preceding comments are only a few of the hundreds on an Instagram post by The Dog's Trust, which shared a plant-based dog treat recipe to celebrate 2018 World Vegan Day. The charity wasn't advocating a vegan diet for dogs but was simply suggesting an idea for a special dog treat in conjunction with an international awareness campaign. You can probably imagine the insults hurled at full-time vegetarian and vegan pet food proponents. It's painfully evident that although the vegan sector is exploding for human food, many people remain skeptical about plant-based meals for pets, particularly about the perceived conflict with an animal's "natural behavior." People understand they must reduce their own animal-meat intake to improve their health and save the planet but worry that eliminating meat from their pet's diet may harm them in some way. They'd like to have a better, healthier, less-damaging protein alternative to animal flesh, but they don't know where to start.

Ethical Feeding Friction

Ernie calls this dilemma ethical feeding friction. Environmentally conscious people or those opposed to the cruelty of factory farming feel guilty each time they open a bag or can of conventional pet food. Although animal meat may never defile their own plates, they continue filling their pet's bowl with the meaty chunks of contradiction. Some concerned pet owners attempt to ease their ethical feeding friction by cooking homemade meals with meat from high-welfare producers that employ "organic," "free-range," and other potentially misleading marketing terms. But even in the best of these animal farms, animals suffer, and the environment is damaged. Killing animals can be a morally uncomfortable and ethically challenging experience, no matter what the pet food industry or packaging claims.

Overcoming this feeding friction is the first step in understanding that pets can be fed an animal-free diet. Animal ethicist and vegan Jessica Pierce admits that buying meat for her pets makes her uncomfortable: "But I do it," she says.[1] Why? Because she worries how her personal beliefs might affect her pets' health. Pierce isn't alone, and research explains why. In 2013, social psychologist Hank Rothgerber conducted research into what vegetarian people feed their pets. Rothgerber was most interested in whether non–meat eaters experienced feeding guilt (ethical feeding friction). He evaluated 515 non–meat eaters to better understand what motivated their pet-feeding practices.[2] As you've learned by now, it's complicated.

Rothgerber's research explored the conflict between feeding one's pet the "healthiest" animal-based diet and ethical concerns over animal welfare and the environment. As we predicted in Chapter 4, Rothgerber found that ethically motivated vegetarians were more likely to own pets than those motivated by personal health concerns. After all, if you love animals enough to refuse to eat them, you're likely to live with one (or more). Rothgerber also found that vegans and ethical vegetarians were more likely to feed their pet a plant-based diet, expressing their concerns over feeding other animals to a pet. He describes choosing a pet food as "a tragic trade-off, contrasting two sacred values: protecting the well-being of their pets and protecting the well-being of other animals and the environment."

Are we *really* stuck between a proverbial "pet food rock and an ethical hard place" today? One might think that in the six years since Rothgerber's research we would have removed the "tragedy" from the situation. Unfortunately, the 2019 Dodd study showed us this isn't the case, with only 27 percent of the over two hundred vegans surveyed feeding their pets a plant-based diet.[3] Frustratingly, pet owners complain that the same challenges remain: lack of availability of vegan pet food, lack of information about the nutritional adequacy of the food, and a worry that plant-based diets are "unnatural" for dogs and cats. Somehow, we're not adequately educating the pet-owning public that these apprehensions have been addressed. Modern plant-based options are making it possible to protect both the well-being of our pets *and* the well-being of other animals, while preserving our environment. Despite these advances, many vegans and vegetarians are still wary. What will it take to convince them to switch their pets to the plant-based diet they themselves feel so passionately about? Is it simply that we need more science published on plant-based nutrition for pets, or do we need a paradigm shift in the way society understands our dogs' and cats' dietary needs? Perhaps it requires a bit of both.

Consider Michelle Cehn and her "vegan dog," Chance. Cehn is used to being an outlier. When her mother told the eight-year-old Michelle that a person who didn't eat meat was a "vegetarian," she learned a new word, one she wouldn't hear again for years, let alone meet one. "I thought I was very alone in that," she tells Alice. "I went vegan in college, but for a very long time I didn't come across another vegetarian. It was a long time before I came across animal advocacy groups. When I did, I thought, 'Wow! There are other people speaking for animals out there, and all this information.'" Her newfound animal-friendly friends fully accepted her own dietary habits; but what about her dog's?

By feeding Chance an animal meat–free diet, Cehn entered a controversial area within her vegan safe space. Whereas those who meet happy, healthy, and energetic Chance don't consider criticizing his diet, the Internet is a different story. "People freak out," Cehn says. "Oh my God, they're so worried about the well-being of my dog, yet not at all understanding of the well-being of the animal I'd be feeding him if I were feeding him meat!" She finds it hard to understand how refusing to feed her dog meat gets her accused of animal abuse by vegans and non-vegans alike, even though these critics seem oddly oblivious to the immeasurable abuses the pet food meat animals experience.

Cehn is one of many who have encountered online and real-life confrontations about vegan pets. When he started VeggieDog in 2013, Klaus Wagner had to do a lot of what he calls "educational work," and he says he's got more to do:

> We will probably have to move on with this educational work for a few more years. Old, established knowledge isn't easy to change. We use social media to explain our reasons and, of course, we experience backlash from people there. . . . We're absolutely aware that the skepticism about a vegetarian diet is essentially deeply rooted in fear. People want to provide their dogs with everything they need and they're just afraid they might harm their dogs with this kind of feeding. But when we talk to dog owners and explain to them that it's absolutely feasible to feed a plant-based food without any problem, we can erase most fears.

As a veterinarian, Ernie has also experienced first-hand highly charged, aggressive, and threatening comments, even when advocating for farmed animals and the environment. Some of his veterinary colleagues, who take an oath "to promote animal health and welfare, relieve animal suffering, [and] protect the health of the public and environment," often omit cows, pigs, chicken, fish, and other farmed animals from their vow, and attack the non–animal meat movement. Ernie believes veterinarians should demand humane and compassionate care for *all* animals, not just dogs, cats, and horses. Ernie jokes: "If you want to start a fight these days, just ask someone what they feed their pet." How did the pet food arena get this combative?

Eliminating animal meats from pet food shouldn't be so contentious. Cehn tells Alice that when she posts about vegan dogs on social media, she gets more comments than she does for any other content:

> Everyone has to leave their opinion. They see it and they're compelled to leave a comment. Suddenly, everyone becomes a veterinarian: they're like, "No! Dogs are carnivores and they're meant to eat meat; you're stupid, you don't understand biology." I'm like, "Do *you* understand biology?" It's such a hugely misunderstood area. Everyone suddenly has a veterinary nutrition degree when they leave these comments.

She finds it tough not to get involved and respond. "Nothing's going to change if nobody explains it to people," she adds. "If I'm able to step in there, I say, 'Hey, you know what? I used to think the same thing. But I did my research and my dog has been vegan for ten years and has a big 'thumbs up' from his vet. Before you make a snap judgment, I encourage you to do some research.'" She points out that once most pet owners realize how deeply they've been deceived about animal meats, many will accept the legitimacy of meat-free dog diets and begin their own research.

VeggieDog's Wagner agrees, telling us that his company now sees consumers commenting on social media in support of plant-based dog diets. Cehn continues to post about Chance's diet, despite the backlash. "It plants a seed," she says, "and that seed just so needs to be planted right now." Others want to kill those seeds before they sprout. In a recent interview with the *New York Times*,[4] Lisa Freeman, a board-certified veterinary nutritionist at Tufts University, was quoted: "We want [our pets] to be eating a diet that is nutritionally balanced. That means it has all the proteins, vitamins and minerals that they need in the correct ratios and with the best quality control. It isn't easy to formulate a high-quality diet for dogs, and it's particularly difficult with a vegan diet." Is that really true?

It's not. The evidence clearly shows that dogs can thrive on a diet without feeding them other animals. An increasing number of reputable vegetarian and vegan dog food brands are providing complete and balanced, AAFCO- and European FEDIAF–approved diets around the globe. Formulating plant-based dog foods is becoming easier and more affordable for pet food companies as plant-based nutritional science expands and ingredients become more accessible. Although the availability of plant-based pet food is still lagging far behind conventional animal-meat foods and treats, it's becoming easier for pet owners to transition to a diet that could have multiple benefits, from reducing pet obesity and disease risk, to making the most ethical choice for planet, farmed animals, and pets. Unfortunately, for some veterinarians and pet owners, the absence of animal meat on a pet food label remains a psychological challenge.

Ingredient Bias

"Ingredient bias" is a term Ernie created to explain why some people reject unfamiliar human or pet food ingredients. Our food preferences are shaped by our life experiences, geography, and culture. Many Americans refuse the French delicacy frogs' legs, and, as we saw in Chapter 4, many Asian people see nothing odd about dining on dog meat. There's no rational (or physiological) basis for these preferences or prejudices; it's simply part of our complicated collective unconsciousness. These same ingredient biases apply to pet food. Most pet owners and veterinarians consider anything that's not beef, pork, poultry, or fish as somehow "inferior" for dogs and cats. This consideration isn't based on nutritional needs; it's rooted in cultural bias. As we saw in the social media battles, pet food has become an emotionally charged topic. A quick examination of the comments section on any plant-based pet food Internet post will prove how passionately pet owners feel about interfering with the "natural diet of dogs," a false fantasy disproved in Chapter 6.

A comment that largely summarizes the confusion was found on @PlantPoweredDog's Instagram account:

> DOGS SHOULD NOT BE VEGAN. My partner and I are vegan however our dog eats an organic, raw diet. Because it's species appropriate. Shame on you for promoting this. Please UNFOLLOW me. I do NOT support this page.

A combination of aggressive pet food marketing and manipulative mythologies about "natural" canine behavior has wrongly convinced even the most dedicated vegans that it's unhealthy to take animal meat out of pet food without a shred of evidence.

This animal meat–based, oversimplified, and reductionist view of pet nutrition is being refuted by research. Ernie, Andrew Knight, and other plant-based pet food proponents cite not only anecdotes, individual cases, and popular books[5] describing animals thriving on plant-based diets, but also scientific studies that support animal meat–free pet diets.[6,7,8] As far back as 1994, PETA published the results of a systematic survey of the health of three hundred vegetarian dogs sourced from thirty-three U.S. states and Canada.[9] Dogs ranged in age from young puppies to nineteen years old and included a wide range of breeds and gender. The study dogs had been maintained on animal meat–free diets for two to over nine years, with an average being fed plant-based food for 5.7 years. Over 80 percent of dogs maintained on vegan or vegetarian diets for 50 to 100 percent of their lifetimes were documented as being in "good to excellent health." The few health problems that *were* found were those also commonly reported within the normal, animal meat–eating dog population.

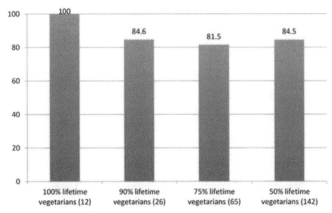

Figure 3: Percentages of dogs in good to excellent health, vs. time as vegetarians (PETA 1994).

This is scientifically rigorous research, providing adequate numbers of animals for the results to be reliably extrapolatable to the wider population. And it was largely ignored when it wasn't being criticized.

Knight was expecting enormous scrutiny and criticism when he presented his more current research to the veterinary world. To his surprise, it didn't happen. He tells Alice that if you base your position on indisputable evidence and sound reasoning, it's hard for scientifically driven veterinarians to dispute:

> Nobody has ever refuted what I've said, because I don't say anything that's not supported by the evidence and by sound reasoning. People often start off with wrong assumptions, and what I do is I show them they're wrong. So, the assumption might be that cats and dogs need meat. No, that's not true. What they need is a specific set of nutrients and, provided they get those, it doesn't matter where they get them from.

Whereas most veterinarians will accept scientific evidence, many pet owners may remain unconvinced. Taking what Ernie says a step further: if you want to start a fight, ask a pet owner to consider a plant-based diet. At least, that's what happened in Los Angeles. The pet rescue and shelter community in Los Angeles, California, was divided in 2017 by a proposal to feed dogs in the city's shelters plant-based meals. This "vegan shelter" movement was initiated after several prominent vegans, including recording artist and social activist Moby, pointed out that the shelters were killing more animals to feed the rescued dogs than they were actually saving. Could switching to a plant-based diet for dogs reduce the number of slaughtered animals and help the city adhere to their pledge to help *all* animals in need? Based on these suggestions, the L.A. animal services commission unanimously voted for a feasibility study and risk analysis.

The initial shelter study was spearheaded by Roger Wolfson, a controversial member of the L.A. Animal Services Commission and a television screenwriter. In 2017, Wolfson told the press that more than 20,000 chickens, 10,000 turkeys, and a thousand lambs die each year in order to feed the 33,000 dogs in L.A.'s public shelters.[10] He estimated that changing shelter dogs to a vegan diet could eliminate up to 30,000 pounds of meat per month. Pointing out that they are the department of *animal* services, not *companion animal* services, Wolfson urged the public to consider the importance of avoiding the unnecessary killing of animals: "If dogs can get their needs met without killing animals, we owe it to the citizens of Los Angeles to try." Wolfson also cited the impact of meat and dairy consumption on deforestation, greenhouse gases, and ocean dead zones. Unfortunately, some conservative veterinarians disagreed. In response to Wolfson's proposal, the L.A. shelter's chief veterinarian, Jeremy Prupas, cited nutritionists, a veterinary toxicologist, and other experts who advised against a "vegan diet for dogs and cats," and suggested that canine diarrhea would be "a big issue."

Not every veterinarian was so close-minded. Armaiti May, another L.A.-based veterinarian, countered that although abrupt changes in diet could lead to loose stools, a gradual transition would likely avoid any major problems. May joins a growing number of veterinarians who believe animal meat–based pet foods are linked to many cancers, obesity, and inflammatory conditions in dogs.

Ultimately, the plant-based dog food proposal was rejected. People who initially supported the animal shelter initiative became concerned over "veganism," "vegan activists," and other exaggerated hypothetical fears. The issue was arguably derailed by terminology and the emotional associations the word *vegan* often carries, especially in the United States. Disappointingly, the fight ended up being a dispute about "vegan activists attacking my meat-based way of life" instead of focusing on environmental impacts, animal welfare, and canine nutrition. The primary rational argument that defeated this plant-based dog food initiative was, "It might cause loose poop." Vegans need to reassess how we're presenting the plant-based message. If we're going to open people's eyes to the *real* issues at stake, we need a new plant-based pet food language.

Vegans Need a New Plant-Based Pet Food Language

Part of the controversy over the concept of "vegan pets" is due to the misuse of the term *vegan*. Our pets are not "vegan." Dogs aren't lying awake at night worrying about farmed-animal suffering, and the cats who live with us aren't ethically conflicted about killing mice. Veganism is a way of life that doesn't begin and end at the dinner table. It's a social justice movement, a commitment to making life better for the billions of animals in the world that suffer not just for our meals, but also for our clothes, cosmetics, household products, and entertainment. For many, it's a personal belief system and lifestyle; others consider it something comparable to a spiritual faith. Veganism is an ethical and moral framework, and even a political persuasion. For most vegans, it's a bit of all of these.

For opponents, veganism becomes whatever the context finds most polarizing. The most successful anti-vegan arguments exploit a single perceived inconsistency to try to destroy the entire structure. In the L.A. shelter example, critics found success by falsely extending the argument to include cats, when the initial proposal was to explore plant-based options for feeding dogs. Vegan advocates were then dragged into defending "veganism" for cats, instead of remaining focused on a proven plant-based diet for omnivorous dogs. Some vegans seized upon the well-publicized controversy as an opportunity to attack the horrors of factory farming and expose the hypocrisy of U.S. animal shelters that "rescue" a few select animal species while killing and feeding them millions of other animals. Unfortunately, the controversy and defeat of the L.A. shelter plant-based pet food movement caused many Americans to conclude that, "for some reason, vegan diets must not be okay for pets." This is why we need a new plant-based language.

The first step toward greater acceptance of animal-free pet foods is to carefully evaluate the terms we use. It's a practical necessity to use the words *vegan* and *veganism* sparingly when talking about our pets. Even when referring to our own diets, some of us may prefer to identify ourselves as "vegan" to friends but substitute "plant-based" when in less-accepting company.

You might worry that this approach inadvertently apologizes for a lifestyle that prevents animal suffering and environmental destruction. In a perfect society, there should be nothing shameful about proclaiming your beliefs, especially when they're based on compassion and don't harm others. However, the world we live in proves there can be disadvantages to playing the "vegan card" too soon, unwittingly self-sabotaging any chance of constructive discussion. Here's an example that Ernie experienced that demonstrates the unintended risks of saying the word *vegan* at the wrong time:

> I was thrilled. Not only had I been presented with a prestigious veterinary service award, but I was about to dine with one of my political heroes. I was a progressive Democrat with future political aspirations (I would later run for state office), and breaking bread with an illustrious U.S. senator was sure to be a highlight of my year. The dinner was held in the good senator's capital city, in a decidedly beef-heavy Midwestern state. I was seated across from the senator, and the group engaged in small talk. The university president formally introduced everyone, and salads were served. People were congratulating me for my presentation earlier in the day, and I was buzzing with admiration for the senator. I took the opportunity to praise the senator for his policies and dedication to the Democratic Party's ideals.

Unfortunately for me, the success of the salad setting couldn't have foreshadowed the disastrous main course to follow. Smiling broadly, engrossed in a medical discussion, I noticed a waiter approaching. "Excuse me, Dr. Ward?" I affirmed I was. "Did you request a vegan dinner? Are you a vegan?"

"Yes, thank you," I replied, as I had a thousand times during my life. I casually turned back to my conversation, oblivious that my dinner was about to dramatically alter.

"Vegan? Did you say you're a vegan?"

It was the senator, barking at me from across the table.

"Yes, sir. I've been. . . ." I was cut off before I could utter another syllable.

"You don't eat meat? How in the world can you be a veterinarian?"

And with that, the senator sat upright, turned his shoulder to me, and never spoke another word in my direction for the remainder of the evening. In fact, no one at the table said more than, "Can you pass the salt?" to me until the next day.

The *vegan* label silenced what might have been an otherwise productive evening building potential alliances in addressing climate change and common-sense gun control, shared passions for Ernie and the senator. What if the waiter had said "vegetarian," "the vegetable dish," "the plant-based starter," "the meat-free option," or any other adjective except "vegan"? Would it have gone unnoticed by the senator? The word *vegan* likely caught the senator's attention because he represented a state dominated by the cattle industry, members of which were likely constantly warning him against "vegan activists" or "animal rights fanatics." The "vegan" interruption to his dinner was intolerable, especially since he'd made assumptions that all veterinarians held the same beliefs as he and his constituents.

This experience greatly influenced how Ernie began using animal-free food terms, especially in the highly controversial vegan pet food space. Although it's easy to say, "Ernie should've used this opportunity to educate the senator about the ills of factory farming," or "Ernie shouldn't hide his veganism!" the reality is quite different. We can't force other people to change; only they can make that decision. What we can do instead is try to build ethical bridges based on commonalities and civil discourse, rather than burning them through altercation and hostility. Militant and violent activism can force change, but we, the authors, believe in leading this advancement with science, logic, and compassion to create consensual and sustainable change. To paraphrase the famous Gandhi quotation: to change the world, you must become the change you seek. And there's also neurolinguistics to consider.

Modern behavioral science proves that when a person encounters a word, an entire linguistic framework is activated in their brain. The brilliant University of California, Berkeley cognitive linguist George Lakoff discovered this in his early fMRI research, popularizing his findings in the clearly titled best-selling *Don't Think of an Elephant!* In simplest terms, when any word is heard or read, an associated network of terms, emotions, and mental images is instantly activated within the subconscious. Each individual has a lifetime of experiences that are connected to the word, so the words *elephant* or *chair* might conjure up slightly different versions of those objects or concepts. In addition to the visual representation of *chair*, there may be emotions, experiences, and metaphors activated, resulting in not only a discrete definition, but also a "feeling" around the word.

A child who sits in a kindergarten school chair and has it unexpectedly break underneath them may forever be primed to sit carefully in any type of chair. Even more interesting, that person may associate *chair* with fear, embarrassment, or pain, causing them to avoid choosing a chair to purchase as an adult: "Honey, can you help me pick out the dining room chairs?" "No, you handle that." The person doesn't know why they aren't interested in chairs and that they have the habit of sitting very cautiously. They don't think: "Why do I feel this way?" They just do. All of this happens nearly instantaneously, without volitional control or awareness deep within the subconscious. This activated brain network that Lakoff uncovered is also the basis of the "gut feeling" described in Malcolm Gladwell's influential best-selling book *Blink* and is the foundation of much of our behavior.[11]

When you consider a still-controversial concept such as veganism with this in mind, you can immediately understand that it activates a wide variety of responses based on previous experiences. For the U.S. senator, the word *vegan* was likely associated with visions of angry mobs, buckets of blood thrown at politicians, and big companies pulling funding. No wonder he gave Ernie the cold shoulder! At the opposite end of the table, Ernie's neurolinguistic network couldn't understand what all the fuss was about. After decades of abstaining from animal meats and living a cruelty-free lifestyle, Ernie's linguistic framework was built on entirely different metaphors. When a long-time vegan's brain hears the word *vegan*, a network of positive images associated with compassion for life creates the definition. Ernie feels happy when he's called "vegan," while others revile the term, and neither is immediately aware why. Blame it on our subconscious; blame it on societal conditioning. Either way, it's the challenging reality the word *vegan* confronts.

Conflating the terms *plant-based* with *vegan* can be reductionist and confusing, equating a diet with a belief system. But it can also be a short-term strategy to open discussions that can influence long-term change. What if by using the word *plant-based* rather than *vegan*, Ernie had been able to have a constructive conversation around reducing meat consumption at his dinner? What if he'd been able to civilly point out that everyone reducing their meat intake by half would be better for the animals than if 20 percent of the world went fully vegan? In this scenario, the senator could preserve his precious cattle industry, reduce national healthcare costs, and save money on environmental disasters. Instead, there was no conversation and no chance for any change. This is the price our minds pay by relying on heuristic shortcuts in an effort to protect us from perceived threats. Emotionally, it's easy to want people to behave a certain way, to share our beliefs and agree with our logic, but the real goal has to be to reduce how many animals are in factory farms and confront climate change. The intention of the animal-free movement is to build bridges, not to carpet-bomb the "opposition." To create lasting change requires changing attitudes and behaviors, and that begins with a certain level of pragmatic compromise about the language we use.

Animal-free pet food company Wild Earth, for instance, has mostly vegan employees—*mostly*, because there are also animal-meat consumers on the team, including co-founder Ron Shigeta. To be certain Wild Earth's food is competing on taste and quality, Ron believes the company needs to have employees who eat animal meat to test and compare. This situation also allows Ernie and Ryan to try out their plant-based messages and concepts on Ron's carnivorous neurolinguistics. Similarly, if meat-free producer Impossible Foods doesn't taste conventional burgers to make sure its plant-based alternative is just as good, the whole enterprise risks failure. Clara Foods likewise needs people to consume real eggs so the company can make delicious egg-free egg whites.

By working together to create cruelty-free, sustainable, animal-free food that tastes just as good as the "real thing," these companies are also reducing the gap between the vegan sensibility and the outsider perspective. It's easy to forget when you're passionate about something that you need to convince others why they should personally care. Describing the horrors of factory farming to people on social media or having an uncomfortable dinner conversation can certainly lead to incremental gains. But to create something that makes the message *appealing*? Well, that's a game changer.

Ideal Diets, Not Ideology

The word *plants* activates a separate linguistic framework from *vegan*. With images of green leaves, healthy vegetables, and vibrant fruits flooding most people's brains, energy and vitality are conjured up. *Plant-based* lights up common brain pathways that lead to *healthy*, *safe*, and *good*, three attributes we demand from pet food. Much of the recent interest in human veganism and vegetarianism is the result of the "plant-based" movement. People hesitant to wade into controversy feel liberated to try a new diet without risk of being labeled *activist* or *troublemaker*. Flexitarians, vegetarians, ecotarians (people who make choices based on environmental concerns), flexi-vegans (those who eat a predominantly plant-based diet with an occasional dish of meat or fish), and plant-based proponents are safe to proclaim they're on a meat-free diet. This is no longer simply a theory. In 2018, 92 percent of plant-based meals were eaten by non-vegans. Market research shows that an increasing number of consumers are opting for a "flexitarian" diet that swaps meat and dairy for plants.[12]

The same applies for those wishing to take animal meat out of their pet's bowl. The term *plant-based* is open for mental framing as environmentally friendly or healthy, bypassing the controversies of animal farming. A 2019 Faunalytics study looked at the most appealing labeling for plant-based meat alternatives, responding to the fact that describing products as *vegan* is increasingly considered "a bad idea."[13] Industry leaders have recommended that companies avoid using "v-words" on their meat-free products (Food Navigator, 2018),[14] putting meat-free options in a separate "vegetarian" section of your menu reduces sales,[15] and the word *vegan* apparently reduces foods' appeal for more consumers than other common labels like *diet, sugar-free,* or *gluten-free.*[16] The term *plant-based* has therefore been widely adopted as an alternative, focusing on what a product contains rather than what it lacks. A poll of 1,163 social media users suggested that *plant-based* might be perceived more positively and as more of a dietary than a lifestyle choice.[17]

However, the Faunalytics study found something quite different: the average person preferred the label *vegan* over *plant-based*, saying that a "vegan burger" sounded better than a "plant-based burger" in a head-to-head comparison. All labels were rated similarly and neutrally on measures of sound and likelihood of purchase, but in a head-to-head comparison, the term *plant-based* rated lower than all other descriptors tested, including *vegan*. Could we be nearing a tipping point in favor of veganism?

There is still plenty of emotional baggage attached to the word *vegan*. Should we worry about confronting humanity with the horrors of factory farms, as we did in Chapter 3? Yes and no. *Feel-good* was the most positively rated term in the Faunalytics study,[18] and there's nothing feel-good about animal cruelty. The goal of the authors of this book is to eliminate animals as food for pets and people. How we achieve that goal, as long as it is ethically and morally sound, is largely irrelevant to us. For some, understanding the immeasurable suffering of a pig sentenced to a miserable life crammed inside in a tiny gestation crate will inspire them to banish pork from their pet's bowl. For others, buying fewer animal meats for their dog in order to help reduce climate change will do the trick. The fear or diagnosis of a pet suffering from meat-related obesity or cancer will push some to reconsider their diet. We, the authors, don't care why folks reduce feeding animals to their pets; we care that they do. That means using a variety of terms and tactics to appeal to different consumers. Based on the current controversy attached to the notion of a "vegan pet," the "v-word" still may not be the wisest choice for pet food.

Regardless of what this meat-free movement is called, it's clear society is on the cusp of something big. Ten years ago, vegans were forced to satisfy themselves with eating soggy bean patties, facing widespread social ostracization, being the subject of persistent ridicule, and drinking cups of black coffee topped only with soy milk. Today, 6 percent of Americans identify as "vegan," compared to just 1 percent in 2014. As many as 30 percent report they proudly leave meat off their plates on a regular basis and are also seeking plant-based meat alternatives.[19] The plant-based meat market is set to reach $5.2 billion by 2020[20] and could make up one-third of the market by 2050.[21]

We're on the brink of a slaughter free–food social revolution. Large-scale attitude changes in society have almost always started with a small minority of extremely dedicated people who think of nothing else in their lives. These outspoken and opinionated individuals can continue for many decades until, at some point, enough like-minded people join them, and the movement reaches a tipping point. This moment often coincides with an event in history that creates wide-scale sympathy or awareness, and everybody else comes flooding in. The "new idea" becomes the general consensus in society, and then things change rapidly. Some of these changes are trivial, like better beer, and some are earth-shattering and take enormous dedication, suffering, and sacrifice, like the abolition of slavery. But change is inevitable.

We're seeing this change now happening with veganism, a classic example of a social revolution. Vegans have been incredibly strong believers for decades, evolving a health-focused diet movement into an ethical way of life. It was vegans who first stepped in to make the new plant-based companies possible by investing in them; we'll meet some of them in the next few chapters. Today, these companies are creating meat-free food for *everyone,* not just vegans. Wild Earth's co-founder Shigeta, a meat-eater, reminds us:

> In the end nothing will withstand these vegans, because they're bringing everything that they have—and as a community, they have quite a bit. It allows people like me, a biotech investor, to join the movement. Because if the money and the confidence is not there, there is no movement, there are companies, no start-ups. There's a gate that we're walking through and that's important. It's a confluence of these sort of catalytic people and their resources, and technology that allows things to exist that have never existed before. Technology is creating products that are viable alternatives to eating meat. This is another very collective thing where lots of people are having ideas and, as these ideas begin to show their potential through technology, the food becomes something that people *want to eat,* that we can really enjoy. We can legitimately say, "Hey, this burger is just as good as any other burger I've had." Then this just catches fire!

Many of the people choosing animal-free options are not doing it for purely "vegan reasons." They might choose plant-based food as a more sustainable way to eat less red meat, or they might care about the welfare of chickens and pigs, but still eat fish. Regardless of their reasons, they're participating in this societal disruption where consuming animal meat has been the norm.

Shigeta points out that the difficult thing about social revolutions is that when the "true believers" have to hand their idea over to everybody, it will change, and sometimes in ways they may not like. "It doesn't belong to them anymore. Sometimes, the true believers feel sad about that," he says. "But the beautiful thing is that to win, it has to be for everybody. So, there's this beautiful, spiritual thing where something that's *true* changes in the way that people believe it. That's how change comes to the world." This means vegans need to be willing to occasionally release the word *vegan*. Nowhere is this clearer than in pet food, where we've already seen that the idea of "vegan pets" causes unnecessary confusion and outrage. We've also seen that dogs and cats are increasingly an integral part of global society. As Donaldson and Kymlicka put it, our pets have become citizens: "Dog and cat members of a mixed human–animal society."[22]

It's clear from the enormous contribution of pet food to the environmental and welfare problems associated with meat consumption that the animal meat–free revolution must include pets. Our pets will never share a cruelty-free vegan ideology, nor will the many people who choose animal-free options for environmental or health reasons. Just because they don't claim veganism doesn't mean they can't join an animal meat–free movement. A more inclusive language means bigger potential for social disruption, and that leads to a greater potential to fix our unsustainable food system. Shigeta puts it simply: "If we can reduce meat consumption by 70 to 90 percent globally, we could halt global climate change."

These aims are bold and ambitious, and perhaps overly optimistic. But something has to change, or our current way of life is in peril. Distinguishing between living a vegan lifestyle and feeding a plant-based diet is *essential* when it comes to talking about companion animals. When we remove animal meat from pet food, we're simply switching our pets to a different nutrient source, one that doesn't use animal flesh. Changing a pet food brand isn't imposing an ideology on the pet owner or pet. Your pet doesn't have to join a movement or sign up to a march. Nor do you. You just feed your dog a different dog food. Many of us will be motivated by ethical or environmental concerns that don't directly affect our dogs or cats. However, it's important to remember that whatever our personal ethics, we're first and foremost acting in our pets' best interests. This book has already shown that an animal meat–free diet can be healthier and safer and is indisputably better for the environment and animal welfare.

What About Cats?

"That's all very well," you might be saying, "but what about my cat? No matter how desirable and healthy it might be to switch our dogs to a meat-free diet, this isn't an option for our carnivorous felines. Is it?" A lot of people are asking that question, including organizations responsible for animal welfare. In November 2018, the Royal Society for the Prevention of Cruelty to Animals (RSPCA) announced that U.K. owners who feed their cats a "vegan diet" could be violating the Animal Welfare Act by not adequately meeting their pet's nutritional needs.[23] Comments published on social media showed that this view is widely supported. Klaus Wagner tells Alice that Green Petfood doesn't yet have a complete meat-free pet food for cats: "Right now, we don't see a vegetarian or vegan food that can cover a cat's nutritional needs, and that's the most important thing for us." Why do so many people believe cats can't be plant-based? Are they right? You may be surprised to learn your cat is more "vegan" than you realize.

A year after his first study, Rothgerber published a second paper seeking to further clarify "the vegetarian's dilemma,"[24] or the ethical feeding friction felt by many pet owners. It questioned whether non–meat eating owners would treat dogs and cats differently, in terms of the percentage of their diet they were happy to derive from animal products. Survey responses from 290 vegans and vegetarians showed that owners fed their dogs a diet significantly more vegetarian than what they fed their cats and reported experiencing less guilt about feeding their cats a primarily animal meat–based diet. This result makes sense given there is more widespread public belief that vegetarian diets are somehow nutritionally inappropriate for cats than there is for dogs. Jessica Pierce summarizes: "Maybe you worry about the suffering of food animals, yet believe a carnivorous diet is the only healthy option for your cat."[25] It's an entirely understandable belief. Whereas it's proven that dogs can thrive on a plant-based diet, cats are more metabolically challenging.

Colleen Patrick-Goudreau, recognized expert and thought leader on the culinary, social, ethical, and practical aspects of vegan living, jokes on her podcast "Food for Thought" that the ultimate solution to the vegan pet owner's ethical feeding dilemma is to adopt a rabbit. Nobody's going to attack you for sharing your plant-based foodstuffs with an herbivore! But even the view that rabbits are pure herbivores has been challenged. Research published in December 2018 documented Canadian hares actually eating *meat* during long winters, when vegetation is scarce.[26] Perhaps we should start calling rabbits and hares "facultative herbivores." Modern science once again proves our current taxonomic terminology is outdated and inaccurate.

Although Patrick-Goudreau says she would readily feed a dog a vegan diet based on the scientific evidence, she doesn't feel the same confidence when it comes to her cats. She believes domestic cats are "obligate carnivores," that old amended taxonomical term used to describe an animal that needs a certain set of particular amino acids and vitamins found primarily in animal flesh to live. Because those specific amino acids and vitamins were originally only found in animal meats, the term "obligate carnivore" stuck to felines. The specific terminology is important, because food technology today is able to produce plant-based, lab-grown, or fungal proteins that contain all essential amino acids a cat (or human or dog) requires, without the animal.

Complicating metabolic matters, cats haven't been "man's best friend" for as long as, well, "man's best friend." Felines were domesticated far more recently than dogs, and as any reluctant recipient of their cat's proud "catch of the day" knows, their instinct to hunt and kill is very much alive and clawing. They lack many of the genetic, biochemical, and behavioral adaptations of the tens of thousands of years of co-evolution that enable dogs and humans to thrive on an omnivorous diet. Whereas dogs require ten essential amino acids from food, cats must obtain eleven amino acids from their meals. Their need for certain proteins extends far beyond the reach of their claws, deep in their cellular energy matrix. For instance, dogs have enzymes that aid in producing arginine. Cats lack these enzymes, meaning even a few missed meals without arginine could be fatal.

But what everyone really wants to talk about in cats is taurine. Taurine is that infamous sulfur-containing beta amino acid that cats must eat in order to survive. It's also been the center of the grain-free dog food heart disease debate. Unlike canines, cats cannot synthesize taurine from its two amino-acid building blocks, cysteine and methionine. Animal tissues, especially skeletal muscles, are rich in taurine, and it is relatively low in plants, insufficient for a feline's complete nutritional needs. If a cat isn't fed adequate taurine, they can develop eye diseases, heart failure, and pregnancy complications.

That's not all that makes feeding a vegan diet to a cat challenging. There's also an issue with certain vitamins. Cats can't synthesize vitamin A (retinol), vitamin B3 (niacin), vitamin D, or arachidonic acid (an essential fatty acid). This means they must consume these nutrients in a "preformed state" because their bodies can't convert them into a usable form. All these factors are commonly cited as reasons cats can't be fed a "meatless" diet.

But are these reasons true? Not necessarily, especially with advances in fungal proteins and cellular meats. We're about to explore how, over the next five to ten years, cellular technologies will blur the lines between what could be considered "meat," "vegan," and "animal-free," resulting in diets that are complete and balanced for cats without killing a single animal. This is important, not only for the health of the planet and other animals, but also for the future human–feline bond to flourish. We've already seen that feeding animal meats to cats, especially fish, is bad for the planet, and there are a lot of cats to feed. Despite a Gallup poll showing that 70 percent of Americans claim to be "dog people," there are actually more cats than dogs in the United States.[27] Recent estimates put the number of flesh-eating felines at around 94 million, edging out the approximately 90 million dogs.[28] That's more "obligate carnivores" that need to be fed by the corporate meat-production machine. Let's return to meat-based cat foods: Are our cats *actually* being fed taurine and other essential nutrients from animal meats in their food? Once again, the answer is complicated.

In the wild, the only source of complete nutrition for cats is another animal, whether that be a mouse, a small bird, or an insect. In a commercial diet, however, all of the nutrients a cat needs can be safely supplemented from non-animal sources. What most cat owners don't realize is that there's usually not enough taurine from animal sources in most commercial pet food for cats to survive. This is partly because taurine is a heat-sensitive and water-soluble compound, and during animal-meat processing, much of it is lost. In fact, cat food regulations in the United States require taurine to be added into feline diets because regulators know there isn't enough remaining in the meat to meet a cat's nutritional needs.[29]

Where does the added taurine come from? A synthetic source. Half of the world's industrial-produced taurine is added to pet food and the other half to pharmaceutical applications.[30] Although it might be true *in the wild* that the only source of taurine is another animal, the taurine that allows the vast majority of pet cats to survive is synthetic. How is a plant-based diet for cats any different? Argue all you want about what is "ancestral," "natural," or "biologically appropriate;" it's on the ingredient label for everyone to see.

Figure 4: Cat Food Label.

Take the label in Figure 4, picked at random from the premium cat food on display at Alice's local grocery store. Aside from the meat and animal derivatives, oils and fats, and "various sugars," we have a long list of additives that provide all the essential vitamins and minerals cats require. This example includes vitamin E supplement, riboflavin supplement, vitamin D3 supplement, potassium iodide, and—significantly—taurine. Do an online search for any commercial cat food and look at the ingredients label: you're likely to see the same thing. There's no reason why the same sources of synthetic vitamins and minerals currently used by animal meat–based pet foods shouldn't be used in a plant-based cat food. Pet food companies have been supplementing the essential nutrients for years,[31] and the practice is widely accepted in feline therapeutic plant-based diets, too.

When veterinarians put cats with food sensitivities on special animal meat–free or protein-hydrolyzed hypoallergenic diets, any missing vitamins and minerals are added to ensure the food is nutritionally complete, identical to meat-based cat food. Why do some pet food companies insist they can't make a "meatless cat food" when they practically already do? The primary source of nutrition that meat ingredients provide is protein, and we've learned that proteins are made up of amino acids. It's the essential vitamins and minerals, the ones cats can't synthesize themselves, that are the real keys in making sure they're eating a healthy diet. The evidence, both direct and indirect, suggests that cats *can* thrive on an animal meat–free diet as long as it's nutritionally complete and balanced.

Lingering doubts remain for many vegan cat owners due to these conflicting messages.[32] Perhaps the biggest challenge to giving cats plant-based diets consists of people who don't take the time to do it safely. Search the Internet for "vegan cat" and you'll quickly encounter pages of feline failures. (The same exercise is true for human vegans.) The vast majority of these anecdotes originate from passionate vegans who decide to stop feeding their cats meat. Not only is that dangerous, but it's also guaranteed to fail. One of the most common reports you'll encounter is "vegan cats get bladder stones." Although that statement is not completely accurate, it's true that cats fed an imbalanced homemade plant-based diet tend to have more alkaline urinary pH, making them susceptible to Feline Urinary Syndrome (FUS), a serious urogenital condition. Most complete and balanced commercial vegetarian cat foods are formulated to avoid this condition. But will cats eat these meat-free diets? Will they like them?

Food always reduces to flavor. If cats, dogs, or people don't like a food's taste, regardless of health benefits, they won't keep feeding it to their animals or eating it themselves. Because cats didn't evolve eating plants, they didn't adapt to their unique flavors. This is why a cat's flavor palette is largely focused on what is savory (meat), while largely ignoring succulent and sweet tastes (vegetables and fruits). Many cat owners have heard that many cats refused early generations of plant-based diets. Vegan spokesperson Patrick-Goudreau witnessed her own two cats, Simon and Schuster, refusing their vegan kibble years ago. This became stressful for Patrick-Goudreau. She would add nutritional yeast to tempt them, but even when she managed to get her cats to eat the food, they were far from enthusiastic. As she summarizes on her podcast:

> Keeping my cats safe from harm, keeping them happy, making sure they're healthy, that they're getting the nutrients and calories that they need to thrive is pretty much my number one priority when it comes to my cats' wellbeing. And having to fight them at every meal kind of negates all of these goals.[33]

This is changing. Not only are modern feline vegetarian diets more appetizing and healthier, but cellular meats will soon arrive. Cultured mouse and chicken meats, and an infinite assortment of animal and fish proteins, are set to appear on pet food shelves over the next two to five years. The distinction between animal-sourced and non-animal proteins is going to shift into simply feeding the healthiest nutrient formulation for a pet, and ethical feeding friction will be a thing of the past.

This book is not recommending that cat owners feed their feline a homemade animal-meat or vegan diet. There's far less leeway in balancing the essential nutrients for a cat than for an omnivorous dog or human. Cat owners experimenting with homemade, nutritionally inadequate diets for their cats have caused much of the bad reputation suffered by plant-based foods. If done *properly*, cats can be maintained on animal meat–free diets as healthily as dogs. Still, it's a bigger leap of faith—and nutritional science. You should also bear in mind that ensuring your cat stays "truly vegan" means keeping him or her indoors *all the time*. If cats are allowed outside, who could blame them for engaging with their inner predator and killing small mammals and birds? In the United States, at least ten times as many rodents and birds are killed each year by pet cats as are used in biomedical research, a shocking toll.[34] The ethics of restricting a cat's freedom in this way is another dilemma feline owners confront each time they close a door or window. Once again, we're seeing that veganism is *our* ideology, not our pets'. A cat's instinct is to hunt, and feeding them a plant-based diet is never going to make them "ethically vegan." It will, however, help reduce the damage humans wreak on the planet.

We've seen that many pet owners feel feeding animal meat to their pets is inconsistent with their values and they'd like to change. Worries about the potentially adverse effects on their pet's health and a lack of understanding on how to make the transition safely have held them back. Shannon Falconer acknowledges: "Although we know, and many others know, that we can get all the nutrients pets need from plant-based sources, there's still a belief, even though it's not true, that all of the nutrients cats need have to come from a source of meat." Yet companies like Because Animals, Wild Earth, V-dog, and Green Petfood, along with veterinarians like Andrew Knight and Ernie, are working to make change increasingly viable. Knight is personally optimistic. He admits: "There are people on the leading edge of social change who are absolutely concerned about feeding meat to cats and dogs." The primary reasons people are switching to plant-based diets themselves are they see it as a healthier alternative, they care about the environment, and lastly, they care about other animals. For now, a reasonable alternative to ease ethical feeding friction for cat owners is to feed a complete and balanced vegetarian cat food one or two days a week. Call it Meat-Free Feline Friday.

The future is even brighter for animal-free pet foods. In the last part of this book we'll explore the novel proteins coming to market that will substitute for conventional animal meat in dog and cat foods. They will do so in a safe and nutritious way that requires no extra effort from their human owners, and will taste just as good, if not better, to cats than beef, chicken, or fish. We'll look at the variety of alternative proteins, from cultured or cell-based meats, to yeast or fungi-based acellular agriculture, to insects and algae, and others soon to become staples in pet food bowls. It's time to elevate the culinary conversation beyond traditional ingredients and embrace new foods that are good for us, our pets, and the environment. The next few chapters of this book explore how we can go about shedding our old ingredient biases and open ourselves to new ways of making food.

9

More Legs, Less Guilt?

Insect-Protein Pet Food

W HAT'S ONE OF the hottest trends in food innovation? Edible insects. Food producers and creative chefs are experimenting with insect protein to satisfy mankind's insatiable palate for meat. Even conventional animal–meat giant Tyson Foods has announced that demand for proteins such as crickets is expected to expand in 2019, "as curiosity and willingness to explore options grows." The market for edible insects in the United States is expected to rise to $153.9 million by 2023, up from $44.1 million in 2018.[1] From gourmet grub restaurants to cricket cookies and cuchamás (green caterpillar) tacos, these crunchy critters are attempting to be less "yuk" and more "yum." Naturally, savvy pet food companies are jumping onto the trend, launching cricket and mealworm dog foods. A 2014 paper analyzed the amino acid content of five insect species as possible protein sources for use in pet foods. Four of these insect species exceeded both the National Research Council's canine and feline mammal requirements for growth of all essential amino acids and crude protein.[2] So, would eating and feeding insects be better for the environment and reduce animal suffering?

We've actually been feeding insects to farmed animals for decades, especially fly larvae and mealworms, as high-protein alternatives to fishmeal. Early studies proved that chickens and pigs raised on fly larvae diets grew just as quickly and large as when fed animal meat or soybean meal,[3] and researchers are now beginning to explore how to further optimize black soldier fly larvae feed to replace fish and soybean proteins.[4] Scientists are also experimenting with ways to use fly larvae to process the biowaste of farmed-animal production.[5] Why the sudden interest in insects? As with most questions, the answer comes down to money.

The animal feed industry is exploring these alternative protein sources not because they fear climate catastrophe or are guilty about animal suffering, but because it could be cheaper. However, when it comes to feeding people and pets rather than livestock, price is only one factor in the corporate calculus. To make a successful food product, a cricket, fly, or mealworm must taste good. Do they? Early indications suggest that people seem to think so. Adventurous omnivores have publicly embraced insect dishes for the past several years. Craving new flavors and textures, as well as a bit of bravado, innovative chefs and experimental home cooks post recipes and videos of frying beetles, scorpions, and spiders on thousands of websites and blogs. These piquant pioneers may be onto something: unique flavors. Many insects have been described as tasting like chicken, beef jerky, bananas, nuts, or popcorn, although it's widely reported that insects tend to adopt or enhance whatever flavors they're cooked in. Clever chefs tap into the visual visceral reaction most people experience when a spindly spider or cluster of crickets adorns their plate to amplify a daring dining experience.

For widespread acceptance of insect proteins, we'll need to transcend theatrics and focus on flavor, health, and cost. Future insect foods are likely to disguise an insect's natural appearance in favor of meals and flours, molding the protein the same as minced animal meats. The resulting foods made from insects will be indistinguishable from any other cuisine. Insect protein promises to be a healthy protein source, rich in amino acids and essential fatty acids and low in fats. The international food industry is recognizing this potential, and insect proteins are generating a huge amount of, ahem, buzz. Global food giant Cargill is investing heavily in insect protein research, forecasting a future protein pinch in which animal meats will be reserved for humans and pets, not fed to farmed animals. Some progressive insect farms are even converting to "human-grade insect" production. Thailand, for example, has about 20,000 domestic cricket farms that produce an average 7,500 metric tons of insects a year for human consumption.[6] Although this is a proverbial cricket drop in the meat bucket, it represents an emerging open-mindedness for alternatives to animal proteins within the human and animal food industries.

The environmental and economic advantages of producing insect proteins are becoming better understood. Growing a kilogram of crickets uses twenty-five times less feed and substantially less water and energy than producing the same amount of beef, according to the United Nations Food & Agriculture Organization. The infographic below[7] summarizes the substantial environmental and greenhouse gas (GHG) benefits of choosing insect meal over vertebrate meal in our pet food.

	Grams of greenhouse gases released per kg of live weight (Oonincx et.al, 2010)	Kilos of feed needed per kg of live weight (Collavo et.al, 2005, Smil, 2002)	Meters sq of land needed per gram of protein (Oonincx & de Boer, 2012)	Liters of water needed per gram of protein (Miglietta et.al, 2015)
Insects (crickets for GHG & feed, mealworms for land & water)	2	1.7	18	23
Chickens	n/a	2.5	51	34
Pigs	1,130	5	63	57
Cows	2,850	10	254	112

Figure 5: Benefits of Choosing Insect Meal Over Vertebrate Meal.

Dried crickets are currently the most popular insect being used to feed pets and people. They contain more protein than beef, chicken, or pork. Each 100 grams of crickets possesses over 20 grams of pure protein, compared to 31 grams of protein in beef.[8]

So why isn't everyone already chowing down on crickets or munching mealworms? Many are. In numerous countries and cultures, insects have been a dietary staple for centuries. It's estimated that about two billion people worldwide enjoy insects as snacks or side dishes.[9] Approximately 1,900 different insects are used in traditional diets, and are most popular in Thailand, Japan, China, Australia, and Peru. Westerners are waking up to the unique benefits insects have as food. Exciting companies like Eat Grub, formed in 2014 by Shami Radia and Neil Whippey, and Dr. Beynon's Bug Farm, with its on-site Grub Kitchen, are sharing insect dishes with people unfamiliar with dining on bugs. Sustainable restaurateurs around the globe, including Helsinki's award-winning Ultima, are joining what is estimated to be a global one-billion-dollar food insect market within the next three years. That's a lot of crickets.

In Europe, the entomophagy (edible insects) market is predicted to be worth $85 million (€65 million) by 2020. If insect foods become more popular, they could potentially reduce consumption of vertebrate meat, moving farming away from intensive animal agriculture. Another strong argument for consuming insects instead of mammals is that these "food bugs" don't transmit mammalian or avian diseases and viruses to humans. What about feeding insects to our dogs and cats?

Species-Appropriate Snacks

We already are. In early 2019, Purina launched a chicken, egg, and cricket recipe dog food under their innovative protein brand, RootLab. Alternative protein startups like California's Tiny Farms and U.K.-based Bug Bakes are also turning to food-grade crickets to replace animal meat in their pet foods. Tiny Farms co-founder Andrew Brentano explains: "The biology of insects is very efficient. They're essentially cold-blooded, so they're not constantly burning calories to keep themselves warm. They very efficiently convert what they eat into their body mass."[10] We've seen that it takes 20 percent less feed to produce one kilogram of crickets than it does to produce the same amount of beef, and a third of the feed needed to grow a pig for slaughter. These savings and efficiencies make crickets attractive as a healthy, novel animal feed and pet food protein.

Canadian cricket supplier Entomo Farms offers animal-meat farmers a "practical, easy solution" to reduce their feed costs. It offers wholesale cricket flour and mealworm flour to be used in livestock and pet feed. Entomo Farms is currently working with a number of global partners, including leading Canadian universities and Canadian food chain suppliers and farmers, to advance its cutting-edge biotechnology, which it calls "Geoentomophagy." Entomo Farms dedicates an entire section of its website to pet food, explaining that trendy raw-meat diets have overburdened the animal protein–production capacity of the planet. They suggest switching the animal meats in pet food to insect proteins, and promise "astronomical benefits for the globe." Entomo envisions a new eco–pet food market that will maximize nutrition for pets while reducing the ecological footprint of pet foods.

Ross Lamond is another young entrepreneur investing his heart and soul in the new insect market. His startup, Bug Bakes, was the first to offer an insect-based dog treat in the United Kingdom. He started the company after graduating from the University of Glasgow, where he'd specialized in international law. It was during an environmental class that he first learned of the planetary devastation caused by animal farming:

I'd heard the message "Reduce the global impact of meat, eat less meat," but I'd always just thought it was just one of those things, like "Yeah, I'm sure you could, but does that really matter?" So, when I actually learned that animal agriculture is the most environmentally damaging practice on the planet, I was totally shocked. It was at this same time that the United Nations wanted us to start adopting insect protein because at a basic level it's the same as livestock: it's just animal protein. It's pretty straightforward. But environmentally it's much less intensive.

Chatting with his parents one weekend about his idea, Lamond mused: "You know what, even if people won't eat insects, our cats and dogs would." The moment he said it aloud, he realized it made perfect sense.

Some quick research revealed that while Entomo was beginning to create insect protein for pets in Canada, nobody had yet brought the concept into Europe or the United Kingdom. Lamond found many Internet forums where scientists declared, "Insects are the future of pet food." However, nobody seemed to actually be doing it. So, fresh out of university, he made a decision: "Someone's going to do this, and there's no reason why I can't at least give it a go. Then I can always say that I made the U.K.'s first insect food for pets. . . . And it's actually going pretty well!"

He's right. Looking at Lamond's impressive website and thriving pet treat subscription business, it's hard to imagine that he started out cooking handmade treats in his mom's oven. His initial plan was to come up with the Bug Bake recipe and outsource the production to a professional producer. The problem was, there were only one or two companies in the United Kingdom willing to work with insects, and unless he ordered more than ten or twenty metric tons of treats, he could only choose pre-made recipes off a menu. Of course, none of those dog treat recipes included insect protein. Lamond quickly realized, "Oh God, I'm going to have to do this myself!"

The first step was to get his home kitchen licensed as an animal-byproduct food production plant, a tedious and time-consuming process. After he made his first batch of oven-baked treats by hand, he used the profits to buy proper cooking machinery. Lamond adds his cricket flour order onto that of his friends at Eat Grub, another U.K. food company that makes high-protein bars from crickets. Because Eat Grub makes human-grade products, Lamond knows his dog treats will get the highest-quality crickets. In fact, he's so confident that this is the case that he's more than happy to nibble on Bug Bake dog treats himself: "They smell quite nice, but they're a bit bland, and very crunchy." He cooks his dog treats at a low temperature long enough for them to thoroughly dry out, meaning they last for well over a year, with zero added preservatives.

After speaking with a food product consultant and several veterinarians (including his brother), Lamond was confident his treats were safe and healthy. His family Leonberger, Lyra, was his first taste tester, and remains the face of Bug Bakes. Lyra is also named as the company's co-founder, and her portrait is the company logo. Sadly, she passed away just a year before we spoke with Lamond. Bug Bakes is more than a corporate business venture for him; it's a way to remember a beloved pet. He tells us:

> On the back of the packet, it says, "Make sure there's drinking water nearby," and on the drawing of the dog bowl I've put her name on it. It's just tiny things like that.

For now, Lamond is still running Bug Bakes from home, but he's got bigger plans. He laughs: "I've got a very understanding family! They think it's a really good idea, so they've been really supportive. I'm now scaling up to create my own dedicated mini-factory. If it works out, it's kind of a cool story."

Pet food companies like Lamond's are actually tapping into the ancient dog- and cat-feeding behavior of eating crickets in the wild. Still, Lamond is wary of falling into the "natural fallacy." Sometimes in our fantasy of "nature is best," we forget that everything "natural" isn't fun, safe, or healthy. As Lamond says, there are a lot of advantages to scientific progress and modern life:

> Cats and dogs would eat insects in the wild: in that sense the food is natural for them. But to be honest, I don't care what's "natural" for them. Antibiotics aren't "natural" for me, but if I'm going to get sick, I'd rather lie in bed for two days than two weeks. Cats and dogs aren't "natural."

Lamond was recently approached by a fellow exhibitor at a pet food show, who challenged him: "You know this food isn't 'natural.' A dog is just like a wolf. I shared a post on my Instagram the other day of a dog's skull next to a wolf's skull, and you couldn't tell the difference." Lamond laughs, pointing out that if you take a breed of dog that's the same size and shape as a wolf, the skull comparison would make sense: "But if you take a pug and put that skull next to a wolf's, I can guarantee you'll be able to tell the difference." One woman selling raw exotic meats for dogs, particularly ostrich and camel tissues, said to him: "When would a wolf ever eat your insect food in the wild?" Lamond replied: "When would a Chihuahua ever catch and kill a camel?"

When you study insect proteins, they're almost indistinguishable from any other animal protein. Veterinarians have also used crickets as a hypoallergenic protein source for pets with food allergies. Germany's Green Petfood, which also produces vegetarian pet food, has launched a complete and balanced dog food, InsectDog, alongside its popular VeggieDog, proclaiming crickets as "the protein source of the future." CEO Klaus Wagner explains:

> Besides providing first-class protein, insects contain valuable fatty acids that support the health of your four-legged friend's skin and coat. An increasing number of dogs are allergic to all kinds of protein sources, particularly animal protein. Their owners try everything from horsemeat to ostrich to kangaroo. Of course, most of these ingredients must be imported from far, far away, which also creates carbon dioxide emissions. Most dogs haven't been in contact with insect protein yet, thus our InsectDog—containing insects raised in Europe—is a real blessing for all dogs that have literally tried everything else. We see it as our social and ecological mission to establish insect protein in dog food, but also in people's mindsets.

And then there's the downright wacky wonder-food of insects, cockroach milk. In 2006, Nathan Coussens, a young scientist at the University of Iowa, noticed shiny crystals spilling out of the gut of a certain type of cockroach embryo (*Diploptera punctata*) during dissection. He noted the unusual finding, but the observation remained shelved for years, dismissed by his colleagues as metabolic waste products. It would later be determined that Coussens was actually observing cockroach milk in a previously unrecognized crystalline form.

Cockroaches have milk? *Diploptera punctata* is the only known type of cockroach that gives birth to live young. A single crystal of their milk has three times the energy of an equal amount of buffalo milk. Similar to other mammalian breast milks, cockroach milk crystals are a complete food source, rich in proteins, fats, sugars, and all essential amino acids. The milk also contains ample stores of essential nutrients such as oleic acid, conjugated linoleic acid, omega-3 fatty acids, short-chain and medium-chain fatty acids, vitamins, and minerals. During digestion of these crystal proteins, amino acids are released at a continuous rate, and the high protein heterogeneity inside a single *in vivo*–developed protein crystal lends it "superfood" properties.[11] An international team of scientists from the United States, Japan, Canada, France, and India recently described the crystalline cockroach milk as a "fantastic" protein supplement.[12] Because these milk crystals are remarkably stable, the milk could be produced in large quantities with the help of a yeast-based growing system. Later, this book will explore other non-animal proteins that can be "brewed" using biofermentation.

Cockroaches may become the new "cows": you can eat them as well as milk them. Another species, the inch-long (25-mm) speckled or lobster cockroach, *Nauphoeta cinerea*, can be ground into a flour and has a protein content over 40 percent more than normal wheat-based flour (63.22 percent versus 9.8 percent).[13] Brazilian food scientists at the Federal University of Rio Grande recently developed a novel method for using special-bred food-grade *N. cinerea* that results in a cheaper, healthier alternative to traditional flours. When viewed alongside plant-based flours, it's impossible to tell the difference. It also reportedly tastes the same, perhaps even better. This "insect flour" contains eight essential amino acids and a relatively high quantity of omega-3 and omega-9 fatty acids. When baked in cakes, breads, or protein bars, people don't notice they're eating an insect until they're told. Then they're a little shaken. Researchers believe these "cockroach superfoods" will play a pivotal role in the solution to food shortage in the decades to come.

Scalability Challenges

Of course, entomophagy can only make a significant difference if insects are mass-produced, and this is proving more of a challenge than expected.[14] Insects still require relatively large amounts of water, approximately twenty-three liters for each gram of protein. Although this is significantly less than the 112 liters used for a gram of beef protein, it's not much less than chicken protein at twenty-four liters per gram. Most challenging, however, is the strong North American and European ingredient bias against eating insects.

For this reason, Andrew Knight is skeptical about insect-based meats, guessing that consumers "who are not willing to endure the minor discomfort of dropping meat as it currently stands because they like the taste" will not be willing to endure the even more discomforting thought of consuming a cockroach. In his view from a marketing perspective, insect-based pet food is "probably dead in the water." Knight also points out that if people in other countries have been eating insects for centuries, surely companies would have invested in this industry a long time ago. For him, the fact that they haven't suggests that it's not possible to scale it up and make a profit by breaking into other countries: "I would guess that that's an indication that insects are not going to fly." Knight laughs. "No pun intended!" Part of the reason for this lack of growth may be that in countries like Thailand where people already eat insects, it's traditionally low-income fare. This is another barrier to encouraging more people to substitute "premium beef" with "poor bugs."

As we mentioned, at least one of the big pet food producers is still optimistic. In early 2019, Nestlé Purina began a campaign to "re-educate" consumers on what "premium" pet food means, promoting new cricket, carp, and chicken-organ dog foods. They created RootLab Chicken, Egg & Cricket Recipe to begin testing the market's appetite for bug-based dog chow. Purina describes the new diet this way:

> We don't view crickets as a trend, but rather a lasting solution for how we bring great nutrition to our dogs while respecting our world. Pound for pound, crickets offer 2 x the protein of beef. A kilogram of crickets only produces 1 gram of greenhouse gas, whereas a kilogram of beef produces 2850 grams. Our crickets are raised in Canada where they're fed an organic, vegetarian, custom-made diet.[15]

Even though science backs bugs as an excellent protein source for dogs, convincing customers that crickets are a "premium ingredient" might be tough, even for a pet food giant such as Purina.

Do Insects Suffer? A Primer on Animal Pain and Suffering

Another concern is whether insects deserve the same welfare protections as vertebrate animals. Do crickets or cockroaches suffer pain, anxiety, and stress? Where do insects lie on the ethical scale for animal advocates and vegans? Chris Bryant of the Cellular Agriculture Society worries that including insects in the same category as plant-based proteins is misleading:

> For me, it probably makes concerns about animal suffering much worse. It's a bit obtuse to think about insect suffering, but I'd hazard a guess that there's something going on: after all, bees know when you piss them off! Maybe they can't formulate complex emotions in the way we can, but they presumably suffer on some kind of a level that warrants caring about at some point. Just by the tiny size, you might have to have a hundred insects for a meal rather than half a chicken or one percent of a cow, so you need many, many more of them. I think clean meat and plant-based meat are a good way to move away from animal suffering, whereas eating insects might address many of the environmental concerns but possibly lead to much more animal suffering.

He's got a point. What if by scaling up food-insect production, we end up harming many more feeling beings? If people like Bryant are right, insect farming could result in the suffering of trillions instead of billions. There are a few convincing arguments against this, but let's address the elephant beetle in the room: Do insects feel pain the same way that cows, pigs, chickens, or fish do? You may have guessed that, once again, it's complicated.

There's mixed scientific evidence about the pain perception of invertebrates. Pain is difficult to study, and the extent of discomfort a nonverbal species experiences is hard to quantify objectively. Even pain assessment in dogs, a species with which we share a unique empathy, is still considered controversial and lacks clear consensus. Although there are numerous ways to investigate pain perception in other beings, let's focus on two general observational elements commonly used: nociception and emotional interpretation. Nociception is the reflex observed whenever an animal encounters a noxious stimulus. They withdraw a limb, flee, or avoid the cause as a means of self-preservation. Nociception doesn't prove something hurts, only that a reflex exists to avoid a dangerous stimulus. This type of pain in humans is often referred to as epicritic pain, and describes the pain experienced when you place your hand on a hot stove and immediately withdraw it due to spinal reflexes. This is a highly localized painful sensation, most often associated with the skin. We can easily observe nociceptive reflexes in other animals: stick a needle in a dog or a cricket, and they squirm and flee.

Some experts say this observation alone is adequate to classify the stimulus as painful, whereas others require additional evidence. Neuropathic pain (pain originating from the nerves or nervous tissue rather than damaged tissues) and somatic pain (skin, muscles, joint, bones, or organs) may also be grouped into the epicritic category. Examples of neuropathic pain include hitting your funny bone, sciatica, and diseases that damage neurons, such as multiple sclerosis, certain cancers and chemotherapy, and spinal cord injuries.

The other general classification of pain is known as protopathic and is related to the second element we often use to interpret animal suffering: emotion. Protopathic pain is not thought of as an acute, highly localized, discrete focus of discomfort, but rather a slow, delayed, and general feeling of ache. The throbbing pain you feel the day after you touch the stove is a classic example of protopathic pain. Remembering that painful sensation and avoiding the stove completes the emotional interpretation of pain. In research, if an animal experiences a painful shock in a certain location, they learn to avoid that spot. That avoidance further supports that the stimulus was painful by human standards.

This is where the pain debate really begins. We can only interpret pain in human terms. This severely, if not conclusively, prohibits humans from ever truly knowing if another being experiences pain and suffering the way we do. Philosophers refer to this as the "argument from analogy," and it applies here because if we see a dog or cricket squirm after a needle-stick, we conclude it is painful to them because that is how humans respond to being stuck. This is contestable because even though many animals may have identical nervous systems, hormonal reactions, and behaviors associated with human pain, since they're animals they may actually have entirely different emotional responses. Critics who argue that animals don't experience pain the same as humans do rely on this sort of logic. But does that argument make biological sense?

If we accept natural selection as the preferred method for life to adapt and progress, then pain seems to be an attribute worth saving. Endogenous opioids, those natural pain-killing hormones, and nervous tissues are found throughout invertebrate and vertebrate species.[16] Sensing and avoiding pain is one of the most basic requirements for self-preservation and species propagation. An animal that can't sense it's overheating or freezing won't survive long. Surely the fact that pain-sensing mechanisms are found in millions of other animal species indicates their utility and value to life. When a cow bleats after branding, that indicates pain to us. When a chicken cowers in a cage as a person approaches, that indicates the remembrance of pain. When a pig squeals a warning when a water hose is raised, we interpret that as the anticipation of suffering.

Pain is a perceptual phenomenon, isolated to the inner workings of an animal's nervous system. Pain is not eliminated or reduced simply because an animal is covered in fur, hooved, or has gills. Pain is woven into the fabric of life as we know it, and it must be our obligation and duty to avoid causing pain and suffering to other humans and animals. And that may include insects. If we neglect the possibility that insects suffer, it is feasible that we will move from one intensive system of animal abuse to another, where conscious animals are cruelly farmed in greater numbers than ever before. There's an emerging body of research that suggests insects such as crickets are conscious. Science has proven for decades that many insects are capable of relatively complex cognitive tasks. Even cockroaches, a lowly bug many squash without hesitation, demonstrate place learning, the process of linking experiences with the locations of occurrence.[17]

Regardless, when it comes to the cognition and welfare of animals and insects, we should revisit Jeremy Bentham's famous observation: "The question is not, Can they reason? nor, Can they talk? but, Can they suffer?" Let's ask a cricket farmer. Dutch insect farmer Bert Nostimos has farmed crickets for pet food for forty years and believes that "the stress is very high inside the boxes and, with medicine, you can reduce the stress." "Medicine" in this case means pumping the cricket boxes full of mood-altering hormones, something not all of us would feel comfortable adding to our pet food. Nostimos describes himself as "thinking like a cricket," sometimes even sleeping in the nursery to prevent his insects becoming, in his words, "depressed."[18] This lifelong cricket farmer's belief in insect distress is not unfounded. Many invertebrates have mechanoreceptors that serve as pain receptors;[19] they produce opioids (key to regulating pain in mammals), avoid sources of potential injury, or struggle when poisoned or restrained, as we've discussed. All or any of these responses could indicate an insect's conscious experience of pain.

Based on all available evidence, it's safe to conclude that insects can certainly experience nociception and epicritic pain. But are insects capable of *consciously suffering* as a result of that pain? Some argue that because insects lack a formed brain, they can't really feel pain. Neuroanatomical research indicates that it's possible. It is accepted within the scientific community that "the absence of a neocortex does not appear to preclude an organism from experiencing affective states."[20] The insect brain supports functions analogous to those of our vertebrate midbrain and basal ganglia structures, which might enable subjective experience,[21] suggesting insects may also possess this "basic consciousness." However, some have argued that because insects continue with normal activities after they've been badly hurt, their experience of pain must be superficial.[22] Yet these interpretations about capacity for pain and suffering are both based on insects' similarity to or difference from vertebrates. Biomedical scientist

Jane Smith warns of the danger of dismissing suffering simply "because we cannot imagine pain experienced in anything other than the vertebrate or, specifically, human sense."[23]

Is Insect Farming an Ethical Option?

Even if insects consciously process pain and distress on a comparable level to vertebrates, many insist that it's more ethical to farm invertebrates because we're not depriving them of "a good life" in the same way as other animals. Whereas farmed vertebrates are slaughtered early in their natural life span, wild insects live very short, arduous lives and typically suffer potentially traumatic, painful deaths. Proponents also argue that it's relatively easy to humanely kill farmed crickets, freezing them into a painless and natural torpor state, and essentially sending them into a deep, terminal sleep. If we farm them responsibly with adequate space, we might consider their lives to be potentially *better* in captivity. This is Green Petfood CEO Klaus Wagner's philosophy:

> We're aware that there's an ethical discussion around this topic. Even vegans don't agree upon the question if the life of an insect can be compared to the one of a vertebrate. Some say yes; some say insects don't have a "soul life" like vertebrates do. Either way, we make sure that our insects are treated carefully. The insects that we use in our InsectDog are specially cultivated for our food. We generally use larvae of the mealworm or of the *hermetia illucens* [black soldier fly]. The insects are kept in a warm, hygienic environment and reproduce naturally. To start the food manufacturing process, they are initially stunned using cold water. Insects already fall into the so-called hibernation (winter sleep) at quite low temperatures. After that, they are processed to meal and oil very quickly. That way, we make sure that the insects don't suffer.

Entomo Farms has developed what it calls "Cricket Condos," which allow crickets (a naturally swarming species that likes being in a dark, warm place) to live in a way that mirrors as closely as possible how they would exist in the wild. They're free to hop from one feeding station to another and can burrow deep into the "condos" if they want. Harvesting time comes near the end of their natural life cycle, which is only six weeks. Bug Bake's Lamond is quick to contrast this humane farming model with traditional livestock farming, highlighting that the only way you can farm physiologically inefficient livestock efficiently is to factory farm the animals, lining them up like sardines in a can. "People say that eating insects is disgusting," he says. "Really, the thing that's truly disgusting is factory farming."

Lamond also points out that there's not many truly humane ways to kill conventional livestock: "When people say, 'Oh with a bolt gun they don't feel it,' well, they do feel the two days in the truck down, queued up for slaughter one-by-one. The actual moment of death might be humane, but the process of actually getting them to the slaughterhouse is not great." By contrast, freezing insects into a coma-like state simply taps into their natural evolutionary response to cold.

Other companies are using black soldier flies and setting up dark, quiet tubes that the maggots will naturally crawl up into when they're ready to transform into beetles. While these flies might be killed slightly before their natural death, Lamond remains confident that this is a preferable demise to anything one would find in a conventional slaughterhouse. "There's no pretty way to kill an animal," he says, "but that's probably the most elegant way I can think of to die." Research by Welsh supplier Bug Farm Foods found that over 70 percent of people who classify themselves as vegan or vegetarian will happily eat insects because "they can be farmed and killed ethically."[24]

Of course, not every vegan agrees, and Lamond has come under attack from some of the remaining 30 percent. He's bemused at why vegans are attacking a tiny startup creating eco-friendly dog treats, especially as he's supportive of a vegan lifestyle: "Nothing is truly black and white, but I genuinely think the vegan diet is really close to what we should be doing in the future." Lamond believes strongly that a plant-based diet marries up perfectly with insect farming, because insects can be fed almost anything. Insects are incredibly efficient at converting organic wastes into protein, meaning you can feed them the vegetable waste we don't eat. Of course, environmental impact isn't the main concern for many vegans, and Lamond has a convincing argument for the ethics of insect farming:

> A lot of vegans will not accept that animals die even in normal agriculture. You have to be aware that insects die on a carrot farm, or on a soy farm, as do mice, badgers, etc. Once a year, there's insect genocide on most vegetable farms. Pesticides kill insects—that's the point—and not in humane ways. At the moment there's not a way to actually farm nutritional resources without having some kind of impact on animal life.

By comparison, farming insects has no accidental casualties, and the "victims" are simply put to sleep in their old age. By Lamond's reasoning, eating insects may be a more "vegan-friendly" option than plants. Farming insects, he believes, is actually consistent with veganism in the sense that nothing or nobody has to be killed to feed them. Because far less land is used than in vertebrate or plant farming, you can leave nature to be nature, which means more respect for wild animals than plowing them down at vegetable harvest or poisoning them with pesticides. For Lamond, the answer is a plant-based future with a practical mindset.

Although smaller, ethical brands may care about their insects' well-being, how likely is this to be the case when insect farming takes place on a large scale? Search Google for "cricket farming" and you'll find thousands of crickets packed into plastic bins, hardly ideal conditions for their welfare. Despite the best efforts of scientific outreach programs and education, the growth in the edible insect industry doesn't necessarily equate to greater empathy toward bugs and their well-being, especially if we're only feeding them to our pets and are unwilling to eat them ourselves.

There is also overwhelming evidence that fish feel conscious pain,[25] but most humans continue to find it difficult to emotionally connect with aquatic species or empathize with their suffering. It's not easy for most humans to relate to animals that aren't "cute and cuddly." Lewis Bollard of the Open Philanthropy Project laments the "dearth of funding" around the welfare of non-charismatic animals like fish, chickens, and others that people don't think about or relate to as easily.[26] This suggests it will be even harder to garner public sympathy for cockroaches and crickets. If we're comfortable with farming insects for pet food *en masse* but care even less about their humane treatment than we do about the treatment of fish and chickens, there may be serious consequences for their welfare. It's possible we will see severely stressed creatures crammed into tiny containers without medication or welfare concerns. Lamond argues that farming insect populations too densely means the yields will suffer, but we've already seen in poultry farming that when animals live short lives before slaughter and can be farmed by the billions, the economies of massive numbers outweigh any individual losses.

Still, insects live for a mere six weeks. Even if they're stuck in a tiny plastic box for that time, how bad can forty days of discomfort be? Although humans may view an insect's life as relatively short and meaningless, it may not feel that way to the insect. Zoologist Kevin Healy believes smaller animals can have superior cognitive abilities because they perceive independent stimuli when larger animals perceive continuous images; research indicates blowflies are capable of incredibly fast brain processing.[27] So fast, in fact, that biologist Donald Broom wonders: "Perhaps blowflies perceive humans as slow and inconsequential."[28]

If farmed insects experience heightened awareness of stimuli, the actions of their human captors would be anything but inconsequential. Even if Healy is wrong, philosopher Bernard Rollin argues that animals with more basic cognition might cope less well with pain, because they are "inexorably locked into what is happening in the here and now." Rollin worries that if insects don't understand their pain will end, "their whole universe is pain; there is no horizon; they are pain."[29] Nostimos may be anthropomorphizing when he worries about the mental health of his crickets. But if future research proves that these trillions of insects do suffer and we have *not* addressed their welfare, the moral consequences of upscaling their use in the pet food industry are appalling. Perhaps the numbers involved, and the evidence of invertebrate stress and pain that we already have, should be enough to advocate a precautionary principle toward farming insects.

* * *

Insects are complicated. There are no easy answers in biology. Insect pet food is arguably a better option than farming vertebrate animals for pet food. If insects can be farmed humanely at large scale, some will agree it is a better option than farming plants. The good thing is, we may not have to choose between animals, plants, and insects for long. In the next three chapters, we'll explore how yeast, fungal, and bacterial proteins along with cellular meats may help us avoid future animal and insect ethical dilemmas. At the 2019 ProVeg New Food Conference in Berlin, Germany, the Good Food Institute's Annie Osborn posited the notion of *cultured insect meat*, suggesting insect cells could be a superior platform for efficient, low-cost production given their durability and scale-up potential, and the fact that there are multiple serum-free media formulations already available commercially for insect cells.[30] Ultimately, insects are just one option in an increasingly exciting food revolution for pets and people.

10

Ancient Proteins for Present-Day Pets

TWENTY-FIVE THOUSAND YEARS ago, a deerskin-clad troop was trekking stealthily through the woods, three large dogs trailing behind. The humans tirelessly scanned the underbrush for bright hues of berries, the twitch of a rabbit, or any potential foodstuffs to fill their bellies and feed their family. The dogs swept the forest floor, seeking the scent of larger game, or perhaps fallen prey. Occasionally, one of the humans would stop and smell a leaf or cautiously taste a root or shoot. The dogs were doing the same, exploring flavors, detecting acidity, and evaluating textures for food. Our ancestors spent nearly every waking moment in pursuit of sustenance, seeking to discover new foods to nourish their families. Thousands of years later, humans are once again embarking on a search for new foods, this time replacing woodland treks with computer simulations, the underbrush with bioreactors, and wild game with cellular matrices. We've come full circle, reviving our ancestral quest for food with fresh eyes and sophisticated technologies.

When it comes to the health of our pets, some essential elements may be missing among the comforts of modern existence. Many scientists refer to this as the "hygiene hypothesis": our sterile, clean homes and living environments fail to adequately stimulate our immune systems or build a healthy microbiota, causing us to become hypersensitive and allergic later in life. A growing body of research supports that the increase in human and pet allergies in recent years is from lack of exposure to a wide variety of antigens and allergens.[1] What is actually "good" may be unrecognized by the body's fortress of receptors, and so the immune system mounts a response to it as "bad."

Humans, dogs, cats, and every other life form on the planet today have successfully co-evolved over billions of years. Our bodies are an elegant expression of co-existence. If we eliminate one of our biological building blocks—for example, by never exposing ourselves to certain primal proteins, bacteria, or fungi—a particular immune response may fail to develop or optimize. Perhaps some of the secrets to modern health and longevity are locked within our ancient dirty past.[2]

In his book *Give Your Dog a Bone*,[3] veterinarian Ian Billinghurst suggests that perhaps the "dirtiest" food source, poop, may actually be a highly valuable nutrient for dogs because it contains beneficial gut bacteria. Some of the gross things your dog eats may actually serve as a natural probiotic, adding missing organisms to the gut microbiome. Coprophagia (eating feces) is often associated with gastrointestinal upset or intestinal infections, and the behavior may actually be a dog's attempt to heal itself. What if we could improve our pets' resistance to allergies and disease by feeding them bacteria, fungi, proteins, and fibers missing in modern commercial pet foods? In this chapter, we'll go on a journey with some of the companies working with some incredibly beneficial microbes and nutrients.

Because Animals: Algae and Superfood Nutrition

The latest generation of pet food companies is revisiting the ancient origins of food and applying biotech to create modern proteins. Good examples of the "ancient made modern" are the algae, seaweed, probiotic (*Bacillus coagulans*), and prebiotic plant-fiber inulins used in Because Animals' pet food supplements. By remixing and reimagining pet foods and nutraceuticals, a new wave of pet food companies is reimagining how we feed pets.

Because Animals is run by scientists-turned-entrepreneurs Shannon Falconer and Joshua Errett. The pair originally volunteered at the same cat rescue charity in Toronto, but only met years later when Falconer was working as a microbiologist at Stanford University and Errett was earning his MBA from Indiana. Falconer had already decided that she wanted to dedicate her scientific training to improving the lives of animals; increasing sustainability by subtracting factory farming from the equation would be a bonus. When she launched her pet food supplement in December 2017, human food innovation was busy, but there were only a handful of biotech pet food companies. "I'd always struggled with feeding my pets the most inhumane, lowest-quality ingredients," Falconer tells us. "So moving into pet food made a lot of sense for this reason, and also because nobody was doing it. There's a huge white space where we could really move the needle, if we could make products that will displace meat-based pet food from the shelves."

Serendipitously, her future business partner, Errett, was also exploring opportunities in the pet food industry. He quickly discovered the horrendous quality of meat ingredients in many commercial pet foods. With Falconer's scientific background and Errett's business acumen, they founded Because Animals to facilitate a shared mission around animal welfare. They're assembling a team passionate about ending animal suffering. Their director of sales, Kevin Lahey, is a long-time animal advocate who used to conduct undercover investigations and exposés of factory farming for Mercy For Animals.

Because Animals' first commercial product is an algae-based food supplement for cats and dogs. The green powder combines marine- and land-derived superfoods to provide several nutrients missing from most commercial companion-animal foods. The company bases its products on the fact that, just like in humans, the intestines of cats and dogs are filled with billions of bacteria. When gut bacteria are in proper ratios and populations, this indicates better overall health, including enhanced immunity. Falconer's pet products use a well-established probiotic patented by Ganeden Biotech, *Bacillus coagulans* GBI-30, 6086, whose safety and benefits to digestive and immune health have been supported by more than twenty scientific studies. Another important ingredient they add is inulin, a natural prebiotic fiber used in therapeutic diets to aid gut health.

Ancient algae are also key ingredients in San Francisco–based New Wave Foods' plant-based shrimp. Their alternative shrimp is made from the microalgae eaten by the shrimp it replaces. With the tagline WE DISRUPT SEAFOOD, NOT OCEANS, the company is bypassing the unsustainable process of breeding and killing marine animals for food and going directly to the superfood nutrients seafood consumes. In other words, if we eat what our food eats, wouldn't that be more efficient and more healthy? Co-founded by marine biologist and ocean conservationist Dominique Barnes and biomedical engineer Michelle Wolf, New Wave Foods combines a deep care for ocean life with future food tech.

We see this combination of compassion and science uniting most food biotech startups. New Wave Foods was funded in 2015 by Bay Area biotech accelerator IndieBio, and New Wave has been perfecting its algae- and plant-based shrimp ever since. The company uses only clean, ocean-sourced, and farmed micro- and macro-algae, with a soy-based protein to make its alternative shrimp. Currently, its product is made for people, but there's no reason why foods such as this couldn't be a healthy option for pets in the near future.

Another company drawing on the power of microscopic organisms for future foods is Sustainable Bioproducts, inspired by "extremophiles" found in the superhot pools of Yellowstone National Park. These microbes have evolved to survive in the most inhospitable and resource-deprived environments on Earth, thriving and multiplying at the "extremes." Recognizing their potential as foods, Sustainable Bioproducts is growing them to produce proteins containing the nine essential amino acids required by humans. Add one more, and we have an ideal protein for dogs. At the beginning of 2019, the company announced it had raised $33 million to accelerate its research. CEO Thomas Jonas is excited about the versatility of the company's protein: "It can be savory; it can be sweet; it can be liquid; it can be dairy-like."[4] He hopes to have a food product to sell by 2021.

Ancient Made Modern: Acellular Innovation

Plant-based food innovation is currently dominating animal-free meat markets. Beyond Meat is selling its vegan burgers, sausages, and mince in mainstream grocery stores, and it and Impossible Foods are now featured on restaurant menus around the world. These two companies have raised over $500 million from investors such as Bill Gates, Google Ventures, Hong Kong's Li Ka-shing, and Tyson Foods; in May 2019, Beyond Meat launched a hugely successful public offering. Whatever you may think about their products, these plant-based powerhouses have captured the public's curiosity and interest in animal-free food.

But plant-based isn't necessarily the only way to a sustainable food future. In fact, growing foods from cells through acellular or cellular agriculture may perhaps be the most promising long-term solution to many of the problems that have been outlined in this book. "Lab-grown," "cultured," or "clean" meats may well eliminate the need for massive land use and create less harmful environmental effects, in addition to removing animals from factory farms.

Before we explore these exciting revolutions in food, let's explain the important distinction between "cellular" and "acellular" agriculture. In simplest terms, cellular foods are made from living or once-living cells, and acellular foods are made of proteins and fats without any cellular or living elements from animals.

Acellular agriculture bypasses the need for animal cells, using yeast, fungi, or bacteria to "grow" a protein or fat. An early example of acellular agriculture is synthetic insulin. For decades, diabetics relied on insulin obtained from macerated pig pancreas to treat their disease. In 1978, synthetic insulin was made by inserting human insulin genes (recombinant DNA) into a non-pathogenic bacterium. The bacterium then produced, or synthesized, human insulin in one of the first major medical biotech breakthroughs. Synthetic insulin is now the most commonly used method to treat diabetes and has saved millions of human (and pig) lives. Its success paved the way for acellular agriculture to be used in a wide variety of applications from vaccines to food.

The most common organisms used in acellular agriculture are yeast and fungi. Microbiology professor Nicholas Money's book *The Rise of Yeast* highlights just how exciting these organisms are—not only converting sugar to carbon dioxide, but also making alcohol in the process, which it uses to keep competing microbes away.[5] Over time, brewers and fermenters have isolated and tested specific strains of yeast and fungi, creating a wide database of distinct flavors and brands of alcohols, kombuchas, sauerkrauts, koji, and more. These ancient microbes are about to become the basis for an entirely new category of food. You simply use genetic analysis to find one of the billions of organisms that already produces the specific fat or protein you're looking for (thanks to evolution) or use genetic manipulation to adapt the organism to create the molecule you need. The resulting lab-grown proteins are identical to those found in animal or plant products, without the animal or plant.

One example is Perfect Day's "clean milk," developed using acellular agriculture to replace cow's milk. Founded by Isha Datar, president of New Harvest, a charitable organization devoted to the research, promotion, and production of cultured animal products, Perfect Day is uncovering genetic secrets to create safer and healthier milk. The genes responsible for the production of the primary milk proteins, casein and whey, are added to yeast using specialized 3D printers. The yeast is then fed sugars, and fermentation begins. After a few hours to days, the fermenters begin pumping out new cow milk–free whey and casein proteins. These proteins, not the yeast itself, are used in Perfect Day's final milk product. And tasters can't tell the difference. Perfect Day's "clean milk" tastes, looks, and smells identical to milk from a cow. As well as being more environmentally sustainable and eliminating animal suffering, this milk is healthier, containing only milk proteins, with no cholesterol or lactose. There's also no risk of hidden antibiotics or growth hormones, and no pesticides or farm pollutants. Finally, there's less risk of bacterial contamination, meaning Perfect Day's milk can be stored longer on grocery store shelves. And it makes delicious ice cream! In July 2019, Perfect Day launched its first animal-free dairy product and sold out within hours.

Global food giant Archer Daniels Midland (ADM) understands the potential this company has to disrupt the dairy industry. In late 2018, it announced a partnership with Perfect Day to scale up production. Being able to produce large quantities of "clean milk" quickly will help this startup fulfill its mission to protect the environment. It only takes the company seventy-two hours to make milk from yeast compared to the two to three years it takes for a calf to produce any milk at all. According to farm industry estimates, over 15 percent of all greenhouse gases are produced by meat and dairy production,[6] and we saw how dairy cows suffer in Chapter 3. Whey and casein have historically been too costly for pet foods and are typically associated with lactose, a sugar many dogs and cats don't tolerate well. If we're able to reduce the cost and eliminate lactose, these prized proteins may become more common in future pet foods.

Perfect Day is also developing other dairy products, particularly cheeses, as are other biotech companies. Cheese is one of the most popular foods in Western society, generating an estimated $118 billion in 2019.[7] Cheese is also an essential element of the destructive dairy industry, and is ripe for disruption. In addition to Perfect Day, fellow California startups BioCurious and Counter Culture Labs are looking to change this, developing vegan-friendly cheese that omits the cow as part of the Real Vegan Cheese project. In fact, name an animal product and we'll show you a startup trying to replace it: Oakland-based Geltor's acellular animal-free gelatin hit the market in mid-2017, while Arturo Elizondo, CEO of San Francisco–based Clara Foods, has produced animal-free egg whites in the lab and is now working on scaling up and putting products on sale by the end of 2019.

Meanwhile, most of us are familiar with the Impossible Burger, now a mainstream option in popular restaurants. This plant-based burger uses biotech to mimic "blood," using a unique hemeprotein. Heme is responsible for beef's ruby-red color, metallic tang, and rich umami flavor. It is a complex iron-containing compound bound to blood proteins and deposited throughout muscle tissues. Slaughtered-animal muscles tend to have high concentrations of heme, giving them a distinctive "meaty" taste and "mouthfeel." Impossible Foods believed if it could crack the "heme code," the company could create a nearly identical animal-meat experience. To accomplish this feat, Impossible Foods looked to soy. Impossible found that soy contains the genes to create a form of heme, leghemoglobin. It extracted the genetic code for "soy heme," inserted it into yeast, turned on its fermentation bioreactor, and, *voilà*, the "heme" was found in an Impossible Burger! And people love it.

Critics point out that by using a genetically modified organism (GMO) to produce its product, Impossible Foods is no better than the factory-farm industry. This seems extreme. The goal must be to eliminate animal suffering and environmental devastation, even if that requires using modern GMO products. It's true that the misunderstandings, misleading optimism, and unfulfilled promises, as well as the mistakes of previous generations of corporatized GMO seeds and foods, have left many skeptical about the safety and utility of GMO foods. Those realities can't be erased, but we *can* demand that the producers of the next generation of GMO foods are more transparent in their practices. Producers need to be sensitive to the fact that combining wildly different organisms in "Frankenfoods" isn't the answer to the many problems that face the planet.

In order to feed ten billion humans and three to four billion pets, there need to be significant improvements in food production, including careful genetic advances. Every scientific breakthrough carries promise and peril. Nuclear energy can power a metropolis, or level it. GM foods can nourish the starving or bankrupt family farms and rake in billions. As our genetic editing abilities improve, particularly using CRISPR-Cas9 to delete specific genes rather than insert new ones, researchers can fully embrace applying science to help solve our future food dilemmas. Using modern genetic deleting techniques, it will be possible to modify the organism without meddling with its fundamental DNA structure, preserving the "natural integrity" of the food. Impossible Foods puts it this way:

Since Impossible Burgers made with leghemoglobin generate 87 percent less greenhouse gases, require 95 percent less land and use 75 percent less water to produce than burgers from cows, it would be grossly irresponsible to the planet and its people not to pursue this path.

We won't have to wait long before we see an "Impossible Pet Food." A handful of vegan pet food companies are already using soy and pea proteins, including Netherlands-based Yarrah, Italy's Ami Pet Food, Canada's Gather, and several U.S. pet food companies, including Wild Earth, Halo, and V-dog. Because Animals is planning to release a doggie "dental cookie" made from a cultured protein, and several large and small companies are set to follow. The real pet food change on the horizon reaches far beyond peas and treats and has the potential to disrupt the entire animal meat–based pet food industry. There are a few maverick companies daring to go where many human food companies won't, making food in bioreactors instead of barns.

Wild Earth: Food as a Bridge

Wild Earth is one such maverick, a Bay Area company with a mission to combine natural products with food biotech. The result? Essential nutrients for pets in tasty, bioavailable forms. Ryan started the company with two friends, including food scientist Dr. Ron Shigeta. He added head of operations Dr. Abril Estrada and Ernie as chief veterinary officer a couple of months later. Wild Earth began working with a variety of bacterial and fungal proteins, and encountered an ancient Asian protein, koji. Koji, or *Aspergillus oryzae*, has been perfected by Japanese farmers over thousands of years. This nutritious and savory fermented food is considered a Japanese national treasure. You're probably more familiar with koji than you think; it's the "secret sauce" of miso, soy sauce, and sake and is added to many dishes to boost that umami flavor we taste in the Impossible Burger.

So how did Wild Earth connect koji and fungal proteins with *pet* food? It has Ron Shigeta, Ryan's long-term business partner and co-founder with Ryan of biotech accelerator IndieBio, to thank for this. IndieBio was investing in startups that were using biology to solve the world's largest problems, including food security. Shigeta is a huge foodie, stemming from his college days, when a girlfriend wrote her thesis on food and its social meanings. Fascinated by this idea, Shigeta discovered a greater appreciation of food, an obsession he came to realize many of us share:

> It was really at IndieBio that we realized that food is a bridge. We were investigating all kinds of crazy things: our mission was that biology should be a motive force for the twenty-first century in terms of how we get things; a new paradigm for manufacturing, for producing everything that we use in a sustainable way. A lot of people in academia were very excited about this.

The companies he and Ryan invested in at IndieBio were solving real-world problems with ingenious science. From cancer and medical therapies to treatments for antibiotic-resistant bacterial infections; from long-acting non-opioid chronic pain medication to ways to protect the bee population; from salt-tolerant, drought-resistant plants to making lab robots that can see and think—IndieBio was the hub for these companies.

In terms of IndieBio's time and investment, however, one company stood out: Clara Foods. Clara was IndieBio's first future food investment, and it garnered as much media attention as all IndieBio's other startups combined. In fact, Clara Foods was the only startup that raised its full funding during the IndieBio incubation. It was at that moment that Shigeta knew there was something unique about future foods, and that food and biotechnology could really have a strong relationship. Previous generations had viewed the synergy of food and technology as incompatible, unacceptable, and plain wrong. Not Ron and Ryan. Their years of working in research, medicine, food, and biotech gave them a perspective previously unseen in traditional food companies. It was time to put their money where their minds were. IndieBio ended up investing in about fifteen future food companies. What made those freshman food companies unique was they had a deeply emotional connection with people in a way that biofuels, solar, and wind tech didn't. "What's really special about food is that it's a space where people can change their minds, in a way that none of these other sustainability technologies can," Shigeta says. "People don't really like change, but food is one place where we can change our minds."

At the turn of the twentieth century, Old Chinatown in San Francisco was a tight-knit community that kept to itself, and other people rarely ventured in. For decades, an entire culture lived separately in one of America's most metropolitan cities. Nobody seemed to have any interest in getting to know their neighbors, dispelling the "American melting pot" metaphor, until the pot was literally turned upside down by the great 1906 earthquake. Old Chinatown was completely leveled. The city elders initially considered moving their tenants to another, perhaps safer, location. But as the community rebuilt from the rubble, they noticed something unusual: tourists were flocking to Chinatown. These weren't sightseers seeking Chinese history or culture, but folks craving Chinese food. In the end, it was food tourism that largely saved San Francisco's Chinatown.

As Shigeta puts it, when you sit down at a table with somebody, you eat with them, their history, and their customs. It's a rare, intimate, and emotionally comfortable place where most of us will happily try something different. He says:

> For me, food is a very special place because it's how we do all of our exploring. Most of us only know Thailand, China, India, through the food. Very few people will actually visit those countries, but they're all familiar with them because of their stomachs and their mouths. So, the idea of food as a point of change, as a turning point relating to global climate change, has me very excited.

Instead of waiting days or years deliberating a decision, people will choose what they want to eat quickly, daringly, and ambitiously. If they decide they'd like to try something different, they can simply try it.

In contrast, if we want people to try electric cars, we have to first build an entirely new infrastructure, with a substantial network of battery-charging systems, and train a new generation of sales and repair technicians. Switching to solar power is even more difficult, as it requires reengineering power grids, installing solar panels in homes, and reconstructing entire industries. It doesn't mean that these changes can't, or shouldn't, be made (they must); it means they take substantial time and effort. This isn't the case with food. Curiosity, and a desire to bring something new into our lives through the meals we put on our tables, makes changing diets nearly frictionless. Shigeta believes that if we can use biotech to produce culinary experiences people want, and higher quality, healthier animal-free foods, we can actually do something about climate change in a way that allows *everybody* on the planet to participate:

> I just find that incredibly empowering. We're not just waiting for some policy change in Paris or Stockholm, which will probably never happen. Anybody can participate in making and eating this food. We might feel completely powerless to do anything about climate change and the environment, but then we can walk into a store or a restaurant and buy or order a veggie burger. We can try it, like it, and be part of change in a keystone way. So, I'm incredibly optimistic about tackling global climate change for the first time in my entire life! And I've been thinking about it since the late seventies.

This doesn't just apply to the food we buy and consume for ourselves. We can change from feeding our pets animal meats to giving them plant-based food in a single pet store visit. The options are available; we just have to be open to them.

Which brings us back to fermentation, fungal proteins, and koji. Shigeta was constantly growing koji and fermenting Asian foods in his lab for his family. Ryan would joke: "Hey Ron, that koji stuff, it grows really fast, so be careful; you might contaminate our other experiments!" One day, Ron realized that koji was a potentially excellent protein source. It was the first time he'd considered fungi as unique protein sources, not just flavoring agents. Ron explored his hypothesis: because fungi are evolutionarily closer to animals than to plants, they have similar protein profiles. Fungi don't have brains, nervous systems, or neural tubes, so they're not sentient and don't perceive pain. Eating fungi is no crueler than eating plants. Because fungal proteins are closer to animal proteins, fungi are an appropriate food for pets and people. Koji and many fungal proteins contain all ten canine essential amino acids in greater concentration than beef. We can grow fungi sustainably, using a fraction of the resources and land needed for beef, pork, chicken, or fish. We can also make fungal proteins for pet foods cheaply, which means they're potentially inexpensive. Ron concluded fungal proteins made perfect sense. Wild Earth had begun.

For the Love of Food: Compassionate Beginnings

Ryan's background is in biotech, funding innovative new companies, with a focus on future foods. As passionate as he is about improving human health and environmental sustainability through technology, he is also fervent about improving the lives of the billions of farmed animals. When Ryan first arrived in Los Angeles as a young, idealistic biotech graduate, he was eager to use his intellect and passion to change the world. He set his sights on biotech, particularly innovating in molecular science and medicine.

Surrounded by equally optimistic colleagues restless for change, he settled in with a group of incredibly talented and energetic scientist activists, including many "outspoken" vegans. He recalls telling himself, "I'll never be one of those vegans." One year later, he was one of those vegans. It was probably inevitable, given his long-time vegetarianism. Ryan was brought up loving animals, sharing his childhood Miami home with dogs, cats, and even monitor lizards and iguanas. His Cuban family members were big meat eaters, dining on *ropa vieja* (a shredded beef dish), *pernil* (roasted pork), and *masitas* (fried pork). Meat was something you ate, not something you cared about. All that changed when Ryan turned ten.

Ryan's father wanted fresh pork for his birthday, and he took Ryan to a local hog farm, where they slaughtered pigs in the "classical" Cuban way.

Ryan remembers the moment they pulled the pig out of the pen, all the other pigs squealing in protest. Young Ryan sensed the pigs understood what was happening as their companion was dragged onto a slab and tied down. He vividly remembers the terrified animal convulsing as the farmer plunged a huge knife through its skull. He watched the pig's eyes roll in agony. He recalls: "I was just watching the pig. Nobody else was looking at him; they were all looking away, but I couldn't stop watching. And I watched him suffer and die. It was so deeply disturbing to me."

Ryan had been taught by his family to protect animals. *How could they stand by and not help this pig?* he asked himself. That was the moment he realized the hypocrisy of slaughtering some animals and loving others. He never ate pork again. For a child growing up within Latin culture, this was a big deal. Refusing pork-based Cuban food and proclaiming to be vegetarian was to associate yourself with femininity, weakness, and emasculation within his community. Yet this stereotype didn't make sense to young Ryan. He was a strong, capable kickboxer, who considered himself tough and brave regardless of whether or not he ate animal flesh. He kept his vow to avoid pork despite the cultural stigma, gradually excluding all animal meats and becoming a vegetarian.

These days, movies like *The Game Changers* (which features top vegan athletes) and muscle-bound vegan celebrities help young men realize you don't have to eat animals to be masculine. Still, there's a large number who still see beef burgers and bloody steaks as integral to their macho self-image. Many of Ryan's guy friends still make fun of him for being vegan. His tactic was always to challenge them to watch the harrowing 2005 documentary *Earthlings* with him and "see how macho they really are," and most refused. If they "were really so tough," he said, "Why wouldn't they watch a sappy film about animals?"

These experiences convinced Ryan that the way to reduce animal suffering is "not by trying to convert people to stop eating meat." Instead, he set out to encourage his biotech connections to create tasty, ethical, and sustainable animal-meat alternatives. He wanted them to make foods superior to animal meat in terms of texture, taste, price, and health benefits without taking the idea of "eating meat" away from people: "You can have your 'meat,' and eat it, too!" This "offer something better" strategy provides benefits for farmed animals and the environment not as its primary focus, but as a positive side effect. We saw this in Because Animals' health-forward messaging, and we see it time and time again in the mission of cellular agriculture startups. Cellular and plant-based meats combine all the ideas that Ryan believes in, including future technologies, ending animal suffering, and, through *really good food*, removing the stigma attached to eating "vegan."

Veganism has come a long way since Ryan first moved to L.A. a decade ago, when vegans were "still fringe." Euromonitor International now ranks America as the top market for vegan food products, followed by Germany, Britain, and Australia. The U.S. plant-based market was worth a combined $3 billion at the beginning of 2018, accounting for two percent of all food sales.[8] The amount, variety, and quality of plant-based meat alternatives in grocery stores are exploding. It's no longer "weird" to be vegan or vegetarian, and slowly both are shaking off their hippie, alternative image to become admirable lifestyle choices for the planet, our own health, and animal welfare.

As we've seen, however, although consumers and manufacturers seem hip to animal-meat alternatives, the same can't be said about pet food— yet. Increased acceptance of vegan and vegetarian foods by pet owners hasn't influenced the leading pet food companies to make more plant-based *pet* foods. Most traditional pet food companies persist in clinging to animal meats simply because it's cheap, easy, and accepted. This is why the clean pet food revolution is being waged by young startups, untethered to tradition and convention. Just because something isn't broken doesn't mean it can't be made better. As somebody used to challenging stigma and committed to using biotech to find solutions, Ryan felt that human and pet food was the obvious space to take on next.

Wild Earth's development of koji and fungal proteins as an alternative to animal meat isn't unprecedented. There is another fungal food many Europeans are familiar with: Quorn. Quorn was originally developed by Gerald Solomons, a scientist in the United Kingdom worried about a worldwide protein deficiency after World War II. His answer was a fungal protein. Solomons' team began by growing yeast and fungi in a bioreactor to determine if they could be used as a "microbial food." They managed to grow a tomato plant pathogen, *Fusarium venenatum* fungus, which turned out to be an excellent protein source.

Solomons had his solution; now he needed a product. His company chose the brand name *Quorn* after the Quorn Hunt, famously held in the eponymous tiny village near the company's location in Leicestershire. Unfortunately for Solomons and Quorn, the product was too far ahead of its time to succeed. After twenty years trying to commercialize this product, the mycoprotein was eventually co-developed by ICI and Rank Hovis McDougall and marketed under Marlow Foods, this time named after the source of the fungus, which was discovered in a soil sample from a field near the Thames at Marlow.

Marlow Foods now enjoys annual revenue of around $260 million selling its vegetarian meat substitutes. Marlow was acquired in 2015 by Philippines-based food manufacturer Monde Nissin Corporation for $831 million. Quorn today is greatly improved from the bland, dry veggie burgers of yesteryear. The story of Quorn inspired Ryan and Ron to begin thinking seriously about the potential for koji and other fungal or yeast proteins. Koji is already known for being tasty and safe for humans; all Ryan and Ron needed were tests to prove it was safe for pets, too. Shigeta began brewing more koji in the lab, and Ernie and Abril Estrada started overseeing the product development and testing. Wild Earth was now a real company.

The Miracle of Koji and Fungal Proteins

Koji and many fungal proteins are remarkable foods. The fact that these microscopic organisms can rapidly produce such large amounts of proteins from a diet of simple sugars and carbohydrates is incredible. That they contain all ten canine essential amino acids makes them even more astonishing. Yeast and fungal proteins, including koji, have been shown to support gut health in humans, providing microbiome-nourishing prebiotics and healthy fibers. They also taste amazing and are considered in the Western world to be exotic, fairly gourmet ingredients for humans. This is *really good* food: safe, nutritious, environmentally friendly, ethically sourced, and affordable, making the modern production of fungal proteins nothing short of revolutionary. Using koji and other yeast and bacteria to make proteins and fats means no animals are harmed; there is no risk of a euthanasia drug, antibiotics, or growth hormones entering your pet's body; and it's possible to produce tremendous quantities of this protein source in a hygienic, secure, and localized setting.

Shigeta explains fungal proteins like this: "Koji is not just a fungus. Koji has been with us for thousands of years, and we use it for so many different things. It's almost like going out to eat a bowl of Thai noodles: it's an experience brought over from another culture that we're enjoying." Shigeta *loves* these fermented proteins, describing it as a culinary experience we can happily share with our four-legged friends. Because there are a lot of fungal proteins already being used in food, the Wild Earth team has found it easy to source it from the same vendors providing it to human food companies. Koji, yeast, and other fungal proteins are actually already used in many pet foods, often added to aid digestive health. Wild Earth is the first company to use fungal proteins as the basis of a high-protein dog food. And that's both innovative and exciting.

Many animal cell–based meats are on the horizon that we'll explore later, but it will be a few years before they reach the pet food market. Shigeta points out that whereas you can sell humans food for $100 a pound (or $20 a pint for Perfect Day's animal-free ice cream), it will be years before cell-based meats are cheap enough for use in pet foods. Meanwhile, with the intention of disrupting the pet food industry sooner rather than later, companies like Wild Earth are beginning with yeast and fungi.

Wild Earth scientists sift through those fungal strains most likely to produce the best dog food, separating each one onto media plates to observe what compounds are produced. They're looking for nutrients such as starches, fibers, vitamin profiles, fats, and amino acids. Once an ideal, naturally occurring fungal strain is isolated, it moves to the product development phase. Shigeta explains that one of the benefits of cellular agriculture is that it produces incredible consistency of product: "If you're growing millions of acres of wheat, finding this consistency is more of a problem. We don't see that at the store, but getting the same loaf of bread year in and year out is something that baking companies work very hard to achieve."

It's also hard to store all that perfect wheat. With cellular agriculture, you don't need enormous silos and storehouses for grain storage; you can literally freeze it forever. Because it's grown in a sterile lab, each yeast or fungal strain is free of contaminants and remains in its pure form. After selecting and growing the best strains of fungi, it's removed from the growing medium and pressed, similar to cheese or tofu. Dr. Estrada, Ernie, and another Wild Earth food scientist, Dr. Yvonne Wang, then formulate the food, either using the fungal protein directly in its wet form or drying and converting it into a flour or meal. The fungal proteins can then be used the same as any other food ingredient. Shigeta says: "We want our whole process to be a kitchen first and a lab second."

In Japan, the traditional way to grow koji is to sprinkle it on rice; it immediately starts eating the rice, spreading a white fuzzy frost as it grows. Unfortunately, traditional rice-grown koji doesn't produce a large volume of usable material, meaning rice isn't a viable growth medium for commercial scale. To make it commercially viable, Wild Earth grows its yeast and fungi on special lab-made media using a variety of nutrient sources. Similar to Perfect Day's "clean milk," growing fungal proteins is fast. It takes about three days to go from start to finished protein, compared to twelve to twenty weeks to grow a broiler chicken, or twelve to thirty-six months for a cow.

Wild Earth isn't the only food company pursuing fungal proteins to replace farmed animals. In the United Kingdom, popular vegan chef Derek Sarno, director of plant-based innovation at supermarket giant Tesco, is attempting to replace animal farms with mushrooms. The American-born Sarno previously worked as the senior global executive chef for Whole Foods Market. Along with his brother, Chad, he's launching a mushroom-based meat company called Wicked Meaty, following the success of his plant-based Wicked Healthy range for Tesco. Don't forget, mushrooms are fungi, too.

And Sarno means business, potentially big business. Sarno previously helped Tesco increase its vegetarian and vegan product sales by 25 percent from 2016 to 2017. In his new role, Sarno will work with chicken farmers to convert their chicken houses into "mushroom grow houses," a solution that seemed obvious when he noticed the similarity between the sheds. Packing mushrooms into high-density barns is a far more ethical solution than battery-farming sentient animals. Mushrooms are popular with other vegan chefs. Israeli Harel Zakaim's vegan shawarma shop in Tel Aviv, named Sultana, replicates lamb meat with wild mushrooms, the texture cooked to be similar to chicken. Also in Israel, vegan startup Terramino Foods raised $4.2 million to replicate meat and seafood with mushrooms. The aim of all of these companies is to provide the same great taste and dining experience without the cruelty.

Sarno and his brother also recently launched a new vegan seafood brand, Good Catch Foods. Good Catch uses legumes and algal oil to provide sustainable proteins and realistic seafood flavor, as well as ample servings of healthy omega-3 DHA. Interestingly, Sarno doesn't call himself a "vegan chef," branding himself and his products very explicitly as FREE FROM ANIMALS rather than VEGAN. In Chapter 8 we explored why this might be an excellent communications strategy, expanding the appeal of his food by avoiding potentially controversial language.

"Veganism," Sarno says, "is an ethical lifestyle. What I'm offering through Wicked Healthy plant-based alternatives is just a food choice."[9] He believes this makes his foods appealing to a wider range of people: "Nobody would listen to me if I said I was vegan," he says. "I chose not to be 'vegan' because I could make a larger impact by not saying I was vegan." He views himself as a "plant pusher, not a meat shamer." By collaborating with chicken farmers to make compassionate reforms, his strategy is to join forces with the conventional meat industry to enact change from within.

* * *

Although these innovative startups may be saving the planet and the animals, great nutrition is at the heart of all these companies' agendas. Shannon Falconer is pragmatic about this:

> Yes, we're a mission-based company, but the reality is that even though myself, and every other pet parent, might love the environment and love farmed animals, our pet's health is always going to be the priority. We are not positioning ourselves as a vegan company (although of course we are). We're not positioning our food as the most environmentally friendly diet you can feed your companion animal (although of course it is). We're simply positioning ourselves as creating the highest quality food you can feed your pet.

Innovative pet food startups such as Because Animals and Wild Earth understand that pet owners, first and foremost, care about the well-being and health of their pets. These companies are committed to offering the best pet food possible. This is also why these companies are starting with "non-controversial" plant-, yeast-, and fungal-based pet foods. These are ingredients long-established as GRAS (Generally Recognized As Safe) by the United States Food and Drug Administration (FDA), merely produced and formulated in innovative ways. By merging the ancient with the modern, pet owners can trust them as credible companies, truly dedicated to animal welfare and health, offering animal-meat alternatives with the highest possible quality. From that foundation, these pet food companies will be able to create products that truly disrupt the factory-farming industry. In the next chapters, we'll take a look at what some of these future foods might be.

11

Clean Pet Food and the Promise of Biotech

W<small>E'VE LEARNED THAT</small> although omnivorous dogs can easily thrive on plant-based proteins, the situation is more complicated for cats, who require nutrients typically found in animal meat. We also saw in Chapter 7 that more than two-thirds of vegan owners are not yet confident about feeding meat-free diets to their pets. If you're concerned about the environment, animal welfare, and pet food safety, but uncomfortable with a plant-based feline diet, what do you feed your cat? In her 2018 book *Fellow Creatures,* Harvard philosophy professor Christine Korsgaard confronts this problem, revealing that her beloved cats have forced her to live "a morally compromised life, feeding them the meat that I will not eat myself."[1] Ethical feeding friction for cat owners is serious.

There are an estimated 88.3 million house cats in the United States, each consuming roughly 250 calories a day. Feline diets tend to be heavily animal meat–based, and, as we saw earlier, house cats have become one of the chief predators of the world's oceans. The average American cat eats about thirty pounds of fish per year, about twice as much as their human caregivers.[2] Animal ethicist Bjørn Kristensen estimates that if it takes eight house cats to equal the caloric intake of a human consuming two thousand calories a day, this means that pet cats in the United States are consuming the same caloric intake as approximately eleven million humans.[3] Unlike human diets, the overwhelming majority of a cat's calories come from animal meats and fish. Our purring kitties require an enormous number of suffering animals to fill their bowls. The number of factory-farmed animals will only increase as more cat owners switch to raw meat diets, high-protein formulations, and human-grade pet food.

Harvard's Korsgaard suggests a solution: "Unless it turns out to be possible to artificially concoct an adequate diet for them, we would have to supply them with meat ourselves, or let them hunt . . . with deleterious effects on wildlife. Perhaps artificially cultured meat will eventually solve this problem."[4] In her essay "Veganism, (Almost) Harm-Free Animal Flesh, and Nonmaleficence: Navigating Dietary Ethics in an Unjust World," ethicist Cheryl Abbate points out that the principle of causing the least harm does not necessarily entail that we should only harvest and eat plants. Rather, she says: "[W]e should consider ways to produce and consume animal products without harming sentient animals."[5]

Absolutely. In fact, the science is already well on its way to providing pets with healthy and wholesome cultured meats, and Korsgaard's "eventually" is going to arrive sooner than many realize. Revolutionary biotechnologies are disrupting the traditional meat industry *as you read this book*. A November 2018 article calls vegan and slaughter-free meat alternatives for cats and dogs "a growing frontier" for the pet industry, announcing that "the future of premium pet food is going high tech to satisfy growing consumer consciousness and sense of personal responsibility."[6] This is what Ryan calls "the second domestication"—meat, without the dead animal. We're entering a post-animal food bio-economy.

In his book *The End of Animal Farming*, Jacy Reese highlights a big question for the animal-free movement: "Which products to focus on first: beef, chicken meat, dairy, eggs, or a nonfood product like leather"?[7] But what about pet food? Because American pets are responsible for up to 30 percent of the environmental impact caused by the consumption of farmed animals, it shouldn't be crazy to put the focus on what our dogs and cats are eating. We've seen the extent of environmental harm caused by our pets' meat consumption, along with the immense animal suffering and potential health hazards. We also saw in Chapter 6 that probing the nutritional science of pet food might have broad-reaching impacts for both pet and human health and longevity. As we'll explore in the next chapter, clean pet food might be the surprise catalyst in the animal-free meat revolution due to its potential for more flexibility in texture, taste, appearance, and, most important, acceptance.

Let's start by introducing clean meat as a concept and explore how it might be the answer to our human and pet food emergency. At the end of this chapter, we'll look in particular at the "clean fish" startups creating cell-based shrimp and tuna for human consumption. Today, what's good enough for us is also good enough for our pets, meaning that human-grade clean fish might well be the solution to the cat food crisis that we've been looking for. But first we must decide how we want to use science to help us solve our looming food crisis.

Bad Versus Good Science: Improving Efficiency *Ethically*

Chapter 2 showed that factory-farmed animal agriculture is unsustainable. At some point in the not too distant future, climate change, food shortages, antibiotic resistance, economic pressure, and emerging pandemics from factory farming will force us to find new ways to feed the world. So far, industry has used science to improve meat efficiency in the most unethical of ways. It has pushed farmed animals far beyond their limits of natural productivity, bred chickens to grow fatter and faster and lay more eggs until they bear little resemblance to their ancestors, and altered cows to make more milk and grow more muscle—all to the detriment of their physical and mental welfare. As many as 68 percent more "normally" growing chickens would be needed to produce the same amount of breast meat as conventional fast-growing birds,[8] a horrifying testament to the extent to which mankind has genetically deformed modern poultry. And there's no end in sight to the Frankenfood creatures humans are creating.

At the end of 2018, a "vitamin super-supplement" was developed by Kansas State University researchers to force even more muscle into already anatomically distorted chickens, with the aim of helping the poultry industry make cheaper meat.[9] More muscle mass on the breast and thighs creates more stress on the bones, ligaments, and feet, leading to what we can only speculate is even more suffering. We have to ask ourselves if *this* is the sort of science we want to fix our broken food system. Packing on more flesh and ignoring the environmental damage and abuse caused by animal farming?

It seems many food researchers think it is and are looking for even more unnatural ways to boost a chicken breast. In December 2018, poultry scientists developed a silicon feed additive to strengthen a chicken's bones, allowing for even faster growing and larger broilers.[10] The scientists' stated goal was to address "economic concerns for the poultry industry," allowing farmers to "increase the production efficiency of the world's most commonly consumed meat."[11] If these advances were intended to reduce suffering and improve welfare, we'd be in full support. Instead, these poultry researchers seem determined to make bigger chickens faster, with little, if any, regard for their welfare beyond the bottom line.

The livestock industry is just getting started with the manipulation of food animals. In addition to hormones, antibiotics, and feed additives, the genes of livestock are being edited to improve animal agricultural productivity, creating fatter pigs, bulkier broilers, gender-specific cattle, liberally lactating heifers, and cashmere goats with longer hair.[12] Since its introduction in 2012, the CRISPR-Cas9 tool has enabled scientists to delete DNA with unprecedented precision and ease. Many scientists agree that CRISPR has the potential to dramatically improve nearly any aspect of life, whether preventing or treating disease (great), improving the quality of life and extending longevity (even better), or creating freakish food animals (terrible). Though no gene-edited animal products have reached U.S. or European markets yet, Big Ag quietly continues investing in and investigating this technology.

And these genetic mutants are also happening in other, less regulated parts of the world. Chinese scientist Kui Li, based at the state-run

Chinese Academy of Agricultural Sciences, has used CRISPR to delete the MSTN gene in pigs, which limits how large their muscles grow, creating humongous hogs. Li's research aims to satiate his nation's infinite appetite for pork. His dozens of gene-edited, extra-lean pigs stare quietly at curious onlookers from their metal cages on a farm outside Beijing. Could these porcine marvels be the future of food?

Unfortunately, an unintended consequence of Li's gene-editing experiment was that approximately one in five of Li's pigs developed an extra spinal bone. Li doesn't know why, and he doesn't seem too concerned about this skeletal deformity. Li's primary objective is to have the experimental pigs classified as "safe to eat." After all, if the pigs can't be killed and eaten, what's the point? Chinese scientists are also experimenting with another valued animal product, cashmere. Cashmere comes from Cashmere goats, a breed long prized for its long, lustrous, weather-resistant coat. Using genetic techniques similar to Li's, these scientists created lambs that are larger and have thicker cashmere coats. They used CRISPR to target two genes, the MTSN that Li edited, and FGF5, the gene associated with hair growth. Once again, there's an unintended consequence. The lambs are growing so large in utero that the scientists must deliver them by C-section. But these CRISPR-ed goats produce up to 20 percent more cashmere, so what's the problem?

The problem is ethics, according to prominent neuroscientist Lori Marino. "I think we've already gone over the line with animals," she says.[13] "We are going in the wrong direction, and we are already way beyond any line of decency and ethics." The ultimate question is whether ethics and a shared sense of decency can overcome consumer demand for cheaper animal meats, skins, and coats, regardless of the cost to the environment or animal. Using science to change the physical characteristics of animals to better fit within the factory-farm system isn't the answer.

Instead, society should be changing the food production system. The fact that animals struggle to survive in intensive farming environments, requiring artificial life support in the form of antibiotics, hormones, and genetic modifications (breeding or biotech), suggests there is something inherently wrong with the machinery, not with the "cogs." It is time humanity accepts that these thinking, breathing, feeling animals were never meant to be part of a machine at all. The priority must be to improve or abolish their restrictive environments, rather than reshape the animals to fit within them.

Reducing an animal's stress responses by giving drugs or hormones, for instance, might allow the animal to tolerate more severe confinement, but we need to question *why* they endure more stress in the first place. Creating stress-resistant or physically stronger animals that can survive increasingly oppressive conditions has obvious economic benefits for the food industry. But is profitability an ethically justifiable barrier to enhancing the environment instead of the animal? The first priority must be to assess animal welfare, with profitability figured out only after suffering has been eliminated.

By modifying animals to withstand intensive food production systems, mankind is also avoiding the questionable morality that allows factory farming to exist in the first place. Animal welfare advocate Paul Shapiro compares modern poultry broilers to "meat-producing machines."[14] We know we must make the animals we eat inanimate and insentient, or the guilt could be too much. Ignoring our ethical feeding friction means denying cows, pigs, chickens, and fish the ability to feel that we attribute to our pets, and allows the immeasurable suffering hidden within factory farms to persist. Historian and philosopher Yuval Noah Harari describes our current animal-food system as producing meats "without any thought about the suffering we inflict on these animals."[15] Food biotech can either make animal meats cheaper and more available or eliminate the need for killing animals altogether. In the first scenario, we continue on a path that races toward the destruction of the planet. In the second, we turn around and save it.

There's another way that technology has previously been used to the detriment of our pets' health. When it comes to food, technological progress has almost always been about making the food cheaper and improving supply-chain efficiency. At the turn of the twentieth century, one of the first large commercial dog food manufacturers, Purina, knew the feedlots and slaughterhouses well. It recognized that after a butcher had taken the cuts off for humans, there was still a substantial amount of red meat that was considered unfit for people and thrown away. As the saying goes, the butcher's dog pounced on these discarded bits, oblivious to their allegedly "inferior" quality, and ate well.

Seizing an opportunity to both improve a cattleman's profit and innovate pet foods, companies such as Purina diverted these cheap carcass remnants into pet food. Over the past hundred years society has used technology to maximize the utility of the animals we kill for food, becoming more precise and profitable. By using computers and automated conveyors and developing specialized meat-cutting systems, there is very little "leftover" in a modern slaughterhouse. The head of a cow, for instance, is subjected to numerous processes that suction, dissolve, and pluck out any flesh that can possibly be used. A beef cow is a very expensive animal, and to make any profit producers have to get as much money out of every ounce as they can. Whatever little remains has very few nutrients in it, none of which are deemed "fit for human consumption."

The same mechanized process applies largely to chickens, pigs, and fish; the bulk of their meat has been removed for human consumption, leaving scarce protein for dog or cat foods. The fact that you can buy bone broth for humans in the grocery store is testament to the fact that producers are wringing every drop of protein profit they can out of meat. The reality is, if an animal meat is in a pet food, it's the absolute cheapest, least desirable source available. This is one of the reasons "human-grade meats" are gaining popularity in pet foods. Pet owners are desperate for actual animal meat to feed their pets.

Biotech gives the world a different option: the chance to make food that is *better* rather than cheaper and *healthier* rather than riskier, while still improving supply-chain efficiency. It's far more efficient to breed and grow a cell, fungus, or yeast so as to improve the nutritional value of pet food than it is to breed and grow an entire animal. Humankind doesn't have to destroy forests to grow crops to feed cells. We don't have to accidentally slaughter wild animals to harvest tons of grain to grow fungi. These future pet foods remove the majority of environmental damage, and ethical friction is taken out of the food equation.

The most exciting aspect of these emerging food technologies is that they *improve* over time, not just in terms of cost, but also by becoming healthier and more delicious. Face it: chicken has one variety . . . chicken. Any animal other than a cow, pig, or fish tastes like, well, chicken. Is that really enough to excite billions of future diners? Future proteins will have limitless taste and textural possibilities, infinitely delighting foodies everywhere. Impossible Foods is already improving their burger formulas, enhancing the taste and texture with each tweak and iteration. You simply can't do that with a cow or pig without seriously manipulating their genetics.

This is a truly revolutionary prospect; future foods will continuously improve. Food technology has historically earned a bad reputation because it's typically been used to do *bad* things to food, focusing on amplifying taste and marketing hype, rather than improving health. These future food companies aren't trying to create cheap junk food or trick your taste buds into craving more, but rather genuinely want to make better food that will sustain the world.

It's important to remember that any food you eat today relies on some kind of technology, whether preservatives, genetic selection, seed generation, pesticides, combine harvesters, stun guns, electrocution baths, logistics, or milking machines. Nothing we eat today is absolutely "natural," nor is what we feed our pets (except any small animals your cats might poach). The difference is that future pet foods have the potential to *intensify* the value of what we put in our pets' bowls and improve pet food's ability to positively influence their health.

Clean Meat, Clean Conscience

Cellular agriculture (cell ag) is transforming the future of animal farming, not only by allowing us to grow proteins from yeast and fungal cells, but also by allowing huge amounts of *real* animal protein to be grown from a tiny cell sample taken from a single donor, forever. This kind of cellular meat, initially grown in a lab, is made from cells that can grow a meat-like protein patty good enough to market as a burger. The resulting cell-based burger or "cell-based meat" can also be modified to include the perfect balance of nutrition and be low in saturated fat, while tasting delicious. The same is true of fungal and yeast-based cellular agriculture. These aren't fake meats; they're clean meats. It's real protein without the cruelty.

Global demand for animal products is forecasted to double by 2050 due to booming human and pet populations and rising standards of living. As countries become wealthier, history proves they increase their animal consumption. What if meat could be produced sustainably? What if meat didn't involve the suffering and slaughter of a living animal? What if DNA from a single cow, chicken, or pig could create more meat than the thousands, even millions, of animals whose lives we currently take to feed ourselves and our pets? What if we could feed the world without destroying it?

We can. Put simply, stem cells from an animal's muscle are originally obtained from a few living donor animals (without, it should be said, killing or even hurting the animal). These stem cells, primed for growth, are placed in enriched media (cell food) and fermented in similar fashion to how you brew beer.

The resulting cells are identical to conventionally derived animal cells: they are composed of the same genes, proteins, and amino acids as the source tissue. This means animal meat and cultured meat are essentially the same thing, just created in a different environment. This cellular similarity has been utilized in human medicine for several years to grow new skin for burn victims and even new organs to cure disease. Clinical experiments and trials using cultured heart muscle, ears, pancreas, bones, eyes, and bladder (first successfully transplanted in a dog)[16] are already underway around the world. Growing meat in a lab is actually much easier than growing organs that must perform complex biological functions and be accepted by the donor. Lab-grown meat only needs to look, taste, and feel like animal meat to serve as nutritious food for people or pets.

Like most biotech innovations, cultured meat was initially created in small laboratory settings. But the term *lab-grown meat* is a bit misleading, making the concept sound more like science fiction than science-based farming. As the science becomes refined and more affordable, production is anticipated to move into a large-scale process that mimics brewing beer. It's likely that clean meats won't be grown in gigantic laboratories lined with rows of petri dishes, but in towering stainless-steel bio-reactors. Inside these tanks, also called "cultivators" or "fermenters," a fermentation-like process will take place that involves adding sugars or other growth substrates to feed the protein-rich cells.

The market-readiness of these products is, relatively speaking, around the corner. Cultured meats produced from cell cultures could be ready to hit the market in a few years, and conventional meat producers like Cargill and Tyson Foods are already invested in this animal free–meat future. In addition to its own plant-based research, Tyson invested $2.2 million in Israeli clean meat maker Future Meat Technologies. Bill Gates and Richard Branson have also made substantial investments in cell-based food companies. San Francisco's Good Food Institute (GFI) has awarded a total of $3 million in funding to fourteen scientists in plant- and cell-based meat research, the most money ever allocated to an open-access plant-based meat program. GFI hopes that soon there will be dedicated plant- and cell-based meat research centers at major universities. Meanwhile, over the next two years, these fourteen scientists will dedicate their careers to understanding new and better ways to meet the demand for meat.[17] The fact that GFI members' research will be published as open-access and be freely available to all means that every company interested in developing more ethical, sustainable alternatives will be able to benefit, accelerating change.

We, the authors, believe humanity is witnessing a transition from an animal product–based economy to one centered on plant-based and both cellular and acellular agricultural alternatives. The latter offers what Lewis Bollard at the Open Philanthropy Project calls "one of the more promising and exciting long-term solutions to really getting rid of farm animal suffering."[18] Over a decade ago, in 2008, an early ethical evaluation of cultured meat concluded it was "something we might be morally required to support."[19] Whether the motivation is moral, ethical, economic, environmental, or health-oriented, we're going to have to dramatically decrease the number of animals we farm. Cultured meats are going to play an important role in what we eat moving forward.

The vanguards of cultured meat include Mosa Meat, a company founded by Dutch scientist Mark Post, who unveiled the first clean-meat hamburger in 2013. In the United States, Memphis Meats, headed by Uma Valeti, and Josh Tetrick's company, Just, are pioneering technologies to create food that will "take down the meat and dairy industries."[20] The goal of producing delicious foods that are safer and healthier unites these ambitious companies. There's huge potential to create healthier versions of any animal meat, ones containing fewer artery-clogging fats, healthier fatty acids, and more cancer-preventing fibers.

However, healthier environmentally friendly foods won't be enough to disrupt the animal-based economy. If we're going to ignite a global human and pet food revolution, clean meat must be affordable and accessible. At first, clean meat will be an expensive luxury option. As of early 2019, it cost the plant-based Impossible Burger an additional $5 to $8 for their burger over what was required to produce a beef patty. Because Impossible Burger and Beyond Meat rely heavily on pea proteins, they will potentially encounter commodity price fluctuations, affecting both their costs and availability. Food companies that create more complete cell-based solutions will avoid many of these market constraints and may eventually prove more successful.

Post predicts that Mosa Meat can lower the manufacturing cost of its cell-based burger to less than $10 by 2021. With the right investments, there's an opportunity to produce clean meat on an industrial scale at a much cheaper cost than the hundreds of billions spent raising whole cows, pigs, and chickens. This is a price *everyone* pays, vegan or meat eater. U.S. farm subsidies cost taxpayers about $20 billion every year, mostly to support enormous corporate farm conglomerates, putting small family farms in peril. Switching to cell- and plant-based meats would greatly reduce the need for these government payouts and could end up saving U.S. taxpayers huge sums of money in the long run.

Although the potential for clean meat to reduce methane emissions is without question, the industry has recently come under fire for its possible future contribution to CO_2 emissions. Methane is a more potent gas than CO_2, but it disappears from the atmosphere faster. It takes twelve years for methane to dissipate, but thousands of years for CO_2. Critics argue this means that large-scale cultured-meat production could release a lot of CO_2, intensifying global warming.[21] However, this assumes that we burn fossil fuels to power the cultured meat plants, as opposed to more environmentally friendly, renewable energies such as wind and solar. Another factor easily omitted in this discussion is that the cattle industry also emits tremendous amounts of CO_2 by shipping cows great distances to feedlots and slaughterhouses. Cell-based facilities won't need to ship their products long distances to consumers, because bioreactors will be built in every city and eventually individual homes. The Good Food Institute concludes that clean meat technology will use 82 to 98 percent less water and 90 percent less land than traditional animal farming.[22]

Growing Cells Ethically and Efficiently

A key question that cellular agriculture critics ask is how to grow cells ethically and economically. Previous standards have been expensive, and concerned consumers don't want products grown using animal-based media, especially fetal bovine serum (FBS). To make FBS, a cow fetus is removed at slaughter and its blood extracted. This fetal blood is then refined, and the resulting extract is FBS. FBS contains special hormonal compounds that signal meat cells to continue growing when they realize they're no longer in a living cow. Without FBS, cow stem cells fail to divide and grow into meat. However, one cow fetus can only provide enough serum for a single kilogram of cultured meat, which means that using FBS is neither a sustainable nor a humane process. Several cellular agriculture companies have already stopped using FBS, replacing it with plant-based or synthetic growth serums or managing to go serum-free.[23] Ultimately, the aim is to scale up ethical animal cell culture alternatives to FBS, eliminating any live animals from the process.

Science, cost, and growth media aren't the only barriers to an animal-free future; there are also cellular scaffolds to conquer. Reproducing meat cells need a physical framework on which to spread and mature into muscle fibers. Currently, the clean meat companies can only create mince-like meat products that can be shaped into burgers, sausages, or meatballs. To grow massive quantities of cultured meats, food scientists are racing to create better growth scaffolds, using plant-based sugar polymers as gels (including alginate, cellulose, and chitin) instead of animal-based collagen to form the muscle tissue. In the United Kingdom, scientists at the University of Bath are growing animal cells on blades of grass,[24] a fitting solution given that the conventional way to grow beef is to feed a cow grass. Eventually, industrial-scale bioreactors will be needed to grow animal-free meats at an affordable commercial scale.

All the current cultured meat companies are confident that they'll make the technological breakthroughs required to bring costs down[25] and that it's a matter of "when" not "if." And that "when" is almost now. Turkish startup Biftek.co has developed a plant-based FBS replacement that they claim lowers costs by over 50 percent. Israel's SuperMeat teased it will soon produce an entire chicken breast, not just separate meat fibers compressed into a "chicken breast," using a proprietary plant-based serum.[26] Science can solve these clean meat and pet food challenges. Unfortunately, science is powerless against the biggest challenge of clean meat: politics.

The main challenge slowing the innovation and adoption of cultured meat is regulation. In October 2018, the United States Department of Agriculture (USDA) and the U.S. Food and Drug Administration (FDA) held a public meeting to discuss the use of livestock and poultry cell lines to develop cell-cultured food products. In a landmark decision, it was concluded that *both* the USDA and the FDA should jointly oversee the production of cell-cultured food products derived from livestock and poultry. On November 18, 2018, the agencies announced a joint regulatory framework wherein the FDA will oversee cell collection, cell banks, and cell growth and differentiation. A transition from FDA to USDA oversight will occur during the cell harvest stage. The USDA will then oversee the production and labeling of food products derived from the cells of livestock and poultry.

The terminology and labeling of clean meat by the USDA is also critically important, because it places cultured meat in the same category as animal meat. The Federal Meat Inspection Act defines *meat* as "the part of the muscle of any cattle, sheep, swine, or goats which is skeletal or which is found in the tongue, diaphragm, heart, or esophagus, with or without the accompanying and overlying fat, and the portions of bone (in bone-in product such as T-bone or porterhouse steak), skin, sinew, nerve, and blood vessels which normally accompany the muscle tissue and that are not separated from it in the process of dressing." Under this definition, meat grown in a lab from animal cells counts as "meat." We agree; there is no physiological difference between cultured meat and conventional meat. The only difference is source. And suffering.

The controversy over the meaning and labeling of "meat" returns us to that need for a new vegan language when it comes to human and pet food. *Clean meat, lab-grown, cultured, fungal, dried yeast, plant-based,* and *cell-based* are just a few of the regulatory terms being proposed to describe the exciting world of animal-free meats. In this book, we're about to meet some of the individuals leading these food innovations; but first, we need to explore the power and potential vulnerabilities of these new terms.

What Is "Meat"?

The debate around the labeling of cultured meat raises a deeper question about how people define meat. A recent article on *Slate* asks, "Is meat the muscle of an animal? Or is it the remains of a living creature? If the former, this lab-grown stuff is meat. If the latter, it's not."[27] As simple as that sounds, it's infinitely more complicated. The confusion begins with an archaic word such as *meat*. If you say "meat" in nearly any language to any living adult, chances are you'll activate a linguistic framework full of cows, hamburgers, bacon, stews, sushi, steaks, and sausages. "Meat" is indistinguishable from animals. But that was before factory farms, biotech, and bioreactors became involved.

Today, words like *beef* and *burger* do not authentically describe the reality of the animal product. The reality is a "burger" is "the shredded flesh of a slaughtered bovine animal." When you consider it that way, it becomes evident that it's preposterous to deny cultured meat companies the right to use terms such as *burger* or *sausage*. For animal rights writer Carol Adams, the iconic American hamburger is "the furthest distance you can go from an animal,"[28] a patty of ground-up "shoulder" meat and other cuts, completely unrecognizable as a cow. Patties, wieners, nuggets, and strips—these are *shapes* of animal proteins, intentionally bearing no resemblance to an actual living animal.

So why does protein-in-a-tube have to come from a corpse to be considered an "authentic sausage"? We need a modern food language. In an open letter responding to an article on meat alternatives in the *Wall Street Journal* titled "A Stampede of Meatless Products Overrun Grocery Store Meat Cases,"[29] Colleen Patrick-Goudreau asserts that the movement toward banning "meat" and other descriptors from plant-based or cultured versions "simply demonstrates how threatened animal-based meat and milk companies are by the success of these products." In other words, the animal-meat industry is using language to confuse consumers and block competitors in order to preserve profits.

Indeed, the main reason for the animal agriculture campaigns against the use of "meat" terminology for plant-based foods is fear of loss of money. Ironically, animal agriculture has been using evasive and inaccurate terminology for decades to sanitize the violent practices behind its products. The meat, egg, and dairy industry wield enormous power through advertising and marketing that use euphemisms and technical language in this way: *maceration* of chicks versus *grinding alive*; *cribs* versus *veal crates*; *beak trimming* or *beak treatment* versus *debeaking* or *beak amputation*; *induced molting* versus *forced molting*; *hen rejuvenation period* versus *starvation stimulus protocol*. Gestation crates become sow accommodation or maternity pens. The pork industry uses "blunt force trauma" instead of "slamming pigs' heads against concrete walls to kill them." By contrast, cultured or plant-based meat has no need to use these misleading, evasive adjectives. In practical terms, the language cell-based pet foods use is more authentic, honest, and transparent.

As Patrick-Goudreau points out: "Meanings evolve, context matters, and consumers aren't stupid." There is actually no need to call animal-free alternatives "fake" or "faux" meat. History supports this notion. The modern English language owes over half its words, including the most common language of everyday speech, to the language of the Anglo-Saxons. Our ancestors used the word *meat* to mean all food, calling animal flesh exactly what it was: cow meat, pig flesh, and so on. It was only when the conquering Normans entered England that Norman and French loanwords entered our language, and these included *beef* for cow, *pork* for pig, and *veal* for calf. Meat ceased to be used in the biblical sense of "food" (although it still persists in phrases like "coconut meat") and started to be applied only to animal flesh.

If we return to the origins of our language, when we talk about "vegan sausage," we're simply talking about grain meat or plant-based meat, rather than animal meat. Perhaps creating another kind of meat, this time cultured meat, will encourage people to use words like *pig*, *cow*, or *chicken* to preface meat once again, removing a significant level of cognitive dissonance. Perhaps we'll soon begin hearing animal advocates pivot from crying, "Meat Is Murder," to Paul Shapiro's "Eat Meat, Not Animals."[30]

Debates around the labeling of clean meat should encourage consumers to think more about what meat actually *is* according to the USDA definition, and to make a link between the living animal that was raised and killed for their burger, nugget, or bacon. Surprisingly, many animal-meat producers argue that people already make this connection, and cultured meat companies "deceive" consumers by calling animal-free products "meat." So why do they call it "bacon" instead of "sliced pig meat?" Because that sounds gross. The animal-meat industry has relentlessly marketed the separation between food product and slaughtered animal. Rarely does the animal-meat industry use an actual animal name, instead hiding behind obfuscating terms such as *beef*, *pork*, and *poultry*. Can you imagine a fast food commercial proclaiming, "Made with 100 percent certified slaughtered cow!" Of course not.

But that's actually the argument the beef industry is making with government regulatory agencies. Animal-meat advocates insist that the concept of the slaughterhouse is central to their definition of "real meat." The U.S. Cattlemen's Association's petition to the USDA (ongoing as of 2019) asks the department to create a new rule that specifically defines meat as "the tissue or flesh of animals that have been harvested in the traditional manner." Lia Biondo, the director of policy and outreach for the Cattlemen's Association, was asked to clarify what "harvested in the traditional manner" meant. She replied, "Harvested in the traditional manner means slaughtered at a slaughterhouse."[31] In other words, only animals killed on a slaughterhouse floor can earn the title of "meat." That seems like an outdated, location-biased, and innovation-stifling definition. Regulations aside, it's still challenging to overcome the linguistic power of "meat." But we can.

When products named Impossible Meats and Beyond Burgers are widely publicized, new neurolinguistic links are made. A small, but importantly different, linguistic connection is created each time a person encounters "meat" or "burger" in the context of "plants" or "not animal." The more that pathway is repeated, the more it becomes reinforced and strengthened. Over time, the word *meat* returns to its etymological origins, extending beyond animal flesh. It might take years, even decades, but this lexemic shift is inevitable. This is why animal-based industries have declared war against "soy *milk*," "nut *cheese*," and lab-grown and plant-based *meats*. They don't want these biotech upstarts to threaten the language that propels their animal products, regardless of how environmentally harmful or cruel they are.

The meat, dairy, poultry, pork, and fish industries are woven into the politics and identities of many cultures and countries, and also fund incredibly wealthy industries. When you confront "big meat," you risk challenging humanity's foundation. We don't expect Big Ag to welcome cultured meats with open food aisles, unless they believe they can make a lot of money with them. After all, they've built economic empires on the broken backs of billions of animals. We hardly expect them to be any less ruthless with "vegan" human and pet food companies.

What exactly is "meat" today, given these recent technological advances? At the most basic level, meat is a food made up of proteins containing amino acids. The term *meat* fails to adequately, accurately, or authentically define many modern protein sources. Even many animal-based meats are so highly processed that they've been reduced to little more than their constituent amino acids. Dogs and cats don't crave "meat"; their bodies thrive on proteins and amino acids, fats, carbohydrates, vitamins, and minerals. We don't feed ingredients; we feed nutrients. One of two societal changes must occur to clarify the meaning of "meat":

1) *Meat* becomes an inclusive term for any animal, plant, or lab-grown protein sources, or,
2) *Meat* is replaced by more specific language that obviates the need for origin, using protein and amino acid terminology.

In reality, we'll most likely see a combination of the two. The easiest way for people and pet owners to understand what they're eating or feeding will be to continue calling protein sources "meat." The change required is specifying the origin of a meat ingredient. Whereas many people say they feed their pet a "meat-based diet," let's challenge them to begin calling it "animal meat–based" or "chicken-based" or "cultured meat." This is important because calling attention to the animal required to feed a pet will encourage some pet owners to investigate the care of these farmed animals. For others, the mounting evidence linking animal meats to climate change or dog and cat illnesses will make it impossible to ignore the relationship between pet food and health.

The second option transcends the barriers of "meat" and precisely identifies the nutritional components. For example, there's likely to be a time when a pet food may be formulated with individualized amino acid profiles based on a pet's unique physiological needs. This personalized diet will be determined by analyzing the pet's genome, digestive tract microbiome, and other biomarkers to create a customized nutrient formulation designed to optimize health and quality of life.

Before you dismiss this as science-fiction food, there are several companies already researching this technology. Another IndieBio graduate, AnimalBiome, led by Dr. Holly Ganz, is well on the way to interpreting how a dog's gut flora can be modified with diet to optimize health and overcome illness. In addition to studying the impact of traditional pet foods on the microbiome, Ganz is working with Ernie and Ryan to unlock the health secrets of fungal proteins. Los Angeles–based Basepaws, led by founder Anna Skaya, is cracking the genetic code of pet health and nutrition, and Ernie serves as a scientific advisor. For humans, nearly a dozen companies are already using a person's DNA to make dietary recommendations. These technologies are in early development, but it's likely that within the next decade you'll be able to submit a saliva, stool, or blood sample from your dog or cat and have the perfect diet or nutritional supplement delivered to your door.

Finless Fish and Slaughter-Free Shrimp: The Startups Disrupting Conventional Seafood

Today, we're seeing clean meat startups all over the globe racing to be first to market, and several of these companies are focusing on fish. Singapore-based Shiok Meats is one of these, growing cell-based shrimp (a first in stem cell research as well as food science) and targeting the Asian market. Shiok is definitely onto something, given that the most recent research on consumer attitudes to cell-based meat suggests significantly higher acceptance of clean and plant-based meat in India and China compared with the United States.[32]

Pet ownership is also on the rise in Asia, with China boasting more than a hundred million pets, closely trailing Japan and the United States. Meanwhile, in India the pet population grew from seven million in

2006 to ten million in 2014, with an average of 600,000 pets adopted every year, according to the India International Pet Trade Fair. Indian pet website DogSpot.in anticipates their pet-care sector will grow over 35 percent every year for the foreseeable future. That's a lot of hungry mouths to feed, in countries and cultures where cultured meat is more likely to be embraced. We'll explore the potential for cultured meats to penetrate the pet food space shortly.

We spoke with Sandhya Sriram, who co-founded Shiok Meats with fellow stem cell scientist Ka Yi Ling in mid-2018. The scientific duo has been working with all kinds of cells, from muscle, fat, and neuro to cardiac muscle, for over ten years, having completed PhDs and then post-doc work in stem cell biology. Sriram had been closely following the clean meat and plant-based meat industries before jumping into the space herself. She tells Alice and Ernie:

> I'm a vegetarian by choice, so I'm super interested to find out about how meat eaters think about plant-based meat and cell-based meat. Will they ever choose a plant-based meat over an actual meat that's in the supermarket, kept on probably the same shelves? That's the question I was reading about a lot—obsessively reading about it I would say!

At the start of 2018, Sriram realized the best way to find the answer was to simply do it. She decided to start in cellular agriculture rather than plant-based. She laughs: "I'm not a plant-based person in terms of the technology. So, I wanted to do something that I'm really good at!" And Sriram is *really* good at cellular agriculture. Identifying a gap in the market for cell-based seafood, Sriram and Ling inadvertently made a challenging choice. There was no existing stem cell research on the common seafood animals. When she sat down in their rental lab space in the first week of August 2018, Sriram's plan was simply to "isolate shrimp cells and see what happens!" After dissecting a couple of shrimp, she realized that you *could* isolate their stem cells, giving her the confidence she needed to incorporate the company and quit her day job, bringing in Ling. Shiok Meats was born, named after "shiok!" in Singapore and Malaysian slang, which means "fantastic!" or "delicious!"

Their challenge had only just begun. Since that day, Sriram and Ling have been spending endless hours in the lab trying to understand shrimp growth, especially how their cells behave outside of their body. Frustratingly, shrimp cells don't grow as fast as the pair expected them to grow (they have a doubling time of six days, which is comparatively slow in the animal world). That means Sriram and Ling's main focus is to understand how to create an environment that allows the cells to grow faster without mutating them. There's no genome or any kind of sequencing data for shrimp available, so they're sequencing shrimp themselves to try to understand why their cells don't proliferate as fast as other animals. Another interesting discovery has been that the shrimp cells don't "die." As Sriram puts it, they just "stay." "They're alive; they don't proliferate fast, but they love staying as stem cells. This is super, super interesting for us."

This revelation isn't as strange as it sounds, given that basic biology tells us that crustaceans and mollusks have high regenerative capacity because they have more and longer telomeres (the parts of the chromosome that keep the cell growing or alive without sentience, like a fuse on a bomb). Many research articles show that longer telomeres help stop cell proliferation and keep the cells in a quietened, stem cell state. You have to "trigger" the stem cells to propel them into the cell growth phase. Shiok Meats is therefore in the midst of trying to figure out what these biological triggers might be, and Sriram and Ling won't know what they are until they find out exactly what genetic information shrimp cells contain. So far, they've been able to differentiate the cells to get them to a state that looks like minced meat, on a lab scale. But Sriram is estimating a minimum of two or three years to get the product to market. She anticipates Shiok's entry point will be one or two high-end restaurants where cell-based shrimp is part of their tasting menu, with supermarket sales about four to five years away.

If shrimp are such tricky animals to model, why has Shiok Meats decided to focus on them? To understand, we need to consider the Asian food market. Whereas Western clean meat startups have been concentrating on cultural favorites such as red meat and chicken, only one or two companies are looking at seafood, the main cuisine in Asia. Given that Asia contains 60 percent of the world's population, Sriram was amazed that companies weren't already targeting that market. She now realizes that the lack of research was probably a big factor stopping other startups, but that was never going to stop her:

> My forte is growing any type of stem cells. I've dealt with a lot of animals over those ten years of my life so I felt quite confident that I could isolate stem cells from any species that you give me!

Instead of lowly shrimp, Shiok's seafood competitors were all looking at finned fish, particularly expensive species such as tuna and salmon. But Sriram didn't want to create something exclusive; she wanted to make food that everybody could afford and enjoy. There are *a lot* of crustaceans eaten in Asia; the shrimp market is a $40 billion industry. Sriram assumed that by starting off with shrimp, a small animal, it would be easy enough to release a prototype in a couple of months, maybe a year, after which the company could move on to crabs and lobsters. "So that's how the whole idea started off," Sriram says with a smile. "I started dreaming about shrimp, talking about shrimp—it was *all* about shrimp at that point!"

But still, why shrimp? Eliminating shrimp aquaculture is a major motivator for Sriram. She's seen a couple of shrimp farms firsthand: "The way that the shrimps are grown in farms isn't supposed to be the way that they should be grown. I have seen them being grown in the dirtiest of waters with excessive use of antibiotics. I've seen shrimps grown in pig farm– and slaughter farm–runoffs. It is truly pathetic." The generous use of antibiotics means that humans can consume these shrimps despite the bacterial contamination. This kind of combined livestock farming and aquaculture is allowed because it helps save a lot of water by reusing the dirty water run-off, and it's convenient because shrimps feed on dirt. It's also cheaper. Good for producers, not so good for consumers. Sriram's blunt opinion of farmed shrimp: "I don't think you should be eating that shrimp at all." She's also horrified by the ratio of shrimp harvesting's ocean bycatch: for every pound of shrimp caught in the ocean, you get twenty pounds of bycatch. That's twenty pounds of dead and discarded ocean creatures for a couple of plates of shrimp hors d'oeuvres:

> Other than that, it's just that the way people are eating meat is definitely unsustainable. Like for example, in the U.S. or Europe, you would probably come across shrimp cocktails, or shrimp and fried rice, or buttered shrimp, but here we use shrimp as shrimp sauce, shrimp paste; we use dried shrimp as seasoning on top of all our dishes. So it's actually a snack, a delicacy, part of your meal, a protein source. . . . We use a lot of crustaceans here. It's a huge market, but none of what people are consuming is healthy.

In addition to conducting novel research, Shiok Meats has experienced other challenges with its location. Whereas in the United States biohackers can fairly easily secure a lab space to rent, that concept is largely unknown in Southeast Asia. Most of the startups formed in Asia are spin-offs from universities or research institutes that give their employees free space to develop their postdoctoral research, using technology from their PhD studies. Sriram and Ling didn't have any technology from their previous jobs, and independent startups like Shiok Meats are "kind of odd in this part of the world." Sriram tells us:

> People thought we were crazy. They were like "What are you doing? Why are you quitting your well-paid jobs and starting this company that doesn't even have IP? You haven't even tried this, what's wrong with you ladies?" "Well," we said, "we're just taking a bet, and we're quite confident that we can get to a point where we'll make this happen."

It took Sriram and Ling over two months to find an option for lab space, and in the end Sriram's former boss saved the day by helping them secure it. Funding their venture was even trickier. Sriram acknowledges that Asian investors are extremely risk averse, which means they're not going to be your first investors. It's only after they see U.S. investment and a proven track record of success that they will invest in a startup. Fortunately, Shiok Meats found a U.S. backer and is now working with Asian investors.

Although space and money may pose challenges to startups in Southeast Asia, there are also huge advantages for the region. For one thing, governmental regulation isn't as burdensome as it is in the United States and Europe. Each Asian country has an agency similar to the FDA or USDA, but far smaller and easier to navigate. Shiok's cell-based meat comes under the "novel food" sector, and as long as there are no GMOs and the meat is cooked before freezing and shipping, there's little regulatory pushback for cultured meats. Shiok Meats has been working with food regulators in Hong Kong, Singapore, and India, and based on these correspondences, Shiok believes the world's first clean meats will be launched in Asia.

There's also a greater chance of consumer acceptance in Asia. Sriram explains: "[P]eople don't want to get panicked by talking about something new in the food industry too early. So, when you're ready with your product, you just launch it, and people will accept it. That's the kind of consumerism that happens in Asia." It's a theory that's recently been backed up by a large-scale consumer survey.[33] In southeastern and eastern Asia, people were found to be excited to try new foods, and in Singapore 95 percent of the food consumed is imported because the country lacks the land to grow many crops. That means residents are enthusiastic about new brands coming in, especially if it's a protein. Sriram explains:

> There are three things that we get super excited about: anything meat, especially seafood; anything that's a snack; and the third is anything that's convenient. So these three are the major factors for us. There

is a section of people, I would say it's a minority, who kind of bother about where their food comes from, how healthy it is, and all of that. But eventually when it comes to food, it's taste and price. If you get that right, people are happy to buy it. That's the kind of mentality in this part of the world.

Even in more food-traditional regions, such as India, the millennial generation is happy to try different foods and ingredients, and it's this demographic that is most excited about plant-based and cell-based meat, according to Shiok's surveys.

Shrimp is also not just for humans. Cats *love* seafood, including shrimp. Purina Fancy Feast gourmet cat food describes itself as a "delicious, silky broth with tender morsels of real tuna, shrimp and whitefish"; Simpson's Premium offers a "Chicken with Salmon & Shrimp" cat food. We saw in Chapter 2 that in many industrialized nations, the average cat eats more fish than the average human does.[34] In 2002, more than 2.9 million tons of fish were fed to house cats globally, an amount that, when the article was published in 2008, was predicted to rise to 4.9 million by 2010.[35] Though conventional fished or farmed shrimp contains ample protein, it's often served with a hefty dose of salt. Cell-grown shrimp promises almost no environmental damage, almost no risk of contamination, and can be produced with low or no added salt and greater healthy omega-3 fatty acid content. We've already seen that pet ownership in Asia is rapidly growing; why shouldn't Shiok seafood include feline consumers?

While Shiok Meats is creating seafood for "everybody," another clean seafood startup is producing food that it hopes people will see as "gourmet." The focus of San Francisco's Finless Foods is bluefin tuna, precisely because it's an extravagant, expensive, and somewhat rare food in human culinary arts. Finless Foods is striving to make sure that people associate cell-based food with very high quality—not because saving the planet requires cell-grown tuna, but because people want more tuna. "I mean, this whole project is essentially useless," Mike Selden, CEO and founder, tells us with a hint of irony:

What we're making? There's no point to it. People can already solve all the problems that we need to solve by just eating vegan food. But people are not interested in that. So, we're trying to make something that goes around all the public perception problems that veganism has and that vegan food has. Which is why we need to do something that people associate with very high quality.

Selden has no interest in changing the way that vegetarians and vegans eat, confident that environmentally they've already solved the problems that cultured meat companies are attempting to solve. Perhaps controversially, he doesn't think cell-based meat will ever be cheaper or better for the environment than plant-based foods. He's also acutely sensitive to the marketing problems associated with the words *vegan* and *vegetarian*, boldly proclaiming their products as "real, fresh fish." We're back to the need for a new vegan language. By advertising a product as vegetarian or vegan, companies risk only reaching an established niche market. That's not the kind of exclusivity Selden is after:

We really want people who are meat eaters to focus on this. So, in terms of messaging, for a long time vegan and vegetarian food has sold itself on morals and ethics, but it seems like people don't really use those markers to buy food. They buy food based on taste, price, convenience, and then, slightly less, nutrition. I think as long as we're trying to sell food based on morals, we're never really going to change the world. It's always going to be virtue signaling for the rich, and really not for anybody else. If we want to make mass change, we need food that competes on its own metrics, the metrics that people actually buy things on.

For Selden, vegan marketing is not a fast enough way to halt the irreparable climate change that mankind is going to have to deal with if we don't change our habits in the next twelve to fifteen years. We need to try something else. Today, Selden avoids the *vegan* label at all costs:

When I was vegan, I would give people food that I made, and they'd have a bite and say, "It's good!" So, I'd ask, "Do you want more?" to which they'd reply, "No, no, I'm not vegan." *But you liked it!* I think when people hear those words, they just think, "Oh, I'm not vegan so it's not for me."

Because of this "vegan food is not for me" attitude, Finless Foods' communications strategy has been shifting away from animal welfare and environmental messaging, simply because the majority of people don't appear to buy food based on those things. Selden also realizes that technological messages are more likely to scare people than intrigue them, describing the idea that Finless Foods is creating "a bit of a fantasy." Instead, they're focusing on *food* as a message, putting the emphasis on culinary tradition. "We want to use this as an opportunity to create things for people that they've never had before—on making any fish production local," says Selden. "There's all kinds of exotic and interesting and delicious fish across the globe that I as an American never had access to until recently."

Just as Ron Shigeta described food as a "bridge" to other cultures, Selden is excited about the concept of bringing new, tasty cuisine that people have never had before, directly to the consumer. Hardcore foodies will no longer need to fly to Japan or Eastern Europe to try seafood delicacies, because Finless Foods will be able to make it for them in their hometown. What's more, this fish will be fresh, high quality, and really *interesting.* These cultured meat companies aren't just trying to make a like-for-like imitation, something "as good as," but products people *crave,* that are uniquely desirable on their own merit.

Selden believes the way to repair our planet is to offer positive, appealing *solutions,* and that includes "good technologies." He cites the way the U.S. once mindlessly killed whales to power our oil lamps, until kerosene was invented to substitute for whale oil. After that technological advancement, in the U.S. killing whales morphed into an inhumane concept. The moral awakening only happened when whale oil was no longer necessary. Ethical change typically follows convenience and practicality. "I don't think we're going to change the world based on moral arguments," Selden summarizes. "I think we have to fix it based on collective action and technological fixes. Then the morals will come after that." We, the authors, agree.

Let's find out more about Finless Foods' "technological fix." Although Selden's background is in biochemistry and molecular biology, his journey to cellular agriculture has been less than orthodox. He graduated from the University of Massachusetts at Amherst, a research-oriented institution a short two-hour's drive from the Atlantic Ocean. He met his future co-founder, Brian Wyrwas, when they were in college researching Panama disease (Fusarium wilt), a major threat to crops such as bananas. After a brief stint in marine conservation in southeast Asia, Selden taught high school chemistry in Taiwan, then worked as a translator in China. Eventually he ended up back in New York, working at Mount Sinai Icahn School of Medicine.

He quickly reunited with Wyrwas, and they started exploring Selden's fascination with the idea of replacing animal products with cell-derived alternatives. It was the seed of an idea planted by a sea creature Selden had run across during his travels: the horseshoe crab. In February 2014, Selden read an article by Alexis Madrigal in *The Atlantic*, titled "The Blood Harvest," which revealed the chilling plight of these intelligent crustaceans that were drained of their blood for use in human medical tests. The article described the difficulties for scientists who had developed synthetic equivalents to horseshoe crab blood and were trying to eliminate horseshoe crab usage. Selden thought: "If you can create synthetic horseshoe crab blood, couldn't you just create synthetic *anything*, any type of meat, and just not eat animals at all?"

It was then that he learned about Mark Post and his cell-grown burger, future food innovators New Harvest, and synthetic leather company Modern Meadow. From there, he says, it was "a slow descent into madness":

It's been kind of wild. I've done a lot of different things, but I haven't done any of them for very long. It's all sort of built up to this somehow. It feels like every single thing I've done has been very much pointed towards this. Working in marine conservation made me more of an environmentalist; working in crop security problems helped me a lot in understanding the importance of agriculture. The work that I was doing in epigenetics helped shape our process here. Working as a high school teacher helped me lead people, and then being a Chinese translator helped me learn Chinese. Our company functions well in China because we're one of the only ones with a bilingual CEO.

After working at New Harvest for a short time, Selden started Finless Foods, the first cell-based seafood company and the third cell-based meat company that still works on cell-based meats in general. Selden soon partnered with Wyrwas, who has a background in primary cell culture, and in September 2017 Finless Foods made the first cell-grown fish ever to be eaten by humans. The funding rolled in after that demonstration, and Finless now has twelve people on staff, with plans to expand. Selden isn't offering any timelines for his foods, wary of putting pressure on regulators, but he's confident that their cultured fish will be "a large chunk of the market within five years." Finless has already made tremendous progress on bluefin tuna, a fish that has an especially effective environmental message as a result of its endangered status. Wild bluefin tuna also contains dangerously high levels of heavy metals and plastics. But, like Shiok with its shrimp, Finless has come across unexpected scientific challenges. Selden reveals:

> Fish cellular biology is such an unexplored field that we've very much had to do a lot of basic research ourselves; we don't have a knowledge base to build off. That's been a journey. In terms of bluefin tuna, the genome is not sequenced. So, we've had to sequence it ourselves. And the genome is not characterized, so we've had to characterize it ourselves (read all the different parts and see what they are). The cellular morphology is completely not understood; nobody's ever bothered to

deal with fish cell differentiation, in terms of lineages, muscle, fat. I guess the tough part is we needed to start from scratch.

The fact that bluefin tuna can't be easily farmed is one of the reasons it's appealing to Selden, as fishing for it is nearly always harmful to the environment. However, that also means that it's extremely hard to acquire cell samples. Whereas cellular meat companies like Mosa Meat and Just can visit any farm to find a variety of cows, pigs, or chickens, finding ideal samples of bluefin tuna is challenging. Finless Foods has had to build labs all over the world—from Asia, to the U.S. east coast, to Europe—and Selden and his team have to fly back and forth to these different labs depending on where bluefin are schooling.

It was also nearly impossible to get funding for future seafood startups until recently. Selden explains that being in the first generation of startups "was seen as a crazy crackpot thing." Crackpot or not, companies like Selden's represent a potential major disruption to the global seafood industry.

* * *

Of course, tuna and shrimp aren't the most common ingredients in most commercial fish-based cat food. We saw earlier that cat food is usually made up of small fish such as anchovies, mackerel, herring, and sardines rather than byproducts of fishing for human consumption. There's no reason why these kinds of lower-grade fish couldn't be cultured for pet foods. The issue is if cell-grown human-grade fish is just as easy to produce, then we may see these "premium ingredients" pushing small fish out of cat food. Clean human seafood and meat companies will be able to bring better, more exciting food to more people; clean pet food companies will also provide our pets with the best ingredients and nutrients. Let's now explore how these alternatives to animal meat are being developed *explicitly* for our pets. The clean pet food revolution is joining forces with the clean meat revolution. Viva la revolucíon!

12

Cultivating a Clean
Pet Food Revolution

THERE'S A CONVINCING argument that clean or cultured meat might be even better suited to pets than it is to humans. As we'll explore later in the chapter, many vegans may refuse to eat clean meat on the basis that it is still an "animal product," even if the cell donor isn't harmed or required: after all, to some, animal DNA is still an animal product. But although these consumers aren't the intended market for clean meat, their *pets* might be. Plant-based, fungal, bacterial, or algal proteins may prove a more acceptable alternative for many vegan dog owners, but for some vegan cat owners, clean meat will produce the high-quality proteins they demand. After all, humans might *want* to eat meat, but we don't *need* to. Cats and other captive carnivores, on the other hand, currently have no choice but to consume the amino acids currently found in animal tissues. That means there are many vegan cat owners still desperately looking for a humane animal-meat alternative.

Bjørn Kristensen, a PhD student at Oregon State University, is fascinated by the ethical dilemma of feeding captive carnivores conventional meat. In his paper "The Moral Problem of Captive Predation," he supports clean meat as an alternative.[1] He believes cultured meat is an ideal solution to replace the farmed animals and extruded kibble currently being fed to captive cats, big and small, around the world. Kristensen argues it is more compelling to feed captive cats (and other pets) cultured meats rather than supplying humans with them, because we are omnivores and can choose to eat plant-based diets. The environmental footprint of a seventy-pound golden retriever eating a raw meat diet is almost *twice* that of an average American eating an omnivorous diet—a convincing reason to address our pets' meat consumption even before our own.

If humans insist on keeping cats (big and small) in captivity, we need to pursue alternative protein sources for them. As we've learned, the average U.S. house cat is fed over thirty pounds of fish a year, double the amount a human adult eats, and their diet is over 31 percent derived from farmed animals,[2] compared to 20 percent animal meats that people consume. Feeding captive and domesticated cats cultured meats (or plant-based alternatives) would be a big step toward protecting the environment and reducing animal suffering.

Other philosophers and animal rights advocates question whether we should keep *any* cats captive unless we feed them non-animal proteins. Kristensen notes the lack of attention paid in philosophical discussion to the suffering caused in order to sustain captive carnivorous animals—not just pet and shelter cats, but also zoo and aquarium animals. He argues that because we have already "interfered with nature" by keeping a carnivore captive, it is morally necessary, as well as practical, to *interfere further* so as to alleviate the additional suffering caused by sustaining captive carnivorous animals. We saw similar arguments from Marc Bekoff and Andrew Knight earlier in this book, who argue that there's nothing "natural" about keeping companion animals, especially apex predators such as felines. We have a duty to use our power and responsibility as "captors" to provide cats with the healthiest, happiest lives possible, even if that means feeding them differently than they would eat in the wild, from which they may have been stolen.

Rich Kelleman, founder and CEO of Bond Pet Foods, based in Colorado, believes clean meat for pets has another clear advantage over cell-grown meat for humans. Companies working on cellular meats for human consumption are trying to get the forms, colors, shapes, tastes, smells, and tactile characteristics "people perfect" because that's the only way the public will embrace it. Pets, he acknowledges, don't seem to worry about much except for texture, smell, and taste. Most pet foods bear little, if any, resemblance to the glistening and succulent foods adorning their packaging. The primary objective of pet food is that it be safe and nutritionally complete. Pet food is about feeding the *nutrients* a pet needs, not the *ingredients* we find appealing. Shigeta puts it this way:

> I think the main reason why dog food is immediately interesting is that if you bring a food out based on a fungus or yeast, even if it's a very well-known food, people may still not want to eat it. . . . But they will try giving it to their dog, so long as it's really healthy and their pet likes it. The dog has no preconceptions about whether something's gross or aesthetically desirable. He will smell it and eat it. A dog is a lot less picky than an average person!

Dogs and cats also don't have the same ingredient biases humans have, making them prime candidates for new foods. Whereas plant-based alternatives to meat have been slow to penetrate the pet food space, cultured meat has an advantage. This is particularly important for cats. As we saw in Chapter 8, a plant-based diet for cats is possible, but many owners remain skeptical. What about clean meat? Well, that's another story. Kelleman points out that cell-based pet food companies don't have to worry about the challenges surrounding cellular scaffolds that most companies must confront when it comes to human-oriented cellular meats. Pet food clean meats would be perfectly satisfactory in a minced or even "baby food" canned consistency.

Cultured-meat pet foods could have far-reaching ethical consequences outside the pet industry: providing chum for zoos, aquariums, sanctuaries, shelters, and any other area where carnivorous animals are held captive. Cellular agriculture could also help wild animals, putting an end to the hunting of endangered species by providing an alternative way to produce exotic foods—including whale, tiger, and seal meats. If we wanted, we could even produce slaughter-free "cultured dog meat" for the Asian market, preventing the well-publicized annual Yulin festival and the cruelties of the dog meat trade we touched on in Chapter 4.

Cultured *dog* meat? Although many of us find the thought revolting, we recognize our inherent ingredient bias and personal ethics are involved. These specific ethical feeding frictions will gradually evaporate as cultured meats become an amalgam of whale-plus-dog-meat dinners or tuna-and-mealworm nuggets. As long as no living animal is harmed and food technologies advance, the future of food is an infinite palette of tastes, textures, and amino acids. Whatever you desire, it can be cooked in a bioreactor!

We also see a time in the next hundred years when the concept of eating a living animal is forgotten, much like whale oil lamps. History will record our hunter/gatherer–farmer/killer days with a mix of nostalgia, regret, and disgust. We may continue to wage war on other humans, but the practicalities and potential of cultured foods will erase factory farming from existence. There may remain a few boutique animal farms that cater to the richest or most decadent desires, but the vast majority of humans and their pets will enjoy healthier, tastier, more accessible, and less expensive food grown in bioreactors. Louis Pasteur famously observed, "Chance favors only the prepared mind." Pet food biotech startups have been preparing, and now may be their chance.

Disrupting Conventional Pet Food: The Wild Earth Journey

Whereas much of the attention being paid to the food of the future has been focused on cell-based meats, there have been other significant advances in alternative protein production. We saw in the previous chapter that fungi, yeast, and bacteria are being used to create novel ingredients and protein-rich sources for both human and pet food. For Wild Earth, koji treats are just the first step, the ultimate goal being to create a constellation of cultured proteins, including cell-based mouse meat for cats. How? To find out, let's go back with Ryan to the beginning.

Wild Earth CEO Ryan Bethencourt has been committed to making a difference in biotech for years. He recalls telling fellow graduate school students: "I'm going to do anything it takes to build companies in the biotech space." Luckily, Ryan's Cambridge Business School professor saw potential and helped guide him during his master's studies. His preparation began to pay off when he finished school and moved to Los Angeles. Ryan firmly believes that every single one of us has the potential to make a difference in the world. This core principle led to what he calls a "series of fortuitous circumstances" that propelled him and his co-founders to create IndieBio, his biotech accelerator.

Ryan's "What have I got to lose?" attitude stems from a childhood spent overcoming dyslexia and plagued with thoughts of "someone's going to make fun of me." After emerging from those years, he realized, "They've been making fun of me my entire life, so it doesn't really matter!" He truly believed he had nothing to lose. It's a testament to this devil-may-care attitude that he moved to Los Angeles in 2008 just as the Great Recession hit, a move that his friends and colleagues called "crazy." Success often boils down to timing, and surely his timing couldn't have been worse. He'd moved to L.A. to be close to his passion, biotech, and all around him biotech companies were going bankrupt. Ryan's optimism didn't falter. Computer technology companies continued to raise funds; if they could succeed, why shouldn't biotech? History said otherwise. Biotech was traditionally ruled by gigantic pharmaceutical and chemical companies, not T-shirt-wearing computer nerds. Ryan dared the unthinkable: he set out to democratize biotech.

Ryan asked a simple question: Why should you have to be part of the life science establishment to start a biotech company? Why did you need a PhD or an MD? Did you *really* need to raise tens of millions of dollars to start? Ryan didn't think so, and he helped catalyze what would later be called the "biohacker movement." What's a biohacker? It's basically someone who hacks the science of biotech with lower-cost tools and novel strategies. Anyone with an undergraduate's understanding of biology and chemistry can do it. Ryan's group began by buying used equipment from early biotech victims of the recession, including a $200,000 cutting-edge laboratory robot he purchased for $3,000 dollars.

Every day, Ryan read headlines making statements like, BIOTECH IS DEAD, FORGET ABOUT BIOTECH, DON'T INVEST IN BIOTECH, and HOW BILLIONAIRES LOSE THEIR SHIRTS: BIOTECH. According to the experts, the biotech bubble had burst before Ryan even made it to California. Yet Ryan remained undeterred: "If all this means we're having fun, we're doing some science, then so be it!" They were enjoying themselves, inventing remarkable science on the cheap, and embracing a rich tradition of citizen scientists: people who are simply curious about the world and find tools and ways of understanding it better. For Ryan, that's the attitude that got him started, and that's what drives him today.

In L.A., Ryan began to meet like-minded people, which led to a group called BioCurious. After BioCurious, he co-founded the nonprofit Counter Culture Labs with Ron Shigeta, who would later rejoin him at Wild Earth. Ryan remained restless and turned his focus toward boosting Northern California's fledgling biohacker scene. In 2013, he founded his first company, Berkeley Biolabs. He was full of ideas and talent, but he lacked an essential ingredient to fulfill his biotech dream: money. Ryan had run lean for over five years and wanted to do more to ignite a widespread biohacker revolution. He and a couple of friends began pitching the idea of a biotech accelerator. In an economic climate where most market analysts cautioned against investing in biotech, they found a believer. A small venture capital firm called SOS Ventures, headed by Sean O'Sullivan, funded their biotech accelerator for about $15 million over a period of four years. This investment allowed Ryan and his co-founders to open up their biohacker lab, IndieBio, a company that would help other innovators "sell science."

It was at this time that Ryan realized that future foods were the science he was most interested in selling. Ryan was there in 2011 when Josh Tetrick, founder of Hampton Creek, raised his first $500,000. Hampton Creek would later change its name to Just and go on to raise over $220 million. However, in 2011, Tetrick was, as Ryan describes him, "just another vegan from L.A." Ryan thought: "If one vegan from L.A. could raise half a million dollars for vegan mayonnaise by replacing eggs with pea protein, why couldn't a biotech guy replace eggs with *biologically the same thing*?" That thought propelled him to fund future food companies at IndieBio, with the ultimate aim of eliminating the need for all animal products.

Ryan was tapping into a concept that would unite his two passions in life: ending animal suffering and developing biotechnology that would improve society. He ran his vegan food idea—to use biotech to replace industrial animal agriculture—by his omnivorous business partner, Shigeta, who was enthusiastic and intrigued. The pair assembled a close-knit group of investors and innovators dedicated to reducing the number of farmed animals and promoting environmental sustainability.

They dubbed themselves the "Vegan Mafia" after the "Paypal Mafia" of the 1990s, whose members included Elon Musk, Peter Thiel (later an early investor in Wild Earth), and Reid Hoffman, as well as others mentioned in this book, and their funders. Kyle Vogt, CEO of self-driving car technology Cruise, joined, along with Kevin Boylan, a former Wall Street trader who co-founded VeggieGrill and PowerPlant Ventures. Boylan's friend and business partner, Mark Rampolla, founder of ZICO Coconut Water, and Jody Rasch of VegInvest (another Wild Earth early investor) became members. Seth Bannon, a social entrepreneur and partner at Fifty Years, and Lisa Feria of Stray Dog Capital, a fund that invests in developing companies (including Wild Earth), pledged support. This group would be instrumental in spreading the biohacker revolution and expanding the national and international conversation around plant-based and future foods.

Ryan is a self-professed "junk food vegan," much to Ernie's consternation and constant prodding. As we saw earlier, Ryan grew up fueled by fast food, hamburgers, and a heaping portion of Cuban meats, and is motivated to replicate the tastes of his childhood and culture without the cruelty of farming animals. Ron, as we likewise saw, is a committed omnivore who loves creating complex flavors and tastes in the laboratory. Both were driven at IndieBio to disrupt the food industry, but for very different reasons. Shigeta's motivation was based on improving the environmental sustainability of food production. He knew humans were destroying the planet by making poor food choices. Ryan's focus was to end animal suffering.

Together, they concluded that eliminating eating animals was the answer. Well prepared, they now needed a chance. It arrived when their friend Isha Datar, from cell-ag startup New Harvest, mentioned "two scientists starting a vegan egg company in need of money." Ryan and Ron met with them, and funded what would become Clara Foods, headed by the brilliant Arturo Elizondo and David Anchel. IndieBio helped Clara Foods raise its first $1.5 million.

After making a media splash with Clara Foods and its egg substitute, IndieBio began attracting larger companies aligned with its mission to disrupt the farmed-animal industry. Ryan realized during Clara Foods' first demo that IndieBio might actually be able to make a massive difference in the world. Shigeta agreed that by leveraging science and entrepreneurship and aligning market forces, their organization could compete against animal agriculture. Competing in business was a very different tactic than the street protests and information and social media campaigns that had been the traditional tactics of vegan and environmental activists. The pair felt that society was beginning to accept the idea of alternative meat proteins.

IndieBio was just getting started. It helped startups researching regenerative medicine, biotech therapeutics companies, biological computation, microbiome researchers, and technologies that could store massive amounts of biological and DNA data. Of these diverse biotech innovators, it was always the animal protein alternatives that earned the most press and attracted the largest amount of funding.

After only a few years, IndieBio was able to offer $200,000 per company in its accelerator, four times its initial $50,000. Once again, New Harvest founder Datar tipped off Ryan about an interesting opportunity. This time it was about Dr. Uma Valeti, a vegan cardiologist who was building animal muscles in his lab. Valeti knew the idea had potential as a product, but he didn't want to leave his post as head of cardiology at the University of Minnesota. Ryan got on the phone that day and urged Valeti to reconsider:

> Look, you could spark a movement if you took the risk. I realize it's a risk, but we're here, the time is now. Uma, what do you want to be remembered for? In thirty years' time, whether the company succeeds or fails, do you want to be the guy who starts a movement or not? You would literally save billions of lives.

A cautious man, Valeti wasn't going to be swayed by a phone call, no matter how impassioned or persuasive. Nonetheless, Ryan sensed Valeti was considering his plea to let IndieBio help. A few days later, Valeti called Ryan back and said, "Okay, we're gonna do it." That's how IndieBio helped start Memphis Meats, supporting the company from scientific hypothesis to the creation of a proof-of-concept product. Shortly after Memphis Meats joined IndieBio, Geltor (working on animal-free collagen) and New Age Meats came on board. These three investments represented about a third of IndieBio's financial engagement. Ryan hoped these strategic investments and their resulting media coverage would catalyze others to participate in the biohacker revolution. He was right. Within three or four months of the announcement of Memphis Meats, Dutch professor Mark Post started Mosa Meat. The global future-food fire was lit.

Ryan and IndieBio did not stop there. Biotech luminaries, he noted, were seeking to revolutionize *human* food, but it was clear this technology had many other applications that could help make lives better, reduce suffering, and address the climate catastrophe. History teaches us that scientific breakthroughs tend to spread far beyond their origins. Harnessing electricity illuminated the way for computers; refrigeration generated advances in food transportation and processing; and beer and bread production gave rise to future fermentation biotechnologies. Seeing the buzz generated by cellular agriculture and how much interest investors, scientists, and the media were showing in the future of food, Ryan began to consider other areas where he could apply food biotech.

As a long-time animal lover, it was natural that his first impulse was to look at pet food. Ryan was fostering with Rocket Dog Rescue in San Francisco and remembers thinking to himself, "What *actually* goes into my dog's food?" The more he looked into pet food production, the more he realized its inherent problems: food safety, its contribution to factory farming, and a lack of sustainability. There was clearly a huge need for an alternative to animal meats for pets, perhaps even more so than in human food. By mid-2017, Ryan, Ron, and former co-founder Kristin Wuhrman of Wild Earth (who would go on to join pet genetic testing startup Basepaws) had prototyped a koji-based pet treat, conducted proof-of-concept experiments, created a cellular mouse meat, and raised some initial seed money. Ernie joined Wild Earth in late 2017, along with food scientist Dr. Abril Estrada. The team was ready to work transforming pet food, protecting the environment, and saving animals. But where should they begin?

The first objective for many ethically minded pet food manufacturers is to replace animal protein with plant proteins. Although in theory this seems simple, ingredient sourcing, production, and cost are complicated and must be carefully considered. Pet food is highly competitive on price, and high-quality, healthy, plant-based pet food is expensive to make. It seems contradictory that raising a cow to kill would be less expensive than growing peas or yeast, but due to taxpayer subsidies and the immense scale that has been discussed in this book, it's true. Here are Wild Earth's first goals:

Step one: Make highly nutritious, safe, and affordable plant-based pet foods.
Step two: Develop and introduce fungal and yeast proteins and cultured meats to pet food.

Wild Earth launched its first dog treat, one containing the fungal protein koji, in late 2018. Despite the advantages discussed in Chapter 10, koji is still much more expensive to produce than poultry or beef, meaning that including high quantities of koji results in more expensive treats and foods. Fungal proteins will become cheaper as bioreactors and "steel time" become more accessible and the processes more efficient. The first part of step two will be fungal and yeast proteins, paving the way for the real future pet food: cultured meats.

> Step three: Grow real meat proteins from cells, making complete and balanced pet food without slaughtered animals.

Cellular mouse and chicken meats and fungal proteins will be cost-prohibitive at first. The real power and potential of cultured proteins is their scalability. The bottom line is that you can produce more protein per gram using far fewer natural resources in a bioreactor than you could ever raise in a feedlot, hen house, hog farm, or salmon fishery. In a bioreactor you can grow proteins in a few days compared to the many weeks or years it takes to raise an animal for slaughter. Some of the larger commercial pet food companies are watching lab-grown meat closely, and many are already investing in them. Once it's clear that companies like Wild Earth and Bond Pet Foods work, it's likely that the pet food industry will aggressively embrace cultured proteins. They will do this because cultured proteins will make them more money in the long run, plain and simple. Wild Earth is doing it because it's clearly good for the environment and the planet and animal welfare. Let's call it a win–win–win proposition.

Pet food is experiencing a biotech transformation similar to human meats. Plant-based, cultured meat, and clean protein pet food companies such as Wild Earth, Bond Pet Foods, and Because Animals are sparking disruption in the pet industry. It's likely that there will be a plethora of plant-based, cultured, and fungal protein dog and cat foods entering the market over the next decade. Within thirty years, it's entirely plausible that most pet foods will be animal-free. There will be a deeper focus on animal health and pet nutrition, and maybe a few startups will even overtake established pet food companies. Many of today's major pet food manufacturers will join the clean pet food revolution, either by partnering with startups or by creating their own animal meat–free proteins. Eventually, the distinction between people foods and pet foods will be blurred to the point that we truly are eating and feeding *nutrients*, not *ingredients*.

Pet Food Producers with a Difference

The alternative pet food space is ramping up. Philadelphia-based Because Animals is planning to release its own clean pet food products, a cell-based line of proteins, to join its plant-based line. In 2019, it brought on board a tissue scientist to develop a mammalian meat for its first feline product, something Because Animals is calling an "ancestral cat food diet," tapping into the marketing messages used by raw-meat cat food advocates and playing them at their own game. CEO Shannon Falconer understands it will take time before most pet owners accept that animal meat isn't a necessary ingredient in pet food, and the only way to initially convince pet owners to switch is to offer them an alternative that's just as good, if not better. As we've seen in the enthusiasm shown for Beyond Meat and Impossible food products, for many consumers that tipping-point product utilizes cellular and molecular science.

Bond Pet Foods, founded by former advertising executive Rich Kelleman, is already promoting "the impossible: real, clean, animal protein with not a single animal slaughtered in the process." Kelleman's background doesn't immediately indicate "pet food" or "clean meat"; his twenty-plus years in advertising included agencies working on everything from Facebook to Chevrolet. He even led his marketing firm's Burger King account, helping the fast food chain rethink the future of its burger, what it represented, and how it was made. Not only did this foreshadow his future involvement in a very different kind of food reinvention, but it also altered how Kelleman viewed the food he was eating. Working with a conventional meat company opened his eyes to the truth about how animal meat–based foods are sourced and made. Kelleman went from a voracious meat eater to a committed vegan while working with Burger King. Flash forward a few years, and his views on food had permanently changed. But he had a problem with his pets:

With this new sensibility, as a pet parent with dogs and cats, I really struggled with that notion of having to harm one animal to feed another. I'm an animal lover in the broadest sense: even spiders in our house, they're no kill! That's the lens that I'm looking at this through. However, I felt like I couldn't turn my dogs and cats vegan, that didn't feel like the best path for their own personal health and nutrition. So that's essentially where this journey began—just seeing if I could try to find a solution for this angst.

Kelleman was experiencing that familiar ethical feeding friction. Nonetheless, his discomfort inspired him to find a solution. Initially, this meant trying to create a better conventional meat-based pet food, building a network of farmers he felt were "doing things a bit better." But the nagging doubt remained, along with the same animal welfare and sustainability concerns. Kelleman realized smaller-scale animal farming wasn't the solution. That's when he heard about Memphis Meats.

When Kelleman discovered Memphis Meats, Clara Foods, and Perfect Day, the companies were so early in their discovery phases that he was able to pick up the phone and chat with their founders. Through conversations with Uma Valeti and others in the space, he connected with the Good Food Institute and New Harvest. "Long story short, I was in awe," Kelleman recalls. "I just thought, this cannot be possible, this is amazing!" He was particularly struck by the idea that if one were to use this sort of acellular or cellular-based process to produce proteins for pets, the technical bar would be significantly lower. There's no need to fully replicate the meat experience for pets; it doesn't have to have the mouth feel, the smell, the taste, the texture, or other characteristics important to humans. The food simply needs to be nutritionally high quality and uniform. Kelleman explains it this way:

> It's solving a different problem—creating an animal protein that is nutritionally equivalent or better. You don't necessarily have to create that same lovely, human experience. Especially with dogs, there's more flexibility with what they'll put in their mouths. It struck me that even

though biotechnology wasn't my wheelhouse, my career path, if I could build a team that had that knowledge and skill-set, and who were passionate about creating a new way to produce proteins for companion animals, then we could do something pretty special.

Armed with this realization, it was an easy pivot from trying to create a more humanely sourced pet food to creating the road map to develop one of the world's first pet foods made through acellular agriculture. Unlike Because Animals and many of the plant-based pet food companies out there, Bond isn't necessarily "anti-meat for pets":

We believe meat can be a beautiful thing for dogs and cats in the sense that it provides the essential amino acids they need to thrive, and it's highly digestible and bioavailable. But meat comes with a lot of downside in terms of its environmental and animal welfare impacts, and with regards to food safety. Crazy things get introduced into processing meat that shouldn't be in there (pentobarbital, antibiotics, other pharmaceuticals).

Like Wild Earth and Because Animals, Bond's goal with its ambitious animal proteins is to replicate the composition of meat through an acellular process so as to help solve some of these problems. Bond is expressing authentic animal proteins in a microbial host. We saw this in Chapter 10 through the work of human food companies like Perfect Day, Clara Foods, and Geltor. Bond Pet Foods is starting with chickens, the most consumed meat in the world for both people and pets. It takes the genetic code from the chicken and isolates its muscle DNA. This DNA is then inserted into yeast or another fungus, where Bond uses the biological machinery of the microbe to create an optimal amino acid profile. That "optimal protein" becomes the cornerstone of Bond's complete pet food recipe. One of the joys of producing a protein through an acellular process is that companies don't have to worry about the Fetal Bovine Serum (FBS) conundrum we discussed earlier. Microbes don't need FBS to reproduce and make these proteins. There's also less pressure from food regulators, because the USDA, FDA, and AAFCO are familiar with fermented enzymes and proteins currently used as ingredients.

Although Bond Pet Foods is still in the early stages of its discovery process, it has already shown that it can express the proteins it's looking for in its microbial host of choice, and the company has filed numerous patents. Like other startups in this space, such as Wild Earth's fungal protein dog food and Because Animals' yeast-based dental chews, Bond plans to launch a first-generation product soon. A pure fungal or bacterial protein is planned for launch in 2019 and will help Bond introduce a "bigger venture." Like the others, Bond hopes to use this ingredient in a dog treat to help people see that it's safe and effective, doesn't cause upset stomachs, and is enjoyed by dogs. Bond's more ambitious pet food proteins should be ready to hit the market in three to four years.

Kelleman receives a steady drumbeat of messages and emails from people saying, "I can't wait until this comes to market!" That's why, unlike most of the other clean pet food startups, Bond is already loudly encouraging its future food products: "We wanted to feed into that excitement and that enthusiasm," Kelleman observes. "Organically, I wanted to start giving people the sense that a new choice is on the horizon, one that's animal-derived, that we're hard at work and building it every day."

In many ways, these young companies are doing for pet food what Dyson did for vacuum cleaners. Nobody thought you could innovate in vacuums until James Dyson reimagined the essence of vacuuming. Dyson asked fundamental questions: *What was the vacuum cleaner's purpose? Was there a way to do it better? Could I improve the experience?* Dyson reinvented how a vacuum cleaner works from the inside out, and, in the process, made the lives of millions of people easier. That's what Wild Earth, Bond Pet Foods, and Beyond Animals are doing with pet food. They're going into an increasingly unsustainable, problematic space and creating something entirely different from the inside out.

These companies are not just talking about a new brand, slogan, or flavor of dog food, but entirely new nutrient sources. That's why Bond advertises its products as offering "optimal nutrition without compromise" through "unapologetically engineered" proteins, and why Wild Earth refuses to disparage modern GM and related food technologies. Because the production process is carefully controlled, these companies can analyze the characteristics and ensure that the composition of their proteins is exactly what they want, depending on a pet's needs for their life stage or general health.

Remember the "biological handshake" introduced in Chapter 6? Bond and Wild Earth are working with teams of veterinarians and nutritionists to create blueprints for "perfect pet proteins" that can be engineered to meet the individual, unique needs of pets. Kelleman explains: "We're asking, how can we modify our approach in some way to yield a better protein composition for dogs and cats? Can we remix the natural feedstock and natural process of growth and harvest?" Ernie puts it even more simply: let's make better pet food.

Within a few weeks of eating these new foods, the pet owner might see her pet's coat look a little shinier or the stool a little firmer. Wild Earth, Because Animals, and Bond are even more excited about the long-term positive impacts that personalized nutrition promises. The proof that these new diets will help pets live longer, healthier lives will come from data. That's why Bond, Wild Earth, and Because Animals are capturing that intelligence as they develop and test their products.

In spite of the incredible promise of these technologies, and the amount of interest and energy in this space, these future pet foods still face many technological challenges. As Kelleman says: "There's obviously a difference between being able to produce something on a very small scale in a small five-liter bioreactor on a bench top, and a 100,000-liter scale." All these companies will need to work through those scale-up considerations as they move forward. Even with acellular production, a very high bar still remains when it comes to proving the ingredients' performance, safety, and efficacy, not just for regulatory agencies, but also for the company's own confidence and the public's assurance.

However, the biggest obstacle may be more psychological than physical. Kelleman shrugs:

> At the end of the day, there's also—not just on Bond's shoulders but everyone in the space—getting the world to go off the drug of conventional meat when it comes to pet foods. Meat is king in the pet food industry. Today everyone is looking for traditional meat protein as the number 1, 2, 3 ingredient—it's something that the public feels connotes quality. So, there's a significant amount of education that needs to be done to enlighten people about new microbial and animal-derived proteins and products.

If you've arrived at this point in this book, you've already been on this journey. You know that these new pet foods are aiming to be better than animal meat–based foods in *every single way*. However, there are those in the industry who still need convincing that clean pet food companies are solving a significant problem, and that the pet food industry could be more than just "recycled and repurposed" human food proteins. Kelleman tells us that some investors still think Bond is not going to have the same significant impact in mitigating environmental and animal welfare concerns that "people food companies" have. We saw early in this book that this isn't true; animal meats in pet food are a major cause of environmental destruction and animal suffering. The fact that this dismissive attitude prevails shows the pressing need for a narrative that challenges the perception of pet food as unimportant or insignificant to our future survival. The future of humanity depends on either feeding pets fewer animals or feeding fewer pets.

Ultimately, clean pet foods are not just solving a problem by replacing like-for-like. They're offering *more*. These alternative proteins will taste better, be safer, and be more nutritious, environmentally friendly, cruelty-free, and affordable. First, these startups make products that don't hurt animals or the environment. Next, they make a better, tastier product. Third, they find ways to make our pets healthier and more functional, improving health outcomes. And last? These companies convince pet

0

owners to try something new and unknown. Once that is achieved, the transition from animal meats to cell-based meats for people may actually be easier and quicker. That's when we truly begin saving the planet and securing our future.

Viva la Revolucíon! Working Toward Wider Transformation

Of course, these small startups are just the beginning. If pet food is to be truly revolutionized, the larger conventional pet food companies will need to join in. We're already seeing small, ethical startups partnering with established conglomerates in the human food industry, such as Boston's plant-based food tech company Motif getting backed in 2019 by $90 million in funding led by Breakthrough Energy Ventures.[3] This fund includes Amazon's founder, Jeff Bezos; Virgin's founder, Richard Branson; and Microsoft's founder, Bill Gates, who named the "cow-free burger" as one of his "Top 10 Breakthrough Technology Innovations of 2019."[4] Motif is helping plant-based food producers reach larger audiences by offering a biotechnology platform that ferments proteins typically derived from animal products. Sound familiar? That's exactly how our pet food startups are making their products. Motif sees biotech and fermentation as the answer to providing slaughter-free, sustainable meat alternatives that compete on price as well as taste.

The same sorts of partnerships are just beginning in biotech pet foods. Wild Earth was one of the first companies chosen for a start-up accelerator co-funded by Mars Petcare, the company behind brands like Pedigree, Whiskas, and Royal Canin. Bond Pet Foods was selected by Nestlé's Purina as a finalist for its 2019 innovation prize and has been working with Purina to develop "strategic opportunities." We saw in Chapter 7 that "people food" meat giant Tyson is embracing alternative proteins, recognizing the looming change, and investing in startups.

As explored earlier, a true social revolution requires broad, far-reaching change, spearheaded by passionate "true believers" but propelled by those who have the power, money, and experience to reach the wider market. Tyson Foods, Mars Petcare, and Nestlé Purina's active participation in cultured meats and plant-based nutrition is a sign of progress and inevitability. The fact that there are numerous news stories detailing the commercial interest in cultured meats makes the topic more widely acceptable and helps consumers reframe their concepts of "meat" and "protein."

As someone who worked with Burger King and then converted to veganism, Rich Kelleman is used to initiating change from the inside out. That's why he's excited about Bond Pet Foods' being a finalist for the Purina Pet Care Innovation Prize, despite his awareness that "some . . . might not see that affiliation and partnership in the best light." Wild Earth harbored the same concerns when it joined the Mars accelerator. Given all we've learned about conventional pet food in this book, it would be easy to vilify these massive conglomerates as ruthless corporate organizations, unconcerned about the environment, animal welfare, and pet health as long as the money rolls in. However, when we examine these corporations on a human level, this isn't the case. As Bond and Wild Earth quickly discovered, most employees at pet food companies honestly want to make a positive difference in pet well-being. Kelleman from Bond says:

> As part of the award, we spent a significant amount of time in St. Louis with a cross-section of folks who work in Purina's innovation nutrition, regulatory, manufacturing divisions—you name it—and they genuinely, as a company, care about our pets (it's not just business). For example, we had a team dinner one night, and literally, a member of their executive team began to cry when he shared what his group was working on; he was so connected to the initiatives they're working on and the difference they're making in pets' lives.

Ernie from Wild Earth recalls a similar experience:

> I was so accustomed to people rolling their eyes as soon as I said, "plant-based pet food," that I was overjoyed when the entire Mars team nodded in agreement. They agreed that it didn't matter where the nutrients originated, as long as they provided the best health for our pets. The

discussion wasn't whether we should use yeast, fungal, or cell-based proteins, only how these new proteins could help us make pet food that was healthier and better for the environment and animal welfare.

Rather than competing, why not join forces and see what lessons can be shared? This pooling of intellectual and practical resources is the beginning of a true revolution. Although we may never know what meetings are like at the highest levels of Mars, Purina, or Hill's Pet Food, it's clear that the majority of their ordinary employees have a genuine desire to make the best pet foods possible, and many are increasingly concerned about factory farming and the environmental damage their products cause. Kelleman points out:

> While other aspects of farm or supply-chain animal welfare could undoubtedly be improved—and perhaps that's why they chose us as part of the 2019 cohort—I firmly believe that collaborations with the largest pet food companies in the world can amplify cellular agriculture's impact, be it through greater access to decades of study and knowledge in pet nutrition, or [by] one day supplying these global brands with cultured proteins to replace animal ingredients in their high-volume, high-reach products. These partnerships can help make faster progress in transforming the food landscape for the better.

Kelleman and Ernie are confident that over time there will be more partnerships and collaborations within the pet food industry, whether through mergers or strategic collaborations. There *have* to be, if the movement away from conventional animal-meat protein is to become more than just a niche segment. To have the global impact that we want and *need* to have, these innovative startups need to do more than just gradually grow their own brands. The need for and efficacy of these revolutionary new ingredients need to be proven if they are to be widely adopted. One of the fastest ways for that to happen is for a large pet food company to place a high-volume order of an alternative protein and declare "we support this." True change starts when we *replace* some of the larger animal-meat products around the world, as opposed to simply competing against them.

Finless Foods is another future food startup that has found itself collaborating rather than competing with the major players, largely due to the exclusive nature of its product. "In the fishing industry, everyone wants to find a way to produce more bluefin tuna, but they can't," CEO Mike Selden tells us. "There's only one company on Earth that knows how to farm it with a closed life cycle, and they're having a lot of trouble scaling up, because bluefin tuna have a very long life cycle." Finless Foods' "sell" to seafood companies is, as Selden puts it: "Hey, we can make incredible amounts of bluefin tuna, whereas currently you can't really increase your levels of production whatsoever." He tells us that rather than fighting against his company, the conventional fishing industry is really excited that they've found a way to make more tuna. In turn, Selden is keen to work with the people who are experts in supply-chain logistics, advertising and marketing, and packaging and who know all of the distributors, co-packers, restaurants, and grocery stores. He explains:

> I think some CEOs and co-founders in this industry see this as a kind of moral crusade against people who have wronged animals. I really don't see it that way. I think that capitalism is really an inherently wrong system that forces people to exploit each other, and exploit animals, and exploit the environment. So, I don't really see anyone's hands being clean, be it mine or anyone else's. . . . With that in mind, I don't see a point in doing anything other than trying to get this product to market as fast as we can, in terms of making sure that it sees the widest possible adoption that it possibly can.

By collaborating with larger, more experienced companies, food biotech startups can outsource as much knowledge as possible, leaving them free to concentrate on developing the best, most ethical, and most sustainable products. Big businesses can then help the startups get their products to consumers quickly and effectively. The more people they can reach, the faster change will happen. The relationship works both ways: smaller startups can inspire bigger companies to do better, to think outside the box. By challenging conventional, tired notions of what makes "good enough" human and pet food, these startups are inspiring industry-wide innovation; by highlighting sustainability and ethics, they're helping hold corporations accountable. Wild Earth, Bond Pet Foods, and Because Animals can show Mars, Purina, Hill's, and others that there's a better way, and these large companies can then help them realize that ambition.

Would You Feed Cultured Meat to Your Pets?

Ross Lamond from Bug Bakes is happy to munch on his cricket-flour dog treats; Shannon Falconer tops up her breakfast smoothie with Because Animals' superfood pet food supplement; and Ryan and Ernie are known to nibble on Wild Earth's canine koji biscuits. What differentiates "people food" from "pet food"? If it's now okay, even desirable, for a pet to eat what its human eats, is it also now socially acceptable to eat food offered to a dog or cat?

A paper by Alison Langdon, an English professor at Western Kentucky University, explores our attitudes toward sharing food with animals.[5] Langdon writes that humans tend to feel uncomfortable sharing food meant for their own mouths with nonhumans. She argues that sharing food with our pets manifests our "medieval unease" with "human animality." She claims this unease is experienced even when we share food with pet dogs, the nonhuman animal with whom we "most intimately share both the procurement and consumption of food." Langdon describes the depiction of food sharing in medieval literature, including the tale of Sir Gowther, whose penance for his many sins is to remain silent and only eat food he receives from the mouth of a dog. The pope allegedly decrees this punishment as a means of reducing Sir Gowther to a lowly state, even lower than a dog. This act of humility becomes the foundation for his future salvation. But is it an act of grace or punishment? Human and pet food sharing is a complicated affair, with Langdon concluding that the categories of animal and human food are "more porous, sometimes transgressing, sometimes reaffirming boundaries." Sometimes people food is okay for pets, and other times pet food is okay for people.

The fluidity and nuances of these arguably arbitrary categories of "pet food" and "human food" are still evident today. Although the majority of social media tends to share cute dog and cat memes and adoring photographs, occasionally a post like this goes viral:

> This lady at my work today told me her ex-husband cheated on her so she made him a "beef and rice" dinner with dog food mixed in and didn't tell him till after he ate the whole thing that if he wanted to act like a dog she would feed him like one & i'm still laughing.

Equating a husband's infidelity to "acting like a dog," the woman punishes her cheating spouse by feeding him dog food. Published in March 2018, the post had received 15,696 "likes" on Instagram at the time of writing. Nearly seven centuries after the tale of Sir Gowther, we still perceive food for a dog as being wholly separate from and unfit for humans. There's a lot of disgust in this Instagram post, not just toward the cheating man, but perhaps inadvertently toward dogs and their food. It suggests that while we claim to feed pets *nutrients* instead of *ingredients*, we may be missing deeper complexities within our relationship with food. Some food *only we eat*, and some food *we only feed*, even when the only physical difference is a label.

Not everyone agrees. Many of the comments under this social media post defend dogs as loyal and innocent and encourage compassionate treatment of the husband instead of vilification. This is new for humans, because historically we've had clear boundaries around food based on who gathered it. In medieval times, agency determined the nature of the food; an animal's kill became animal food, and a human's kill (or harvest) became human food.[6] Today, we feed our dogs and cats meals we purchased. Even if the pet food contains a dead animal, we didn't kill the animal, nor did our pet. Whose food is it?

The main differences between people foods and pet foods have more to do with processing than nutrients. For starters, human food is held to a higher safety standard than pet food. There are more rigorous food safety–testing requirements, and companies have potentially higher liability should a problem occur. Food animals deemed diseased, dying, or disabled are forbidden for people food yet considered acceptable by the FDA for animal feed. Human foods must be processed, packaged, and transported in near-sterile environments, as opposed to pet food manufacturing, which can be less clean. In general, people food is usually a bit safer than that for pets. In reality, however, the differences aren't as significant as you might think. Food is food. What we call it has more to do with the risk of contamination from processing than ingredients or nutrients.

The clean pet food revolution is about tearing down pet food taboos by removing potentially unsafe ingredients and contaminants. Animal meats, as we've seen throughout this book, are the main source of pet food contamination. Removing animal flesh from pet food is the first step toward clean pet food. But is that enough for consumers? How can future food companies address the worry that cultured meats will inadvertently introduce other risks? Chris Bryant, who studies consumer attitudes to clean meat for a living, believes that if people won't eat clean meat themselves, they are highly unlikely to feed it to their pets. Bryant's research reveals that some of the reasons for consumer rejection of clean meat are the perception of it as either unnatural or unsafe, or concerns that it is inferior in terms of taste and aesthetics.[7]

Bryant's findings suggest that women are generally less likely to try clean meat than men. He says: "I suspect that the main factor driving rejection is perceived risk. Women tend to be more risk averse than men, particularly when it comes to food and especially in the context of feeding their families." And pets are part of our families, making food choices more important than ever. Andrew Knight agrees, pointing out that most people view their companion animals as surrogate children and want to safeguard them. He concludes that if people have concerns about a product for themselves, they won't want to feed it to their animals.

Not everyone agrees with Bryant and Knight, and consumer perceptions about plant-based foods are rapidly changing. More recent surveys indicate consumers are beginning to accept the idea of "clean meat." The Good Food Institute (GFI) partnered with Faunalytics in 2018 to develop a comprehensive study to gauge U.S. public opinion regarding clean meat, entitled "Messages to Overcome Naturalness Concerns in Clean Meat Acceptance: Primary Findings."[8] Funded by Animal Charity Evaluators, the study is the first considered by food experts to be a scientifically rigorous survey of the public's opinion of cultured meat. Overall, the results were encouraging: "66 percent of respondents stated they were willing to try a clean meat product; 53 percent were willing to eat clean or cultured meat as a replacement for animal meat; and 46 percent said they would be willing to buy it regularly."

GFI also wanted to investigate what would encourage more people to switch to clean meats. These results were even more intriguing. Researchers initially assumed people would switch to clean meats when shown how animals were raised and slaughtered. Messages revealing the use of hormones and antibiotics in animal meats were the most effective, but not overwhelmingly. Apparently, many people already knew that animal meats are steeped in controversy but felt there were no viable alternatives. In other words, consumers knew meats were bad, but what choice did they have when they craved a burger? So GFI asked them what they feared about clean meats.

Interestingly, the researchers found that people were generally receptive to the idea of animal-meat alternatives and reported few reservations. In fact, the results indicated no universal "ick" factor regarding clean meat, meaning future foods are likely to succeed. GFI uncovered that most people are uncomfortable with conventional meat and are looking for an alternative that competes on taste, price, and convenience. Give consumers a choice, and clean meat wins, which bodes well for clean pet foods: 62 percent of Americans are likely to try a food made using technology, rising to 71 percent among younger millennials.[9] Once the regulatory process is sorted out, it seems likely that fears around safety will disappear altogether. Still, Bryant suspects that the taste and aesthetics of clean meats could remain an acceptance barrier to clean pet foods. "A lot of people are very infatuated with their pets and want to feel like they're treating them all the time," he says. "So if consumers perceive clean meat to be a sacrifice on taste and texture, even if they're not the ones eating it, it could put them off buying it." Ernie challenges this supposition by inviting pet owners to open a bag or can of conventional pet food and identify the "real meats." Most pet owners will be left asking, "Where's the beef?" Future pet foods have the opportunity to reframe what proteins look, feel, and taste like and be more transparent about processing.

Ernie and Ron are confident that public perception of lab-grown meat is going to change quickly as people realize it has immediate benefits for them and their pets. Ron compares this to the controversy over GMO soy and corn years ago. Despite being two very successful products today, in terms of public relations they were complete failures. Ron believes the controversy stemmed from the fact that the technology was focused on improving supply-chain efficiency, with no direct and obvious benefits to the consumer. If you asked what the GMO or technological improvement accomplished, the answer went as follows: "It makes it easier and cheaper for corporations to grow more."

This response might have been terrific for the corporation, but it showed no benefit for the consumer. Nor were there any health, taste, or nutritional benefits to justify the food's genetic tinkering, which is not a good position for a food. The result was confusion and controversy, and both ultimately derailed an entire technology. The failure of this technology shows that even a 30 percent cost reduction means little when you have a plate of food in front of you and an emotional idea of what you're putting into your body: "Wait, I'm putting some Frankenfood in my body so a rich corporation can make more money? No, thank you!"

What if you learn that technology is going to make food *better* for you or your pet? Not better for the food executives, but better for *your* health, the health of your family, or that of your pet. Ernie, Ron, and other future food scientists believe that message has the potential to transform how new food technologies are accepted. Shigeta summarizes: "When the food actively participates in your health and helps you become a healthier person, people will flock to it." Ernie also emphasizes his belief that people are increasingly concerned about climate change, and purchasing animal-free foods will allow consumers to be a part of the solution. This is why the clean pet food pioneers believe they will succeed. For Kelleman, Bond's immediate market is vegans or vegetarians struggling with the same ethical feeding friction that inspired him to start the company. Wild Earth is confident that clean pet food will appeal to the "Meatless Monday" crowd and flexitarians, people who are beginning to critically evaluate their own food choices. These are people who shop at places like Whole Foods and are mindful about the foods they purchase. Kelleman agrees:

> They're reading pet food labels, educating themselves about the ingredients and options, with an eye on super-premium products because they feel those brands are more of an open book in how they're sourced and made. This is the audience we'll initially be courting with our brand and products.

Over time, as Bond's products and others gain momentum, Kelleman is confident that people will start to reassess the nutritional profile of their pets. They'll see that their neighbors are feeding Wild Earth, Bond Pet Foods, or Because Animals products to their pets, that they're healthy and thriving, and they'll want the same. Pet owners who see clean pet foods as a healthy choice don't need to be attached to sustainability or animal welfare issues. They will simply see that their neighbor's dog is doing well without animal meat, so they'll give it a try.

Even health, safety, and affordability aren't going to convince everyone to switch to a cellular-meat pet food. Some are content with plant-based foods, and that's absolutely fine. Some vegans dislike the idea of consuming anything that came from an animal, no matter how distant or removed from an actual living being. Bryant believes that although some vegans and vegetarians may be less likely than omnivores to try clean meat, they also tend to be more supportive of it as a concept for meat-eaters, given its capacity to reduce animal suffering. People concerned about animal welfare will likely be happy to feed clean meat pet foods, viewing it as a solution to the ethical feeding friction discussed in Chapter 8.

Many pet owners believe cats are the perfect species for the first cultured meats, as the comments on vegan-leather Beyond Skin's post "Would you eat lab grown meat?" suggest:

"No way . . . can't do that anymore, even if it's false. But for my pet, if it's safe, OK why not?"

"Feeding my cats meat feels really wrong but I don't think there's been enough research to be able to trust they'd be okay on a vegan diet. This seems like the perfect solution."

"Oh, good point about the cat food!"

"I would not eat it but would buy it for my cat."

"No, but I bet my cat would!"

"One thing I'd LOVE 'cruelty-free' meat for? Feeding to my own dog!"

This notion of "I would not eat it, but I would buy it for my cat" could potentially backfire, creating harmful boundaries between clean meat pet food and conventional meat human food. It has been argued by several clean meat startups that if companies like Wild Earth and Bond Pet Food bring *clean meat pet food* to the market first, people will associate clean meats with a "substandard" or at least "different" category of food, and will be less likely to eat it themselves. "I don't think that cell-based fish should be used for pet food, ever," Mike Selden of Finless Foods tells Alice. "I think it's bad for the industry. I just think it will be really difficult to sell something as dog food and then have the rest of the industry sell it as people food." Nearly all of the clean pet food pioneers confirm that some investors feel their companies' efforts could potentially slow the movement if they bring clean pet food products to market sooner than clean human food products. Sounds like Sir Gowther's story all over again. Can we ever truly share food with an animal?

Unsurprisingly, people like Ernie and Kelleman aren't worried that if we feed pets clean meat, we may discourage humans from eating it. Their focus is solely on improving the health of pets and reducing animal suffering as quickly and effectively as possible. For those working in future pet foods, cell-based meat is the future, for both humans and animals. The most important thing is to bring *better* pet food choices to market to benefit all animals. Ron Shigeta sees pet food as an excellent way to accelerate the next generation of microbe-based human food that can actually compete against the conventional contenders.

First, companies like Wild Earth will succeed with animal food. Then, Shigeta believes, microbe-based food for people will catch on. Shigeta sees biotech pet food companies as paving the way for producers to make cultured foods that one day everybody, people and pets, will enjoy. Ultimately, the argument that clean pet foods will somehow sour human clean foods only works if we ignore the public's increasing demand for "human-grade pet foods." As Chris Bryant says, there's no logic to the resistance against clean meat pet food today: "In theory, I can't see why clean pet food should reduce the appeal of clean meat for humans: if my dog eats beef, that doesn't make me want to eat beef any less." Kelleman agrees:

> The pet food industry has evolved so much over the last decade. If you go to any pet industry conference today and look at the foods people are clamoring for, you'll think that pet foods are meant for your own cupboards and consumption. Natural, organic, traceable, sustainable, certified humane, etc. There's a humanization in what people are looking and asking for in pet food. There's an opportunity to satiate this interest and demand.

For Ernie, "Food is food. I'm interested in optimizing nutrients to benefit pets and people."

If there's one former advertising executive who may be able to sell clean pet food without encroaching on human foods, it's Kelleman:

> A lot of love, care, and effort have gone in to create something that's better than what's out there right now. If it's positioned like that, I don't think any of the human food companies have anything to worry about. In fact, I wholeheartedly believe it could help their cause.

In these days of human-grade, gourmet pet food, feeding your dog a certain type of food doesn't make humans less likely to eat it, as long as it's high quality and safe. The huge success of fresh pet food companies such as The Farmer's Dog and Just Food for Dogs is built on dog owners sharing the same prime cuts of beef and fresh vegetables they pile on their own plates. Because Animals' human-grade products are further validation of this burgeoning sentiment. The clean pet food revolution is counting on it.

Mike Selden argues that because plants and fungi are better for the environment, cheaper, and easier to produce, it would be better simply to stick to those ingredients for pet food. He says that pets aren't picky about food technology and confirms that dogs *love* Wild Earth's koji fungal proteins. Selden points out that pets don't psychologically understand the difference between animal meat and something else; they just need the right nutrients, and it needs to taste good, qualities you can achieve without growing animal cells. He explains:

> People have psychology. If they're convinced that they need meat, they need to be convinced that what they're eating is meat, whatever that means to them. Pets don't have that hangup, as far as I can tell.

Of course, this argument misses an important point: pets might not have any hangups about what they're eating, but their owners do. Although dogs and cats may eat whatever we give them, *people*, not pets, buy the food. Most pet owners continue to believe that their dogs and cats desire animal meat, and they want to give them the best quality possible. This now includes meats they would eat themselves.

A common complaint against the terminology "clean meat" is that it implies conventional animal meat is "dirty." The "dirty" is most often associated with animal proteins and their associated contamination. As we've seen, cultured meat avoids almost all the risks of animal meat, making it a safer and "cleaner" alternative for both humans and pets. Both Wild Earth and Because Animals are helping to preserve cultured meats such as beef for humans by creating species-appropriate animal cells such as mouse and small bird meats. Using cell lines exclusively associated with dog and cat prey will aid in eliminating consumer confusion. Bond Pet Foods is more confident this "clean prey meat" strategy isn't necessary, focusing instead on cultured chicken, the meat most consumed by both humans and pets. Ultimately, the promise of biotech is that *any* of these protein sources can be developed, safely and sustainably, for human or animal consumption. Kelleman is optimistic: "If we have this conversation again in a year's time [2020], I'm sure instead of talking about a handful of companies doing some interesting things in this space, it will be a dozen or more." He adds:

> The next generation of pet food is going to be exciting—and transformative—for the world. Multiple companies with different approaches, different voices, different points of view, and [different] ways to create pet foods through cellular agriculture. That's going to be very interesting.

It's going to be more than interesting. It's going to be revolutionary.

13

Saving Pet Food's Secret Victims

Cruelty-Free Pet Food Testing

O N A DARK night in 1965, Julia and Peter Lakavage's Dalmatian, Pepper, disappeared from their rural Pennsylvania backyard. Heartbroken, Julia spent the next week scouring the surrounding terrain, sending search parties through the woods, and driving to the top of Blue Mountain to desperately call her name. No trace was found. Julia persisted in her search, and eventually received a tip that a van had been spotted in the area carrying two large Dalmatians. Julia raced to find the van.

By the time Julia discovered the whereabouts of her beloved Pepper, it was too late. Pepper had already been implanted with an experimental cardiac pacemaker, having been abducted and sold to a medical lab in Philadelphia. Pepper died during the experimental heart surgery, and her body was cremated. This Dalmatian's story kicked off a national media sensation around the theft of pets for biomedical research. Ultimately, the tragedy helped modernize animal-testing protocols. In response to the "midnight dog thefts," animal researchers began relying on outside companies to supply them with animals bred specifically for research. No more dognapping. But what about the welfare of animals sentenced to be born and die in the name of science? And what does this have to do with pet food? A lot more than you might think.

After Pepper's story broke, researchers in North America and Western Europe stopped turning to shady procurement for their research animals. In the early 1970s, U.S. companies such as Marshall BioResources and Sinclair BioResources began breeding and selling genetically standardized, mass-produced dogs, cats, pigs, and rodents, shipped and delivered directly to laboratories. Need a dog for your study? No problem. These companies can provide your lab with a limitless supply of beagles—more specifically, Antibody Profile Defined/Specific Pathogen Free (APD/SPF) Marshall Beagles.

Pepper's case clearly demonstrates that the line between "pet dog" and "laboratory dog" is easily crossed—and forgotten. Most pet owners would search high and low, as Pepper's did, to find their missing dog. When it was discovered that Pepper had been used for research and killed, her outraged pet parents started a movement to change attitudes and laws. What was lost in the fury was that Pepper's owners, and society as a whole, were silent on the suffering of other "parentless" dogs used in research. It seems that most dog owners are okay with dogs being used in testing, as long as the animal in question isn't *their* dog.

It's time we stopped this hypocrisy when it comes to animal ethics and moral attitudes. Why are we okay with some animals being bred, confined, and killed for testing, while simultaneously snuggling with others and calling them our "children"? We need a little more consistency with our beliefs. Which leads us back to pet food and animal research.

No matter how much specialized breeding the *bioresource* (that's the inanimate term used within the research industry for "test animal") has, he or she is still a living, breathing, affectionate dog, cat, or other animal. The apparent ethical boundary between research animals and the ones we keep in our homes is only a name: *pet* versus *bioresource*. Reminds us of *beef* versus *cow*; *bacon* versus *piglet*. By removing the animal name from a food or experiment, it somehow makes it morally acceptable and ethically allowable. We, the authors, disagree, and many others do, too.

One of the more disturbing aspects of animal testing is that it's not only medical research that is being performed on dogs and cats. Every day across the United States, thousands of "purpose-bred beagles" awake to languish in isolated laboratory colonies, waiting to take their turn in *pet food feeding trials*. These dogs were bred to do one thing: live in confinement, their bodies exploited for experimentation. There are no loving owners to collect these animals and take them home to play. Their "purpose" is to sit in cages, day in, day out, testing different foods for our own companion animals. Yes, there are a few high-welfare pet food feeding trial facilities beginning to appear, and we applaud their efforts. They're taking the well-being and quality of life of their beagles more seriously and sensitively than previous generations of testing facilities. It's a step in the right, humane, direction. Yet despite offering better living conditions, these facilities continue using beagles bred exclusively for research. We believe scientists and producers need to do even better. And they can, with recent breakthroughs in biotech and innovative laboratories such as PetMech.

PetMech: Finding a Better Way

Tim Bowser is trim and reserved, with eyes that reveal the impressive intelligence hidden beneath his unassuming Midwestern accent. If you met Bowser, you would be hard-pressed to imagine him in a white lab coat, immersed in food research at Oklahoma State University. Bowser is one of only a handful of leading scientists seeking to provide humane animal testing, a vocation he attributes to his religious upbringing. Raised to treat all animals and people with compassion, it's religion that Bowser credits for his progressive view on animal testing. He's quick to quote Bible verses from Exodus and Proverbs that exhort mankind to "treat animals kindly," but as he began his doctoral research, his faith started to conflict with what he was witnessing in the lab.

He observed research animals being treated poorly and handled roughly with little regard for their comfort and well-being. About that time, he became friends with an iconic professor of psychology, Dr. Charles Abramson, who was also concerned about animal research. One day, after Bowser shared his discomfort with a particular animal-testing protocol, Dr. Abramson issued a challenge: "Is there a different way to do this? Why are we hurting them? Is there a better way?" Bowser set out to find the answer to the last question. In 2005, he founded PetMech, a "humane, in-home product testing company," described on its website as recognizing "a need for humane pet and animal food and product testing using in-home testing techniques."[1]

There's another reason that Bowser has focused on using laboratory analysis and in-home testing of volunteer pets, instead of traditional "kennel farms" (a term he uses casually, revealing the current standard and comfort level among most laboratory researchers). He feels in-home pet testing is not only more humane but also provides more accurate results. Bowser has been closely involved with the shift in human medical research toward computational models and *in vitro* testing and sees this being applied to pet food tests, too. "Many of these newer non-animal testing models can be better than live animal testing," he says. "We're just beginning to see the trickle-over from human research."

PetMech was one of the early animal feed testing labs to switch from using the traditional, yet barbaric, food digestibility testing known as "gavage" to *in vitro* tests simulating the stomach and intestinal tract's digestive processes. In the past, to determine how digestible a pet food was, you'd insert a known amount into a porous bag, force feed it to the dog or cat, and retrieve it at set intervals. You'd weigh the food pouch and the difference was the "digestibility." A dog could be subjected to these painful tests over and over again for days to weeks as a pet food formulation was adjusted. Bowser asked himself whether there might be a different way to obtain these results, and concluded the answer was "yes"—by providing animal-free, *in vitro* laboratory analysis for pet food digestibility. Thanks to the efforts of Bowser and others, *in vitro* digestibility testing is quickly becoming the preferred method for pet food companies. Plus, it's faster and cheaper than the torturous old way.

Pet food palatability is another criterion Bowser identified a better way to evaluate. Most pet food companies outsource the determination of whether or not a pet enjoys their food to one of those specialized "kennel farms." Some of the larger pet food manufacturers will conduct feeding trials with their *own* laboratory animals on-site, and the conditions these animals are kept in are often hidden from public view. In either scenario, dogs and cats purpose-bred for research are offered a food, and their response is recorded. Bowser questioned the necessity of a dog living in confinement for the sole purpose of palatability tests. He also realized that volunteer pet dogs better represented the variety of taste preferences of real-life dogs, and that research beagles may not signal accurate canine acceptance. Those captive beagles might love a certain treat flavor, but your rescue mutt may not find it as appetizing. Tim started experimenting with pets volunteered by their owners to conduct palatability research. Once he refined his methodology, he discovered pet food companies that were uncomfortable with research "kennel farms" began seeking out his particular type of testing.

Wild Earth has been working with Bowser to revolutionize pet food feeding trials. Many veterinarians advise pet owners to choose a pet food stamped, ANIMAL FEEDING TESTS USING AAFCO PROCEDURES SUBSTANTIATE THAT _____ PROVIDES COMPLETE AND BALANCED NUTRITION FOR _____. To earn that badge, the pet food must undergo live animal feeding trials. In simplest terms, a pet food is fed to a colony of research dogs for six months. Concurrently, a colony of control dogs is fed a known, approved diet. Throughout the test, the dogs are checked weekly for weight loss. As long as the dogs don't lose more than 15 percent of their body weight while being fed the diet, pass four basic blood tests, and show no signs of obvious illness, the pet food is considered "animal feeding trial approved." And what happens to the colonies afterward, when the dogs can no longer be used? Some facilities will try to find homes for dogs they can't use, but this isn't the case for all. Many end up euthanized.

Some feeding trials are deadly. Remember the pet food–pentobarbital contamination we discussed at the beginning of this book? To determine whether the level of pentobarbital found in pet food was harmful to pets, the Center for Veterinary Medicine conducted an eight-week feeding trial using forty-two beagle puppies. Jessica Pierce relays how these young dogs were fed pentobarbital-laced food, then killed and their organs "evaluated."[2] The fact that researchers found no obvious harm to the forty-two puppies might reassure owners that the pet food is safe. Unfortunately for those puppies, the pet food study was lethal.

Pet food companies can do so much better than this. For starters, the feeding trial methodology is severely limited and outdated. PetMech and Wild Earth are calling for pet food testing agencies to demand more thorough biochemical analyses, along with complete urinalysis and fecal microbiome testing. Current AAFCO requirements for feeding trials are limited to testing hemoglobin (HGB), packed cell volume (PCV), serum alkaline phosphatase (ALP), and serum albumin (ALB), measured and recorded at the beginning and end of the test period. That's it. We have thousands of modern medical biomarkers that can precisely measure and detect abnormalities much earlier and more accurately than these few archaic tests. Our pets deserve better testing for their foods, and that doesn't have to mean more beagles suffering.

Bowser and Ernie are pushing to allow *in-home* pet food feeding trials. This has only been done once with a fresh pet food, California-based Just Food for Dogs, in 2013. Just Food for Dogs conducted the experimental study with Cal Poly Pomona's Animal Health Science Department. Bowser wants to make this a commercial reality, allowing any pet food company to easily conduct humane feeding studies. Ernie explains their proposal:

> Our goal is to provide completely cruelty-free pet food. To us, that means not only making food without harming animals, but also without lab animal experiments. That's why we're encouraging the entire pet food industry to rethink laboratory animal feeding trials and begin using in-home pet feeding studies. We start by verifying the pet food is nutritionally complete and balanced based on AAFCO chemical analysis and formulation guidelines. Chemical nutritional analysis has been proven for decades to be a safe and effective means to ensure nutritional adequacy in pet foods, and is the current method by which most pet foods are approved for sale in the U.S. These foods carry the AAFCO statement: FORMULATED TO MEET THE NUTRITIONAL LEVELS

ESTABLISHED BY THE AAFCO DOG (OR CAT) FOOD NUTRIENT PROFILES. It also doesn't require any testing on animals.

After the food passes these requirements, pet owners can volunteer their healthy adult pet to participate in a 26-week feeding trial. The feeding trial dogs are then fed the test diet exclusively during the study period, with extensive veterinary examinations and blood, urine, and fecal testing performed throughout. I believe testing should not be limited to only the start and end points of the feeding trial, as the current guidelines require. I think AAFCO should call for repeated and more comprehensive tests throughout the 26-week period to optimize our understanding of the diet and detect any subtle physiological shifts.

These feeding trials require a committed and trustworthy pet owner. In our experience, we've been pleasantly surprised by the number of owners eager and willing to help. For the control dogs eating a previously AAFCO feeding trial diet, a cohort from the community may be used. The FDA and state pet feed regulators can accurately determine if a food passes based on study participants' physical and biochemical results. We know that humane, in-home feeding trials are more challenging, but based on [our] own experience and that of Just Food for Dogs, we know it can, and should, become the standard.

Why aren't other companies following this example and removing captive research beagles from pet food testing altogether, allowing actual pets to trial nutritionally approved food by consuming it at home and leading normal lives? By broadening testing to include a wide variety of breeds, in-home feeding trials could better uncover "real-world" issues of mixed-breed and other purebred dogs and cats. In the human drug–testing space, the risks of relying on medical trials conducted only on Caucasian males have been evident. Drug reactions in females and various ethnic groups aren't recognized until the drug is launched.

By combining existing chemical nutritionally guaranteed analysis with modern biomarkers and in-home testing, it should be possible to produce the safest and most nutritious pet foods. Wild Earth is collaborating with Bowser to ensure that the company's in-home testing protocols meet and exceed all current research dog colony standards. Wild Earth is also working closely with government regulatory agencies to follow and, in some cases, establish additional nutrition and safety codes. Ernie says many of his colleagues within large pet food companies and governmental agencies are also concerned about animal welfare and are eager to explore ways to reduce and eliminate animal testing.

Love Animals? Don't Support Animal Testing

> We must painfully acknowledge that, precisely because of its great intellectual development, the best of man's domesticated animals—the dog—most often becomes the victim of physiological experiments. . . . The dog is irreplaceable; moreover, it is extremely touching. It is almost a participant in the experiments conducted upon it, greatly facilitating the success of the research by its understanding and compliance.—**Ivan Pavlov**, 1893

In 1935, the Nobel Prize–winning scientist Ivan Pavlov, of "Pavlov's Dogs" infamy, approved the design for his commemorative monument outside the Institute of Experimental Medicine in St. Petersburg, Russia. The plaque depicts several of Pavlov's research dogs tied to wooden frames in the laboratory, their "Pavlov's Pouch," a surgical opening into their stomach for experimentation, gorily gaping at viewers. It's hard to imagine approving that sort of image today. Many believe such brutal, inhumane experiments are a thing of the past. Most people don't find experimenting on dogs "touching." However, a certain idea lingers and is actively promoted by organizations, including the Foundation of Biomedical Research (FBR), that these dogs are willing, compliant, and understanding participants. These pro–lab animal research groups describe the conditions as similar to a home environment, with exceptional care taken to ensure each animal's happiness. If your idea of "home" is a maximum-security prison, then you'd probably feel welcome in most animal research facilities.

Beagles are the most commonly used dog breed because they are easy to train, and will passively lift a paw for an I.V. or injection or step into a restraint harness without complaint. Because beagles are so trusting, it's easy to argue they "enjoy" experimentation. If they didn't like what humans were doing to them, wouldn't they put up more of a fight? FBR and its spokespeople, including Dr. Temple Grandin, argue these beagle experiments are an extension of our love for animals. They say that loving animals means supporting testing on them. No joke.

In October 2017, the FBR campaign LOVE ANIMALS? SUPPORT ANIMAL RESEARCH FEATURING DR. TEMPLE GRANDIN celebrated "how medical discoveries made with animal research have helped our companion animals live longer, happier, healthier lives." Without animal research, they say, our pets would not have immunizations against rabies, distemper, parvo, or feline leukemia; we wouldn't be able to treat heartworm, brucellosis, cancer, or canine arthritis. Okay, so perhaps some animal research is necessary, even for other animals. What is questionable is the implication that the animals being experimented on should somehow be happy and honored to be experimented on. What if we were talking about nonconsenting human test subjects, innocent people "taking one for the team" so their luckier cousins could benefit? The ethics don't hold up to us. Furthermore, it's one thing to justify life-saving research on animals to save a human or animal life; it's quite another to try to justify thousands of dogs bred and imprisoned in kennel farms for a new variation of pet food. Scientific progress is meant to improve lives, not perpetuate outdated methodologies.

Brutally invasive testing on dogs has also occurred in the last twenty years, at least in America. In 2002 and 2003, undercover investigators from People for the Ethical Treatment of Animals (PETA) uncovered inhumane suffering of dogs at a U.S. testing facility contracted by a large pet food company.[3] Dogs were filmed confined in inadequately sized cages with feces- and urine-covered flooring, and videos were taken of dogs being piled on the ground after having their vocal cords surgically removed. The U.S. Department of Agriculture investigated PETA's complaints and found the laboratory did not provide minimum veterinary care and pain relief to suffering animals, failed to provide animals with adequate living space, and did not adequately train laboratory personnel on basic animal handling and care.[4] These findings, along with about forty other violations of the federal Animal Welfare Act, resulted in a paltry $33,000 (£59,000) fine. Since then, the pet food company implicated has discontinued using the convicted research center, but animal welfare and rights advocate Lorie Grefski hastens to add that "they do still conduct animal experimentation that many consider cruel."[5] The past decade of legislative changes protecting animal facilities through ag-gag laws has made it incredibly difficult and dangerous to determine the current extent of testing on dogs, cats, and other sentient species.

It shouldn't be acceptable to experiment on one animal and snuggle with another, especially when both are dogs or cats. We must insist that the food we feed our pets has not been produced at the expense and suffering of another, less-privileged animal. We must abolish sentencing one dog or cat to a life of confinement and experimentation in order to feed another. Just Food for Dogs, PetMech, and Wild Earth are innovating pet food testing in order to safely feed them without having to breed and sacrifice thousands of "farmed" dogs and cats.

Conclusion

I think the beautiful thing about this space, for both human and pet foods, is that there are so many different ways of producing proteins and delivering on nutrition that will come into the fold over the next decade. And there's room for all of it. It's not just one microbial protein or one cultured option; there's going to be a suite of options that different companies are going to bring to market, and I think at the end of the day, that's all good: that *choice* for pet owners, for people, just weighing what's important to them when it comes to product format and nutrition, and everything in between.

—**Rich Kelleman**, Bond Pet Foods

MAYBE YOU'VE MADE it to the end of this book and still wish to feed your pet human-grade or homemade meat-based meals, sprinkled with Because Animals Superfood. You might be happy to try Wild Earth's plant- and fungi-based dog food, but plan to steer clear of cultured animal meat. Maybe insect-based pet food appeals most to you. Or perhaps you're excited at the thought of a future where your cat can enjoy seafood without harming any real fish. Well, all of those options are okay with us. Our message is *and* not *or*. These revolutionary pet food companies aren't taking any of your diet choices away. Instead, they're making new options that owners can try and their pets will crave. You might feed your dog a vegetarian diet but supplement it with the occasional cut of beef. Perhaps you stick to your current chicken kibble but buy koji cookies for treats. Essentially, these new pet food companies are competing in a global market to make the food that you give your pets *better*.

Technology never compels anybody to buy anything. It's only what the technology does for you or your pet that makes it worth buying. That's the pet food revolution that's happening right now: animal-free pet food to compete with animal agriculture. Clean pet food startups are rewriting the genetic code of food to grow entirely new ingredients for our pets.

Our future is an Earth populated by ten billion people, plus their billions of pets. This could be a disaster, or it could be an opportunity to thrive. We can be more sustainable than we are today if we use biotechnology for *good*. Big bioreactors will grow clean meats that we can safely share with our pets, as old battery farms replace chickens with mushrooms. Today, roughly a billion people go to sleep hungry, unable to feed themselves, let alone a pet. Tomorrow, we'll be able to feed them all—more nutritiously, more safely, and less expensively. The clean pet food revolution will be won for our planet and all of its animals.

Acknowledgments

ONE OF THE most rewarding parts of writing this book was having an excuse to spend time with some of the brilliant minds behind the biotech startups in the clean pet food space. Huge thanks to Shannon Falconer, CEO of Because Animals, whose superfood algae mix Alice sprinkles onto her dog's food every morning; to Ron Shigeta, co-founder of Wild Earth, whose koji-based protein dogs literally go wild for; to Ross Lamond, the inspiring young founder of Bug Bakes dog treats; to Klaus Wagner, whose Green Petfood plants trees to offset their carbon emissions; and to Rich Kelleman, CEO of Bond Pet Foods, who (along with Wild Earth and Because Animals) is aiming to develop cell-based meat for pets—real animal protein without the animal cruelty. A special mention goes out to Mike Selden, CEO of Finless Foods, and Sandhya Sriram, founder of Shiok Meats in Singapore, who spoke with us at length about their work creating seafood from the cells of bluefin tuna and shrimp, eliminating the environmental and ethical horrors associated with ocean bycatch, aquaculture, and fish slaughter. It was clear in our discussions that each of these innovators is motivated not by profit but by fierce concern and compassion. Whether trying to make the planet a better place for farmed animals, pets, or people, these companies are using science to disrupt and rebuild our broken food system. We're in awe of them, and if you haven't checked out their companies, we urge you to do so.

We should also acknowledge the other experts we had an excuse to pester with questions during the writing of this book. Thank you to sociologist Chris Bryant, who shared his research on consumer attitudes towards cell-based meat and how his findings might translate to willingness to feed this to our dogs and cats, too. The chapters on plant-based pets would have been very hard to write without the insights of Andrew Knight, professor of animal welfare and ethics and founder of Vegepets.info, a source for evidence-based science on the benefits of removing animal meat from your pets' diet. We also owe a large part of the final chapter to Tim Bowser of PetMech, who spoke passionately with Ernie about ending the cruelties of animal testing in the pet food industry. Alice loved talking with Michelle Cehn, a vegan influencer whose dog Chance has thrived on a plant-based diet since she adopted him from a rescue shelter twelve years ago. Finally, Marc Bekoff, professor of ecology and evolutionary biology, gave us some real (pet?) food for thought discussing how his dogs loved to share his own vegan food, peanut butter and jelly bagels powering them over the Boulder mountain trails.

We must also acknowledge Martin Rowe at Lantern, who "saw" our vision from the outset and enhanced our story immensely. Lantern, a publisher dedicated to creating a better world, is the natural home for our project. We're enormously grateful to join their portfolio. Thanks also to Amy Trakinski and VegInvest for their support of Wild Earth and our shared vision of a clean pet food revolution and a more compassionate, sustainable, and livable planet.

Of course, we owe a universe of thanks to our family, friends, and colleagues who read, edited, and offered support (and helpful criticism) during this journey. We can only imagine how annoying our infinite texts, messages, and emails must've been! To all these busy people who gave up their precious time to talk with us, fueled us with coffee and tea, and tolerated our incessant yammering about our environment and animal welfare, we cannot thank you enough. And last but not least, thank you to our four-legged companions who inspired this book in the first place: JD the cavalier, Harry and Ginny (Ward, not Potter, but still magical), and the revolving door of Ryan's foster dogs.

Viva la revolucion!

Notes

Introduction

1   AAPA. "Pet Industry Market Size & Ownership Statistics." Products & the Law Overview, 2018. <www.americanpetproducts.org/press_industrytrends.asp>.

2   Serpell, James A. "How Social Trends Impact Pet Ownership," cited in *The End of Animal Farming: How Scientists, Entrepreneurs, and Activists Are Building an Animal-Free Food System* by Jacy Reese (Boston: Beacon, 2019).

3   Rollin, Bernard E. "Ethical Behavior in Animals." In *Pets and People: The Ethics of Companion Animals*, edited by Christine Overall (New York: Oxford University Press, 2017), 99.

4   AAPA. "Pet Industry Market Size & Ownership Statistics."

5   Ibid.

6   Research by American Express, found in Wells, Liz. "UK Spends £12bn on Man's Best Friend," *Talking Retail*, November 28, 2018. <https://www.talkingretail.com/news/industry-news/uk-spends-12bn-mans-best-friend-study-reveals-28-11-2018/>.

7   Mordor Intelligence. "Brazil Pet Food Market—Segmented by Product, Pricing Type, Animal Type, Ingredient Type, and Sales Channel—Growth, Trends, and Forecast (2018–2023)." <https://www.mordorintelligence.com/industry-reports/brazil-pet-food-market>.

8   Grand View Research (2018). "Pet Food Market Size Worth $98.81 Billion By 2022 | CAGR: 4.3%." <https://www.grandviewresearch.com/press-release/global-pet-food-market>.

9   IPCC. "IPCC Global Warming Special Report 2018." <https://www.ipcc.ch/sr15/>.

10 Springmann, Marco, et al. "Options for Keeping the Food System within Environmental Limits." *Nature* (October 10, 2018) 562: 519–525.

11 Okin, Gregory S. "Environmental Impacts of Food Consumption by Dogs and Cats." *PLOS ONE* (August 2, 2017) 12(8).

12 Marlon, Jennifer, et al. (2018). Yale Climate Opinion Maps. <http://climatecommunication.yale.edu/visualizations-data/ycom-us-2018/>.

13 Fox, Jennifer Barnett. "No Break for Bacon Love." *Meat + Poultry*, September 19, 2018 <https://www.meatpoultry.com/articles/20172-no-break-for-bacon-love>.

14 Okin, "Environmental Impacts of Food Consumption by Dogs and Cats."

15 World Atlas (2018). "How Many Dogs Are There in the World?" <https://www.worldatlas.com/articles/how-many-dogs-are-there-in-the-world.html>.

16 PDSA Animal Wellbeing (PAW) Report (2018). "How Many Pets Are There in the U.K.?" <https://www.pdsa.org.uk/get-involved/our-campaigns/pdsa-animal-wellbeing-report/uk-pet-populations-of-dogs-cats-and-rabbits>.

17 Xinhua. "Clampdown on Dog Ownership Begins in East China." GB Times, November 23, 2018. <https://gbtimes.com/clampdown-on-responsible-dog-ownership-begins-in-east-china>.

18 Packaged Facts (2018). "Gen Z and Millennials as Pet Market Consumers: Dogs, Cats, Other Pets." <https://www.packagedfacts.com/Millennials-Gen-Pet-Consumers-Dogs-Cats-Pets-11268949/>.

19 Herzog, Hal. *Some We Love, Some We Hate, Some We Eat: Why It's So Hard to Think Straight About Animals* (New York: HarperCollins, 2010).

20 Ferguson, Donna. "Pawsecco, Anyone? Millennials Splurge on Pampered Pets." *Guardian*, October 27, 2018. <https://www.theguardian.com/lifeandstyle/2018/oct/27/millennials-pampered-pets-pyjamas-cakes>.

21 Pierce, Jessica. *Run, Spot, Run: The Ethics of Keeping Pets* (Chicago: University of Chicago Press, 2016).

22 Herzog, *Some We Love, Some We Hate, Some We Eat.*

23 Ferguson, "Pawsecco, Anyone? Millennials Splurge on Pampered Pets."

24 Rowan, A., and T. Kartal. "Dog Population & Dog Sheltering Trends in the United States of America." *Animals* (April 28, 2018) 8(5): pii: E68. doi: 10.3390/ani8050068.

25 Ibid.

26 Herzog, *Some We Love, Some We Hate, Some We Eat*, 74.

27 Pierce, Jessica. *Run, Spot, Run: The Ethics of Keeping Pets* (Chicago: University of Chicago Press, 2016), 71.

28 Linder, Deborah E. "Why Are So Many of Our Pets Overweight?" *Petfoodology*, January 18, 2018. <http://vetnutrition.tufts.edu/2018/01/why-are-so-many-of-our-pets-overweight/>.

29 Corrieri, Luca, et al. "Companion and Free-Ranging Bali Dogs: Environmental Links with Personality Traits in an Endemic Dog Population of South East Asia." *PLOS ONE* (June 2018) 5: 13.

30 Arnold, Jennifer. *Love Is All You Need: The Revolutionary Bond-Based Approach to Educating Your Dog* (New York: Spiegel & Grau, 2016), 4.

31 Turner, Dennis C., and Patrick Bateson. *The Domestic Cat: The Biology of Its Behaviour* (Cambridge: Cambridge University Press, 2000).

32 Bekoff, Mark. "As Dogs Go Wild in a World Without Us, How Might They Cope?" *Psychology Today*, September 2, 2018.

Chapter 1: A Dollop of Deadly

1   Murawski, John. "Florence Kills 5,500 Pigs and 3.4 Million Chickens. The Numbers Are Expected to Rise." *The Charlotte Observer*, September 18, 2018. <https://www.charlotteobserver.com/news/state/north-carolina/article218610365.html>. See also North Carolina Department of Agriculture and Consumer Services (2016). "NCDA & CS Mass Animal Mortality Management Plan for Catastrophic Natural Disasters." <http://www.ncagr.gov/disaster/documents/massmortalityguicanceplan.pdf>.

2   North Carolina Department of Agriculture and Consumer Services (2018). "Flooded Crops Cannot Be Used for Human Food. NCDA & CS, NCSU to Help Farms Divert Crops to Animal Feed with Proper Testing." <https://www.ncagr.gov/paffairs/release/2018/Floodedcropscanntbeusedforhumanfood.htm>.

3   Clean Label Project. "Pet Food Project Summary, 2017." <https://www.cleanlabelproject.org/pet-food/>.

4   Cernansky, Rachel. "The High-Protein Craze May Actually Carry Some Risks." *Washington Post*, October 27, 2017. <https://www.washingtonpost.com/national/health-science/the-high-protein-craze-may-actually-carry-some-risks/2017/10/27/d0e40cb6-dda8-11e6-918c-99ede3c8cafa_story.html>.

5   Chignell, Andrew, Terence Cuneo, and Matthew C. Halteman (eds.). *Philosophy Comes to Dinner: Arguments about the Ethics of Eating* (Oxford: Routledge, 2015).

6   WHO. "Q&A on the Carcinogenicity of the Consumption of Red Meat and Processed Meat," October 2015. <https://www.who.int/features/qa/cancer-red-meat/en/>.

7   Phillips-Donaldson, Debbie. "Pet Food Protein: How Much Is Too Much? Adventures in Pet Food." *Pet Food Industry*, May 29, 2018. <https://www.petfoodindustry.com/blogs/7-adventures-in-pet-food/post/7231-pet-food-protein-how-much-is-too-much>.

8   Böswald, L. F., E. Kienzle, and B. Dobenecker. "Observation about Phosphorus and Protein Supply in Cats and Dogs Prior to the Diagnosis of Chronic Kidney Disease." *Journal of Animal Physiology and Animal Nutrition* (2018) 102: 31–36.

9   Hyogo, H., and S. Yamagishi. "Advanced Glycation End Products (AGEs) and Their Involvement in Liver Disease." *Current Pharmaceutical Design* (2008) 14: 969–972.

10   Osher Center for Integrative Medicine (UCSF) (n.d.). "Animal Protein and Cancer Risk." <https://osher.ucsf.edu/patient-care/integrative-medicine-resources/cancer-and-nutrition/faq/animal-protein-cancer-risk>.

11   Greger, Michael. "Animal Protein Compared to Cigarette Smoking." *Nutrition Facts*, August 22, 2016, Vol. 32. <https://nutritionfacts.org/video/animal-protein-compared-cigarette-smoking/>.

12   Snyderwine, E. G., and Schut, H. A. J. "DNA Adducts of Heterocyclic Amine Food Mutagens: Implications for Mutagenesis and Carcinogenesis." *Carcinogenesis* (March 1999) 20(3): 353–368.

13   National Cancer Institute (n.d.). "Chemicals in Meat Cooked at High Temperatures and Cancer Risk." <https://www.cancer.gov/about-cancer/causes-prevention/risk/diet/cooked-meats-fact-sheet>.

14   Van Rooijen, C. et al. "The Maillard Reaction and Pet Food Processing: Effects on Nutritive Value and Pet Health." *Nutrition Research Reviews* (December 2013) 26(2): 130–148.

15   Becker, K. "What's Wrong with Feeding Fresh Food to Your Pet?" *Healthy Pets*, May 22, 2017. <https://healthypets.mercola.com/sites/healthypets/archive/2017/05/22/feeding-pets-fresh-food.aspx>.

16   AAFCO (2019). "What Is in Pet Food?" <https://www.aafco.org/Consumers/What-is-in-Pet-Food>.

17   Nestle, Marion, and Malden C. Nesheim. *Feed Your Pet Right: The Authoritative Guide to Feeding Your Dog and Cat* (New York: Simon and Schuster, 2010).

18   Meeker, D. L., and J. L. Meisinger. "Rendered Ingredients Significantly Influence Sustainability, Quality, and Safety of Pet Food." *Journal of Animal Science* (February 20, 2015) 93: 835–847.

19   FDA (2018). "Guidance for Industry." <https://www.fda.gov/AnimalVeterinary/GuidanceComplianceEnforcement/GuidanceforIndustry/default.htm>.

20   Meeker and Meisinger, "Rendered Ingredients."

21   National Renderers Association (n.d.). "FAQ." <http://www.nationalrenderers.org/about/faqs/#products-safe>.

22   Pitcairn, Richard. "What's REALLY in Meat-Based Pet Foods?" *Plant-Powered Dog*, February 6, 2019. <https://www.youtube.com/watch?v=uPdp_yQ-vq0>

23   Okuma, Tara A., and Rosalee S. Hellberg. "Identification of Meat Species in Pet Foods Using a Real-Time Polymerase Chain Reaction (PCR) Assay." *Food Control* (April 2015) 50: 9–17.

24   Shanker, Deena. "Premium Pet Food Is Really Expensive—and Not Actually Better for Your Pet." *Quartz*, September 26, 2015. <https://qz.com/504943/premium-pet-food-is-really-expensive-and-not-actually-better-for-your-pet/>.

25   Meeker and Meisinger, "Rendered Ingredients."

26   Ibid.

27   Kerasote, Ted. *Pukka's Promise: The Quest for Longer-Lived Dogs.* (New York: Houghton Mifflin Harcourt, 2013), 194–203.

28   Meens, Rob. "Eating Animals in the Early Middle Ages: Classifying the Animal World and Building Group Identities." In *The Animal/Human Boundary: Historical Perspectives*, edited by Angela Creager and William Chester Jordan (Rochester, NY: University of Rochester Press, 2002), 3–38.

29   Statista (2019). "Pet Food Sales Worldwide from 2010 to 2017 (in billion U.S. dollars)." <https://www.statista.com/statistics/253953/global-pet-food-sales/>.

30   FDA (2018). "Pet Food." <https://www.fda.gov/AnimalVeterinary/Products/AnimalFoodFeeds/PetFood/UCM2006475>.

31   AAFCO (2012). "The Business of Pet Food." <https://petfood.aafco.org/>.

32   Misseri, Robert. "Guardians of Rescue: Uncovering One of New Jersey's 'Dirtiest Secrets' at Bravo Packing Plant." Cision PR Newswire, December 20, 2010. <https://

www.prnewswire.com/news-releases/guardians-of-rescue-uncovering-one-of-new-jerseys-dirtiest-secrets-at-bravo-packing-plant-112188169.html>.

33   Spencer, Richard. "China Accused over Contaminated Baby Milk." *Telegraph* (UK), September 15, 2008. <https://www.telegraph.co.uk/news/worldnews/asia/china/2963808/China-accused-over-contaminated-baby-milk.html>.

34   Pierce, Jessica. *Run, Spot, Run: The Ethics of Keeping Pets* (Chicago: University of Chicago Press, 2016), 74.

35   Baur, Gene. "Gene Baur of Farm Sanctuary Reveals the Truth about the Rendering Industry." *Plant-Powered Dog*, February 12, 2019. <https://www.youtube.com/watch?v=HSmV4HHb2ek>.

36   Yang, Haixia, et al. "A Common Antimicrobial Additive Increases Colonic Inflammation and Colitis-Associated Colon Tumorigenesis in Mice." *Science Translational Medicine* (May 30, 2018) 10(443).

37   Fox, Matthew W. "An Antibacterial Threat to Pets." *The Truth About Pet Food*, June 8, 2018. <https://truthaboutpetfood.com/an-antibacterial-threat-to-pets/>.

38   Jeong, San-Hee, et al. "Risk Assessment of Growth Hormones and Antimicrobial Residues in Meat." *Toxicological Research* (December 2010) 26(4): 301–313.

39   FDA. "Food and Drug Administration/Center for Veterinary Medicine Report on the Risk from Pentobarbital in Dog Food," February 28, 2002. <https://www.fda.gov/AboutFDA/CentersOffices/OfficeofFoods/CVM/CVMFOIAElectronicReadingRoom/ucm129131.htm>.

40   Ibid.

41   Pendell, H. (2008). "Former AAFCO President Admits Pet Food May Contain Pets." *WeeMiniMoose*, August 3, 2008. <https://www.youtube.com/watch?time_continue=43&v=RuoSxSJ94RY>.

42   Thixton, Susan. "FDA Says Sorry—We Don't Have the Budget to Enforce Law." *The Truth About Pet Food*, September 28, 2018. <http://truthaboutpetfood.com/fda-says-sorry-we-dont-have-the-budget-to-enforce-law/>.

43   Sandøe, Peter, Sandra Corr, and Clare Palmer. *Companion Animal Ethics* (Oxford: John Wiley & Sons, 2015), 226.

44   Grant, Harriet. "Legal Plastic Content in Animal Feed Could Harm Human Health, Experts Warn." *Guardian*, December 15, 2018. <https://www.theguardian.com/environment/2018/dec/15/legal-plastic-content-in-animal-feed-could-harm-human-health-experts-warn>.

45   The Johns Hopkins Center for a Livable Future (2007). "Feed for Food-Producing Animals: A Resource on Ingredients, the Industry, and Regulation." <https://clf.jhsph.edu/sites/default/files/2019-05/animal_feed.pdf>.

46   Bouvard, V., et al. "Carcinogenicity of Consumption of Red and Processed Meat." *The Lancet Oncology* (December 2015) 16(16): 1599–1600.

47   Song, M. et al. (2016). "Association of Animal and Plant Protein Intake with All-Cause and Cause-Specific Mortality." *JAMA Internal Medicine* (October 2016) 176(10): 1453–1463.

Chapter 2: How Pet Food Is Destroying the World

1 Rangananthan Janet, et al. "Shifting Diets for a Sustainable Food Future: Creating a Sustainable Food Future (Installment Eleven)," April 2016. World Resources Institute. <http://www.wri.org/publication/shifting-diets>.

2 National Climate Assessment (NCA) (2018). "Fourth National Climate Assessment. Volume II: Impacts, Risks, and Adaptation in the United States." <https://nca2018.globalchange.gov>.

3 Thornes, Tobias. "Animal Agriculture and Climate Change." In *Ethical Vegetarianism and Veganism*, edited by Andrew Linzey and Clair Linzey (Oxford: Routledge, 2018), 245.

4 Springmann, Marco, et al. "Analysis and Valuation of the Health and Climate Change Cobenefits of Dietary Change." *Proceedings of the National Academy of Sciences* (April 12, 2016) 113(15): 4146–4151.

5 Davenport, Coral, and Kendra Pierre-Louis. "U.S. Climate Report Warns of Damaged Environment and Shrinking Economy," *New York Times*, November 23, 2018. <https://www.nytimes.com/2018/11/23/climate/us-climate-report.html>. "Scientists who worked on the report said it did not appear that administration officials had tried to alter or suppress its findings. However, several noted that the timing of its release, at 2 p.m. the day after Thanksgiving, appeared designed to minimize its public impact."

6 IPCC (2018). "IPCC Global Warming Special Report." <https://www.ipcc.ch/sr15/>.

7 Climate Analytics (n.d.). "Global Warming Reaches 1°C above Preindustrial, Warmest in More than 11,000 Years." <https://climateanalytics.org/briefings/global-warming-reaches-1c-above-preindustrial-warmest-in-more-than-11000-years/>.

8 Tilman, David, and Michael Clark. "Global Diets Link Environmental Sustainability and Human Health." *Nature* (November 27, 2014) 515: 518–522.

9 Goodland, Robert, and Jeff Anhang. "Livestock and Climate Change." Worldwatch Institute, November/December 2009. <www.worldwatch.org/node/6294>.

10 Harwatt, Helen. "Including Animal to Plant Protein Shifts in Climate Change Mitigation Policy: A Proposed Three-Step Strategy." *Climate Policy* (November 26, 2018) 19(5): 1–9.

11 Thornes, "Animal Agriculture and Climate Change," 247.

12 Springmann, "Analysis and Valuation of the Health and Climate Change Cobenefits."

13 Willett, Walter, et al. "Food in the Anthropocene: The EAT–*Lancet* Commission on Healthy Diets from Sustainable Food Systems." *The Lancet* (February 2, 2019) 393(10170): 447–492. <https://www.thelancet.com/journals/lancet/article/PIIS0140-6736(18)31788-4/fulltext#articleInformation>.

14 OECD/FAO. "OECD-FAO Agricultural Outlook, 2018–2027." (Paris/FAO, Rome: OECD Publishing, 2018). <https://doi.org/10.1787/agr_outlook-2018-en>.

15 Springmann, Marco, et al. "Options for Keeping the Food System within Environmental Limits." *Nature* (October 10, 2018) 562: 519–525.

16   American Pet Products Association. *2015–2016 APPA National Pet Owners Survey* (Greenwich, CT: American Pet Products Association, 2016).

17   Okin, Gregory S. "Environmental Impacts of Food Consumption by Dogs and Cats." *PLOS ONE* (August 2, 2017) 12(8).

18   Kumcu, Aylin, and Andrea E. Woolverton. "Feeding Fido: Changing Consumer Food Preferences Bring Pets to the Table." *Journal of Food Products Marketing* (2015) 21(2): 213–230.

19   Swanson, Kelly S., et al. "Nutritional Sustainability of Pet Foods." *Advances in Nutrition* (March 2013) 4(2): 141–150.

20   Makkar, Harinder P. S. (2012). "Biofuel Co-products as Livestock Feed: Opportunities and Challenges." FAO report, Rome. Available at <http://www.fao.org/3/i3009e/i3009e.pdf>.

21   Popp, Jószef, et al. "Biofuels and Their Co-Products as Livestock Feed: Global Economic and Environmental Implications." *Molecules* (February 29, 2016) 21(285). <https://dea.lib.unideb.hu/dea/bitstream/handle/2437/234274/FILE_UP_0_molecules-21-00285.pdf>.

22   Harris, Chris. "Impact of Biofuels on Meat Production." *The Beef Site,* September 30, 2008. <http://www.thebeefsite.com/articles/1691/impact-of-biofuels-on-meat-production/>.

23   Oldham, Scott. "What's the Average Miles Driven Per Year? (Car Lease Guide)." *Autogravity,* November 1, 2018. <https://www.autogravity.com/blog/money/whats-average-miles-driven-per-year-car-lease-guide>.

24   Ketler, Alanna. "Factory Farming Is Destroying Our Environment." *Collective Evolution,* March 4, 2013. <https://www.collective-evolution.com/2013/03/04/eating-meat-destruction-of-environment/>.

25   Marlow, H. J., et al. "Comparing the Water, Energy, Pesticide and Fertilizer Usage for the Production of Foods Consumed by Different Dietary Types in California." *Public Health Nutrition* (September 2015) 18(13): 2425–2432.

26   EPA (2017). "Nutrient Pollution" <https://www.epa.gov/nutrientpollution/where-occurs-lakes-and-rivers>.

27   Pelletier, Nathan, and Peter Tyedmers. "Forecasting Potential Global Environmental Costs of Livestock Production 2000–2050." *Proceedings of the National Academy of Sciences* (October 26, 2010) 107(43): 18371–18374.

28   Poore, J., and T. Nemecek. "Reducing Food's Environmental Impacts through Producers and Consumers." *Science* (June 1, 2018) 360(6392): 987–992.

29   Vale, Robert, and Brenda Vale. *Time to Eat the Dog? The Real Guide to Sustainable Living* (London: Thames & Hudson, 2009).

30   McGill, Andrew. "The Shrinking of the American Lawn." *The Atlantic,* July 6, 2016. <https://www.theatlantic.com/business/archive/2016/07/lawns-census-bigger-homes-smaller-lots/489590/>.

31 Meeker, D. L., and J. L. Meisinger. "Rendered Ingredients Significantly Influence Sustainability, Quality, and Safety of Pet Food." *Journal of Animal Science* (February 20, 2015) 93: 835–847.

32 Sandøe, Peter, Sandra Corr, and Clare Palmer. *Companion Animal Ethics* (Oxford: John Wiley & Sons, 2015).

33 World Wildlife Fund (WWF). "The Living Planet Report 2018." WWF-UK. <https://www.wwf.org.uk/updates/living-planet-report-2018>.

34 De Silva, Sena S., and Giovanni M. Turchini. "Towards Understanding the Impacts of the Pet Food Industry on World Fish and Seafood Supplies." *Journal of Agricultural and Environmental Ethics* (October 2008) 21(5): 459–467.

35 FAO. FAOSTAT. "Live Animals 2016." <http://www.fao.org/faostat/en/#data/QA>.

36 Willett, "Food in the Anthropocene."

37 Durisin, Megan, and Sruti Singh. "Americans Will Eat a Record Amount of Meat in 2018." *Bloomberg*, January 2, 2018. <https://www.bloomberg.com/news/articles/2018-01-02/have-a-meaty-new-year-americans-will-eat-record-amount-in-2018>.

38 Reisinger, Andy, and Harry Clark. "How Much Do Direct Livestock Emissions Actually Contribute to Global Warming?" *Global Change Biology* (April 2018) 24(4), 1749–1761.

39 Harwatt, "Including Animal to Plant Protein Shifts in Climate Change Mitigation Policy."

40 Pimentel, David, and Marcia Pimentel. "Sustainability of Meat-Based and Plant-Based Diets and the Environment." *American Journal of Clinical Nutrition* (2003) 78(suppl): 660S–663S.

41 Harwatt, "Including Animal to Plant Protein Shifts in Climate Change Mitigation Policy."

42 Poore and Nemecek, "Reducing Food's Environmental Impacts through Producers and Consumers."

43 Okin, "Environmental Impacts of Food Consumption by Dogs and Cats."

44 Roser, Max, and Hannah Ritchie (2017). "Yields and Land Use in Agriculture." *OurWorldInData.org*. <https://ourworldindata.org/yields-and-land-use-in-agriculture>.

45 Cassidy, Emily S., et al. "Redefining Agricultural Yields: From Tonnes to People Nourished per Hectare." *Environmental Research Letters* (August 1, 2013) 8(3): 034015.

46 Shepon, Alon, et al. "The Opportunity Cost of Animal Based Diets Exceeds All Food Losses." *Proceedings of the National Academy of Sciences* (April 10, 2018) 115(15): 3804–3809.

47 Springmann, Marco, et al. "Health-Motivated Taxes on Red and Processed Meat: A Modelling Study on Optimal Tax Levels and Associated Health Impacts." *PLOS ONE* (November 6, 2018) 13, e0204139.

48 De Silva and Turchini, "Towards Understanding the Impacts of the Pet Food Industry."

49 Ibid.

50   Kaschner, Kristin. "Marine Mammal and Seabird Consumption of Small Pelagic Fishes." In *On the Multiple Uses of Forage Fish: From Ecosystems to Markets*, compiled by Jackie Alder and Daniel Pauly. Fisheries Centre Research Reports, 2006, 14(3).

51   De Silva and Turchini, "Towards Understanding the Impacts of the Pet Food Industry."

52   FAO (2016). "The State of World Fisheries and Aquaculture." <http://www.fao.org/3/a-i5555e.pdf>.

53   Worm, Boris, et al. "Impacts of Biodiversity Loss on Ocean Ecosystem Services." *Science* (December 2006) 314(5800): 787–790.

54   Bergqvist, Jenny, and Stefan Gunnarsson. "Finfish Aquaculture: Animal Welfare, the Environment, and Ethical Implications." *Journal of Agricultural and Environmental Ethics* (February 2013) 26(1): 75–99.

55   Bollard, Lewis. "Fish: The Forgotten Farm Animal." *Open Philanthropy Project*, January 18, 2018. <https://www.openphilanthropy.org/blog/fish-forgotten-farm-animal>.

56   Bergqvist and Gunnarsson, "Finfish Aquaculture."

57   De Silva and Turchini, "Towards Understanding the Impacts of the Pet Food Industry."

58   Bergqvist and Gunnarsson, "Finfish Aquaculture."

59   Singer, Peter. "Fish: The Forgotten Victims on Our Plate," *Guardian*, September 14, 2010. <https://www.theguardian.com/commentisfree/cif-green/2010/sep/14/fish-forgotten-victims>.

60   Digre, Hanne, et al. "The On-Board Live Storage of Atlantic Cod (*Gadus morhua*) and Haddock (*Melanogrammus aeglefinus*) Caught by Trawl: Fish Behaviour, Stress and Fillet Quality." *Fisheries Research* (May 2017) 189: 42–54.

61   Diana, James S. "Aquaculture Production and Biodiversity Conservation." *BioScience* (January 2009) 59(1): 27–38.

62   Herzog, Hal. *Some We Love, Some We Hate, Some We Eat: Why It's So Hard to Think Straight About Animals* (New York: HarperCollins, 2010), 77.

63   Pitcairn, Richard, and Susan Hubble Pitcairn. *Dr. Pitcairn's Complete Guide to Natural Health for Dogs & Cats* (New York: Rodale, 2017).

64   Alonzo, Austin. "Pet Food's Future May Depend on New, Old Proteins." *PetFoodIndustry.com*, April 20, 2016. <https://www.petfoodindustry.com/articles/5771-pet-foods-future-may-depend-on-new-old-proteins>.

65   According to the Department of Environment, Land, Water and Planning report, released under freedom of information to the Australian Society for Kangaroos. Reported in Martin, Lisa. "Kangaroo Pet Food Trial: One Million Animals Killed and Fraud and Bribery Alleged," *Guardian*, March 13, 2019. <https://www.theguardian.com/world/2019/mar/13/kangaroo-pet-food-trial-one-million-animals-killed-and-and-bribery-alleged>.

Chapter 3: *Who* Are We Feeding to Our Pets?

1   Baggini, Julian. "The Ethics of Pet Food: Why Are We So Selective in How We Show Animals Our Love?" *The Independent*, March 31, 2015. <https://www.independent.

co.uk/property/house-and-home/pets/features/the-ethics-of-pet-food-why-are-we-are-so-selective-in-how-we-show-animals-our-love-10147366.html>.

2   Okin, Gregory S. "Environmental Impacts of Food Consumption by Dogs and Cats." *PLOS ONE* (August 2, 2017) 12(8).

3   Humane Society of the United States (n.d.). "An HSUS Report: The Welfare of Animals in the Meat, Egg, and Dairy Industries." <https://www.humanesociety.org/sites/default/files/docs/hsus-report-welfare-animals-meat-egg-dairy-industry.pdf>.

4   Animal Protection Index. "USA." <https://api.worldanimalprotection.org/country/usa>.

5   Sandøe, Peter, Sandra Corr, and Clare Palmer. *Companion Animal Ethics* (Oxford: John Wiley & Sons, 2015), 221.

6   Figures cited by Reese, Jacy. *The End of Animal Farming: How Scientists, Entrepreneurs, and Activists Are Building an Animal-Free Food System* (Boston: Beacon, 2018), 115.

7   Laverdure-Dunetz, Diana. "Save Animals and the Planet—Raise Your Dog Vegan." *PETA Prime*, October 2018. <https://prime.peta.org/2018/10/save-animals-and-the-planet-raise-your-dog-vegan>.

8   Food Marketing Institute and North American Meat Institute. *Power of Meat Conference: An In-Depth Look at Meat through Shoppers' Eyes* (Arlington, VA: Food Marketing Institute, 2017). <http://www.meatconference.com/sites/default/files/books/Power_of_meat_2017.pdf>.

9   2012 Farm Sanctuary brochure, quoted in Thibodeau, Lucille Claire. "'All Creation Groans': The Lives of Factory Farmed Animals in the United States." In *Ethical Vegetarianism and Veganism*, edited by Andrew Linzey and Clair Linzey (Oxford: Routledge, 2018), 140.

10 Animal Charity Evaluators. "Why Farmed Animals?" <https://animalcharityevaluators.org/donation-advice/why-farmed-animals/>.

11 Mercy For Animals. "Four Out of Five Americans Want Restaurants and Grocers to End Cruel Factory Farming Practices," *PR Newswire*, July 13, 2017.

12 Thibodeau, "'All Creation Groans.'"

13 Ibid.

14 Tischler, Joyce S. "Rights for Nonhuman Animals: A Guardianship Model for Dogs and Cats." *San Diego Law Review* (1977) 14(2): 484.

15 Ibid.

16 "Death on a Factory Farm," directed by Tom Simon and Sarah Teale (2009). <https://en.wikipedia.org/wiki/Death_on_a_Factory_Farm>.

17 Rollin, Bernard. "Guest Commentary: Animal Welfare in the Dairy Industry." AGWEB. *Farm Journal*, November 14, 2017. <https://www.agweb.com/article/guest-commentary-animal-welfare-in-the-dairy-industry/>.

18 Amaral-Phillips, Donna M., et al (n.d.). "Feeding and Managing Baby Calves from Birth to 3 Months of Age." ASC-161, University of Kentucky Cooperative Extension Service.

<https://afs.ca.uky.edu/files/feeding_and_managing_baby_calves_from_birth_to_3_months_of_age.pdf>.

19 American Veterinary Medical Association (AVMA). "Literature Review on the Welfare Implications of Hot-Iron Branding and Its Alternatives," April 4, 2011. <https://www.avma.org/KB/Resources/LiteratureReviews/Documents/hot-iron_branding_bgnd.pdf>.

20 American Veterinary Medical Association (AVMA). "Literature Review on the Welfare Implications of Electroimmobilization," March 3, 2008. <https://www.avma.org/KB/Resources/LiteratureReviews/Documents/electroimmobilization_bgnd.pdf>.

21 American Veterinary Medical Association (AVMA). "Literature Review on the Welfare Implications of Dehorning and Disbudding of Cattle," July 15, 2014. <https://www.avma.org/KB/Resources/LiteratureReviews/Pages/Welfare-Implications-of-Dehorning-and-Disbudding-Cattle.aspx>.

22 Stafford, Kevin J., and David J. Mellor. "Addressing the Pain Associated with Disbudding and Dehorning in Cattle." *Applied Animal Behaviour Science* (December 15, 2011) 135(3): 226–231.

23 Winder, C. B., et al. "Clinical Trial of Local Anesthetic Protocols for Acute Pain Associated with Caustic Paste Disbudding in Dairy Calves." *Journal of Dairy Science* (August 2017) 100(8): 6429–6441.

24 Stock, M. L., et al. "Bovine Dehorning: Assessing Pain and Providing Analgesic Management." *Veterinary Clinics: Food Animal Practice* (March 2013) 29(1): 103–133.

25 Lymbery, Philip. *Dead Zone: Where the Wild Things Were* (London: Bloomsbury, 2017), 54.

26 University of Kentucky College of Agriculture, Food and Environment (n.d.). "Extension: Small and Backyard Flocks: Frequently Asked Questions." <http://www2.ca.uky.edu/smallflocks/FAQs.html>.

27 "Unlike most domestic hens, who have been selectively bred to lay eggs year-round, wild fowl breed and lay primarily in spring. The Red Jungle Fowl lays 10–15 eggs per year, and the average size of each brood is 4–6 chicks." Humane Society of the United States (n.d.). "About Chickens." <http://www.humanesociety.org/assets/pdfs/farm/about_chickens.pdf>.

28 Follensbee, M. E., et al. "Quantifying the Nesting Motivation of Domestic Hens." *Journal of Animal Science* (1992) 70(1): 164.

29 Duncan, I. J. H. "Welfare Problems of Poultry." In *The Well-Being of Farm Animals: Challenges and Solutions*, edited by G. John Benson and Bernard Rollin (Oxford: John Wiley & Sons, 2004).

30 Grandin, Temple, and Catherine Johnson. *Animals in Translation: Using the Mysteries of Autism to Decode Animal Behavior* (New York: SUNY Press, 2005).

31 Knowles, Toby G., et al. "Leg Disorders in Broiler Chickens: Prevalence, Risk Factors and Prevention." *PLOS ONE* (February 6, 2008): 3. <https://journals.plos.org/plosone/article?id=10.1371/journal.pone.0001545>.

32   Shapiro, Paul. "Sixth Viewpoint: An Activist's Perspective on Animal Welfare." In *Animal Welfare in Animal Agriculture* (2d. ed.), edited by Wilson G. Pond, Fuller W. Bazer, and Bernard E. Rollin (Boca Raton, FL: CRC Press, 2011).

33   Gabbatt, Adam. "Turkeys Pin Hopes on Trump Pardon—Just Don't Ask about Last Year's Birds," *Guardian*, November 19, 2018. <https://www.theguardian.com/lifeandstyle/2018/nov/19/turkeys-trump-thanksgiving>.

34   Webster, John. *Animal Welfare: A Cool Eye Towards Eden.* (Oxford: Wiley-Blackwell, 1995), 156.

35   Davis, Karen. Quoted in "Disengaged Journalism and the Disparagement and Disappearance of Animals." In *For the Animals: From Exploitation to Liberation* (New York: Lantern, 2019), 238.

36   Johnson, Jeff. "Welfare and Productivity in Animal Agriculture." In *Ethical Vegetarianism and Veganism*, edited by Andrew Linzey and Clair Linzey (Oxford: Routledge, 2018), 165.

37   Baggini, "The Ethics of Pet Food."

38   Alonzo, Austin. "Study: Slower-Growing Birds Would Harm Environment." *WATTAgNet*, March 14, 2019. <https://www.wattagnet.com/articles/37152-study-slower-growing-birds-would-harm-environment>.

39   Abbate, Cheryl. "Veganism, (Almost) Harm-Free Animal Flesh, and Nonmaleficence: Navigating Dietary Ethics in an Unjust World." In *The Routledge Handbook of Animal Ethics*, edited by Bob Fischer (Oxford: Routledge, 2019).

40   Hartcher, K. M., and B. Jones. "The Welfare of Layer Hens in Cage and Cage-Free Housing Systems." *World's Poultry Science Journal* (December 2017) 73(4): 767–782.

41   Humane Society (n.d.). "Cage-Free vs. Battery-Cage Eggs." <https://www.humanesociety.org/resources/cage-free-vs-battery-cage-eggs>.

42   Reese, Jacy. *The End of Animal Farming.*

43   Ibid.

44   Duncan I. J. H. et al., "Behavioral Consequences of Partial Beak Amputation (Beak Trimming in Poultry)." *British Poultry Science* (September 1989) 30(30): 479–489.

45   Soisontes, Sakson. "An Alternative Use of One Day-Old Male Layer Chicks: The Case of Thailand." Science and Information Centre for Sustainable Poultry Production (WING), August 2015. <https://www.researchgate.net/publication/307925554_An_alternative_use_of_one_day-old_male_layer_chicks_the_case_of_Thailand>.

46   Krautwald-Junghanns, M. E., et al. "Current Approaches to Avoid the Culling of Day-Old Male Chicks in the Layer Industry, with Special Reference to Spectroscopic Methods." *Poultry Science* (March 2018) 97(3): 749–757.

47   Elder, Max. "The Moral Poverty of Pescetarianism." In *Ethical Vegetarianism and Veganism*, edited by Andrew Linzey and Clair Linzey (Oxford: Routledge, 2018), 110.

48   Linzey, Andrew, and Clair Linzey. "Introduction: Vegetarianism as Ethical Protest." In *Ethical Vegetarianism and Veganism*, edited by Andrew Linzey and Clair Linzey (Oxford: Routledge, 2018), 12.

49   Voiceless: The Animal Protection Institute. "The Voiceless Animal Cruelty Index." <https://vaci.voiceless.org.au/>.

50   Fitzgerald, Amy J., et al. "Slaughterhouses and Increased Crime Rates: An Empirical Analysis of the Spillover from 'The Jungle' into the Surrounding Community." *Organization & Environment* (June 2009) 22(2): 158–184.

Chapter 4: Four Legs Good, Four Legs Bad

1   Serpell, James A. "James Serpell: Dogs as the Animal Kingdom's Ambassadors," on George Miller's podcast *The Hedgehog and the Fox*, May 3, 2018. <https://www.podularity.com/thehedgehogandthefox/2018/05/03/james-serpell-dogs-animal-kingdoms-ambassadors/>.

2   Treleaven, Sarah. "How Your Dog Could Go Vegan and Still Stay Healthy," *Popular Science*, November 26, 2018. <https://www.popsci.com/vegan-dog-food>.

3   Serpell, "James Serpell: Dogs as the Animal Kingdom's Ambassadors."

4   Lockwood, Randall. "Tracking the 'State of the Animals': Challenges and Opportunities in Assessing Change." In *The State of the Animals III*, edited by Deborah J. Salem and Andrew Rowan (Washington, DC: Humane Society Press, 2005), 1–14.

5   Dodd, Sarah A. S., et al. "Plant-Based (Vegan) Diets for Pets: A Survey of Pet Owner Attitudes and Feeding Practices." *PLOS ONE* (January 15, 2019). <https://doi.org/10.1371/journal.pone.0210806>.

6   Humane League Labs. "Report: Diet Change and Demographic Characteristics of Vegans, Vegetarians, Semi-Vegetarians, and Omnivores" (April 2014). <http://www.humaneleaguelabs.org/static/reports/2014/04/diet-change-and-demographic-characteristics1.pdf>.

7   Rothgerber, H., and F. Mican. "Childhood Pet Ownership, Attachment to Pets, and Subsequent Meat Avoidance: The Mediating Role of Empathy toward Animals." *Appetite* (August 2014) 79: 11–17.

8   Humane League Labs, "Report: Diet Change and Demographic Characteristics."

9   Bratanova, B., et al. "The Effect of Categorization as Food on the Perceived Moral Standing of Animals." *Appetite* (August 2011) 57: 193–196.

10   Serpell, James A. "Having Our Dogs and Eating Them Too: Why Animals Are a Social Issue." *Journal of Social Issues* (July 2009) 65(3): 633–644.

11   Rothgerber and Mican, "Childhood Pet Ownership."

12   Dugnoille, Julien. "To Eat or Not to Eat Companion Dogs: Symbolic Value of Dog Meat and Human–Dog Companionship in Contemporary South Korea." *Food, Culture & Society* (March 2018) 21(2): 214–232.

13   Koreandogs.org. "Royal Canin: Speak Out Against the Dog Meat Trade Operating Outside Your Facility in Korea!" Action Alert campaign, August 23, 2017. <http://koreandogs.org/royal-canin/>.

14   Vega, Sharon. "Humane Society Shuts Down Dog Meat Farm That Was Also a Puppy Mill." *One Green Planet*, 2019. <https://www.onegreenplanet.org/animalsandnature/humane-society-shuts-down-dog-meat-farm-that-was-also-a-puppy-mill/>.

15 Ibid.

16 Herzog, Hal. *Some We Love, Some We Hate, Some We Eat: Why It's So Hard to Think Straight About Animals* (New York: HarperCollins, 2010), 265.

17 Pelluchon, Corine. "Food Ethics and Justice toward Animals." In *Ethical Vegetarianism and Veganism*, edited by Andrew Linzey and Clair Linzey (Oxford: Routledge, 2018).

18 Donaldson, Sue, and Will Kymlicka. *Zoopolis: A Political Theory of Animal Rights* (Oxford: Oxford University Press, 2011), 5–6.

19 Thelander, Jeanette. "Our Ambivalent Relations with Animals." In *Ethical Vegetarianism and Veganism*, edited by Andrew Linzey and Clair Linzey (Oxford: Routledge, 2018), 219.

20 Coren, Stanley. *The Intelligence of Dogs: A Guide to the Thoughts, Emotions, and Inner Lives of Our Canine Companions* (New York: Simon & Schuster, 2006).

21 Quoted in Herzog, Hal. *Some We Love, Some We Hate, Some We Eat*, 12.

22 Woien, Sandra. "Americans Spend $70 Billion on Pets, and That Money Could Do More Good." *The Conversation*, October 15, 2018 <http://theconversation.com/americans-spend-70-billion-on-pets-and-that-money-could-do-more-good-102467>.

23 Runkle, Nathan. "Here Are the Legal Loopholes That Allow Farmed Animals to Be Abused and Killed." *Alternet*, August 30, 2017. <https://www.alternet.org/animal-rights/here-are-legal-loopholes-allow-farmed-animals-be-abused-and-killed>.

Chapter 5: Paying a Premium

1 Zion Market Research. "Pet Food Market (Wet Food, Dry Food, Nutrition, Snacks and Others) for Cats, Dogs and Other Animals: U.S Industry Perspective, Comprehensive Analysis and Forecast, 2016–2022," January 4, 2017. <https://www.zionmarketresearch.com/market-analysis/pet-food-market>.

2 Packaged Facts. "Gen Z and Millennials as Pet Market Consumers: Dogs, Cats, Other Pets," February 16, 2018. <https://www.packagedfacts.com/Millennials-Gen-Pet-Consumers-Dogs-Cats-Pets-11268949/>.

3 Bedford, Emma (n.d.). "Blue Buffalo Pet Products' Net Sales in the United States from 2013 to 2017 (in Million U.S. Dollars)." *Statista*, last edited August 7, 2019. <https://www.statista.com/statistics/810236/blue-buffalo-pet-products-net-sales-us/>.

4 Sprinkle, David. "Presentation: Premiumization Trends in the U.S. Pet Market." *China International Pet Show. Packaged Facts*, 2019. <https://www.packagedfacts.com/Content/Presentation-Premiumization-Trends-in-the-US-Pet-Market>.

5 FDA. "Pet Food Labels—General," 2017. <https://www.fda.gov/animal-veterinary/animal-health-literacy/pet-food-labels-general>.

6 Pierce, Jessica. *Run, Spot, Run: The Ethics of Keeping Pets* (Chicago: University of Chicago Press, 2016), 75.

7 Shanker, Deena. "Premium Pet Food Is Really Expensive—and Not Actually Better for Your Pet." *Quartz*, September 26, 2015. <https://qz.com/504943/premium-pet-food-is-really-expensive-and-not-actually-better-for-your-pet/>.

8   Pet Food Industry. "Report: 95% Say Pets Are Part of the Family." March 9, 2016. <https://www.petfoodindustry.com/articles/5695-report---say-pets-are-part-of-the-family>.

9   Buff, P. R., et al. "Natural Pet Food: A Review of Natural Diets and Their Impact on Canine and Feline Physiology." *Journal of Animal Science* (September 2014) 92(9): 3781–3791.

10   AAFCO. Official Publication. Association of American Feed Control Officials, 2013. Champaign, IL.

11   The US District Court for the Northern District of Illinois. Class Action Complaint. <https://www.locklaw.com/wp-content/uploads/2019/03/2019-02-28-Taste-of-the-Wild-Complaint-IL.pdf>.

12   The US District Court for the Northern District of Illinois. Class Action Complaint. <https://truthaboutpetfood.com/wp-content/uploads/2019/03/TasteoftheWild-2019-lawsuit.pdf>.

13   The US District Court Central District of California. Class Action Complaint. <https://www.locklaw.com/wp-content/uploads/2019/02/2019-02-22-Solid-Gold-Cat-Food-Order-regarding-Motion-to-Dismiss.pdf>.

14   The US District Court Southern District of New York. Class Action Complaint. <https://www.manatt.com/Manatt/media/Documents/Articles/Parks-v-Ainsworth-Pet-Nutrition,-LLC.PDF>.

15   AAFCO. Official Publication. Association of American Feed Control Officials, 2013. Champaign, IL.

16   Mueller, Ralf S., et al. "Critically Appraised Topic on Adverse Food Reactions of Companion Animals (2): Common Food Allergen Sources in Dogs and Cats." *BMC Veterinary Research* (January 2016) 12(9).

17   Hoffman, Jan. "Popular Grain-Free Dog Foods May Be Linked to Heart Disease," *New York Times*, July 24, 2018. <https://www.nytimes.com/2018/07/24/health/grain-free-dog-food-heart-disease.html>.

18   Mansilla, Wilfredo D., et al. "Special Topic: The Association Between Pulse Ingredients and Canine Dilated Cardiomyopathy: Addressing the Knowledge Gaps before Establishing Causation." *Journal of Animal Science* (March 2019) 97(3): 983–997.

19   Hoffman, "Popular Grain-Free Dog Foods May Be Linked to Heart Disease."

20   Remillard, R. L. "Homemade Diets: Attributes, Pitfalls, and a Call for Action." *Topics in Companion Animal Medicine* (August 2008) 23(3): 137–142.

21   Stockman, J., et al. "Evaluation of Recipes of Home-Prepared Maintenance Diets for Dogs." *Journal of the American Veterinary Medical Association* (June 2013) 242(11): 1500–1505.

22   Oliveira, M. C. C., et al. "Evaluation of the Owner's Perception in the Use of Homemade Diets for the Nutritional Management of Dogs." *Journal of Nutritional Science* (September 2014) 3. doi: 10.1017/jns.2014.24.

23   Lefebvre S. L., et al. "Evaluation of the Risks of Shedding Salmonellae and Other Potential Pathogens by Therapy Dogs Fed Raw Diets in Ontario and Alberta." *Zoonoses Public Health* (October 2008) 55(8–10): 470–480.

24 Donnelly, Grace. "Dog Food Recall: What Pet Owners Should Know." *Fortune*, February 16, 2018. <http://fortune.com/2018/02/16/pet-food-recalls/>.

25 FDA. "Get Facts: Raw Pet Food Diets Can Be Dangerous to You and Your Pet." February 22, 2018. <https://www.fda.gov/animal-veterinary/animal-health-literacy/get-facts-raw-pet-food-diets-can-be-dangerous-you-and-your-pet>.

26 LeJeune, Jeffrey T., and Dale D. Hancock. "Public Health Concerns Associated with Feeding Raw Meat Diets to Dogs." *Journal of the American Veterinary Medical Association* (November 1, 2001) 219(9): 1222–1225.

27 Van Bree, F. P. J., et al. "Zoonotic Bacteria and Parasites Found in Raw Meat–Based Diets for Cats and Dogs." *Veterinary Record* (January 2018) 182(2): 50. doi: 10.1136/vr.104535.

Chapter 6: Where Do Your Pets Get Their Protein?

1   Knight, Andrew, and Madelaine Leitsberger. "Vegetarian versus Meat-Based Diets for Companion Animals." *Animals* (September 2016) 6(9): 57.

2   Derr, Mark. "Dogs and Humans Are Evolutionary Partners." *Psychology Today*, January 2, 2019. <https://www.psychologytoday.com/us/blog/dogs-best-friend/201901/dogs-and-humans-are-evolutionary-partners>.

3   Yeomans, Lisa, et al. "Close Companions: Early Evidence for Dogs in Northeast Jordan and the Potential Impact of New Hunting Methods." *Journal of Anthropological Archaeology* (March 2019) 53: 161–173.

4   Jung, Christoph, and Daniela Pörtl. "Scavenging Hypothesis: Lack of Evidence for Dog Domestication on the Waste Dump." *Dog Behavior* (2018) 4(2): 41–56.

5   Clutton-Brock, Juliet. "Origins of the Dog: Domestication and Early History." In *The Domestic Dog: Its Evolution, Behaviour and Interactions with People*, edited by James A. Serpell (Cambridge: Cambridge University Press, 1995).

6   Derr, "Dogs and Humans Are Evolutionary Partners."

7   Montague, Michael J., et al. "Comparative Analysis of the Domestic Cat Genome Reveals Genetic Signatures Underlying Feline Biology and Domestication." *Proceedings of the National Academy of Sciences* (November 2014) 111(48): 17230–17235.

8   Gergely, Anna, et al. "Auditory–Visual Matching of Conspecifics and Non-conspecifics by Dogs and Human Infants." *Animals* (January 2019) 9(1): 17.

9   Overall, Karen. *Manual of Clinical Behavioral Medicine for Dogs and Cats* (St. Louis, MO: Elsevier Health Sciences, 2013).

10 Beetz, Andrea, et al. "Psychosocial and Psychophysiological Effects of Human-Animal Interactions: The Possible Role of Oxytocin." *Frontiers in Psychology* (2012) 3: 234.

11 Axelsson, Erik, et al. "The Genomic Signature of Dog Domestication Reveals Adaptation to a Starch-Rich Diet." *Nature* (March 2013) 495: 360–364.

12 Arendt, M., et al. "Amylase Activity Is Associated with AMY2B Copy Numbers in Dog: Implications for Dog Domestication, Diet and Diabetes." *Animal Genetics* (October 2014) 45(5): 716–722.

13 Ollivier, M., et al. "Dogs Accompanied Humans During the Neolithic Expansion into Europe." *Biology Letters* (October 2018) 14(10).

14 Ollivier, M., et al. "*Amy2B* Copy Number Variation Reveals Starch Diet Adaptations in Ancient European Dogs." *Royal Society Open Science* (November 2016) 3(11).

15 Barboza, Perry S., et al. "Feed Intake and Digestion in the Maned Wolf (*Chrysocyon brachyurus*): Consequences for Dietary Management." *Zoo Biology* (1994) 13(4): 375–381.

16 Allen, Mary E. "Maned Wolf Nutrition Management." In *Husbandry Manual for the Maned Wolf Chrysocyon brachyurus*, edited by N. B. Flerchall, M. Rodden, and S. Taylor. (Silver Spring, MD: American Association of Zoos and Aquariums, 1995). <https://nagonline.net/wp-content/uploads/2013/12/Maned-Wolf-Nutrition. pdf>.

17 Laidlaw, Rob. *Gray Wolf: A Comparison of Husbandry and Housing Practices*. Zoocheck Canada Inc., World Society for the Protection of Animals, Ontario Zoo Working Group, February 2000. <http://www.zoocheck.com/wp-content/uploads/2015/06/ Wolfreport.pdf>.

18 Serpell, James A. "How Happy Is Your Pet? The Problem of Subjectivity in the Assessment of Companion Animal Welfare." *Animal Welfare* (February 2019) 28(1): 57–66.

19 Grier, Katherine C. *Pets in America: A History* (Orlando: Harcourt Books, 2006).

20 Dodds, W. Jean, and Diana R. Laverdure. *Canine Nutrigenomics: The New Science of Feeding Your Dog for Optimum Health* (Wenatchee, WA: Dogwise Publishing, 2015).

21 Salt, C., et al. "Association between Life Span and Body Condition in Neutered Client-Owned Dogs. *Journal of Veterinary Internal Medicine* (January 2019) 33(1): 89–99.

22 Turner-McGrievy, G. M., et al. "Comparative Effectiveness of Plant-Based Diets for Weight Loss: A Randomized Controlled Trial of Five Different Diets." *Nutrition* (February 2015) 31(2): 350–358.

23 Dinu, M., et al. "Vegetarian, Vegan Diets and Multiple Health Outcomes: A Systematic Review with Meta-analysis of Observational Studies." *Critical Reviews in Food Science and Nutrition* (November 2017) 57(17): 3640–3649.

24 Swanson, K. S., et al. "Nutritional Genomics: Implications for Companion Animals." *Journal of Nutrition* (October 2003) 133(10): 3033–3040.

25 Montague, "Comparative Analysis of the Domestic Cat Genome."

26 Bekoff, Marc. "Oh Goodness, Why'd My Dog Erin Just Eat Something So Foul?" *Psychology Today*, February 26, 2019. <https://www.psychologytoday.com/us/blog/ animal-emotions/201902/oh-goodness-whyd-my-dog-erin-just-eat-something-so-foul>.

27 Swanson, "Nutritional Genomics."

28 Heath, Sarah Elizabeth, et al. Nutritional Supplementation in Cases of Canine Cognitive Dysfunction: A Clinical Trial." *Applied Animal Behaviour Science* (July 2007) 105(4): 284–296.

29 Chorney, Saryn. "Senior Dogs Can Suffer from Dementia Just Like People Do; Find Out If Your Older Pup Needs Help." *People*, January 14, 2019. <https://people.com/pets/senior-dogs-dementia-alzheimers-disease-canine-cognitive-dysfunction/>.

30 Purina Institute. "Canine & Feline Brain Health: Groundbreaking Nutritional Science from Purina." August 2018. <https://www.purinainstitute.com/sites/g/files/auxxlc381/files/2018-08/canine-feline-brain-health.pdf>.

31 Jackson, Janet, and Gary Pan (n.d.). "DogSmarts: 'The Bright Mind Effect.'" *Slate* (podcast). <http://www.slate.com/podcasts/dogsmarts/the_bright_mind_effect.html>.

32 Pan, Y. "Enhancing Brain Functions in Senior Dogs: A New Nutritional Approach." *Topics in Companion Animal Medicine* (February 2011) 26(1): 10–16.

33 V-dog Testimonials (n.d.). <https://v-dog.com/blogs/testimonials/tagged/seniors-arthritis>.

34 Laursen, Lucas. "Interdisciplinary Research: Big Science at the Table." *Nature* (December 2010) 468: S2–S4.

Chapter 7: Plant-Powered Pets

1   Quoted in Carroll, Rory. "Health Mutt: Proposal to Put Shelter Dogs on Vegan Diet Divides Los Angeles," *Guardian*, December 29, 2017. <https://www.theguardian.com/us-news/2017/dec/29/los-angeles-vegan-dog-diet-animal-shelters-moby>.

2   Knight, Andrew, and Madelaine Leitsberger. "Vegetarian versus Meat-Based Diets for Companion Animals." *Animals* (September 2016) 6(9): 57.

3   Plant-Powered Dog Food Summit. <https://www.plantpowereddogfoodsummit.com/>.

4   Knight and Leitsberger, "Vegetarian versus Meat-Based Diets for Companion Animals."

5   ODPHP. "Scientific Report of the 2015 Dietary Guidelines Advisory Committee." <https://health.gov/dietaryguidelines/2015-scientific-report/>.

6   Government of Canada (2019). "Canada's Food Guide." <https://food-guide.canada.ca/en/>.

7   Tyson (2019). "Food Trends on the Tip of the Tongue in 2019." <https://www.tysonfoods.com/the-feed-blog/food-trends-2019>.

8   Brown, W. Y., et al. "An Experimental Meat-Free Diet Maintained Haematological Characteristics in Sprint-Racing Sled Dogs." *British Journal of Nutrition* (November 2009) 102(9): 1318–1323.

9   Brown, W. Y. "Nutritional and Ethical Issues Regarding Vegetarianism in the Domestic Dog." *Recent Advances in Animal Nutrition—Australia* (2009) 17: 137–143.

10 Wakefield, L. A., et al. "Evaluation of Cats Fed Vegetarian Diets and Attitudes of Their Caregivers." *Journal of the American Veterinary Medical Association* (July 2006) 229(1): 70–73.

11 Leon A., et al. "Hypokalaemic Episodic Polymyopathy in Cats Fed a Vegetarian Diet." *Australian Veterinary Journal* (October 1992) 69(10): 249–254.

12 Bednar, G. E., et al. "Selected Animal and Plant Protein Sources Affect Nutrient Digestibility and Fecal Characteristics of Ileally Cannulated Dogs." *Archiv für Tierernaehrung* (2000) 53(2): 127–140.

13 Vegepets.info (n.d.). "Meat-Based Diets: Appendices." <http://vegepets.info/diets/diets/meat-based-appendices.html>.

14 Gallegos, Jenna. "Grain-Free Pet Foods Are No Healthier, Vets Say. Focus on This Nutrition Issue Instead," *Washington Post*, August 15, 2017. <https://www.washingtonpost.com/news/animalia/wp/2017/08/15/grain-free-pet-foods-are-no-healthier-vets-say-focus-on-this-nutrition-issue-instead/>.

15 Mueller, Ralf S., et al. "Critically Appraised Topic on Adverse Food Reactions of Companion Animals (2): Common Food Allergen Sources in Dogs and Cats." *BMC Veterinary Research* (January 2016) 12(9).

16 Pitcairn, Richard, and Susan Hubble Pitcairn. *Dr. Pitcairn's Complete Guide to Natural Health for Dogs & Cats* (New York: Rodale, 2017).

17 Sprinkle, David. "2019 State of the Veterinary Profession." VMX conference, January 22, 2019. <https://www.vet-advantage.com/2019-state-of-the-veterinary-profession/>.

18 Berschneider, H. M. "Alternative Diets." *Clinical Techniques in Small Animal Practice* (February 2002) 17(1): 1–5.

19 Dodd, Sarah A. S., et al. "Plant-Based (Vegan) Diets for Pets: A Survey of Pet Owner Attitudes and Feeding Practices." *PLOS ONE* (January 15, 2019). <https://doi.org/10.1371/journal.pone.0210806>.

20 Pierce, Jessica. *Run, Spot, Run: The Ethics of Keeping Pets* (Chicago: University of Chicago Press, 2016).

21 Coates, Jennifer. "Can Dogs Stay Healthy on a Vegetarian Diet?" *PetMD*, January 2014. <https://www.petmd.com/blogs/nutritionnuggets/jcoates/2014/jan/can-dogs-stay-healthy-on-a-vegetarian-diet-31188>.

22 Bekoff, Marc. "Oh Goodness, Why'd My Dog Erin Just Eat Something So Foul?" *Psychology Today*, February 26, 2019. <https://www.psychologytoday.com/us/blog/animal-emotions/201902/oh-goodness-whyd-my-dog-erin-just-eat-something-so-foul>.

23 Kurihara, Kenzo. "Umami the Fifth Basic Taste: History of Studies on Receptor Mechanisms and Role as a Food Flavor." *BioMed Research International* (June 2015). <https://www.hindawi.com/journals/bmri/2015/189402/>

24 Kurihara, K., and M. Kashiwayanagi. "Physiological Studies on Umami Taste." *The Journal of Nutrition* (April 2000) 130(4S Suppl): 931S–934S.

25 FDA. "Pet Food Labels—General, 2017." <https://www.fda.gov/animal-veterinary/animal-health-literacy/pet-food-labels-general>.

26 Meeker, D. L., and J. L. Meisinger. "Rendered Ingredients Significantly Influence Sustainability, Quality, and Safety of Pet Food." *Journal of Animal Science* (February 20, 2015) 93: 835–847.

27   Donaldson, Sue, and Will Kymlicka. *Zoopolis: A Political Theory of Animal Rights* (Oxford: Oxford University Press, 2011), 149–150.

Chapter 8: Challenges for Plant-Based Feeding

1   Pierce, Jessica. *Run, Spot, Run: The Ethics of Keeping Pets* (Chicago: University of Chicago Press, 2016).

2   Rothgerber, H. "A Meaty Matter: Pet Diet and the Vegetarian's Dilemma." *Appetite* (September 2013) 68: 76–82.

3   Dodd, Sarah A. S., et al. "Plant-Based (Vegan) Diets for Pets: A Survey of Pet Owner Attitudes and Feeding Practices." *PLOS ONE* (January 15, 2019). <https://doi. org/10.1371/journal.pone.0210806>.

4   McDermott, Marie Tae. "The Vegan Dog," *New York Times*, June 6, 2017. <https:// www.nytimes.com/2017/06/06/well/family/the-vegan-dog.html>.

5   Peden, James A. *Vegetarian Cats and Dogs* (3d ed). (Troy, MT: Harbingers of a New Age, 1999).

6   Brown, W. Y., et al. "An Experimental Meat-Free Diet Maintained Haematological Characteristics in Sprint-Racing Sled Dogs." *British Journal of Nutrition* (November 2009) 102(9): 1318–1323.

7   Brown, W. Y. "Nutritional and Ethical Issues Regarding Vegetarianism in the Domestic Dog." *Recent Advances in Animal Nutrition—Australia* (2009) 17: 137–143.

8   Wakefield, L. A., et al. "Evaluation of Cats Fed Vegetarian Diets and Attitudes of Their Caregivers." *Journal of the American Veterinary Medical Association* (July 2006) 229(1): 70–73.

9   Vegetarian Canine Diets, n.d. <http://www.vegepets.info/diets/veg-canine.html #population-studies>.

10   Carroll, Rory. "Health Mutt: Proposal to Put Shelter Dogs on Vegan Diet Divides Los Angeles," *Guardian*, December 29, 2017. <https://www.theguardian.com/ us-news/2017/dec/29/los-angeles-vegan-dog-diet-animal-shelters-moby>.

11   Lakoff, George. *Don't Think of an Elephant! Know Your Values and Frame the Debate— The Essential Guide for Progressives* (White River Junction, VT: Chelsea Green, 2004). Gladwell, Malcolm. *Blink! The Power of Thinking Without Thinking* (New York: Back Bay Books, 2007).

12   Chiorando, Maria. "92% of Plant-Based Meals Eaten by Non-Vegans Last Year, Says Data." *Plant Based News*, February 19, 2019. <https://www.plantbasednews.org/ post/92-of-plant-based-meals-eaten-by-non-vegans>.

13   Anderson, Jo. "What to Call Plant-Based Meat Alternatives: A Labeling Study." *Faunalytics*, January 23, 2019. <https://faunalytics.org/what-to-call-plant-based-meat -alternatives-a-labelling-study/>.

14   Michail, Niamh. "Avoid the 'V' Word, and Other Tips to Boost Meat-free and Dairy-free Sales." *FoodNavigator*, January 15, 2018. <https://www.foodnavigator.com/Article/2018/01/15/ Avoid-the-V-word-and-other-tips-to-boost-meat-free-and-dairy-free-sales>.

15 Bacon, Linda, and Dario Krpan. "(Not) Eating for the Environment: The Impact of Restaurant Menu Design on Vegetarian Food Choice." *Appetite* (June 2018) 125: 190–200.

16 Morning Consult (2018). "Consumer Trends in the Food and Beverage Industry." <https://morningconsult.com/wp-content/uploads/2018/05/Morning-Consult-Consumer-Trends-In-The-Food-and-Beverage-Industry.pdf>.

17 Michail, "Avoid the 'V' Word."

18 Anderson, "What to Call Plant-Based Meat Alternatives."

19 Report Buyer. "Top Trends in Prepared Foods 2017: Exploring Trends in Meat, Fish and Seafood; Pasta, Noodles and Rice; Prepared Meals; Savory Deli Food; Soup; and Meat Substitutes." <https://www.reportbuyer.com/product/4959853/top-trends-in-prepared-foods-2017-exploring-trends-in-meat-fish-and-seafood-pasta-noodles-and-rice-prepared-meals-savory-deli-food-soup-and-meat-substitutes.html>.

20 Markets and Markets (2018). "Meat Substitutes Market Worth 6.43 Billion USD by 2023." <https://www.marketsandmarkets.com/PressReleases/meat-substitutes.asp>.

21 Lux Research. "WhooPea: Plant Sources Are Changing the Protein Landscape," December 22, 2014. <https://members.luxresearchinc.com/research/report/16091>.

22 Donaldson, Sue, and Will Kymlicka. *Zoopolis: A Political Theory of Animal Rights* (Oxford: Oxford University Press, 2011) 149–150.

23 Quine, Oscar. "Pet Owners Who Force Their Cats to Be Vegan Could Risk Breaking the Law," *The Telegraph*, November 23, 2018. <https://www.telegraph.co.uk/news/2018/11/23/pet-owners-feed-cats-vegan-diet-could-face-prosecution/>.

24 Rothgerber, Hank. "Carnivorous Cats, Vegetarian Dogs, and the Resolution of the Vegetarian's Dilemma." *Anthrozoös* (2014) 27(4): 485–498.

25 Pierce, *Run, Spot, Run*, 18.

26 Peers, Michael J. L., et al. "Scavenging by Snowshoe Hares (*Lepus americanus*) in Yukon, Canada." *Northwestern Naturalist* (December 2018) 99(3): 232–235.

27 Herzog, Hal. *Some We Love, Some We Hate, Some We Eat: Why It's So Hard to Think Straight About Animals* (New York: HarperCollins, 2010), 26.

28 American Pet Products Association (2019). "Pet Industry Market Size & Ownership Statistics." <https://www.americanpetproducts.org/press_industrytrends.asp>.

29 Spitze, A. R., et al. "Taurine Concentrations in Animal Feed Ingredients; Cooking Influences Taurine Content." *Journal of Animal Physiology and Animal Nutrition* (August 2003) 87(7–8): 251–262.

30 Tully, Paul S. "Sulfonic Acids." In *Kirk-Othmer Encyclopedia of Chemical Technology* (New York: John Wiley & Sons, Inc., 2000).

31 Ami Pet Food. "Ami Cat." <https://amipetfood.com/en/products/products-for-cats/amicat>.

32 Gray, Christina M., et al. "Nutritional Adequacy of Two Vegan Diets for Cats." *Journal of the American Veterinary Medical Association* (December 2004) 225(11): 1670–1675.

33   Patrick-Goudreau, Colleen (2015). "Vegan with Cats and Dogs." *Food for Thought* (podcast).

34   Herzog, *Some We Love, Some We Hate, Some We Eat.*

Chapter 9: More Legs, Less Guilt?

1   Tyson (2019). "Food Trends on the Tip of the Tongue in 2019." <https://www. tysonfoods.com/the-feed-blog/food-trends-2019>.

2   McKusker, S., et al. "Amino Acid Content of Selected Plant, Algae and Insect Species: A Search for Alternative Protein Sources for Use in Pet Foods." *Journal of Nutritional Science* (2014) 3. <https://www.ncbi.nlm.nih.gov/pmc/articles/ PMC4473169/>.

3   Onsongo, V. O., et al. "Insects for Income Generation Through Animal Feed: Effect of Dietary Replacement of Soybean and Fish Meal with Black Soldier Fly Meal on Broiler Growth and Economic Performance." *Journal of Economic Entomology* (August 2018) 111(4): 1966–1973.

4   Van Huis, Arnold. "Edible Insects Contributing to Food Security?" *Agriculture & Food Security* (December 2015) 4(20).

5   Gold, M., et al. "Conceptual Model of Biowaste Processing with Black Soldier Fly Larvae." 2nd International Conference: "Insects to Feed the World" (IFW 2018), Wuhan, China, May 15–18, 2018. Abstracts published here: <https://www. wageningenacademic.com/doi/10.3920/JIFF2018.S1>.

6   Hanboonsong, Yupa, et al. "Six-Legged Livestock: Edible Insect Farming, Collection and Marketing in Thailand, Bangkok." Food and Agriculture Organization of the United Nations, Regional Office for Asia and the Pacific, March 2013. <http://www. fao.org/3/i3246e/i3246e00.htm>.

7   de Souza, Agnieszka, et al. "Bugs Are Coming Soon to Your Dinner Table." *Bloomberg*, July 5, 2018. <https://www.bloomberg.com/graphics/2018-insects-as-food>.

8   Payne, C. L. R., et al. "Are Edible Insects More or Less 'Healthy' Than Commonly Consumed Meats?" *European Journal of Clinical Nutrition* (2016) 70: 285–291. <https://www.nature.com/articles/ejcn2015149>.

9   Thompson, Derek. "Will We Ever Stop Eating Animal Meat?" *The Atlantic*, September 20, 2018. <https://www.theatlantic.com/ideas/archive/2018/09/will-we-ever-stop -eating-animal-meat/570874/>.

10   Ibid.

11   Niaz, Kamal, et al. "Highlight Report: *Diploptera functata* (Cockroach) Milk as Next Superfood." *EXCLI Journal* (2018) 17: 721–723.

12   Banerjee, S., et al. "Structure of a Heterogeneous, Glycosylated, Lipid-Bound, In Vivo-Grown Protein Crystal at Atomic Resolution from the Viviparous Cockroach *Diploptera punctata*." *International Union of Crystallography, Issuing Body* (June 2016) 3(Pt4): 282–293.

13   Niaz, "Highlight Report."

14 Van Huis, A., et al. "Insects to Feed the World." *Journal of Insects as Food and Feed* 1: 3–5. <https://www.researchgate.net/publication/272355428_Insects_to_feed_the _world>.

15 Rootlab (n.d.). "Chicken, Egg & Cricket Recipe." <https://www.rootlabpetfood.com/ recipes/chicken-egg-cricket/grain-free>.

16 Harrison, L. M., et al. "The Opiate System in Invertebrates." *Peptides* (1994) 15(7): 1309–1329.

17 Mizunami, M., et al. "Mushroom Bodies of the Cockroach: Their Participation in Place Memory." *Journal of Comparative Neurology* (December 1998) 402(4): 520–537.

18 *The Bug Grub Couple* (2017). "Our Lives." Directed by BBC. UK: BBC. <https://www. bbc.co.uk/programmes/b0911ydt>.

19 Broom, Donald M. *Sentience and Animal Welfare* (Wallingford: CABI, August 2014).

20 Low, Philip, et al. "The Cambridge Declaration on Consciousness" (Francis Crick Memorial Conference, Cambridge, England, 2012). <http://www.fcmconference.org>.

21 Klein, Colin, and Andrew B. Barron. "Insects Have the Capacity for Subjective Experience." *Animal Sentience* (2016): 100.

22 Eisemann, C., et al. "Do Insects Feel Pain?—A Biological View." *Cellular and Molecular Life Sciences* (February 1984) 40(2): 164–167.

23 Smith, Jane A. "A Question of Pain in Invertebrates." *ILAR Journal* (1991) 33(1–2): 25–31.

24 Bug Farm Foods (n.d.). "Why Eat Insects?" <https://www.bugfarmfoods.com/ why-eat-insects/>.

25 Jabr, Ferris. "It's Official: Fish Feel Pain." *Smithsonian.com*, January 8, 2018. <https:// www.smithsonianmag.com/science-nature/fish-feel-pain-180967764/>.

26 Bollard, Lewis. "Ending Factory Farming as Soon as Possible." *80,000 Hours* (podcast, September 27, 2017), edited by Robert Wiblin. <https://80000hours.org/podcast/ episodes/lewis-bollard-end-factory-farming/>.

27 Healy, Kevin, et al. "Metabolic Rate and Body Size Are Linked with Perception of Temporal Information." *Animal Behaviour* (October 2013) 86(4): 685–696.

28 Broom, *Sentience and Animal Welfare*.

29 Rollin, Bernard E. *The Unheeded Cry: Animal Consciousness, Animal Pain and Science* (Oxford: Oxford University Press, 1989).

30 Osborn, Annie. "Should We Eat More Insects?" ProVeg New Food Conference (Berlin, Germany, 2019). <https://proveg.com/new-food-conference/#programme-day-two>.

Chapter 10: Ancient Proteins for Present-Day Pets

1 Barberán, Albert, et al. "The Ecology of Microscopic Life in Household Dust." *Proceedings of the Royal Society B: Biological Sciences* (September 2015) 282(1814). <https://royalsocietypublishing.org/doi/pdf/10.1098/rspb.2015.1139>.

2 Robb Dunn Lab (n.d.). "Wild Life of Our Homes." <http://robdunnlab.com/projects/ wild-life-of-our-homes/>.

3   Billinghurst, Ian. *Give Your Dog a Bone: The Practical Commonsense Way to Feed Dogs for a Long Healthy Life* (Mundaring, Western Australia: Warrigal Press, 1993).

4   Quoted in McBride, Sarah. "Do These Tiny Organisms Hold the Key to Lab-Grown Food?" *Bloomberg*, February 4, 2019. <https://www.bloomberg.com/news/articles/2019-02-04/do-these-tiny-organisms-hold-the-key-to-lab-grown-food>.

5   Money, Nicholas P. *The Rise of Yeast: How the Sugar Fungus Shaped Civilisation* (Oxford: Oxford University Press, 2018).

6   GRAIN and the Institute for Agriculture and Trade Policy (IATP). "Emissions Impossible: How Big Meat and Dairy Are Heating up the Planet." *GRAIN*, July 18, 2018. <https://www.grain.org/article/entries/5976-emissions-impossible-how-big-meat-and-dairy-are-heating-up-the-planet>.

7   Natural Products Insider. "Global Cheese Market to Hit $118 Billion by 2019," February 21, 2014. <https://www.naturalproductsinsider.com/branding-marketing/global-cheese-market-hit-118-billion-2019>.

8   Plant-Based Foods Association (n.d.). "2018 Retail Sales Data for Plant-Based Foods." <https://plantbasedfoods.org/consumer-access/nielsen-data-release-2018/>.

9   The Chickpeeps. "Episode 19: Wicked Healthy with Derek Sarno" (podcast, April 1, 2018). <https://www.thechickpeeps.com/episodes/2018/4/1/ep-19-wicked-healthy-with-derek-sarno>.

Chapter 11: Clean Pet Food and the Promise of Biotech

1   Korsgaard, Christine. "Fellow Creatures: Kantian Ethics and Our Duties to Animals." *Tanner Lectures on Human Values* (2004) 24: 77–110.

2   Urbina, Ian. "'Sea Slaves': The Human Misery That Feeds Pets and Livestock," *New York Times*, July 27, 2015. <https://www.nytimes.com/2015/07/27/world/outlaw-ocean-thailand-fishing-sea-slaves-pets.html>.

3   Kristensen, B. "Toward the Research and Development of Cultured Meat for Captive Carnivorous Animals." In *Professionals in Food Chains* (The Netherlands: Wageningen Academic Publishers, 2018), 152–156.

4   Korsgaard, "Fellow Creatures."

5   Abbate, Cheryl. "Veganism, (Almost) Harm-Free Animal Flesh, and Nonmaleficence: Navigating Dietary Ethics in an Unjust World." In *The Routledge Handbook of Animal Ethics*, edited by Bob Fischer (Oxford: Routledge, 2019).

6   Treleaven, Sarah. "How Your Dog Could Go Vegan and Still Stay Healthy." *Popular Science*, November 26, 2018. <https://www.popsci.com/vegan-dog-food>.

7   Reese, Jacy. *The End of Animal Farming: How Scientists, Entrepreneurs, and Activists Are Building an Animal-Free Food System* (Boston: Beacon, 2018), 60.

8   Alonzo, Austin. "Study: Slower-Growing Birds Would Harm Environment." *WATTAgNet*, March 14, 2019. <https://www.wattagnet.com/articles/37152-study-slower-growing-birds-would-harm-environment>.

9   K-State Research and Extension. "K-State Researchers Find Vitamin Compound That Boosts Growth," December 11, 2018. <http://www.ksre.k-state.edu/news/stories/2018/12/muscle-growth-chickens.html>.

10 Scholey, D. V., et al. "Bioavailability of a Novel Form of Silicon Supplement." *Scientific Reports* (November 2018) 8: 17022.

11 "Silicon Supplement Could Improve Bone Strength and Welfare of Millions of Chickens a Year," Nottingham Trent University, November 2018. <https://www.ntu.ac.uk/about-us/news/news-articles/2018/11/silicon-supplement-could-improve-bone-strength-and-welfare-of-millions-of-chickens-a-year>.

12 Rana, Preetika, and Lucy Craymer. "Big Tongues and Extra Vertebrae: The Unintended Consequences of Animal Gene Editing," *Wall Street Journal*, December 19, 2018.

13 Quoted in Rana and Craymer, "Big Tongues."

14 Shapiro, Paul. "Sixth Viewpoint: An Activist's Perspective on Animal Welfare." In *Animal Welfare in Animal Agriculture* (2d ed.), edited by Wilson G. Pond, Fuller W. Bazer, and Bernard E. Rollin (Boca Raton, FL: CRC Press, 2011).

15 Harari, Yuval Noah. Foreword to Shapiro, Paul. *Clean Meat: How Growing Meat Without Animals Will Revolutionize Dinner and the World* (New York: Gallery Books, 2018), xi.

16 Oberpenning, F., et al. "De Novo Reconstitution of a Functional Mammalian Urinary Bladder by Tissue Engineering." *Nature Biotechnology* (February 1999) 17(2): 149–155.

17 Zampa, Matthew (n.d.). "The Good Food Institute Is Disrupting the Meat Market for Good." *Sentient Media.* <https://sentientmedia.org/the-good-food-institute-is-disrupting-the-meat-market-for-good/>.

18 Bollard, Lewis. "Ending Factory Farming as Soon as Possible. *80,000 Hours* (podcast, September 27, 2017), edited by Robert Wiblin. <https://80000hours.org/podcast/episodes/lewis-bollard-end-factory-farming/>.

19 Hopkins, Patrick D., and Austin Dacey. "Vegetarian Meat: Could Technology Save Animals and Satisfy Meat Eaters?" *Journal of Agricultural and Environmental Ethics* (2008) 21: 579–596.

20 Carrington, Damian. "The New Food: Meet the Startups Racing to Reinvent the Meal," *Guardian*, April 30, 2018. <https://www.theguardian.com/environment/2018/apr/30/lab-grown-meat-how-a-bunch-of-geeks-scared-the-meat-industry>.

21 Lynch, John, and Raymond Pierrehumbert. "Climate Impacts of Cultured Meat and Beef Cattle." *Frontiers in Sustainable Food Systems* (February 2019) 3. <https://www.frontiersin.org/articles/10.3389/fsufs.2019.00005/full>.

22 Simon, Matt. "The Confounding Climate Science of Lab-Grown Meat." *Wired*, February 19, 2019. <https://www.wired.com/story/the-confounding-climate-science-of-lab-grown-meat/>.

23 Shapiro, Paul. *Clean Meat: How Growing Meat Without Animals Will Revolutionize Dinner and the World* (New York: Gallery Books, 2018), 62.

24   Briggs, Helen. "Artificial Meat: UK Scientists Growing 'Bacon' in Labs." *BBC News*, March 19, 2019. <https://www.bbc.co.uk/news/science-environment-47611026>.

25   Shapiro, *Clean Meat*, 20.

26   Reese, *The End of Animal Farming*, 87.

27   Eveleth, Rose. "Is Lab-Grown Meat Really Meat? *Slate*, July 11, 2018. <https://slate.com/technology/2018/07/should-lab-grown-meat-be-called-meat.html>.

28   Adams, Carol J. "There Is Nothing More American Than the Veggie Burger," *New York Times Sunday Review*, June 30, 2018. <https://www.nytimes.com/2018/06/30/opinion/sunday/there-is-nothing-more-all-american-than-the-veggie-burger.html>.

29   Bunge, Jacob, and Heather Haddon. "A Stampede of Meatless Products Overrun Grocery Store Meat Cases," *Wall Street Journal*, June 10, 2018. <https://www.wsj.com/articles/a-stampede-of-meatless-products-overrun-grocery-store-meat-cases-1528653236>.

30   Shapiro, *Clean Meat*, 24.

31   Eveleth, "Is Lab-Grown Meat Really Meat?"

32   Bryant, Christopher, et al. "A Survey of Consumer Perceptions of Plant-Based and Clean Meat in the USA, India, and China." *Frontiers in Sustainable Food Systems* (February 2019). <https://www.frontiersin.org/articles/10.3389/fsufs.2019.00011/full>.

33   Ibid.

34   World Wildlife Fund (WWF). "The Living Planet Report 2018." WWF-UK. <https://www.wwf.org.uk/updates/living-planet-report-2018>.

35   De Silva, Sena S., and Giovanni M. Turchini. "Towards Understanding the Impacts of the Pet Food Industry on World Fish and Seafood Supplies." *Journal of Agricultural and Environmental Ethics* (October 2008) 21(5): 459–467.

Chapter 12: Cultivating a Clean Pet Food Revolution

1   Kristensen, Bjørn R. "The Moral Problem of Captive Predation: Toward the Research and Development of Cultured Meat for Captive Carnivorous Animals." In *Professionals in Food Chains* (The Netherlands: Wageningen Academic Publishers, 2018), 152–156.

2   Okin, Gregory S. "Environmental Impacts of Food Consumption by Dogs and Cats." *PLOS ONE* (August 2, 2017) 12(8).

3   Starostinetskaya, Anna. "Jeff Bezos, Bill Gates, and Richard Branson Lead $90 million Investment to Create Next Vegan Impossible Burger." *VegNews*, February 2019. <https://vegnews.com/2019/2/jeff-bezos-bill-gates-and-richard-branson-lead-90-million-investment-to-create-next-vegan-impossible-burger>.

4   Lamb, Catherine. "Bill Gates Names Meat-Free Burgers in Top 10 Breakthrough Technologies of 2019." *The Spoon*, February 27, 2019. <https://thespoon.tech/bill-gates-names-meat-free-burgers-in-top-10-breakthrough-technologies-of-2019>.

5   Langdon, Alison. "Fit for a Dog? Food Sharing and the Medieval Human/Animal Divide." *Society & Animals* (2018) 1: 1–17.

6   Ibid.

7   Bryant, Christopher, and Julie Barnett. "Consumer Acceptance of Cultured Meat: A Systematic Review." *Meat Science* (September 2018) 143: 8–17.

8   Faunalytics. "The Faunalytics Resource Hub: Clean Meat," August 1, 2018. <http://faunalytics.org/clean-meat/>.

9   Carrington, Damian. "The New Food: Meet the Startups Racing to Reinvent the Meal," *Guardian*, April 30, 2018. <https://www.theguardian.com/environment/2018/apr/30/lab-grown-meat-how-a-bunch-of-geeks-scared-the-meat-industry>.

10   Faunalytics, "The Faunalytics Resource Hub."

Chapter 13: Saving Pet Food's Secret Victims

1   PetMech, LLC: Humane In-Home Product Testing (n.d.). "About Us." <http://www.petmech.com/about-1.html>.

2   Pierce, Jessica. *Run, Spot, Run: The Ethics of Keeping Pets* (Chicago: University of Chicago Press, 2016), 77.

3   Forest, Dylan. "P&F, Iams Fire Testing Lab over PETA Disclosures." *Animal People*, April 1, 2003. <https://newspaper.animalpeopleforum.org/2003/04/01/pg-iams-fire-testing-lab-over-peta-disclosures/>.

4   Brown, Katy (2010). "A Nation of Animal Lovers?" Ethical Consumer Research Report, p. 14. <http://www.vegepets.info/resources/Publications/Diets-Brown-Ethical-Consumer-2010.pdf>

5   Grefski, Lorie (2015). "Is Your Pet's Food Tested on Animals?" *One Green Planet*. <http://www.onegreenplanet.org/animalsandnature/is-your-pets-food-tested-on-animals/>.

Index

NOTE: Page references ending in "f" indicate figures.

New Harvest, 199, 242, 256

New Wave Foods (biotech food company), 197

New York Times, 93, 153

nitrates, 31

North Carolina Department of Agriculture, 1

Nostimos, Bert, 188

nutrient balance

    and Canine Cognitive Dysfunction, 126

    and genomic research, 127–129

    in homemade pet foods, 96–97

    in insect-protein foods, 182–183

    and origin of nutrients, 231–232

    personalized nutrition, 232, 257, 259

    and taurine deficiency, 91–92, 93, 94

nutritional yeast, 119, 122, 145, 172

obesity, xvi, 2, 117, 122–123, 136

obligate carnivores, 116, 168

ocean bycatch, 41, 236

Office of Disease Prevention and Health Promotion, 135

Okin, Gregory, 26, 27

omnivores, 117–118

    dogs as, 109–112

    wolves as, 112–113

"Ones Who Walk Away from Omelas, The" (Le Guin), 67–68

Operation Opson (2011), 7

organic labeling, 7, 96

Organization for Economic Cooperation and Development (OECD), 25, 26

Osborn, Annie, 193

Oven, Alice, x, 99, 101, 103–104, 134

oxytocin, 110

pain perception, by insects, 185–189. *See also* suffering and animal welfare

palatability, 141–146, 278–279

Paris Agreement (2016), 24

Patrick-Goudreau, Colleen, 168, 172, 228, 229

Pavlov, Ivan, 282

Pelluchon, Corine, 79, 80

Pendell, Hersch, 15

pentobarbital, 11, 14–16, 279–280

people food vs animal food, 6, 8, 16, 95–96, 265–267, 271–273

Perfect Day (biotech food company), 199–200, 210

personalized nutrition, 232, 257, 259

PETA (People for the Ethical Treatment of Animals), 154, 155f, 283

pet food industry

    amount of pet food produced by, 47

    conflicts of interest in, 16–17

    cost in, 253–254

    and factory farming, 47

    investment in cultured proteins, 254, 261–263

    market value of, 84

    meat-centrism in, ix–x

    start of, 8

pet food meats, environmental impact of, viii–x, 20–45

    contributing to climate change, 20–21, 24–25, 29–31

    and fish-based pet foods, 36–42

    need for rapid changes in, 21–24

    and overconsumption of animal meats, 25–29

    and switch to plant-sourced protein, 32–36, 43–45

pet food meats, ingredients/contaminants of, xii, 1–19

    and AAFCO, 10, 15, 16–17

    antibiotics and hormones, 13–14

    euthanasia drugs, 10, 11, 14–16, 279–280

    flavoring, 144–145

    health risks of, 17–19, 121

    meat byproducts, 2–3

    and mislabeling/fraud, 5, 7

Index

Sustainable Bioproducts (biotech food company), 197
Sylar (dog), 81

taurine, 91–92, 93, 94, 169, 170
teflubenzuron, 38–39
Terramino Foods, 212
Tesco, 211, 212
Tetrick, Josh, 249–250
Thelander, Jeanette, 80
Thibodeau, Lucille Claire, 52
Thixton, Susan, 15
Thornes, Tobias, 25
thyroid problems, 13, 136, 137
Time to Eat the Dog? The Real Guide to Sustainable Living (Vale and Vale), 31
Tischler, Joyce, 52–53
Topics in Companion Animal Medicine, 96
Tosh Farms, 62
triclosan (TCS), 13
Trump, Donald, 24
tuna, cell-based, 238–239, 240, 242–243
Turchini, Giovanni M., 37
turkeys, 1, 60, 61, 156
Turner, Dennis, xvii
Twenty-Eight Hour Law (1873/1994), 53
Tyson Foods, 135, 175, 223, 261

umami flavor, 143, 200
United Egg Producers, 58
United Kingdom
    animal feed guidelines in, 18
    insect-based pet foods in, 179–181
    number of pet dogs and cats in, vii, x
    pet expenditures in, viii
    plant-based pet foods in, 134
United Nations
    Food & Agriculture Organization (FAO), 37–38, 177
    Intergovernmental Panel on Climate Change (IPCC), viii, 23
United States
    animal welfare standards in, 47–48, 69
    environmental performance of, 23
    meat consumption in, 25
    number of pet dogs and cats in, vii, x, xiii
    pet expenditures in, vii
    plant-based market in, 208
United States Department of Agriculture (USDA), 27, 226–227, 230, 284
Unleashing Your Dog: A Field Guide to Giving Your Canine Companion the Best Life Possible (Bekoff), 143
U.S. Cattlemen's Association, 230
U.S. Farm Bill, 28–29
U.S. National Climate Assessment, 21, 22, 34

Vale, Brenda, 31
Vale, Robert, 31
Valeti, Uma, 251–252, 256
V-dog (pet food company), 127, 202
vegan and vegetarian diets. *See* plant-based diets
VeggieDog (Green Petfood brand), 151, 182
veterinarians
    and canine cancer rates, 17
    and DCM, 90–91, 93
    and homemade pet food recipes, 97
    opposition to plant-based feeding, 151–152, 156
    support for plant-based feeding, 132, 134, 136
    See also Knight, Andrew; Ward, Ernie
vitamin A, 118, 169
vitamin B3, 169
vitamin D, 94, 97, 169
Voiceless Animal Cruelty Index (VACI), 69
Wagner, Klaus
    on animal husbandry, 63, 64
    on backlash to veganism, 151

331

About the Authors

Photo: Laura Ward

Ernie Ward, DVM is an internationally recognized veterinarian and the author of three books, including *Chow Hounds: Why Our Dogs Are Getting Fatter.* He writes "The Vet Is In" monthly column for *Dogster Magazine.* He is pictured with Ginny (left) and Harry.

Photo: Emily Nicholson

Alice Oven is a freelance writer on animal welfare and ethics, and the senior acquisitions editor at Taylor & Francis for veterinary and life science books. Alice lives in London, UK, with her adopted King Charles Cavalier, JD.

Photo: Wild Earth

Ryan Bethencourt is the co-founder of Wild Earth, a dog food company, and founder and former program director of the biotech incubator IndieBio.

About the Publisher

LANTERN BOOKS was founded in 1999 on the principle of living with a greater depth and commitment to the preservation of the natural world. In addition to publishing books on animal advocacy, vegetarianism, religion, and environmentalism, Lantern is dedicated to printing books in the U.S. on recycled paper and saving resources in day-to-day operations. Lantern is honored to be a recipient of the highest standard in environmentally responsible publishing from the Green Press Initiative.

lanternbooks.com